THE AMERICAN NEGRO
HIS HISTORY AND LITERATURE

IN
FREEDOM'S
BIRTHPLACE

John Daniels

ARNO PRESS and THE NEW YORK TIMES
NEW YORK 1969

General Editor
WILLIAM LOREN KATZ

In 1899 THE UNIVERSITY OF PENNSYLVANIA published Dr. W. E. B. Du Bois's trailblazing study, *The Philadelphia Negro*. Similar studies followed, among them surveys of Negro communities in St. Louis and Columbia, Missouri, and Pittsburgh, Pennsylvania. The first in-depth study on Boston, *In Freedom's Birthplace*, was the work of John Daniels. Begun in 1905, when the author held a South End House Fellowship at Harvard University, the volume was published in 1914, with the professional guidance of Dr. Robert E. Park, an outstanding sociologist, and the advice and counsel of Mr. Robert A. Woods of the South End House. The study itself grew out of the experiences associated with the establishment of a small branch of the South End House in the midst of the Negro ghetto, from which humble beginning also developed the famous Robert Gould Shaw House. According to Woods (who wrote the original introduction to Daniels' book), the main purpose of the study was to turn the attention of Bostonians to the Negro "problem" at home, rather than continuing to focus upon assistance, pecuniary or otherwise, to southern blacks.

The book is an ambitious undertaking; the scope is broad, the method historic and descriptive. Daniels surveys the Negro in Boston from his introduction in 1638 as a slave to the outbreak of World War I. The first two chapters furnish the general background; they treat the Negro's introduction into Massachusetts, briefly indicating the difference between the institution of slavery there and in other colonies, show the gradual rise of a free Negro class and its efforts at self-help, and call attention to the Negro's contribution to the winning of American independence. These chapters also deal with the nation-wide controversy over slavery, noting the importance of the Boston Negro in the antislavery movement, and the role of Bostonian and other Negroes in defending the Union. Much of the material in these chapters was not generally known at the time the book appeared.

In the following seven chapters the author discusses the economic, social, religious, and political strivings of Boston Negroes after the Civil War. On the vital problem of employment, Daniels noted that Negroes were confined largely to the most servile jobs. In 1910, more than 70 per cent of all black males were servants or other menials; for Negro women the concentration was higher. Prejudice of white workmen and employers, lack of skill on the part of Negro workers, and the hostility of trade unions all served, then as now, to adversely affect the hiring of Negroes. Difficulty in securing credit and lack of business training and capital kept Negro businesses small and mainly restricted to the field of service enterprises. Those in the professional class were insignificant in number.

Housing, one of the most pressing problems for

Negroes today, and the cause of much of the violence that has wracked Boston and other cities in recent years, was much the same in 1910. Most Negroes at that time were confined to ghettos, as today they are largely restricted to the Roxbury area. Daniels believed Negroes should be able to live any place they desired and could afford in order to bring up their children in a healthy environment, and therefore that they should be able to acquire real estate. However, while a few Negroes escaped to the suburbs, prejudice in the form of white opposition or inflated property values held their number to a minimum.

The educational picture was brighter. Daniels believed that mixed schools were far superior to separate schools, and was gratified to note that Negroes attended the same schools as whites. But once an education was obtained, Negroes frequently had to go south to secure employment. And in 1914 Boston Negroes were represented in the school system by only one principal, six teachers, and a few officials. (Mental capability, Daniels pointed out, could not be counted as a factor, since Negro children equalled or surpassed white children in scholarship.)

The Negro church also came under Daniels' careful scrutiny, and the author includes some caustic comments on it and its ministers. He was not blind to the awesome potential of the Negro minister in a community depressed by poverty and prejudice, and stated that ministers could become the "most dangerous incendiaries were they so minded," but, he added, all they advocate is "patience and unbounded charity." Unfortunately, the Negro minister generally was illiterate and immoral, a criticism, which despite mitigating circumstances, at that time could hardly be refuted. Daniels found that most Negro churches were debt-ridden and that the Negro community was "over-churched." Yet one Boston Negro church made itself outstanding. The Joy Street Baptist Church, outgrowth of The African Meeting House, became a symbol of liberty for Boston Negroes. This "Negro Cradle of Liberty" was used for abolition meetings. The New England Antislavery Society was organized there and eighteen of the first seventy-two persons who signed the constitution of the society were Negroes.

Around this time fraternal and social benefit organizations, such as the Masons, Elks, and Odd Fellows, were formed for self-help. Negro women also established clubs (one of which evolved into the National Federation of Colored Women's Clubs) and a great deal of relief work was carried on by Negroes. Although these Negro groups worked for social uplift, there was a division as to the best means of preparing the Negro for full acceptance into American society. This cleavage revolved about the philosophies of Booker T. Washington and Dr. W. E. B. Du Bois. Most upper-class Negroes in Boston disagreed with Washington's advocacy of the policy of establishing an economic foundation before seeking the ballot. The mass of Boston's Negroes, however, accepted Washington's philosophy, which was congenial to both southern and northern whites. Washington's main Boston opponent was Monroe Trotter, a Harvard-trained journalist, who sided with Du Bois. Both Du Bois and Trotter agreed that the right to vote was essential to the Negro's acquiring full citizenship rights, as well as every other opportunity open to white Americans. They thought of Washington as an "appeaser." (On one occasion, in July, 1901, Trotter and his followers even went so far as to break up a meeting when Washington tried to speak. Trotter was fined $50.00 and sentenced to thirty days imprisonment.)

After presenting the idealogical and environmental conflicts then prevalent, Daniels assumes a prophetic role (a common practice at the time), examining what the future held for the Negro in Boston and the United States. How could the status of the Negro be further elevated? Daniels mentions first the right to vote, then interracial associations, advances in education, good manners, and appropriate dress and demeanor. He believed that the admission of Negroes to theatres and other public and semi-public institutions would also help. Economic progress he saw as essential, and felt the Negro should adopt the business philosophy set forth by Booker T. Washington's National Negro Business League. He advocated industrial education for Negroes, but unfortunately, like Washington, was unaware that traditional craft education was already obsolete.

The volume concludes with an Appendix in which the author has assembled valuable material in the form of vital statistics, property holdings, and population, emigration, and immigration figures. In addition, there are biographical notes on William Lloyd Garrison and outstanding Boston Negroes, and finally, although the author did not include a bibliography, an ample index.

In general, *In Freedom's Birthplace* received a favorable reception. *The Nation* found it "a painstaking inquiry into a local problem," and sociologist Robert Park, who had initially suggested the survey, referred to it as "unquestionably the best study that has ever been made thus far of the Negro in Northern communities." The reviewer in *The Annals of the American Academy of Political and Social Science,* however, accused Daniels of falling into the trap of seeing too literally and missing "the reality that lies in the unseen fact."

Daniels' book was written against a background of all-pervasive national racism. Scientists, novelists, poets, essayists, social scientists, journalists, ministers, and politicians vied to brand the Negro with the mark of inferiority—physically, mentally, and morally. Well has this period, 1890–1914, been referred to by historian Rayford W. Logan as the Negro's "nadir." It would have been phenomenal indeed had Daniels been able to resist falling back on the cliches and stereotyped thoughts then current. He wrote that the average Negro was inferior to the average white man in "reproductive power; resistance to disease and to general wear and tear; stability; self-control; trust-worthiness; responsibility; accuracy, thoroughness; persistence; constancy of purpose; initiative; self-reliance; positive morality and defined ethical standards." Therefore, when Daniels discussed the future of the Negro, he tried to reconcile his "racist" philosophy with his sociological scholarship. The mounting prejudice against Boston Negroes he ascribed to the excesses of the Negro in the South during Reconstruction, a thesis now descredited by John Hope Franklin, Kenneth Stampp, and other scholars. Further, Daniels erroneously believed that after Emancipation the Negro was really given every civil and economic opportunity equal to those given white citizens. He regarded Booker T. Washington's philosophy of self-help as a super-event, even "providential," and believed that the Negro was making progress, raising the standards of his church, and raising his economic status by buying houses and opening businesses. Daniels even said that the Negro's inferiority was decreasing. He said this inferiority was of a peculiar sort, not like that of lower animals, but like that of a growing child. It was therefore, reducible. Of course, Daniels considered the word "Negro" an acceptable appellation and not a term of reproach. He did not foresee that though once accepted, the term would be rejected today in favor of "black" or "Afro-American."

In spite of his racism, however, in analyzing the status of Boston's Negroes, Daniels made some judgments and observations that accurately reflect the mood of today. For example, he said that the Negro's advance must be based on race pride. Negroes should learn to act together, but first to respect themselves. They must not be ashamed of their race, even though whites had demeaned and debased them and taught them to view themselves with contempt, but must develop pride in their race. This was a precept advocated by men like Carter G. Woodson and Marcus Garvey, and today, by black militants who demand that courses in Afro-American history be instituted in schools and colleges.

The efforts of such men as Prince Hall, Charles Lennox Remond, William C. Nell and Monroe Trotter to elevate the condition of their fellowmen are paralleled today by the many Negroes working for similar ends. The militant David Walker, exhorting his enslaved brethren to rise up and slay their masters, if necessary, to win their freedom, finds echo today in the advocacy of violence by black extremists. And foreshadowing the idealogy of some black activist groups, Daniels believed that "separateness" would lead ultimately to articulation of the Negro into the general community, and that once articulated, the Negro would enrich American society with his gifts. Although Daniels could visualize great poets and eloquent orators rising from the Negro ranks, unfortunately his bias prevented his seeing eminent historians, physicians, statesmen, journalists, teachers, congressmen, judges, and scientists. Nevertheless, he was convinced that his conclusions were not only valid for Boston Negroes, but could be applied to Negroes all over the nation.

Although, from a vantage point of more than fifty years' hindsight, Negroes and many liberal whites may reject Daniels' racist views, the book has merit. Its value has long been recognized, and over the years it has often been cited in works dealing with Negroes in the North. *In Freedom's Birthplace* fills a gap in the urban social history of an important northern community and offers a basis for comparing the problems of Negroes in cities today with their condition a half century ago.

Lorenzo J. Greene
PROFESSOR OF HISTORY
LINCOLN UNIVERSITY

IN FREEDOM'S BIRTHPLACE

IN FREEDOM'S BIRTHPLACE

A STUDY OF THE BOSTON NEGROES

BY

JOHN DANIELS

*Sometime Holder of the South End House Fellowship
in Harvard University; now Secretary of the
Social Service Corporation, Baltimore*

BOSTON AND NEW YORK
HOUGHTON MIFFLIN COMPANY
The Riverside Press Cambridge
1914

PREFACE

To Mr. Robert A. Woods, of the South End House, the writer desires to acknowledge his deep gratitude for constant guidance in connection with the making of the present study. Also to Mr. Albert J. Kennedy and to Mr. William I. Cole, both till recently of the staff of the above Settlement, the writer is greatly indebted, particularly for the painstaking reading and candid criticism of his manuscript preceding its final revision. The plan of casting the account mainly in the historical and the descriptive, rather than the argumentative, mould, to the extent which has been done, was suggested by Dr. Robert E. Park, now of the sociological department of Chicago University.

Any adequate roll of those among the Negro people who have assisted would be impossible to call in the space here permitted. Some, however, have contributed an especially generous quota of their time. Grateful acknowledgment for such service is due Mr. William L. Reed, Mr. Butler R. Wilson, Mr. William H. Lewis, Mr. Archibald H. Grimké, Mr. William M. Trotter, Mr. William H. Dupree, Mr. Robert M. Coursey, Mr. Joshua A. Crawford, Mr. Joseph W. Houston, and Miss Eliza Gardner, — all of Boston. Beyond this, however, the writer wishes to record that the source from which in general he has derived his measure of sympathetic understanding and of close-range information, with regard to the conditions herein described, as well as constant encouragement for the continuance and completion of his inquiries, has been found in the Negro people themselves. To them, their achievements, and their higher and broader future, this study is sincerely dedicated.

In the interest both of accuracy and also of possible subsequent attention to this same subject, the writer will welcome any corrections, amplifications, or suggestions, in connection with the present narrative. For this purpose, he may be addressed in care of the publishers.

CONTENTS

INTRODUCTION

THE residents of the South End House, early in the development of their work, were struck by a curious anomaly in the attitude of Boston citizens toward the Negro. Very large sums of money were annually contributed to schools for appropriate and effective measures of improvement among colored people in the South, while practically no specific attention was paid to the serious problem of the steadily increasing Negro population of Boston itself. A few descendants of the Abolitionists, natural or spiritual, continued to have a care for the broad rights of the Negro, but this somewhat abstract concern seemed to make it the more difficult for them to find that there were once again new occasions bringing new duties; to realize that the issue was no longer merely one of equality but of contact.

For the sake of a more human and more timely relation, the South End House undertook in 1904 a small branch in a street inhabited almost entirely by an isolated cluster of colored families; an experiment which by gradual stages led to the establishment, on an independent basis, of the Robert Gould Shaw House, in the midst of the great Negro quarter of the city.

The present study was begun among experiences associated with that development; and has been continued by Mr. Daniels, as other work would permit, for a period of nine years. It is hoped that this presentment may help the citizens of Boston to focalize their traditional devotion to the cause of the Negro in greater degree upon conditions that are immediate in time and place. It may also be of service in cities and large towns throughout the country where the most distinctive of all our American problems is coming into its urban phase.

It is, indeed, entirely possible that the issue, which for a century has run tantalizingly athwart every large motive of broad national progress, may proceed to play this same rôle, with unexpected variations and complications, in the life of our municipalities. As ever stronger magnets to unskilled labor, the cities of the North inevitably draw the Negroes to them. Even in the South it is anticipated that, with the development of cotton-picking machinery, an increasing proportion of Negroes will be driven from the farming regions to the towns.

It cannot be doubted that the feeling of aversion on the part of the whites in the cities is increasing. Even the incoming immigrants begin to express it. It is often pathetically urged by Negro leaders that this sentiment is imparted to the newcomers by native Americans who have stifled in themselves the sentiments inculcated by their fathers; but the actuality of the color prejudice is shown by the fact that some of the immigrants, notably the Italians, bring it with them.

The city situation may be protected from this new danger, and it may be the means of shifting the Negro problem for the country as a whole into a normal and ultimately manageable angle, if the Negroes can be considered as an unassimilated social factor analogous to the different immigrant nationalities; and the people of the city as a whole, including the colored population, be accustomed to look upon the color line, in many of its aspects, as simply a much more extreme form of the cleavage which separates the different types of immigrants from the natives and from one another. It is true that this analogy is incomplete: — at the point of racial intermixture it ceases. But its practical value can be very great.

In the case of each immigrant nationality, bitter prejudice has been encountered; but such experience has only more firmly established and specialized certain forms of economic, political, and religious allegiance within the nationality group. This formation has, on the whole, eased the process of assimilation; has brought resource more quickly to the hand of the stranger; and made it possible to bring up within the shortest possible time trained and powerful leaders who have secured for themselves, and then for their congeners, a solid and abiding foundation of influence and consideration throughout the community as a whole. This path beaten down by the footsteps of the great multitude of the new Americans is open to the Negro, and it is his only dependable way of entrance into the broad fellowship of American city life. The cities of the country, in their community relations, are, for better or worse, decisively organized on the basis of racial distinctions, and of a particular method for overcoming them. The Negro must adopt the method or rule himself out of the game.

The great secret is that of learning the power of association based on racial loyalty. The immigrants have even proved that a certain sort of segregation, amid all the conflicting currents of city life, is provisionally a blessing. They have also learned the relative futility of scattered pleas for a flat parity of opportunity, and the indomitable quality of collective power in hand. Here is the test of whether the Negro of the cities can develop the urban type of intelligence through which city dwellers maintain themselves and make advances. The present measure of his capacity for registering in thought and purpose the indications of reality is in such achievements and such failures as he is making in organization. If the Negroes of Boston could, for instance, consolidate their purchasing power, and direct it as they collectively chose, they could quickly double or treble the number of their representatives who should be holding responsible positions in industrial and mercantile establishments. Mr. Daniels's treatment will be found particularly suggestive as to whether in economic opportunity the Negroes do not, in spite of prejudice, have almost as much as they on the average and collectively merit.

That the Negroes as a type do not force conviction to the mind of the citizen as an economic asset is to-day very largely owing to the relative incapacity for loyal, continuous, result-getting team-work among themselves. Their minor leaders are destroyed by the jealousies of such as should gladly be their followers; and those who are otherwise equipped to be their major leaders see in all forms of internal organization a truculent surrender of the principle of social equality.

One would be far from forgetting that the Negro suffers under a cruel load of injustice; but the point of incidence of this infliction is not where he thinks it to be.

It is not fundamentally in the outward hindrance to vocational success or cultural recognition, but in the confusion and ineptness with which color prejudice affects the productive moral faculty of a whole racial group. The one great return to be made by the white urban citizen to the Negro for the wrongs which he has suffered is to bring to him in pervading and infectious ways the stirring incentive to group capacity and group achievement, through the long, relentless drill of systematic, purposeful association.

Out of such constructive discipline would emerge a type of Negro leader who would no less sternly fight in defense of every accomplished right of his brethren, but would also gradually and surely place them where they would steadily be gaining a stronger, freer, and fuller life in terms of the indisputable material and moral currency of the city as it is.

ROBERT A. WOODS.

IN FREEDOM'S BIRTHPLACE

CHAPTER I

SLAVE, PATRIOT, AND PIONEER FREEMAN

THE Negro has had his part in the history of Boston almost as long as his Caucasian fellow-citizens. He came into the community in 1638, only eight years after the original settlement.

The first Negroes, apparently but a few in number, were brought to Boston by a trading-vessel, the De-sire, as part of a cargo which, it is interesting to note, consisted for the rest of tobacco and cotton, the two commodities which have become the staples of the Negro's labor in America. These Negroes were brought directly from Providence in the Bahamas, where presumably they had undergone a brief season-ing, but they were in all probability native Africans, who not long before had been captured in the jungle. They were purchased by the people of Boston as slaves.[1]

[1] For the account of the first landing of Negroes in Boston, see Winthrop's *New England*, vol. I, p. 254 (p. 305, Savage edition). There is reason to believe that Negroes had been brought to the vicinity of Boston even before 1638. See *Mass. Hist. Coll.* vol. I, p. 194. One of the earliest writers on New England (Josselyn, author of *Two Voyages to New England*) had occasion to visit Noddle's Island in the harbor, in October, 1637. He found, in the possession of one Maverick, three Negroes, two women and one man. Neither of the women could speak English. One of them seemed to have been a person of high rank in Africa. This writer observed that "the people are well accommodated with servants, some English, others Negroes."

Thus there arose, simultaneously with the Negro's advent, a contradiction between the abstract profession of the white citizens of Boston and their concrete treatment of this race. The Puritans had founded the town in devotion to the cause of spiritual freedom. Yet they did not refrain, within a few years, from placing Negroes in a state of bondage, in which not only was the negation of spiritual freedom implicit, but which took away physical freedom as well. This contradiction was speedily to give trouble to the Puritan conscience, and was to have momentous consequences, in bringing that conscience to bear as a lever to change the Negro's lot. It was a contradiction, moreover, which in modified degree and form has survived to the present, and which still troubles the Boston community.

These first Negroes were not, however, the first slaves in Boston. Indian captives had already been held in slavery. This fact naturally suggests the query as to why Indian slavery did not preclude, or at least continue to coexist with, Negro slavery. The most immediate reason why the enslavement of Indians was not kept up was that the Indian tribes made this practice one of the grievances for their constant wars with the colonists, and in the treaties which were made stipulated its discontinuance. The more intrinsic reason, however, was that the Indian did not prove to be so good a slave as the Negro. On the one hand, the Indian's time-honored traditions had instilled in him the idea that manual toil was degrading, and his characteristic pride made him rebellious against such toil, and still more against the disgrace of being held in subjection. On the other hand, his equally characteristic

sulkiness, his obstinacy in clinging to his own ways and in resisting the civilized ways of the white man, and his laziness, made him unsatisfactory in point of service. The Negro, however, though he lacked the innate pride which in itself commanded respect, was of a cheerful disposition, quick to imitate, readily teachable, and, while somewhat given to loafing and inviting his soul, was for the most part industrious. Curiously enough, it appears from the old records that the Negroes brought to Boston by the Desire had been purchased with the proceeds from the sale of fifteen Indian boys and two squaws whom the vessel had carried away on her outward voyage from her home port, near-by Salem;[1] that is, Indians were practically exchanged for Negroes, — a transaction the inference of which is obvious.

Though these two peoples were not to undergo a common experience in slavery, their destinies were nevertheless interlinked by the white man's coming to America; — destinies strangely alike, yet opposite. The Negroes were to be taken away from their immemorial home-land. The Indians were to have their immemorial home-land taken away from them. There is a suggestion of elemental sympathy in the fact that from the beginning the two races intermarried. To-day, hundreds of Negroes in Boston are imbued with an Indian strain. The Negroes may boast the unique distinction of having more aboriginal American blood flowing through their veins than any other racial group except the present-day Indians themselves. Should the "noble red man" eventually pass into ex-

[1] Winthrop's *New England*, vol. I, p. 234 (p. 279, Savage's edition).

tinction, it will be the Negro who will transmit his heritage to the modern American composite.

There is one further aspect from which the Negro in Boston is a significant figure. His advent in that city followed by only nineteen years the first appearance of Negroes in the colonies.[1] His history in Boston, going back two hundred and seventy-five years, is therefore very nearly coextensive with, and so within bounds representative of, the history of the Negro people in the United States.

For the first century and a half, roughly, from 1638 down to the Revolution, the chronicles bearing upon the subject in hand have to do chiefly with slavery and the slave-trade, and their suppression.

The first slave-ship fitted out in the colonies is believed to have sailed from Boston in 1646.[2] Thereafter not a few Boston merchants engaged in the traffic. Some ships carried barrel-staves, fish, and rum to the Madeiras and the Canaries, and brought back Negroes from the Guinea coast and Madagascar, for sale chiefly in the West Indies, whence cargoes of sugar and molasses were taken home to be manufactured into rum for further trade.[3] Other ships took miscellaneous cargoes to the West Indies and bartered for slaves, which were sold in the Southern colonies.[2] Direct importation of Negroes into Boston remained slight till the close of the century, and never became large. More were obtained indirectly, from the South, and from the Dutch in New York. In 1680, Governor

[1] The first Negroes brought into the colonies were slaves landed at Jamestown, Virginia, in 1619.

[2] U.S. Census, 1860, vol. 2, p. iv.

[3] Reuben Gold Thwaites, *The Colonies*, p. 185.

Bradstreet of Massachusetts stated, "There hath been no Company of blacks or Slaves brought into the Country since the beginning of this plantation, for the space of Fifty yeares,[1] only one small Vessell about two yeares since, after twenty months' voyage to Madagasca, brought hither betwixt Forty and fifty Negro's, most women and children Sold here for 10£ 15£ and 20£ apiece, which stood the merchants in neer 40£ apiece one with another. Now and then, two or three Negro's are brought hither from Barbados and other of his Majesties plantations, and sold here for about twenty pounds apiece. So that there may be within our Government about one hundred or one hundred and twenty." [2] In 1708, Governor Dudley gave four hundred as the number of slaves in Boston, adding that half of these had been born here.[3] The others had been brought in since 1698.[4] From that year to 1727, when, it is recorded, "the traffic in slaves appears to have been more an object than at any period before or since,"[5] from twenty-five to fifty Negroes were brought in annually. Thenceforth there was a steady decline.

The lot of the slaves in Boston, however, was not severe. Most of them were house and body servants, and in fact the less forbidding term "servant" soon came into common use. The Massachusetts Body of

[1] Governor Bradstreet apparently used the expression "Fifty yeares" roughly, or else the Negroes brought to Boston in 1638 were not sufficient in number to be referred to as a "Company."

[2] *Mass. Hist. Coll., Third Series*, VIII, p. 337.

[3] *Thirty-fourth Annual Report of the Mass. Bureau of Statistics of Labor*, p. 230.

[4] Drake's *History of Boston*, p. 574.

[5] *Ibid.*

Liberties of 1641 contained the imperative declaration
that the slaves should be accorded "all the liberties
and Christian usages which the law of God established
in Israel doeth morally require," and the instructions
from the Crown to Governor Andros in 1668 required
him to have a law passed restraining brutality on the
part of masters and overseers, and making wilful killing of slaves punishable by death.[1]

Hardly had slavery got a foothold, moreover, before
opposition to it, on humanitarian grounds, began. As
early as 1701, citizens of Boston had appealed to their
representatives in the colony's Legislature, "to put a
period to negroes being slaves," and to encourage the
bringing in of white servants.[2] The same sentiment
was further evidenced by persistent efforts to stop the
rating of Negroes as live stock for purposes of taxation.
About 1712, Judge Samuel Sewall, the leader of the
anti-slavery agitation of that period, wrote a tract entitled "The Selling of Joseph," which greatly furthered
the movement toward manumission. The slaves themselves entered upon a determined effort to obtain their
freedom. In 1770, James, a slave of Richard Lech-
mere, of Cambridge, brought an action against his
master for detaining him in bondage. The Negroes
raised money enough to employ counsel and push the
matter through to a conclusion. They won a victory,
and from that time on there were many such suits and
the majority of them were successful.[3] A pamphlet
containing an account of the famous Sommersett case,

[1] *Thirty-fourth Annual Report of the Mass. Bureau of Statistics of
Labor*, p. 220.
[2] *Mass Hist. Coll., Second Series*, VIII, p. 184.
[3] Address of Charles Sumner, U. S. Senate, June 28, 1854.

which occurred in England in 1772, and in which the court had ruled that no one could be held in bondage in that country, was widely and effectively circulated in Massachusetts, as well as in the other Northern colonies. In 1773[1] and again in 1777[2] groups of slaves petitioned the Legislature to enact emancipation.

The fact that there were free Negroes — or, as they were styled to distinguish them from the slaves, "free persons of color" — in the community, helped to undermine slavery. As has been mentioned, some Negroes were bound as slaves for a term of years only. Others gained their freedom through exceptional industry or the exhibition of superior qualities. Not a few were set at liberty in return for military service. Some escaped, and, thanks in large part to a public sentiment inclined to be sympathetic, contrived to evade capture and return. Negroes already free often purchased the freedom of kinsmen still held in bondage. Practically from the beginning, moreover, a considerable proportion of slaves were manumitted by more than ordinarily kind-hearted masters. In 1708, according to the town officials' lists, there were thirty-three free Negroes in Boston, and thenceforth their number rapidly increased. The presence of this class prevented slavery from coming to be accepted either by the Negroes or the whites as a foreordained and necessary institution.

Slavery got its death-blow, however, from the rights-of-man fervor which inspired the Revolution.

---

[1] *Mass. Legislative Report on Free Negroes and Mulattoes,* January 16, 1822.

[2] William C. Nell, *Colored Patriots of the Revolution.*

Enthusiasm for the principles of equality could scarcely avoid being brought hard up against the paradox of the Negro's status. Augmented by appreciation of the service which, as will appear, the Negro rendered in the war, that enthusiasm finally assured the Negro his freedom. Though an exact date has never been set to mark the termination of slavery in Massachusetts, the approximate time of its disappearance is sufficiently certain. "How, or by what act particularly, slavery was abolished in Massachusetts, whether by the adoption of the opinion in Sommersett's case, as a declaration and modification of the common law, or by the Declaration of Independence, or by the constitution of 1780, it is not now very easy to determine, and it is rather a matter of curiosity than utility; it being agreed on all hands, that if not abolished before, it was so by the declaration of rights." [1] The declaration of rights here referred to was that drafted by John Adams and adopted by the Massachusetts Constitutional Convention of 1780, the first article of which read: "All men are born free and equal, and have certain natural, essential and unalienable rights: among which may be reckoned the right of enjoying and defending their lives and liberties; that of acquiring, possessing and protecting property; in fine, that of seeking and obtaining their safety and happiness." The slave-trade was formally prohibited in 1788, twenty years before similar action was taken by the Federal Government. In 1790 the first national census showed not a single slave in the state. Though

[1] Statement by Chief Justice Shaw in 1836; — *Commonwealth v. Aves*, 18 Pickering, p. 209.

several other Northern states had by that time adopted acts of conditional emancipation, in the complete elimination of slavery Massachusetts had attained a unique distinction.

This was the first great result wrought by the disturbance which slavery had produced in the Puritan conscience. Boston, as the active center of the movement which brought slavery to an end in Massachusetts, became the birthplace of the Negro's freedom in America, in point of time. There, nearly a century and a half ago, the Negro first came into the estate of a free citizen. Some fourscore years later, Boston was to prove his freedom's birthplace in point of relation to his emancipation throughout the land.

While slavery was being stamped out in Massachusetts, the historic events which terminated in the American Revolution were taking place. It seems like something more than mere coincidence — like a natural intervolution of kindred issues, indeed — that the Negro's first attainment of freedom was contemporaneous with the colonists' victorious struggle for their own independence; and that in this struggle the Negro took a worthy and in truth a memorable part.

The momentous incident which finally drove the colonists to the extreme decision of separation from the mother country was the Boston Massacre. The central hero of that incident was a Negro, or a Negro-Indian half-breed, Crispus Attucks.[1] English troops

---

[1] Attucks was an escaped slave, who had run away from his master, a resident of Framingham, Massachusetts, in September, 1750. In an advertisement for his apprehension, which appeared in the Boston *Gazette* on October 2 of that year, he was described as a mulatto, over six feet in height, and well proportioned.

had been quartered in Boston since October, 1768, to repress any violent opposition to the obnoxious Taxation Act of the previous year. The presence of these troops was most offensive to the citizens and provoked ominous friction. On the evening of the 5th of March, 1770, some soldiers leaving the main guard at the head of King (now State) Street, were met by a crowd armed with cudgels. The resulting row swelled the numbers of the crowd, which soon set itself to harrying the sentinel on duty before the custom house, opposite the head of the street. Finally this sentinel, in exasperation, struck a boy with the butt of his musket. The boy ran off and set up an alarm, and in a few minutes a furious crowd, headed by Attucks, rushed upon the scene. The sentinel was joined by other soldiers, till ten were in line. At last they fired, killing Attucks and two of his companions, James Caldwell and Samuel Gray, and mortally wounding two others, Samuel Maverick and Patrick Carr. The alarm bells of the city clanged, the British drums beat to arms, and the streets were thronged with soldiers and enraged citizens.

Lieutenant-Governor Hutchinson prevented further bloodshed by placing the ten soldiers under arrest and inducing the officers to send the troops back to barracks. But next day a town meeting was held, and the citizens voted "that nothing can rationally be expected to restore the peace of the town and prevent blood and carnage but the immediate withdrawal of the troops." This action forced the removal of the troops to Castle Island in the harbor. Two days later, March 8, a public funeral was held. The four bodies were deposited together in a single grave. Over the grave was erected a stone with this inscription: —

"Long as in Freedom's cause the wise contend,
Dear to your country shall your fame extend,
While to the world the lettered stone shall tell,
Where Caldwell, Attucks, Gray and Maverick fell."

This marked grave lies in the northeast corner of the old cemetery between the Park Street Church and the Tremont Building, close to the grave of Samuel Adams, signer of the Declaration of Independence and Governor of the commonwealth. In a prominent position on the Common, midway facing Tremont Street, stands a more conspicuous memorial, in the form of a monument, erected by the State in 1888. A figure of Liberty holds in her left hand a broken chain, in her right the flag, and at her feet crouches the American eagle. The scene of the massacre is represented on a bronze tablet, the British soldiers with smoking muskets still raised, Attucks lying dead on the ground, and the others falling back into the arms of their fellows. Above, to the left, are carved the words of Daniel Webster, — "From that moment we may date the severance of the British Empire"; and to the left, those of John Adams, — "On that night the foundation of American independence was laid." The Fifth of March was, in fact, celebrated as the chief American holiday till the Fourth of July took its place.

When the Revolution broke out, the question arose as to whether Negroes should be allowed to serve as soldiers. At that time a considerable proportion of the Negroes in Massachusetts, the majority of those in the other Northern colonies, and nearly all of those in the Southern colonies, were still slaves. The opposition to their enlistment appears to have been due mainly to recognition of the obvious inconsistency of calling upon a slave class to help in a war for independence. Because the inconsistency involved was less direct, there was less opposition to enlisting free Negroes. The element that wanted slavery abolished pressed strongly for general emancipation, urging that this was the policy dictated by national self-interest. The proposal was broached in the first Provincial Congress in 1774, but was allowed to subside. In May, 1775, the Committee of Safety passed a resolve that in their opinion "the admission of any persons, as soldiers, but only such as are freemen, will be inconsistent with the principles that are to be supported, and reflect dishonor on the Colony, and that no slaves be admitted into the army upon any consideration whatever." Washington, having assumed command of the army around Boston on July 3, 1775, on the 10th issued instructions to the recruiting officers not to allow any Negro to enlist. At a council of war on October 8, it was agreed unanimously to reject all slaves, and, by a great majority, to reject Negroes altogether, and in November, Washington issued further instructions to that effect.

Whatever may have been the nominal policy in this matter, however, the fact is that Negroes were allowed to serve in the Revolutionary army from the outset, and in increasing numbers till the war's close; for the reason, evidently, that their military service was too badly needed to be refused. Bancroft states that, at Cambridge, "Free Negroes stood in the ranks by the side of white men." On September, 1775, the Continental Congress debated whether to order all Negro soldiers, slave and free, then in service, to be discharged, and apparently because of their number, decided against such action. In December, Washington issued general orders as follows: "As the General is informed that numbers of free Negroes are desirous of enlisting, he gives leave to the recruiting officers to entrain them, and promises to lay the matter before the Congress, who, he doubts not, will approve of it." Congress, in January, 1776, ordered that "the free Negroes who have served faithfully in the army at Cambridge may be reinstated therein, but no others." Though it thus appears that the relaxation applied mainly to free Negroes, yet there is no doubt that a considerable number of slaves served as soldiers, and that many slaves in fact earned their manumission thereby. From an official document dated August 24, 1778, it is known that altogether there were 755 Negroes distributed through the main army under Washington's immediate command.[1] An additional number, it may be assumed, were enlisted in subsidiary corps. Besides, there were at least two fighting bodies composed entirely of Negroes. One of these was the famous Rhode Island regiment, which successfully defended Red Bank at Bunker Hill — 400 Negroes against 1500 Hessians.[2] The other was a Massachusetts company known as "The Bucks of America," and commanded by "Colonel" Middleton, a Boston Negro, who was a

[1] For the account of Negroes in the Revolutionary army, up to this point, the facts have been taken from the *Thirty-fourth Annual Report of the Mass. Bureau of Statistics of Labor*, pp. 227–28.

[2] *Ibid.*, p. 228.

horse-tamer by vocation, and apparently a picturesque character. After the war a banner in recognition of bravery was presented to this company by the Governor.[1]

Of the individual Negro soldiers from Boston and vicinity, the names of several have come down by reason of their exceptional valor or other distinction. Two who made honorable records were John T. Hilton and Seymour Burr, the latter a slave who gained his freedom by serving in the army.[2] Tradition has it that about a dozen members of the Lew family, which appears to have combined valor, musical ability, and thrift, formed themselves into a guerrilla fighting organization known as "Lew's Band." Barzalai Lew was a fifer at Bunker Hill.[3] Primus Hall, of Boston, was body-servant to Colonel Pickering, of Massachusetts, with whom Washington was on the most intimate and confidential terms. There is a story that one evening Washington came to Pickering's tent, to talk over plans, and remained so late that he decided to stay all night. Some time after he had retired, he awoke and saw the Negro sitting up awake. He asked him why he was not in bed, and then, realizing that he himself was occupying the only extra bed, he compelled Hall, in spite of protestations, to share it with him.[4]

The Negro who won most note in the Revolution was Peter Salem, of Framingham, which is not far from Boston. At the Battle of Bunker Hill, he shot and killed the British major, Pitcairn, at the moment

---

[1] W. C. Nell, *Colored Patriots of the Revolution.*
[2] *Ibid.*   [3] *Ibid.*   [4] *Ibid.*

when the latter, leading one of the enemy's most desperate charges, mounted the walls, shouting, "The day is ours." For this exploit he was specially presented to General Washington. In the celebrated picture by Colonel Trumbull, who saw the battle from Roxbury and who made a painting in 1786, the figure of Salem stands out conspicuously, and other Negroes may be discerned among the white soldiers.[1] A representation of Salem also appeared on some of the bills of the old Monumental Bank of Charlestown and of the Freeman's Bank of Boston.[2] When the statue of General Joseph Warren was dedicated on the 17th of June, 1857, the Honorable Edward Everett said, in his address: "It is the monument of the event of the Battle of Bunker Hill; of all the brave men who shared its perils, — alike of Prescott and Putnam and Warren, the chief of the day, and the colored man, Salem, who is reported to have shot the gallant Pitcairn as he mounted the parapet. Cold as the clods on which they rest, still as the silent heavens to which it soars, it is yet vocal, eloquent in their undivided praise."[3]

Such was the account that the Negro rendered of himself in the crisis which determined the future of the land to which he had been brought as a slave, and in which for the most part he was still held in bondage. In that crisis, he did not desert or turn against his enslavers, though he had abundant opportunity so to do. Neither did he prove a coward or a parasite. He made common cause with the white colonials, and fought

---

[1] George Livermore, *Negroes as Slaves, Citizens, and Soldiers.*
[2] W. C. Nell, *Colored Patriots of the Revolution.*
[3] Edward Everett, *Orations and Speeches,* vol. III, p. 259.

loyally by their side as a patriot soldier. Therein was his both an honorable and a substantial part in the birth of the American nation.[1]

Having entered into Boston's history first in the rôle of slave, and then in that of Revolutionary soldier, what part was the Negro to have in the community's upbuilding in ways of free citizenship and peaceful industry? In the years of the nation's beginnings, what advance was the Negro making on his own account?

With respect to the size of the Negro population, the first reliable information had been obtained in 1742. According to a rough census, there were in that year 1374 Negroes in Boston, slave and free. A similar enumeration ten years later showed 1541, forming about ten per cent of a total population of 15,731. In 1754, a special count of slaves was made, and 989 were listed in Boston. At that time, therefore, the free Negroes must have formed a proportion of somewhat over one third. Owing to the decline of the slave-trade and a high mortality, the number of Boston's Negro inhabitants diminished through the remainder of the century. By 1765, it had fallen to 848, and by 1790,

[1] Previous to the Revolution, the Negro had fought in the wars which the colonists waged with the French and their Indian allies. The Lew family also had one or two members in those early conflicts.

Later, in the War of 1812, which tried and proved the strength of the young nation, the Negro again rendered sturdy service. A picturesque story of loyalty is told about one Richard Seavers, of Boston. He had entered the British navy, but at the outbreak of the war he refused to remain with the enemy and gave himself up as a prisoner. He was a man of giant physique and strength, and by virtue of these qualities made himself the "King" of the four hundred and fifty blacks in Dartmoor Prison.

to 766, or only four per cent of the total population. Thenceforth, though the proportion remained practically the same, there was a slow but constant growth in number; to 1174 in 1800, 1468 in 1810, and 1690 in 1820. The increase was due in most part to the coming in of free Negroes, chiefly from other parts of the North, but to some extent from the South. Inasmuch as by 1804, emancipation had taken place in all the states north of Maryland, and the free Negroes had come to form thirteen per cent of the total Negro population of the country, it is clear how the Negro community of Boston was able to draw substantial accessions from this free element.

In the earliest days most of the Negroes who did not, as slaves and servants, live in white households, were congregated about the wharves at the extreme northern tip of the North End, opposite Charlestown. This locality was customarily referred to as "New Guinea." Till about 1820, probably a majority of the Negroes continued to live in various parts of the North End and of the middle portion of the city, now the downtown business section, for the reason that these were till then the only thickly settled districts.[1] Even before 1800, however, there had begun a shifting of the Negro population to the comparatively new and open West End.

The economic status of the Negro at that period is suggested by a most interesting section of the census

[1] For a long time the western portion of the Copp's Hill Burying Ground, which overlooks the harbor, was reserved for slaves and freedmen, the earthly remains of over a thousand of whom lie buried there.

of 1790. This section consisted of a complete list of heads of families, with their names and the number of persons in their households. The fact that the majority of the 766 Negroes in Boston were not entered independently by name, but simply as "Negroes" attached to the respective white households, implies that the passing of slavery had not produced any sweeping change in the local economic and industrial position of this race. Further evidence to the same effect, and applying, moreover, to conditions which still prevailed forty years later, has come down from another source. The city directories of the time used to list the Negroes separately. The directory for 1829 contains the names of 224 Negroes, with their occupations. The total Negro population of that year must have been close to 1690, which was the number shown by the census of the year following. Assuming even that each one of these names was that of a head of a family, and that there were four additional non-working members to each family, nearly 600 persons would still be left unaccounted for. The inference is that at least these 600 Negroes, or approximately a third of the Negro population, were not reckoned of sufficient importance to be hunted up and entered in the directory. They were no doubt family servants, or laborers of lowest grade, who picked up an uncertain living in whatever way they could.

That the Negro was beginning to make industrial and economic progress, however, is also plain. Of the 224 Negroes listed in the directory of 1829, 54 were designated as "laborers." These were doubtless street laborers, care-takers of buildings and estates, and the like. The number of waiters, bootblacks, cooks, window-cleaners, sweeps, wood-sawers, coachmen, and unspecified "servants," was 30; that of laundresses, 8. There were 36 sailors. The trades were represented by a cordwainer, a housewright, a grain-measurer, a soap-maker, a hair-renovator, and a boot-maker. The Negroes had almost a monopoly of the barbering business. The directory gave the names of 32 "hairdressers," most of whom were owners of shops, situated in every part of the city. There were 2 handcart men, 14 clothes shops, most of them on Brattle Street, 4 tailors, a junk-shop, a provision shop, a general shop, and 4 boarding-houses. Thus at that early day a promising proportion of the Negroes had become business proprietors. The sole representatives of the professions were two ministers. The fact that 26 persons were given as having independent residences, but no occupations, and that some of these were widows, warrants the surmise that a few Negroes must have met with sufficient material prosperity to enable them to live on their savings and to leave their families provided for.

The higher field of cultural accomplishment was as yet unentered, save by one interesting figure who will always retain a unique place in the history of her people. This was Phillis Wheatley, the poetess. She was brought to Boston from Africa on a slave-ship in 1761, a little girl of eight or nine years, and was purchased by one John Wheatley as a servant for his wife. She showed a fondness for books, and, encouraged by her mistress, soon acquired what was at that time a superior education. Expression of her thoughts in

verse was natural to her, and at the age of fourteen she
had written poems which indicated her latent ability.
When she was nineteen she was taken to England on a
visit, and was there made much of. A volume of her
poems, dedicated to the Countess of Huntington, and
prefaced by the signed statement of the governor and
the lieutenant-governor of Massachusetts and fifteen
prominent citizens of Boston, witnessing that the writer
was in truth a Negro servant, was published in London in 1773, and subsequently passed through several
editions, in England and America. On her return to
Boston in 1775, Phillis was given her freedom. She
became a member of the congregation which wor-
shiped at the Old South Meeting-House. Soon afterwards the Wheatley family was broken up by death,
and Phillis married a "Dr." Peters, a Negro of more
show than substance, who had a small shop on Court
Street. She fell into severe want, her health failed, and
she died in Boston in 1796.[1] Her volume of verse had
been called, "Poems on Various Subjects, Religious
and Moral," and all her poems had a deeply religious
character. One, entitled "On Being Brought from
Africa to America," is not only typical in this respect,
but because of the author's own life history and the
Negro's position in the community, possesses also a
peculiar interest. It is as follows: —

> " 'T was mercy brought me from my pagan land,
>   Taught my benighted soul to understand
>   That there's a God — that there's a Saviour, too:
>   Once I redemption neither sought nor knew.

[1] For Phillis Wheatley, see William Wells Brown, *The Black Man;*
W. C. Nell, *Colored Patriots of the Revolution;* and the *Encyclopædia
Americana.*

Some view our sable race with scornful eye —
'Their color is a diabolic dye.'
Remember, Christians, Negroes black as Cain
May be refined, and join the angelic train."

Social organization had its beginning among the
Negroes in 1784, in the formation of a Masonic lodge
with fifteen original members. Moreover, this lodge, it
is maintained, was the first, either white or Negro, established in the United States under a charter from the
Masonic body in England.[1] The founder of the lodge
was Prince Hall, one of the small number of Negro
heads of families listed in the federal census six years
later. By vocation he was a soapmaker, by avocation
a preacher, and apparently he was a man of character
and ability, who held the position of leader among his
people. Above his grave in the old Copp's Hill Burying Ground stands a commemorative shaft placed
there in 1895 by the Prince Hall Grand Lodge of Massachusetts (Negro Masonic), which numbers to-day
over six hundred members.

A further and more important advance in organization was made with the founding of the first Negro
church, originally called the African Meeting-House,
in 1805.[2] Previously the Negroes had attended the
same churches as the whites. In the earliest days,
while slavery was still in existence, they were restricted
to certain pews or to a slave gallery, like the one which
may still be seen in the Old North Church. Even after

[1] The author has not gone into the annals of Masonry to ascertain whether this claim is amply supported by evidence.

[2] This church may have grown out of an "African Society," of
which the author has been able to find no other mention than that it
was formed in 1797, with forty-four members.

slavery went out of existence, as a general rule Negroes were expected to sit in the less desirable and least conspicuous seats. It was, apparently, not such discrimination, however, but rather the increase of the Negroes as an element in the population and the growth of a community of interest among them, which led to the formation of a separate Negro church. This church was erected in Smith Court, off Belknap (now Joy) Street, in the West End. The building is said to have been put up entirely with Negro labor.

The establishment of the African Meeting-House had a decisive influence on the Negro colony in two ways apart from its religious life. In the first place, the fact that it was located in the West End no doubt greatly accelerated the movement of the Negroes to that section. Furthermore, by providing the Negroes with the only good-sized gathering place of their own, it naturally became their principal rallying-point, not only for religious purposes, but for whatever other object might bring them together. In this way it did much to promote their general group development.

As in the case of church attendance, so it was also in the case of school attendance; — for a long time Negro children went to the public schools with the white children, though apparently they were kept more or less apart from them. The number of Negro children who took advantage of this common privilege, however, was very small, one of the alleged reasons therefor being that they were ridiculed and at times mistreated by the white children. In 1798, some of the more ambitious Negro parents made the independent move of opening a private school, in the support of which friendly white persons soon assisted. Shortly after the erection of the African Meeting-House, in 1805, the school was transferred thither, and there continued in existence twenty-nine years. In 1800, the next step was taken; a petition, signed by sixty-six Negroes, asking that the city establish and support a separate school for Negro children, was submitted to the school committee. This request was refused, apparently on the ground that Negro children were still free to attend the general public schools, until 1820, when the city did start a Negro primary school. The fact that even then, however, after a school had been especially founded, not more than a third of the Negro children attended,[1] shows that previously it must have been lack of ambition, combined with economic pressure, on the part of the majority of Negro parents, rather than unpleasant treatment of their children at the hands of white children, which was mainly responsible for keeping the Negro boys and girls away from the public schools. Though so far as available records show, no formal action was taken to revoke the Negro's privilege of attending the general schools, that privilege practically lapsed into disuse soon after the establishment of the separate school.

The Negro's effective right to the franchise is said to have been established by the test case of Paul and John Cuffe, in 1778. These two thrifty Negroes, of whom the former, Paul Cuffe, was a successful ship-owner and far-ranging navigator,[2] were called upon by

[1] *Report of the Primary School Committee*, June 15, 1846.
[2] Booker Washington, *The Story of the Negro*.

the Town of Dartmouth, not far from Boston, to pay
a personal tax. They demurred, contending that inasmuch as they were not allowed to vote, they should
not be held to pay taxes. After protracted argument,
the town authorities admitted that taxpaying and the
privilege of voting should go together. The case was
regarded as establishing a precedent.[1] Any further
question as to the Negro's rights was settled by the
adoption of the Body of Liberties of 1790, which guar-
anteed manhood suffrage, without regard to race. Yet
at that period very few of the Negroes in Boston exercised the franchise, or took any interest in political
affairs.

The founding of the Negro Masonic lodge, the
Negro church, and the Negro school, and the successful protest of the Cuffes against taxation without representation, are most of all significant as bearing witness to the rise of a spirit of self-reliance on the part of
the Negroes. Previously they had been dependent, as
slaves or servants, on the whites, with little initiative
of their own. Their budding independence therefore
first led them naturally into a centripetal movement
of separate organization among themselves. Any hostility on the part of the whites was apparently a
secondary factor in this result.

What, however, were the actual relations between
the Negro and his white fellows at that time? What
place did the Negro then occupy in the community?

---

[1] W. C. Nell, *Colored Patriots of the Revolution.* It is not entirely
clear, however, whether this case established the positive right to
vote, or only the negative right to withhold taxes unless allowed to
vote.

The very names which many of the race bore, as shown by the heads of families section of the 1790 census, are suggestive of the Negro's status.[1] "Crum" Barnes, "Cuff" Bennett, and "Sambo" Jackson are not appellations which conjure up individuals of any great degree of dignity and respect. And in fact the Negro's position at that time, generally speaking, appears to have been not far above the level of such names. It was a position too inferior to carry a suggestion of any sort of equality with the whites. For this very reason, the Negro was not the object of the kind of animosity on the part of the whites which in later years the suggestion of equality aroused. Rather, he was looked upon as belonging to a lower order, and as being the ordained serving-man of the community. As such he was treated for the most part with condescending good humor. But he was also made the butt of jest and sport, and sometimes the victim of brutal outbursts.

Testimony to both the ill usage the Negro suffered, and the way he himself felt regarding the treatment

[1] This census is interesting also as shedding light on the derivation of Negro names and revealing them in process of formation. Many are Biblically inspired, as, for instance, "Adam" Rowe, "Joel" Harding, "Luke" Taylor, and "Samson" Brown. "Solomon Isaac" assumed or was burdened with more than his fair share of responsibility for perpetuating the memory of the Old Testament worthies. Another large class of names hark back to the heroes of ancient secular history and even to the gods of mythology; as, for instance, "Cato" Moore, "Nero" Davis, "Cyrus" Eustis, and "Jupiter" Smith. Other names were apparently geographically derived. "Boston" occurs both as a surname, as in "Philip Boston," and as a first name, as in "Boston Roby," "York" Ruggles, "Charlestown" Fluckes, "Glouster" Haskins, and "Hampshire Dennie." The majority of the surnames are those of the white families in which the bearers or their parents had served.

meted out to him, is afforded by an extract from a "Charge to the African Lodge" which Prince Hall, to whom reference as the founder of that lodge has been made, delivered to his fellow-Masons in 1797, and which was subsequently published in pamphlet form. The extract in point is as follows: —

Now, my brethren, as we see and experience, that all things here are frail and changeable and nothing here to be depended upon: Let us seek those things which are above, and at the same time let us pray to Almighty God, while we remain in the tabernacle, that he would give us the grace of patience and strength to bear up under all our troubles, which at this day God knows we have our share. Patience, I say, for were we not possessed of a great measure of it, you could not bear up under the daily insults you meet with in the streets of Boston; much more on public days of recreation, how are you shamefully abus'd, and that at such a degree, that you may truly be said to carry your lives in your hands; and the arrows of death are flying about your heads; helpless old women have their clothes torn off their backs, even to the exposing of their nakedness. . . . My brethren, let us not be cast down under these and many other abuses we at present labour under: for the darkest is before the break of day.

Absence of bitterness, enduring patience, simple religious faith, and persistent hopefulness were the qualities evinced in this exhortation. And these qualities had in fact characterized the Negro from the beginning and have continued to characterize him, in his reaction to the adversities of his lot.

From time to time various attempts had been made to stop the immigration of Negroes to Boston and even to get rid of those already here, on the ground that poverty, disease, and crime were rife among them. In

1788, during the same session of the Legislature which adopted the act prohibiting the slave-trade, a law was passed for the suppression and punishment of " rogues, vagabonds, common beggars, and other idle, disorderly, and lewd persons." By Section V of this law it was provided, "that no person being an African or Negro, other than a subject of the Emperor of Morocco, or a citizen of some one of the United States (to be evidenced by a certificate from the Secretary of the State of which he is a citizen), shall tarry within this Commonwealth for a longer time than two months."[1] And in the "Massachusetts Mercury" of September 16, 1800, appeared the following "Notice to Blacks": —

The officers of police having made return to the subscriber of the names of the following persons, who are Africans or Negroes, not subjects of the Emperor of *Morocco* nor citizens of the United States, the same are hereby warned and directed to depart out of this Commonwealth before the 10th day of October next, as they would avoid the pain and penalties of the law in that case provided, which was passed by the Legislature March 26th, 1788. Charles Bullfinch, *Superintendent*, by order and direction of the selectmen.

This and other similar efforts to get rid of the Negroes by a policy of intimidation failed of their object, however, because they did not after all represent the final decision of the community. The more deliberate attitude received expression in the report in 1822 of a legislative committee appointed the year before to draft a bill restricting the admission of free Negroes into the state. In submitting that report the chair-

---

[1] *Thirty-fourth Annual Report of the Mass. Bureau of Statistics of Labor*, p. 223.

man of the committee, Theodore Lyman, Jr., of Boston, first admitted that no doubt the severe "Black Laws" of most of the other Northern states were driving Negroes into Massachusetts, where they received comparatively humane treatment; that his colleagues and himself could not but be alarmed by "the increase of a species of population, which threatened to become both injurious and burdensome"; that "the black convicts in the State Prison, on the first of January, 1821, formed $146\frac{1}{2}$ part of the black population of the State, while the white convicts, at the same time, formed but 2140th part of the white population"; and that "it is believed a similar proportion will be found to exist in all public establishments of this State; as well Prisons as Poor-Houses."

Nevertheless, he stated, his committee had been unable to report the repressive measure requested. Referring to the law of 1788, he said: —

This law has never been enforced, and ineffectual as it has proved, they [i.e., his committee] would never have been the authors of placing among the Statutes a law so arbitrary in its principles, and in its operation so little accordant with the institutions, feelings, and practices of the people of this Commonwealth. The history of that law has well convinced the Committee that no measure (which they could devise) would be attended with the smallest good consequence. That it would have been a matter of satisfaction and congratulation to the Committee if they had succeeded in framing a law, which . . . should have promised to check and finally to overcome an evil upon which they have never been able to look with unconcern. But a law which should produce that effect would entirely depart from that love of humanity, that respect for hospitality and for the just rights of all classes of men, in the constant and successful exercise of which the inhabitants of Massachusetts have been singularly conspicuous.[1]

That is, — the whites did not like the Negro, they looked upon him as an objectionable element in the community, and they would have been glad to be rid of him. But they could not bring themselves to the point of open and avowed persecution. There was the same old contradiction between principles and practice. There was the same troubling of the Puritan conscience. Conscience again prevailed, with the result, this time, that Massachusetts left her doors open to Negroes seeking refuge from oppression in other states.

While the question of the Negro was thus a subject of debate and a cause of more or less uneasiness, it was still, however, a question which came up only intermittently, which on such occasions was discussed without excitement, and which, furthermore, was regarded as predominantly local in its bearings. It neither deeply agitated nor seriously divided the community. This, in substance, was the situation in Boston at that early period, as the first half-century following the Declaration of Independence neared its close.

But an epoch-making advance beyond this largely passive attitude was close at hand.

---

[1] *Legislative Report on Free Negroes and Mulattoes*, January 16, 1822.

CHAPTER II

A RACE DELIVERED

Section 1. The Abolition Struggle

The Abolition Movement arose in Boston, and till the end had its moral center in that city. It forced the question of the Negro before the community in a way that would not down, and which no longer permitted its discussion in calmness. It changed that question from one of mainly local bearing to one of vital import to the nation. It agitated Boston, the North, and the whole country, to the foundations. It hastened and was, indeed, one of the chief provoking causes of the Civil War. And ultimately it accomplished the eradication of slavery throughout the reëstablished Union.

The Boston Negro, himself first among his people to have experienced freedom, had a specific share in the struggle which gave freedom to his brethren.

Fully to understand this movement which proved so far-reaching, it is necessary to trace the previous course of public opinion with regard to the institution of slavery. Though it is doubtful if the sentiment against slaveholding reached equal strength elsewhere so soon as it did in Boston, the early expressions of such sentiment in New England were not the exclusive nor even the original ones. The initial protests representing any considerable body of opinion were voiced by the Pennsylvania Quakers, in logical accord with their religion of brotherly love, and the earliest anti-slavery society

was organized by them in 1775.[1] By the close of the
Revolution, whose dominant principle of the natural
rights of man, and whose disenslavement of large numbers of Negroes in compensation for military service,
entered in as conclusive factors in the result, the
movement toward emancipation was progressing rapidly in the northern part of the country, and what is
more, was making steady advance in the South. In
1787, Congress passed, with slight Southern opposition, the famous Northwest Territorial Government
Ordinance, precluding slavery from the great Northwest Territory ceded by England, and as yet the only
addition beyond the thirteen original states.[2] Soon
thereafter societies favoring manumission were formed
in Maryland and Virginia. In 1794, the advocates of
emancipation from various parts of the country, South
as well as North, began to meet frequently in convention. Thenceforth, too, the submission to Congress of
petitions, some seeking the further regulation of the
slave-trade, others the suppression of slaveholding in
the District of Columbia, but all of a distinct, though
limited, anti-slavery character, became increasingly
frequent. All the Northern states had adopted emancipation acts by 1804.

By that time it had come to be assumed in the
North, and apparently agreed to in the South, that at
least slavery would not be extended beyond its then
existing boundaries, and that in every new state

[1] The Pennsylvania Society for Promoting the Abolition of Slavery, the Relief of Free Negroes unlawfully held in Bondage, and Improving the Condition of the African Race.

[2] Comprising the present states of Ohio, Michigan, Illinois, In-
diana, Wisconsin, and part of Minnesota.

created from territory outside the original thirteen, it would be expressly forbidden. Furthermore, the majority opinion in the North was that even in the South the institution would eventually come to an end, partly through its own gradual decline, and partly through federal action. Though it was granted that the Federal Government had no constitutional power to exclude slavery from any of the original states, it was expected that in time a sufficient number of additional free states would be admitted to insure the adoption of a constitutional amendment conferring that power.

Meanwhile, however, had occurred an event, of an immediately industrial character, which was speedily to reverse and to alter this course of affairs. That event was the invention by Eli Whitney, in 1793, of the cotton gin.

Cotton was the South's principal slave product. Formerly, it had been necessary to prepare the cotton for manufacture, separating the fiber from the seeds, either by hand or by clumsy contrivances which improved but little upon hand labor. Inasmuch as the process when thus carried out was exceedingly slow, it involved such an amount of slave labor as to leave the planter's margin of profit small. Whitney's invention effected a revolution. It provided machinery which prepared at least a thousand pounds of cotton in place of every five or six which had been possible before. In 1793, the entire export of cotton from the South was 500,000 pounds; only seven years later, in 1800, the export to England alone had multiplied to 16,000,000 pounds.

The basic reason why slavery had previously been losing ground in the South was because it had not proved a sufficiently paying investment. Following the introduction of Whitney's cotton-gin, however, it began to yield huge profits. As a result, the South became commercially wedded to the maintenance of the slave system, and Southern talk of emancipation soon ceased, except on the part of a small number of reformers. The South also commenced to show increasing resentment toward all Northern discussion of an anti-slavery character. Inasmuch, moreover, as Northern textile manufacturers used a large part of the supply of raw cotton, the North on its own account came to have a considerable commercial interest in slavery. This fact worked in the direction of reconciling Northern public opinion to the continuance of the "peculiar institution," at least for an indefinite period, within the Southern states; it still being tacitly assumed, however, that it would not be extended elsewhere.

So the matter rested till 1818, when Missouri applied for admission to statehood. Then the South showed plainly that it was no longer content to have slavery let alone where it already existed, but that it meant to engraft it upon such new territory as appeared suitable for its growth.

Missouri was a part of the Louisiana Purchase, acquired from France in 1803.[1] For that vast tract,

---

[1] Comprising the present states of Louisiana, Arkansas, Missouri, Oklahoma, Nebraska, Iowa, North Dakota, South Dakota and the greater part of Kansas, Colorado, Wyoming, Montana, and Minnesota.

which was still the only annexation besides that of the Northwest Territory, already mentioned, no specific and decisive action, either permitting or forbidding slavery, had yet been taken. The North now proposed that the prohibition of slavery be made a condition of Missouri's admission. A majority of her inhabitants, however, were Southern emigrants, who wanted to see slavery established. The South as a unit showed the same intention. The North arrayed itself quite as solidly on the side of free soil. Much more was actually at stake, be it said, than whether slavery should or should not prevail in Missouri. There was the same question with reference to the rest of the Louisiana Purchase. Furthermore, there was what the South held to be the most important question of all: — the right of the Federal Government to make admission to statehood dependent upon the extraordinary condition of slavery's exclusion. So the issue was joined, for two years contested with increasing bitterness, and at last brought to a termination only by a compromise, — the memorable Missouri Compromise of 1820. By that agreement, Missouri was to be admitted with no restriction as to slavery. In the remainder of the Louisiana Purchase, slavery was to be allowed in the comparatively small section south of latitude 36° 30',[1] and to be prohibited in all the immense area, except Missouri, lying north of that parallel.

This struggle marked the first open clash, on a national scale, between the anti-slavery and the pro-

[1] Comprising the present state of Louisiana, and the greater part of Arkansas and Oklahoma.

slavery forces. Its results were momentous. It put an end once and for all to the complacent belief that there was no danger of slavery's extension. It enraged the North, which charged the South with having broken implicit faith with the nation. It made the South realize more fully than ever before the strength of Northern opposition to slavery. At the same time, by virtue of winning Missouri and the region south of 36° 30′ from the North as slave soil, it engendered in the South a fatal confidence in its power to overcome that opposition. It gave rise to a consciousness of fundamental and perilous difference and divergence between the two sections. In the heat of congressional debate and the excitement of popular clamor, prophecies and threats of disunion and civil war had in fact been uttered. Finally, the struggle left neither side satisfied. Its net result was simply to leave the question of slavery in suspense.

The Compromise did, however, for the time being, remove that question from the field of immediate and violent contention. After the vent of passion, there came, as if half from exhaustion and half from a sense of imminent danger in forcing the conflict further, a reaction and a lull. Both North and South seemed to enter into a mutual conspiracy of silence regarding what each recognized as the paramount issue between them. In the North, anti-slavery discussion of any pronounced character was thereafter looked at askance, and agitation was actively discouraged. The anti-slavery conventions of Quakers and others, which had lapsed from 1808 to 1820 and had then been revived by the Missouri excitement, were abandoned after 1829.[1] The opposition to slavery became quiescent.

Such was the situation on the eve of the Abolition Movement.

The Negroes of Boston, interestingly and appropriately enough, were in a sense this movement's immediate forerunners, and one of their number stood in a sort of John the Baptist relation to its founder. About 1826, some of the most progressive Negroes of Boston and the state at large organized the General Coloured Association of Massachusetts, which had for its purpose promoting the welfare of the race, principally by working for the destruction of slavery.[2] At the Association's convention in 1828, David Walker, a leader among his people in Boston, delivered a stirring anti-slavery address, which subsequently appeared in "Freedom's Journal," the first Negro paper in the United States.[3] In September of the following year, Walker published a booklet of some eighty pages, entitled "An appeal in Four Articles, together with a Preamble to the Coloured Citizens of the World, but in Particular, and very Expressly, to Those of the United States of America." It opened thus: "Having

[1] Except for a last formal meeting in 1833, by which time this earlier anti-slavery movement had been practically absorbed by the Abolition Movement proper. For a brief account, with dates, of the early movement, see *William Lloyd Garrison, the Story of his Life, Told by his Children*, vol. i, p. 89, footnote.

[2] Some of the Society's more prominent members were Hosea and Joshua Easton, John E. Scarlett, Thomas Cole, James G. Barbadoes, William G. Nell, Thomas Dalton, John T. Hilton, Fred Brimley, Coffin Pitts, and Walker Lewis. W. C. Nell, *Colored Patriots of the Revolution*.

[3] Published at New York City; W. C. Nell, *Colored Patriots of the Revolution*.

travelled over a considerable portion of these United
States, and having in the course of my travels, taken
the most accurate observations of things as they exist
— the result of my observations has warranted the full
and unshaken conviction that we (Coloured people of
these United States) are the most degraded, wretched,
and abject set of beings that ever lived since the world
began." The author then proceeded to set forth the
reasons for this unprecedented misery in four "Articles," or chapters, and the causes he assigned were:
first of all, slavery, with its legion of evil consequences;
second, the Negro's own ignorance; third, the upholding of the slave system by so-called Christian ministers;
and fourth, the colonizing, or Liberian plan, which, by
its proposal of removing the Negroes to some other
country, prevented them from feeling that they were
an integral part of the American nation and from being regarded as such by the whites. The language is
clear and forceful, the argument substantial. The following passage from the second "Article" is impressive
not only as being sufficient unto the day and conditions which called it forth, but as perhaps far antici-
pating the future: "Your full glory and happiness . . .
shall never be fully consummated, but with the entire
emancipation of your enslaved brethren all over the
world. . . . For I believe it is the will of the Lord that
our greatest happiness shall consist in working for the
salvation of our whole body. When this is accomplished a burst of glory will shine upon you, which will
indeed astonish you and the world."

The "Appeal" contained also much bitter denunciation of the slaveowners, together with inflammatory

exhortation of the slaves to rise, throw off their bonds, and defend themselves against their oppressors. Withal, it was the first anti-slavery explosion that broke upon the brief period of constrained silence following the Missouri Compromise. It passed rapidly through three editions and was read and discussed throughout the country. The effect it produced in the South was immediate and tumultuous. The slaveowners were furious that a Negro, the son of a slave, should make this open attack upon them.[1] The Virginia Legislature passed a special act prohibiting the "Appeal's" circulation. The Legislature of North Carolina went into secret session to devise means of counteracting its influence. The governor of Georgia wrote to the mayor of Boston requesting him to suppress it. The latter replied that he should be well enough pleased to do this, but that he did not have the necessary legal power. A reward of a thousand dollars was offered in the South for Walker's dead body, and ten times as much for him alive. His wife and his friends urged him to go over the border into Canada, but he preferred to remain in Boston and take his chances. The following year, 1830, he died, at the age of thirty-four.[2]

[1] Walker was born in Wilmington, North Carolina, in 1785, the child of a free mother and a slave father. As a boy, he had become imbued with a violent hatred for the institution of slavery, and had left the South and come to Boston, where he applied himself diligently to study and self-culture. In 1827, he became proprietor of a clothing shop on Brattle Street. He was a very generous man, and had the name of being always ready to help the poor and needy of his race. In many ways he had labored against slavery, but it was his "Appeal" which brought him into sudden prominence.

[2] For the above and further facts regarding Walker and the *Appeal*, see *William Lloyd Garrison*, vol. I, pp. 159–61, 231.

The man who now advanced, to fulfill the mission of giving the slaves their freedom, attached so much importance to Walker's "Appeal" that he characterized it as "one of the most remarkable productions of the age." [1] It came into his hands shortly after its publication, and before he had fully determined upon his own course.[2] In all probability, it appreciably influenced him, and thus bore not only a precedent and perhaps prophetic, but in some degree a causative, relation to his subsequent crusade.

This man was William Lloyd Garrison, and the definitive beginning of the Abolition Movement, as history distinguishes it, was the appearance in Boston, on January 1, 1831, of the first number of his weekly paper, "The Liberator," with this pithy announcement of the editor's purpose:

"Assenting to the self-evident truth maintained in the American Declaration of Independence, 'that all men are created equal, and endowed by their Creator with certain inalienable rights — among which are life, liberty, and the pursuit of happiness,' I shall strenuously contend for the immediate enfranchisement of our slave population."[3]

On the one side, the Declaration of Independence; on the other, slavery: what was this? Nothing more and nothing less than the reappearance of that contradiction which from the beginning had been the Nemesis of the Puritan conscience. That conscience had

---

[1] *William Lloyd Garrison*, vol. I, p. 231.

[2] *Ibid.*, vol. I, p. 160.

[3] For a brief sketch of Garrison's previous career, and the events leading up to his establishment of *The Liberator*, see Appendix, pages 443–46.

been compelled to do away with slavery first in Massachusetts, then in the whole North. Now it was to be mercilessly pursued till it should have put an end to slavery throughout the nation.

Immediate freedom for all the slaves, in every state and territory of the Union: — that was the new and epochal element in Garrison's demand. When he raised that demand unequivocally, the North's dormant hostility to slavery related almost wholly to its further extension, and hardly at all to its continued existence in the area which it had already occupied. The most that earlier anti-slavery sentiment had sought was gradual abolition. Neither of these exigencies had greatly alarmed the slaveholders. The one afforded abundant opportunity to compromise, the other to temporize. Now, however, the South was quick to perceive that once the moral sense of the North should respond to the contention that the slaves were entitled to freedom forthwith, the institution of slavery would be engripped in a struggle for life and death.

A determined moral appeal to the North and the turning of this moral power upon the South, through every peaceful channel, was what Garrison proposed. He did not urge that the federal authorities should at once abolish slavery in the Southern States by the use of force. He granted that while the National Government could and should prohibit slavery in the territories and the District of Columbia, it did not have the constitutional power to exclude it from any of the states. And being a non-resistant, he was in principle opposed to coercion. He uttered the warning, however, that if the destruction of slavery by peaceful means should prove impossible, a bloody war would be inevitable.

The slow but certain enlargement through the North, in the face of apathy and even violent opposition, of the movement which Garrison started; the steadily growing number of great leaders who enlisted under the banner he unfurled, and whose names have rightfully taken place beside his own; the many degrees of hostility to slavery, and the confusing differences over constitutional and political aspects of the question, which ere long divided the Abolitionists into a political-conservative wing that broke away from Garrison, and a moral-radical wing that still followed him and continued the agitation in its original form to the end; the bitter struggles over the admission or exclusion of slavery from new territory, which conspired with the Abolitionists in forcing the issue unavoidably before the nation; the rapid incensement of the South to the verge of rebellion; the Union-saving panic which then seized the North, aggravating to its maximum the denunciation of the Abolitionists as enemies of the national welfare; the South's acceptance of the election of a Republican President as the virtual triumph of abolition doctrine; secession; the infuriation of the North by the attack upon Fort Sumter; the outbreak of the "irrepressible conflict"; and, at last, President Lincoln's Emancipation Proclamation: — all these momentous stages, in the progress toward slavery's destruction, necessary limitations of space make it impossible here more than barely to suggest. It will be necessary from this point to focus attention upon the events of the Abolition struggle in Boston, taking account of those in the national arena only so far as they particularly influenced, or were particularly influenced by, the course of affairs in that city. Still more especially is it the present purpose to note the part taken by the Negroes of Boston.

The "Liberator" immediately became the object of an onslaught of invective from the South and of censure in the North. Its suppression by force was urged upon the mayor of Boston.[1] That official replied that, as a result of his inquiries, he found the paper had only an "insignificant countenance and support"[2] in the community, and that it "had not made, nor was likely to make, converts among the respectable classes."[3] He said he had "ferreted out the paper and its editor; that his office was an obscure hole,[4] his only visible auxiliary a Negro boy, and his supporters a very few insignificant persons of all colors."[5]

One year following the establishment of the "Liberator," however, these "insignificant persons" took the first stride in the Abolition Movement's effective working organization, by launching the New England Anti-Slavery Society. The meeting at which this

[1] Harrison Gray Otis, who was also the one that had been petitioned to suppress Walker's *Appeal*.

[2] *William Lloyd Garrison*, vol. I, p. 242.

[3] *Ibid.*, vol. I, pp. 244–45.

[4] This phrase inspired Lowell's poem "To W. L. Garrison", the first stanza of which is as follows: —

> "In a small chamber, friendless and unseen,
>   Toiled o'er his type one poor, unlearned young man;
>   The place was dark, unfurnitured and mean; —
>   Yet there the freedom of a race began."

[5] *William Lloyd Garrison*, vol. I, p. 245.

society was formed, on the evening of January 6, 1832, took place in the old African Meeting-House, which thereby, and also because of its subsequent use for abolition gatherings, may be said to have become to the Negroes in particular the "Cradle of Liberty" which Faneuil Hall is to the community at large. Though the twelve signatures affixed to the previously drafted declaration of principles were those of white men, about one quarter of the seventy-two first signers of the constitution were Negroes.[1]

This society immediately entered upon an aggressive campaign of agitation. During its first year, it was probably responsible for more anti-slavery addresses and petitions throughout New England than had taken place during the preceding forty years.[2] It became the prototype of similar societies which from that time forth sprang up in constantly increasing numbers all over the North. It is interesting to observe in passing that among the specific objects of this organization was that of raising funds to establish a manual training school for Negro youth.[3] Even the pioneer band of Abolitionists, notwithstanding their apostolic zeal for the Negro's abstract rights, recognized what was to become increasingly obvious as the years went by — namely, that practical preparation for earning a livelihood had a vital relation to the Negro's welfare. Little came of the effort in this direction in Boston, however, if indeed any persistent effort was made.

---

[1] For fuller details regarding the society's formation, see *William Lloyd Garrison*, vol. I, pp. 279–82.

[2] *Ibid.*, vol. I, p. 283.   [3] *Ibid.*, vol. I, p. 282.

The position which the Boston Negroes occupied at
that period has been described at an earlier point in
the present narrative. Though they had been free for
a long time, they were still looked down upon, in common with the free Negroes throughout the North, as
an inferior caste, to whom their liberty was in fact
more of an evil than a good, and whose lot was if anything worse than that of the slaves. This despised
element of the population no one had previously
thought of addressing as though they had any independent interests of their own, and any importance in
the affairs of the community. Garrison, however,
made as direct and full an appeal to them as he did to
his own race, calling upon them to consecrate themselves to the cause of their brethren's emancipation.
While striving for the abolition of slavery in the South,
his own companion purpose was "to elevate our free
colored population in the scale of society" in the
North.[1] He advised that class to cultivate self-respect,
as their good example would break many fetters, and
their temperance, industry, peaceableness, and piety
would prove the safety of granting freedom to their
fellows. They should put their children in school and
educate themselves; form societies for general improvement, — among the women as well as the men,
for "no cause can get along without the powerful aid
of women's influence"; they should put aside jealousies, support each other in trade dealings, and have
some sort of national organization. They should
stoutly maintain all their legal rights, inasmuch as the
Constitution of the United States made no "invidious

[1] *William Lloyd Garrison*, vol. I, p. 234.

distinction with regard to the color or condition of free inhabitants." Wherever they possessed the franchise they should go to the polls, vote for those friendly to their cause, and, if possible, for intelligent and respectable men of their own color. They should constantly exercise in their own behalf the privilege of petition. All thought of leaving America, and colonizing themselves in Africa, Haiti, or elsewhere, should be abandoned. They should once and for all look upon America as their country, be patriotic, and observe Independence Day with fasting and prayer. Finally, they should put their supreme trust in God, for they of all peoples "needed the consolations of religion to sustain them in their grievous afflictions." "My countrymen and friends," he declared, "I have solemnly dedicated my health, and strength, and life, to your service. I love to plan and to work for your social, intellectual, political, and spiritual advancement. My happiness is augmented with yours: in your sufferings I participate. . . . I believe, as firmly as I do my own existence, that the time is not far distant when you and the trampled slaves will all be free — free in the spirit as well as in the letter — and enjoy the same rights in this country as other citizens." The success of their cause, he told them, was part of the "signs of the times," in harmony with the French and Belgian revolutions, the Polish insurrection, the agitation over the Reform Bill in England, and the steps toward emancipation of the Negroes in the Danish, Portuguese, French, and British colonies. "The whole firmament is tremulous with an excess of light." [1]

[1] *William Lloyd Garrison*, vol. I, pp. 255-58. The foregoing ex-

The Boston Negroes responded to this appeal as to a "trumpet call."[1] For the first time, they felt they could draw themselves up to the stature of men. They began to express themselves through the columns of the "Liberator," of whose supporting corps of subscribers they soon came to form a substantial contingent. At the outset of the Abolition Movement they nevertheless felt constrained, in view of their previous slight association with the whites, to keep for the most part by themselves. A Boston committee was appointed by the first annual convention of free Negroes, held at Philadelphia in June, 1831 — a gathering which was addressed by Garrison, and which had in fact been brought about as a joint result of his agitation and the circulation of Walker's "Appeal."[2] That committee had the double function, apparently, of promoting the welfare of the free Negroes and coöperating in the anti-slavery campaign.[3] Subsequently, the Negroes themselves formed a number of abolition societies, which carried on an active propaganda among their own people from that time forth.[4]

tracts are taken chiefly from Garrison's address before the First Annual Convention of Free Colored People, Philadelphia, 1831.

[1] *William Lloyd Garrison*, vol. I, p. 233.

[2] This convention was attended by delegates from the five states of Pennsylvania, New York, Maryland, Delaware, and Virginia. Massachusetts, as it happened, was not directly represented. W. C. Nell, *Colored Patriots of the Revolution.*

[3] The committee consisted of Hosea Easton, Robert Roberts, James G. Barbadoes, and the Rev. Samuel Snowden, pastor of the Methodist Church on May Street, which had been organized in 1828. The latter and the Rev. Thomas Paul, pastor of the African Meeting-House, were the only Negro ministers in Boston at that time, and both were active in the Abolition cause. *Ibid.*

[4] Two of these, for instance, whose names have come down, were the African Abolition Free-Hold Society, and the African Female Anti-Slavery Society.

But while such separate organization was continued for its supplementary value, the Negroes were speedily welcomed into close union with the white Abolitionists. In January, 1833, the General Coloured Association of Massachusetts sought to be affiliated with the New England Anti-Slavery Society as an auxiliary. Not only was the request cordially granted, but a representative of the Negroes was elected to the society's board of counselors. Within the next few years four more Negroes were placed on that board, and two were chosen vice-presidents [1] One of the latter, Charles Lenox Remond, also president of the Essex County Society, came later to have a prominent part in the movement, and was the first Negro to take the platform as an anti-slavery speaker. Such fraternization, of course, laid the white Abolitionists open to severe criticism, even from quarters otherwise inclined to be sympathetic. But they did not compromise. At the annual meeting of the New England Society in January, 1836, the following resolution was adopted:

Resolved, That we consider the Anti-Slavery cause the cause of philanthropy, with regard to which all human beings, white men and colored men, men and women, citizens and foreigners, have the same duties and the same rights.

The author of the resolution thus expressed the views of his colleagues and himself: —

We have been advised, if we really wished to benefit the slave and the colored race generally, not unnecessarily to shock the feelings, though they were but prejudices, of the white people, by admitting colored persons to our Anti-

[1] For names and other information concerning these Negro Abolitionists, see W. C. Nell, *Colored Patriots of the Revolution.*

Slavery meetings and societies. We have been told that many who would otherwise act in unison with us were kept away by our disregard of the feelings of the community in this respect. . . . But what, I would ask, is the great, the single object of all our meetings and societies? Have we any other object than to impress upon the community this one principle, that the colored man is a man? And, on the other hand, is not the prejudice which would have us exclude colored people from our meetings and societies the same which, in our Southern States, dooms them to perpetual bondage? [1]

Thenceforth the Negro's participation in the Abolition Movement steadily enlarged. Though its generals and upper officers were, with a few exceptions, of the other race, some of the sturdiest of its second lieutenants and corporals, as well as the most devoted body of its privates in the ranks, were of the lowly people whom it was to raise to the free estate of manhood. The Negro's unflinching loyalty was an ever-present consolation and support to Garrison and his co-laborers, "outweighing mountains of abuse from other sources." [2]

In December, 1833, through Garrison's initiative, the formation of the American Anti-Slavery Society was effected at an assemblage in Philadelphia, attended by representatives of ten states. One of Boston's six delegates was a Negro. [3] This national organization united all the anti-slavery agencies throughout the North in a common crusade. [4] With this measure of expansion, however, came a still larger

[1] W. C. Nell, *Colored Patriots of the Revolution.*

[2] *William Lloyd Garrison*, vol. I, p. 255.

[3] James G. Barbadoes. *William Lloyd Garrison*, vol. I, p. 395, footnote.

[4] With headquarters at New York, and an official publication called the *Emancipator.*

measure of persecution. One of the chief methods by which the Abolitionists now undertook to exert "moral pressure" consisted of flooding the South with their papers and tracts. Southerners condemned this as an outrageous piece of insolence, and as a covert design to incite the slaves to insurrection. They denounced the "unprincipled fanatics," who were interfering with their "domestic policy," and warned the North to silence them, lest the Union be imperiled. The cry of danger to the Union, thus raised for the first time since the bitter Missouri controversy, produced in Boston, as elsewhere, a wave of indignation against the Abolitionists, as alleged mischief-makers. A great anti-Abolitionist mass meeting was held in Faneuil Hall on the evening of August 21, 1835, and was presided over by the same Theodore Lyman, Jr., now in the capacity of mayor, who thirteen years before, in the State Legislature, had bespoken a show of humanity toward the Negroes. But the Abolitionists had gone insufferably beyond his degree of humanity! Resolutions were adopted expressing Boston's sympathy with the Southern protests, belittling the number and importance of the agitators, and recommending the discouragement of their activity by all legal and orderly means.

An omen that the public animosity might get beyond the bounds of order, however, was afforded soon afterwards in the nocturnal erection in front of Garrison's house of a gallows with two nooses, one for himself and the other for George Thompson, an English lecturer in the anti-slavery cause, and the object of special objurgation as a "foreign emissary." This omen came true. On October 21, a mob — if that is not too crude a term to apply to a gathering composed in fact of the thoroughly respectable element! — assembled before a building where an anti-slavery meeting, at which Thompson was mistakenly supposed to be present, was in progress. The mob shouted to have Thompson delivered over to them for chastisement. Mayor Lyman then appeared, announced that Thompson was not there, and in a timid and perfunctory way asked his fellow-citizens to disperse. But the disappointment at not catching Thompson only made the rioters more clamorous. As it happened, the "Liberator" office was next door. So they set up a yell for Garrison. The latter, reluctantly and only upon the insistence of those in the office with him at the time, had taken refuge in another building near by. In spite of the mayor's feeble protestations, he was hunted out, and but for the unexpected intervention of several strong-armed protectors, would doubtless have suffered serious injury. As it was, he was hustled to the rear of the Old State House, and there gibed, insulted, and partly stripped of his clothing; and was rescued only by being rushed into the mayor's office and thence hurried away to a cell in the jail, for safety till the excitement subsided.

An undercurrent of sympathy for the Abolitionists, however, followed in the wake of this abuse of them, which in fact overreached itself. At the same time an anti-Southern reaction was taking place in the North. It had its rise in the feeling that the South, for its own sectional advantage, was demanding too great a sacrifice of fundamental national principles: — the freedom of the mails, liberty of speech and publication, and, most trying of all, the cherished right of petition. That right became an issue as a result of the second leading means utilized by the Abolitionists in bringing moral influence to bear; namely, the petitioning of Congress to abolish slavery in the territories and the District of Columbia. In 1835, a Southern Congressman moved that thenceforth such petitions should not be received. After a prolonged and heated debate in the following year, the South was placated, while infringement of the right to petition was nominally avoided, by the decision to lay all anti-slavery petitions on the table and to take no further action upon them. This notorious "gag rule" served only to spur the Abolitionists to greater activity, and by 1838 the number of petitions increased tenfold. Two years later a rule not to receive such petitions at all was forced through Congress. But Southern encroachment had gone too far, and in 1844 the restrictions which had been imposed were removed. Meanwhile, the North had become alarmed at the actual and imminent extension of slavery into new soil. In 1836, Arkansas was admitted as a slave state. The plot for the annexation of Texas, which had been colonized largely by Southern slaveholding emigrants, was already being hatched, and the contingency of a war with Mexico, bringing still further additions to slavery's area, was foreseen.[1] Under these conditions Northern anti-slavery sentiment was revived, and grew apace.

The Abolitionists profited by this change of feeling,

---

[1] In 1836, Texas revolted from Mexico and became an independent republic.

which, while still far from reaching their own extreme attitude, was surely tending in their direction. From 1840 on, though differences and division entered their ranks, the progress of their cause as a whole was rapid; and though public hostility to their agitation remained sufficiently in evidence and was to have its further eruptions, still from that time forth they were borne up by a consciousness that they were moving with the tide rather than struggling against it.

An event from which the Abolition Movement derived a broader moral confirmation was the assembling of a World's Anti-Slavery Convention at London in 1840, at which representatives from the British Isles, the Continental countries, and other quarters of the globe, joined with those of the United States in a common appeal against slavery wherever it was still in existence. This convention proved equally memorable, moreover, by reason of an unforeseen by-result. Among the American delegates from Boston and elsewhere were a considerable number of women, for whose full participation in abolition activities Garrison had stood out determinedly. But in England at that time such equal recognition of women was unknown. All the female delegates, therefore, though the credentials they held from their respective societies were as formal and complete as those of the men, were excluded. When Garrison, who arrived some days late, learned of this action, he felt obliged to refuse to take any part in the proceedings himself; — "to the great scandal" of the gathering, "for what sort of a World's Convention was it in which the founder of the greatest anti-slavery movement of the age, or of any age, was

debarred from taking his seat?"[1] The whole episode aroused so much feeling, pro and con, and led to so much debate on the general question of the position of women in affairs, that it is regarded as marking the decisive beginning, both in the United States and in England, of the movement for woman suffrage.[2] That such should have been the genesis of the demand for the civil and political equality of the sexes introduces another of those strikingly suggestive inter-relations between the emancipation of the Negro and other great human advances toward freedom's fuller realization.

Not a few Negroes were sent as delegates to the London Convention.[3] Of these, Charles Lenox Remond, whose early connection with abolition events has been mentioned, had the most noteworthy experience. On the voyage — the captain of the ship being a Virginian — he was consigned to the steerage. His reception in England, however, was in marked contrast. "Our colored friend Remond invariably accompanies us," wrote Garrison, "and is a great favorite in every circle.[4] . . . Prejudice against color is unknown here."[5] Not only was he much in demand as a speaker at public meetings, but he was warmly received and made much of by many persons of high rank. His stay was prolonged to a year and a half, and he traveled in England, Scotland, and Ireland. On his return, in December, 1841, he brought with him a remarkable document, — an "Address from the Irish People to

---

[1] *William Lloyd Garrison*, vol. ii, p. 374.
[2] *Ibid.*, vol. ii, p. 381, footnote.   [3] *Ibid.*, vol. ii, p. 353.
[4] *Ibid.*, vol. ii, p. 388.   [5] *Ibid.*, vol. ii, p. 383.

their Countrymen and Countrywomen in America."[1]
Sixty thousand names,[2] with that of Daniel O'Connell
at the head, were appended to this monster memorial,
which called upon Irish-Americans to treat the Negroes as brethren, and to unite everywhere with the
Abolitionists. It was expected that the appeal would
have substantial results, but that hope was not fulfilled.

Meanwhile, another Negro Abolitionist, the most
remarkable of them all, had made his appearance.
This was Frederick Douglass, who only a few years
before had escaped from slavery in Maryland.[3] He
became a reader of the "Liberator," and soon afterwards, at a meeting in New Bedford, Massachusetts,
where he had taken refuge, he heard Garrison speak.
How he was affected he himself has told: "'You are
the man — the Moses raised up by God to deliver his
modern Israel from bondage,' was the spontaneous
feeling of my heart as I sat away back in the hall and
listened to his mighty words — mighty in truth,
mighty in their simple earnestness."[4] Garrison did
not become acquainted with Douglass then, — in fact,
did not even know of his existence. But in 1841, at
another meeting in Nantucket, the two men came together. Douglass had been induced to tell the story
of his slave days and his escape. It was the first time

[1] *William Lloyd Garrison*, vol. III, p. 43 *et seq.*

[2] Presumably including those of grandparents and parents of
some of the members of Boston's present large Irish-American population.

[3] The escape was made in 1838.

[4] *William Lloyd Garrison*, vol. II, p. 292. The date of the meeting
was April 15, 1839.

he had spoken before a white audience. "It was with difficulty that I could stand erect," he wrote afterwards, "or that I could command and articulate two words without hesitation and stammering. I trembled in every limb. I am not sure but that my embarrassment was the most effective part of my speech, if speech it could be called. . . . The audience sympathized with me at once, and, from having been remarkably quiet, became much excited."[1]

What followed, another eyewitness has narrated: —

When the young man [Douglass] closed, late in the evening, though none seemed to know or care for the hour, Mr. Garrison rose to make the concluding address. I think he never before nor afterwards felt more profoundly the sacredness of his mission, or the importance of a crisis. . . . The crowded congregation had been wrought up almost to enchantment during the whole long evening, particularly by some of the utterances of the last speaker, as he turned over the terrible apocalypse of his experiences in slavery. But Mr. Garrison was singularly serene and calm. . . . He asked only a few simple, direct questions. . . . The first was: "Have we been listening to a thing, a piece of property, or a man?" "A man! A man!" shouted fully five hundred voices of women and men. "And should such a man be held a slave in a republican and Christian land?" "No, no! Never, never!" again swelled up from the same voices, like the billows of the deep. But the last [question] was this: "Shall such a man ever be sent back to slavery from the soil of old Massachusetts?" — this time uttered with all the power of voice of which Garrison was capable. Almost the whole assembly sprang with one accord to their feet, and the walls and roof of the Athenæum seemed to shudder with the "No, no!" loud and long continued in the enthusiasm of the scene.[2]

[1] *William Lloyd Garrison*, vol. III, pp. 18–19.
[2] From an account by Parker Pillsbury, a leading Boston Abolitionist, *William Lloyd Garrison*, vol. III, p. 19.

Douglass, at Garrison's instance, was at once secured as an agent of the Massachusetts Anti-Slavery Society, and in this capacity he traveled and lectured in the New England States for the next four years. His "Narrative of my Experience in Slavery," published in Boston in 1844, did much to further the abolition cause. In 1845, he went to Europe, and spent two years in the British Isles making anti-slavery addresses. He proved the most eloquent and powerful apostle of freedom that his race produced, and in virtue of his long and brilliant career came generally to be regarded as the foremost representative of his people.[1]

A third Negro recruit at this juncture, who quickly rose to prominence, was William Wells Brown. He, too, was an escaped slave.[2] He came to Boston about 1845, and soon took an active part in the Abolitionist agitation, as a speaker and writer. His first book, the "Narrative of W. W. Brown, a Fugitive Slave," appeared in 1847, and his second, "The Anti-Slavery Harp," a collection of songs and verses, in 1848. Both had a wide circulation. In 1849, Brown visited England and the Continent, in the dual capacity of delegate to a congress on international peace and representative of the Abolitionists.[3]

[1] Douglas died in 1895, at the age of seventy-eight.

[2] He was born in Lexington, Kentucky, of a slave woman, Elisabeth, who was the mother of seven children, no two of whom — such were the contingencies in the lives of female slaves — had the same father. William escaped from a boat at Louisville, Kentucky, when twenty-one years old, and was helped in his flight by a Quaker, William Wells, who gave the young man his own name. He secured employment on a Lake Erie steamboat, and from May to December, 1842, assisted sixty-nine fugitives to cross the Lake into Canada. *Narrative of W. W. Brown, a Fugitive Slave.*

[3] His experiences were described in his third book, *Three Years in*

Douglass and Brown were but two very exceptional cases of the runaway slaves who sought refuge in Boston, and whose number increased rapidly after 1840. This city was of course one of the principal stations of the celebrated "Underground Railway," by which slaves were mysteriously conveyed, stage by stage, to points of comparative safety in the Northern states, or across the line into Canada.[1] Those who came to Boston were hidden and cared for by the Abolitionists, and chiefly by the Negro contingent.[2] The secret councils, to devise ways and means of protection and general assistance, were most frequently held at the shops or homes of Negroes. A barber shop of one Peter Howard, situated at the corner of Cambridge and Irving Streets, in the West End, was an early rendezvous. Later on, one of the favorite gathering-places was another barber shop, on the corner of Howard and Bulfinch Streets in the same section, of which the proprietor was John J. Smith, a free Negro from Richmond, Virginia.[3] The most popular resort of all, however, as well as one of the chief places of concealment for runaways, was the home of Lewis

Europe, published in 1852. Then came *Clotel,* in 1852; *St. Domingo,* in 1854; *The Fugitive in Europe,* in 1855; and *The Escape,* in 1858. Other books were published after the War.

[1] See Wilbur H. Siebert, *Light on the Underground Railway.*

[2] Eliza Gardner, one of the few members of Boston's present Negro colony whose memory goes back to those days, recalls that her father's little cottage often sheltered as many fugitives as it could hold, and that the situation was the same in many other Negro homes.

[3] Smith came to Boston in 1848. It is said that when Charles Sumner, the noted Senator and Abolitionist, could not be found at his home or office, he could usually be located at Smith's shop.

Hayden,[1] who came to Boston as a fugitive from Kentucky in 1844, and who by virtue of his native strength of character soon became, and remained till his death, a dominating figure in the local Negro colony.[2]

Several of the most famous fugitive slave cases occurred in Boston. The first of them all was the Latimer case of 1842. By way of preface, it should be said that the question of fugitive slaves had been more or less troublesome ever since slavery's disappearance in the North, but had become acute with the growth of the Abolition Movement. The federal laws were entirely in favor of the slave-owners. They required but little evidence in support of alleged ownership of a runaway, and made the rendition of the slave obligatory not only upon federal but also upon state officials. The North grew to resent this compulsion, and began to take the attitude that its state officials were not constitutionally subject to such federal control. That was the contention of the Abolitionists in Boston when the Latimer case arose.

George Latimer, a fine-looking man, almost white in complexion and at least half-white in blood, escaped to Boston from Norfolk, Virginia, with his wife and child. On the complaint of his owner he was arrested without a warrant, put in jail, and remanded for trial without a jury before a federal court, on the ground that only federal courts had jurisdiction. The Abolitionists at once called a meeting in Faneuil Hall. Many of the pro-Southern element, however, were

[1] On Philips (then Southac) Street, in the West End.
[2] Hayden died in 1889.

present, and by their disturbance did their utmost to break the meeting up. Remond especially was hissed and hooted when he tried to speak. Nevertheless resolutions were adopted, denouncing the fugitive slave laws and calling for counter-legislation by the state. Following this action, the illegality of Latimer's confinement in jail was established to the satisfaction of the county sheriff, with the result that he was released. In the confused debate over the affair he would probably have gone scot free anyway, but as it was, he and his family were ransomed with funds contributed from philanthropic sources.[1]

The Abolitionists made the most of the public indignation which this case aroused. "Latimer meetings" were held throughout the state. A "North Star and Latimer's Journal," issued every other day from Boston, fired the excitement. Then a Latimer and Grand Massachusetts Petition, calling for the prohibition of state or municipal assistance in the return of fugitives, was submitted to the State Legislature.[2] So successful was this agitation that the following year, 1843, the Legislature passed a personal liberty act, which forbade state judges or justices to take part in the capture of fugitive slaves, and enjoined sheriffs, jailers, and constables from detaining them. This was an extremely radical piece of legislation, and its adoption shows the advanced stage which the anti-slavery feeling had reached. It was the first law of that character. Other Northern States soon followed Mass-

---

[1] For a more detailed account, see *William Lloyd Garrison*, vol. III, pp. 66–67, footnote.

[2] *Ibid.*, vol. III, p. 67, footnote.

achusetts' lead. Slave-hunters found it increasingly difficult to recapture the runaways. The South renewed its threats of secession.

Then came the short-lived Compromise of 1850, by which, in return for the admission of California as a free state, and certain other "concessions," the North was forced to consent to the enactment of the notorious Fugitive Slave Law.[1] That law went beyond all former bounds. The entire federal machinery, from courts to army, was enjoined for its execution, and a large force of special marshals and commissioners appointed. The marshals were liable to a fine of $1000, plus the value of the slave, if the latter escaped or even if he were forcibly rescued. Bystanders were guilty of treason in refusing to assist. The claimant's oath was full evidence, the alleged fugitive was shut out from all defense, and the right of *habeas corpus* denied him. Obstruction, rescue, or concealment was punishable by six months imprisonment and $2000 fine. If the claimant suspected an attempt to rescue the slave, the marshal must take the latter to the claimant's own state before surrendering him. Finally, an affidavit and general description made in the claimant's state was sufficient for reclamation in any other state.

Never were expected effect and actual effect of a law more opposite. The enactment which the South confidently believed would force the North into submission had the result instead of goading the North to fury. Undoubtedly, this was the element which defin-

[1] California was part of the territory acquired in 1848 as a result of the war with Mexico.

itely decided the trend of events toward civil war. In Boston, the excitement was intense. The passage of the law was immediately followed by an exodus northward, usually to Canada, of escaped slaves who had taken refuge in the "border" states, and even of those who had got as far north as New England. Well knowing that Boston would be the slave-hunters' chief point of attack, most of the refugees who were abiding in that city joined in the common flight.[1] Vigilance committees were at once organized to assist the fugitives. The Negroes, at a meeting at the Old Joy Street church,[2] determined if necessary to offer armed resistance. The first encounter came in 1850 over two celebrated fugitives, the Crafts, the Georgia agents in pursuit of whom were foiled by their being spirited off to England.[3] In February, 1851, occurred the sensa-

[1] Fifteen families from Boston joined the refugee colony established at Biddulph, near Little York, Canada, by J. C. Brown, a Negro who had purchased his own freedom for $1800. Booker T. Washington, *The Story of the Negro*, vol. I, p. 227.

[2] As the African Meeting-House had by that time come to be known.

[3] Ellen Craft, being almost white in complexion, disguised herself as an invalid going North for medical treatment, with her darker husband (William) passing as her Negro servant. Thus they traveled openly in first-class conveyances from Georgia to Philadelphia, and thence made their way to Boston, where they figured in a great Faneuil Hall mass meeting in 1849. *William Lloyd Garrison*, vol. III, page 247. After the war, the Crafts returned to America. For some time they lived at Cambridge, where their children were educated, and then they went back to their native state, Georgia, where they passed their old age in a comfortable home near Savannah. One of the sons is now living in England, and a daughter is the wife of the late W. D. Crum, who was collector of customs at Charleston, South Carolina, under President Roosevelt, and subsequently United States Minister to Liberia, in which country he met his death from fever. A grandson, Henry K. Craft, graduated

tional "rescue" of Shadrach. This runaway slave's
case was being heard in the courtroom, before a federal commissioner, and a decision practically remand-
ing him to bondage had been given — when a Negro
lawyer, Robert Morris, and a number of others, mostly
of the same race, compassed his escape. How it was
done has been told by an eyewitness:[1] —

Scarcely was the decision announced when the courtroom
door was opened by Mr. Morris and a signal given to the
crowd . . . who filled the corridor, anxiously waiting the result of the hearing. The uncontrollable mass swarmed in,
heedless of all attempts of the officers to keep them back; the
genial deputy marshal took refuge under the table, and
with a suddenness and a fervor which might almost be compared to the chariot of fire that swept away the prophet
Elijah, Shadrach, enveloped in the cloud which darkened the
whole room, disappeared from the view of those who claimed
to own him, and was next heard of in Canada.

The leaders in this affair were indicted by a federal
grand jury, but were triumphantly acquitted, for lack
of sufficiently tangible evidence of guilt.[2]

The surcharged conditions which prevailed at that
time were vividly portrayed in a letter written by one
of the foremost of the Abolitionists, Wendell Phillips:[3]

from Harvard University in 1908, and is now in charge of the electrical plant and the teaching of electrical engineering at Tuskegee Institute. Booker T. Washington, *The Story of the Negro*, vol. I, p. 230.

[1] Thomas Harlow, a leading member of the Suffolk Bar at that
time.

[2] Those indicted included Morris, Lewis Hayden, and other
Negroes, and also Charles Sumner, Theodore Parker, and Richard
H. Dana, Jr. *Colored American Magazine*, September 1901, article
on Robert Morris. Henry Clay was especially horrified because this
escape had been effected by "a band who are not of our own people,"
thus raising the question "whether the government of white men is
to be yielded to a government of blacks." *William Lloyd Garrison*,
vol. III, p. 326, footnote.

[3] In March, 1851.

In Boston, all is activity — never before so much since I knew the cause. The rescue of Shadrach has set the whole public ablaze. I had an old woman of seventy ask my advice about flying, though originally free and fearful only of being caught up by mistake. Of course, in one so old and valueless there was no temptation to mistake, but in others it is horrible to see the distress of families torn apart at this inclement season, the working head forced to leave good employment and seek not employment so much as the chance of it in the narrow, unenterprising and overstocked markets of Canada. Our Vigilance Committee meets every night. The escapes have been providential. Since Shadrach's case nigh a hundred have left the city. . . . I need not enlarge on this; but the long evening sessions — debates about secret escapes — plans to evade where we can't resist — the door watched that no spy may enter — the whispered consultations of the morning — some putting property out of their hands, planning to incur penalties, and planning also that, in case of conviction, the Government may get nothing from them — the doing and answering no questions — intimates forbearing to ask the knowledge which it may be dangerous to have — all reminds one of those foreign scenes which have hitherto been known to us, transatlantic republicans, only in books.

So things continued, and public feeling grew constantly more inflamed, till on May 26, 1854, it passed all previous limits and broke out in open armed attack upon the Government authorities which were executing the rendition of Anthony Burns. The latter had been arrested as a fugitive slave two days before. Immediately the popular excitement mounted to fever pitch. The ensuing week is said to have been without a parallel in Boston since the days of the Revolution. The Abolitionists, the woman suffragists, and several other organizations were holding their anniversary meetings, and the city was thus crowded with visitors. Also, from the country roundabout, even as far as

Worcester, forty miles away, men poured in for the express purpose of thwarting the slave-hunters. A call was issued for volunteers to rescue Burns, at the risk of death if need be, and among the large number who responded were many Negroes. On the evening of the 26th, a great anti-slavery mass meeting was held at Faneuil Hall, and Abolitionist orators made impassioned speeches. As that meeting broke up, a part of the crowd, by prearrangement, rushed to the court-house where Burns was held a prisoner, and using a beam as a battering-ram, broke down one of the doors and surged in. They were finally driven back, however, though one of the deputy marshals was killed in the mêlée. All the military forces within reach were at once concentrated to prevent a second attack. A few days later the victim was delivered over to his master, and amid tumultuous counter-demonstrations, was borne down State Street between armed files to the point of embarkation.[1]

This local incident, combined with the enraged outcry throughout the North against the simultaneous action of Congress in opening Kansas and Nebraska as fighting ground for slavery, gave the Abolitionists, for the time, almost complete control of the situation.[2]

[1] The Rev. Leonard A. Grimes, pastor of the (Negro) Twelfth Baptist Church, and a very active anti-slavery worker, followed Burns and his captors, and with funds which had been provided for the purpose, succeeded in purchasing his freedom; — for, once the slaveholders had compelled his rendition, they had gained their most important object, and were more than willing to be rid of one who might cause them further trouble. Burns subsequently became a minister of the Gospel.

[2] The so-called Kansas-Nebraska Act of May 22, 1854, was forced through Congress by the South, and, though both these

Going further than they had ever dared to go before, they demanded and in the spring of 1855 obtained from the Legislature a drastic extension of the state's personal liberty law. Claimants of runaway slaves were thenceforth required to give full proof of ownership, and a fair trial was assured to the fugitives. For a state officer to issue a warrant for a slave's arrest was made a cause for his removal. For an attorney to assist the claimant was equivalent to his disbarment. For a state judge to help the slave-hunters rendered him liable to impeachment. No sheriff, jailer, or policeman could help arrest a runaway, and no jail could receive him. These provisions put so many obstacles in the way of a slave's recapture as practically to nullify the Federal Fugitive Slave Law of 1850, so far as Massachusetts was concerned. The reclamation of runaways who took refuge in that state was, indeed, from this time next to impossible. The South stormed against such obstruction as an insufferable defiance of the Constitution, and its threats of secession grew still louder.

The first act of secession was now in fact close at hand. The Republican victory at the polls in 1860 was the signal for it. Though that newly-born party, formed in 1856 by a coalition of the Whigs, Free-Soilers, Northern Democrats, and other elements, was

territories were in the free-soil zone, as being north of the Missouri Compromise line of 36° 30', left the question of slavery within their borders to be decided by their inhabitants. The South was sure that in Kansas slavery would be firmly established. Contrary to expectation, however, and owing largely to the organization of emigrant aid societies, great numbers of Northerners settled in that territory, armed conflict with the slaveholding settlers ensued, and the forces of freedom were victorious.

actually so timorous in its attitude toward slavery as
to incur the bitter condemnation of the Abolitionists,
it was of course the party of the North as opposed to
the displaced Democracy of the South.[1] At any rate,
the South, doubtless making up in prevision what it
lacked in logic, chose to regard Republican triumph as
tantamount to the North's indorsement of abolition-
ism. On December 20, 1860, South Carolina set the
fatal example to her sister states, by withdrawing
from the Union. The ordinance by which this action
was taken, recited, as grounds for it, that the non-
slaveholding states had "denounced as sinful the institution of slavery," "permitted the open establishment
. . . of societies whose avowed object is to disturb
the peace and to eloign the property of the citizens
of other states," had "encouraged and assisted thousands of our slaves to leave their homes," and had incited
the rest, "by emissaries, books, and pictures," to
"servile insurrection." "For twenty-five years," it
charged, "this agitation has been steadily increasing,
until it has now secured to its aid the power of the common Government."[2] In other words, the Abolition
Movement was declared to be the cause of secession.

Now a Union-saving panic seized the North. Desperate attempts were made to stay the South. Conciliation, concession, and subserviency stopped short
of no extreme. The Abolitionists were made the
scrapegoats. Once more — though not for long, and

[1] The Republican platform came out only against the doctrine,
enunciated in the Dred Scott decision of 1857, that the Constitution
carried slavery into the territories, and against the suggested re-
opening of the slave-trade. On the other hand, it made many concessions to the South.

[2] *William Lloyd Garrison*, vol. III, pp. 506, 507.

for the last time — they had to suffer as the victims of public abuse and popular passion. In Boston, in January, 1861, rioters forced an anti-slavery meeting in Tremont Temple to adjourn, and the mayor refused to allow it to reassemble.[1]

But then, in April, came the Southern attack upon and capture of Fort Sumter, and the hauling down of the Stars and Stripes from its ramparts. This event was expected to complete the intimidation and demoralization of the North. But never was there a more electrical transformation. There burst forth "a whirlwind of patriotism that swept all before it," and "such an uprising in every city, town, and hamlet of the North, without distinction of sect or party, as to seem like a general resurrection from the dead."[2] The day following Sumter's fall, President Lincoln issued the call for troops.[3] The "irrepressible conflict" had come at last.

The purpose of the war, however, was not to destroy slavery, but to suppress the rebellion. President Lincoln at once made that manifest beyond possible doubt. Nor did he stop there. However deep was his own antipathy toward slavery, he felt still more deeply that as head of the nation his one supreme duty was to do everything in his power to preserve the Union. He therefore made it plain also that if this paramount object could be achieved by consenting to the continuance of slavery, such consent would be given. First before the actual clash at arms, and then for nearly two years afterwards, every opportunity, every in-

---

[1] *William Lloyd Garrison*, vol. IV, pp. 5–7.
[2] *Ibid.*, vol. IV, p. 19.   [3] April 15.

ducement, was held out to the South to return to the
old allegiance, with her "domestic institution" un-
touched. Lincoln's attitude was that of the great
majority of the North. "The Union!" was everything. It seemed as though the Negro's freedom
might after all be offered up in sacrifice.

The Negro's champions, however, knew that the
logic of the situation was with them. For though
secession was the immediate occasion of the conflict,
slavery was without question its fundamental cause.
And though the restoration of the Union was its professed object, how could durable union possibly be re-
established, except by doing away with the element of
inevitable contention? So the Abolitionists set themselves determinedly to their final task of committing
the Government to slavery's destruction. They in-
voked the President and Congress to use their war
power to proclaim emancipation. The "Liberator"
and all the other anti-slavery journals made that demand their shibboleth. Abolition meetings were held
on every hand. The orators of the cause, with Wendell
Phillips at their head, exerted all their eloquence.
Resolutions, petitions, and memorials without number
were poured into Washington, and deputation upon
deputation was sent to the Capitol and the White
House. The President's evident willingness to con-
ciliate the South by yielding on slavery, and his apparent hesitancy and vacillation even after all hope of
conciliation had been practically abandoned, were
censured unsparingly. "To refuse to deliver those
captive millions who are now legally in your power,"
declared Garrison in an editorial addressed to the

President and his Cabinet, "is tantamount to the crime of their original enslavement."[1] In a great meeting at Boston, prophetic application was made of the Scriptural text: "Therefore thus saith the Lord; Ye have not hearkened unto me, in proclaiming liberty, every one to his brother, and every man to his neighbour: behold, I proclaim a liberty for you, saith the Lord, to the sword, to the pestilence, and to the famine."[2] And the Negroes in their churches and in their homes fervently prayed that victory should be withheld from the Union arms till the slaves were set free.

The military exigencies of the war, as well as Lincoln's own inmost convictions, were on the Abolitionists' side. At last, in September, 1862, the President announced that on the first day of the new year he would issue an edict of freedom to the slaves in all states or parts of states still in rebellion against the Federal Government.

In Boston, that New Year's Day was one of joyful thanksgiving and celebration.[3] Two great gatherings were held; one at the Old Music Hall, in the afternoon, and the other in Tremont Temple, through the whole day and evening. Inspiring music —including Mendelssohn's "Hymn of Praise" and Händel's "Hallelujah Chorus" — and the reading by Ralph Waldo Emerson of a poem which he had written for the occasion,[4]

[1] *William Lloyd Garrison*, vol. IV, p. 35.

[2] Jeremiah, XXXIV, 17. *William Lloyd Garrison*, vol. IV, p. 20.

[3] Solemn services had taken place the evening before in all the Negro churches.

[4] The *Boston Hymn*. Greatest applause greeted the stanza referring to the proposal of compensated emancipation: —

> " Pay ransom to the owner,
> And fill the bag to the brim.
> Who is the owner ? The slave is owner,
> And ever was. Pay him ! "

were the features of the afternoon meeting. At first there was painful suspense, mingled with vague fear, for the reason that no tidings of the Proclamation had yet been received. When this suspense was relieved, however, by the announcement that the text of that edict was coming over the wires, the gathering broke into a storm of applause, culminating in nine tremendous cheers for Lincoln, and three more for Garrison.

Still more memorable was the concluding evening session in the Temple. This was in charge of the Negroes themselves, and two of the speakers — John S. Rock, a lawyer distinguished for his eloquence, and the renowned Frederick Douglass — were of the race to whom that day brought promise of deliverance.[1] The climax of enthusiasm came when, a few minutes after nine o'clock, one of the Abolitionists rushed in, breathless, with a newspaper proof-sheet — which he had contrived to get into his hands and to make off with before he could be stopped! — of the Proclamation. First amid hushed silence, then with outbursts of applause, this was read:[2] from the beginning, "Now, therefore, I, Abraham Lincoln, President of the United States," through the central clause, "do order and declare that all persons held as slaves . . . are and hereafter shall be free," to the solemn conclusion, "And upon this act, sincerely believed to be an act of justice, warranted by the Constitution upon military necessity, I invoke the considerate judgment of mankind and

[1] The other speakers were Edward Atkinson, Anna E. Dickinson, and Charles W. Slack.

[2] As the newspapers did not publish the proclamation till the following day this was probably the first time it was read anywhere in the country outside of Washington.

the gracious favor of Almighty God." While shouts
and cheers filled the hall, Douglass — a man of noble
mien and figure — advanced to the front of the platform, with a gesture brought the multitude to their
feet, and led them in singing, with fervor unrestrained,
the old hymn, "Blow ye the trumpet, blow!"

> "Let all the nations know
> To earth's remotest bounds
> The year of jubilee has come."

The meeting then ended, but the Negroes thronged to
their churches for services of prayer and praise that
lasted far into the night.[1]

Surely it was a striking and appropriate coincidence,
if nothing more, that as the first step in the Abolition
Movement's working organization, — namely, the
formation of the New England Anti-Slavery Society,
— was taken in a Negro church, so the concluding
celebration of that movement's crowning achievement,
and the first reading of the immortal Proclamation in
Boston, should have occurred at a gathering under the
auspices of the Negro people; and that the spontaneous pæan of victory on that occasion should have been
raised by one of that race who in his own life experience embodied the rise from slavery to freedom.

The cause of the Union and the cause of the Negro's
liberty were now one and inseparable. But the ultimate triumph or defeat of this double mission was entrusted to the soldier in the battlefield. There the
Negro was to have a vital part.

[1] The foregoing account of the celebrations is based on an article,
"Emancipation Day in Boston, 1863," by Francis Jackson Garrison, which appeared in the *New York Evening Post*, Dec. 28, 1912.

Section 2. The War

When the Emancipation Proclamation was issued, the military situation was critical for the North. The Union forces had been repulsed at Fredericksburg and at Vicksburg, and had fought the battle of Stone River at tremendous cost. Some sixty-five thousand troops were due to be discharged during the ensuing summer and fall. Volunteering was at a standstill. The political opposition to the war had grown formidable, and the advocates of peace at any price were active for mediation and compromise. The Confederates, on the other hand, had filled their ranks, and were never better prepared for keeping up the conflict.

In the face of this crisis, the Government decided upon a general arming of the Negroes, in separate regiments, under white officers.[1] Emancipation of the slaves in the rebellious states, opening the way for their enlistment in the Federal ranks, was thus in truth a measure of "military necessity."

The first body of Negro troops organized after the adoption of this policy was the Fifty-fourth Massachusetts. The unique significance which attached to that regiment was emphasized in a letter written to the father of Robert Gould Shaw, its young colonel, by the famous Abolitionist "War Governor" of the State, John A. Andrew: —

[1] This decision was tentatively arrived at in October, 1862. Though three scattered Negro regiments had already been organized, — the First Kansas Colored, in the summer of that year; the Louisiana Native Guards, in September; and the First South Carolina, in October, — the enlistment of Negroes on a large scale and as a general policy had not previously been undertaken. Luis F. Emilio, *A Brave Black Regiment.*

As you have seen by the newspapers, I am about to raise a colored regiment in Massachusetts. This I cannot but regard as perhaps the most important corps to be organized during the whole war, in view of what must be the composition of our new levies; and therefore I am very anxious to organize it judiciously, in order that it may be a model for all future colored regiments. I am desirous to have for its officers — particularly for its field-officers— young men of military experience,of firm anti-slavery principles, ambitious, superior to a vulgar contempt for color, and having faith in the capacity of colored men for military service. Such officers must necessarily be gentlemen of the highest tone and honor; and I shall look for them in those circles of educated anti-slavery society which, next to the colored race itself, have the greatest interest in this experiment.[1]

Recruiting was begun February 16, 1863, in quarters situated in the midst of the West End Negro colony.[2] That evening a meeting to arouse enthusiasm was held in the old Joy Street church. Enlistment followed immediately, and camp was established at Readville, near Boston. Soon many additional recruiting offices were opened, not only at other points in Massachusetts, but throughout the Eastern and Middle Western states. Frederick Douglass, William Wells Brown, Charles Lenox Remond, Lewis Hayden, John S. Rock, and other Negroes served as general recruiting agents. Within three months, the enrollment of the necessary number of volunteers was completed.

On May 18, Governor Andrew, in the presence of Garrison and Wendell Phillips, delivered the state and

---

[1] Letter written January 30, 1863, to Francis G. Shaw. Luis F. Emilio, *A Brave Black Regiment.*

[2] At the corner of Cambridge and North Russell Streets, on the site now occupied by the Negro Odd Fellows Hall.

national colors to Colonel Shaw, at the Readville camp, with the declaration that he should "stand or fall, as a man and a magistrate, with the rise or fall in history" of those Negro troops. Ten days later he reviewed the regiment as it marched through the streets of Boston, displaying a soldierly discipline and bearing unsurpassed by any other regiment Massachusetts had sent to the war, and receiving enthusiastic greetings from the crowds assembled all along the route and about the wharf, where it embarked for the South.[1]

Meanwhile the organization of the state's second Negro battalion, the Fifty-fifth Massachusetts, which was commanded by Colonel Hallowell, of Boston,[2] and in which one of Garrison's sons was a second lieutenant,[3] had been proceeding rapidly. On July 21, that regiment took its departure for the field of war, but under somewhat different circumstances. Anti-Negro riots were being stirred up by the pro-Southern ("Copperhead") element in various Northern cities, and such an outburst was feared in Boston. For this reason, no dress parade was held in the case of the Fifty-fifth, which made its way to the pier with loaded muskets, ready for a possible attack.[4] The Fifth Cavalry, the third and last body of Negro soldiers from Massachusetts, took the field in May of the following year.

Not only in these three Massachusetts regiments, but in others organized under the auspices of other

[1] *William Lloyd Garrison*, vol IV, p. 81.
[2] Still living in a suburb of Boston in his strong old age, and still the Negro's loyal friend.
[3] George T. Garrison.
[4] *William Lloyd Garrison*, vol. IV, pp. 82–83.

states, and also in the navy, Negroes from Boston and
the immediate vicinity enlisted; and altogether five
hundred or more entered the Union ranks.[1] The patriotism and bravery of these Negro soldiers and their
white officers were the greater, because the Confederates had served warning that they would enslave all
the Negroes taken captive, and would put the officers
to death as leaders of servile insurrection. In spite,
however, of this special risk which was required, the
Government at first allowed the Negro troops only the
wages of military "laborers," instead of the full pay of
soldiers. With remarkable spirit and fortitude, and at
the cost of severe hardship to their families, the men
of the Fifty-fourth and Fifty-fifth refused to receive any
payment at all until their claim to the full amount was
at last recognized.[2] This dignified stand did much
to raise the Negro to a higher place in the esteem of
the general public.

[1] How many of the 1343 men of the Fifty-fourth were from
Boston cannot be exactly determined, but it may be assumed that
most of the fifty or more volunteers at the Boston office, during the
first fortnight of recruiting, and some of those who enlisted elsewhere after the Boston office was closed, were from Boston and
vicinity. In the Fifty-fifth there were at least eighty men from
Boston. Adding the still larger number in the Fifth Cavalry, and
a considerable proportion of the 1954 Negro soldiers from Massachusetts in other regiments and of the 1360 enlistments at the
Charlestown Navy Yard, it would appear that the total from
Boston must have been five hundred or more, as above stated.

[2] The pay of "laborers" was ten dollars a month, that of soldiers
thirteen dollars. Congress eventually voted full pay to all Negro
soldiers from January 1, 1864; and in the case of the Fifty-fourth and
Fifty-fifth, by a subsequent decision of the Attorney-General, the
full amount was allowed from the time of enlistment. The soldiers
of these regiments meanwhile declined to let Massachusetts make up
the amount withheld by the Government. *William Lloyd Garrison*,
vol. IV, p. 96, footnote.

The Fifth Cavalry was organized too late to take part in any of the heavy fighting, though it was present at the final closing in on Richmond. The Fifty-fifth acquitted itself valiantly, particularly in the famous battle of Honey Hill, in South Carolina, where it bore the brunt of the conflict and by its determined resistance in the face of the enemy's advance saved large numbers of the white troops from annihilation. But it was the Fifty-fourth which — as though in fulfillment of a high destiny as the first Negro regiment to take up arms after the proclamation of the Negro's freedom, and as the body of soldiers to which all who believed in the Negro's worth looked to justify their faith — won glory above that of any other Negro battalion of the war, and displayed heroism unsurpassed by any other troops, of either race. The occasion at which this fame was achieved was that of the assault upon Fort Wagner, in South Carolina, on July 18, 1863.

"To the Fifty-fourth Massachusetts Colored was assigned the honor of leading the attack, and after the troops were formed on the beach, ready for the assault, the order to advance was withheld until the Fifty-fourth could march by and take position at the head of the column."[1] And this is the account, from the pen of an eyewitness, of what followed: —

When the inaction had become almost unendurable, the signal to advance came. Colonel Shaw walked along the front to the centre, and giving the command, "Attention!" the men sprang to their feet. Then came the admonition,

[1] William F. Fox, Lieutenant Colonel, U.S.A., *Regimental Losses in the Civil War.*

"Move in quick time until within a hundred yards of the fort; then double-quick; and charge!" A slight pause, followed by the sharp command, "Forward!" and the Fifty-fourth advanced to the storming. . . . Darkness was rapidly coming on. . . . With eyes strained upon the colonel and the flag, they pressed on toward the work, now only two hundred yards away. At that moment Wagner became a mound of fire, from which poured a stream of shot and shell. . . . Men fell in numbers on every side, but the only response the Fifty-fourth made to the deadly challenge was to change step to the double-quick, that it might the sooner close with the foe. . . . As the swifter pace was taken, and officers sprang to the fore with waving swords barely seen in the darkness, the men closed the gaps, and with set jaws, panting breath, and bowed heads, charged on. . . . Every flash showed the ground dotted with killed or wounded. . . . Nothing but the ditch now separated the stormers and the foe. Down into this they went, through the two or three feet of water therein, and mounted the slope beyond in the teeth of the enemy; some of whom, standing on the crest, fired down on them. Both flags were planted on the parapet, the national flag carried there and gallantly maintained by the brave Sergeant William H. Carney of Company C.[1] . . . Colonel Shaw had led his regiment from first to last. Gaining the rampart, he stood there for a moment with uplifted sword, shouting, "Forward, Fifty-fourth!" and then fell dead, shot through the heart.[2]

Though the stormers were at last forced back and the assault failed, for lack of proper support of the splendid charge of the Negro troops, and because of

[1] Sergeant Carney was from New Bedford, Massachusetts. He planted the flag on the parapet of the fort, and in the retreat, though wounded in the head and shoulder and both legs, he bore it back to the Union lines and handed it over with the words which made him famous: "They got me, boys, but the old flag never touched the ground." After the war, Carney lived in Boston, and some years later was appointed to the position of messenger to the Massachusetts Secretary of State. In December, 1908, he was crushed in an elevator accident. On the day of his death, the flags on the State House were lowered to halfmast.

[2] Luis F. Emilio, *A Brave Black Regiment*, p. 79 *et seq.*

the overwhelming numbers defending the fort, it was one of those failures which go down in history as great moral victories for the vanquished. The sacrifice was heavy ; besides Colonel Shaw, 2 officers and 31 men killed, 11 officers and 135 men wounded, and 92 reported missing — either killed or captured — out of a total of 650 engaged.[1]

When the Fifty-fourth returned to Boston, in September, 1865, it received a remarkable ovation. "The demonstrations of respect were rather more than have usually been awarded to returning regiments, even in Massachusetts, which cherishes her soldiers with an unforgetting affection. They were so honored in this case, we presume, because the regiment is a representative one. There were regiments from that state which had seen more fighting than this, though none which had done any better fighting when occasion offered; none which had a higher reputation for discipline, patient endurance, and impetuous valor. . . . It made Fort Wagner such a name to the colored race as Bunker Hill has been for ninety years to the white Yankees. . . . The name of Colonel Robert Gould Shaw is forever linked with that of the regiment which he first commanded, and which he inspired with so much of his own gentle and noble spirit as to make it a perpetual legacy to the men who fought under and loved him."[2]

On the battlefield before Fort Wagner, the body of Colonel Robert Gould Shaw lies buried in the same trench with the bodies of a score of the Negroes of the

[1] Luis F. Emilio, *A Brave Black Regiment.*
[2] Extract from editorial which appeared in the New York *Tribune* at the time.

regiment. At the northwest corner of the Boston Common, opposite the State House, stands the Robert Gould Shaw Memorial, erected by citizens of the state in honor of the Fifty-fourth. No monument in the city is visited more frequently. The sculptural design is the work of Saint-Gaudens, who gave twelve years of thought to the task. The architectural construction was planned by Charles F. McKim, of the firm of McKim, Mead, and White. On the side facing the Capitol is represented, in raised bronze figures on a great tablet, the regiment on the march, with Colonel Shaw in advance and an angel close overhead leading the way. On the reverse side is cut in the stone this inscription, the words those of Dr. Charles W. Eliot, then president of Harvard University: [1] —

TO THE FIFTY-FOURTH   OF MASSACHUSETTS
REGIMENT   INFANTRY

THE WHITE OFFICERS
TAKING LIFE AND HONOR IN THEIR HANDS▲CAST IN THEIR LOT WITH MEN OF A DESPISED RACE UNPROVED IN WAR AND RISKED DEATH AS INCITERS OF SERVILE INSURRECTION IF TAKEN PRISONERS▲ BESIDES ENCOUNTERING ALL THE COMMON PERILS OF CAMP MARCH AND BATTLE ·

THE BLACK RANK AND FILE
VOLUNTEERED WHEN DISASTER CLOUDED THE UNION CAUSE▲SERVED WITHOUT PAY FOR EIGHTEEN MONTHS TILL GIVEN THAT OF WHITE TROOPS▲ FACED THREATENED ENSLAVEMENT IF CAPTURED▲WERE BRAVE IN ACTION▲ PATIENT UNDER HEAVY AND DANGEROUS LABORS▲AND CHEERFUL AMID HARDSHIPS AND PRIVATIONS ·

TOGETHER
THEY GAVE TO THE NATION AND THE WORLD UNDYING PROOF THAT AMERICANS OF AFRICAN DESCENT POSSESS THE PRIDE COURAGE AND DEVOTION OF THE PATRIOT SOLDIER ▲ ONE HUNDRED AND EIGHTY THOUSAND SUCH AMERICANS ENLISTED UNDER THE UNION FLAG IN MDCCCLXIII ▲ MDCCCLXV ·

[1] The monument was erected in 1897.

The Union was saved, and in every state in the Union slavery was destroyed. Boston, the city where in the days of the Republic's dawn the slave first attained his liberty, and where a half-century afterwards the determined movement for his nation-wide emancipation had its rise, was by the results of 1865 fully confirmed in history as the birthplace of the Negro's freedom.

And what of the Negro himself? As he had responded with ready patriotism to his country's call in the War for American Independence, so likewise did he respond again in the War for the Preservation of the Union. His part in the establishment of the nation had been substantial. His part in saving the nation from being rent in twain was vital. For, in view of the military crisis which had arisen at the time when emancipation was proclaimed, it must be regarded as in all probability the fact, that without the one hundred and eighty thousand Negro volunteers who came to the rescue the Union forces could not have won the victory. Union defeat would have meant slavery's indefinite continuance. Thus, while by his part in the Revolution the Negro had contributed to his consequent emancipation throughout the North, by his part in the Civil War he himself proved the decisive factor in the establishment of his freedom throughout the nation.

CHAPTER III

At the conclusion of the war, a number of factors combined in making public sentiment in the North vastly more favorable to the Negro than it had ever been before.

The admirable manner in which the Negro troops had acquitted themselves compelled both respect and gratitude. The noteworthy part which the Negroes had taken in the anti-slavery campaign, especially as speakers on public platforms, and the marked progress they had made during the same period, raised them appreciably in popular estimation. The zeal of the Abolitionists, moreover, had modified somewhat the attitude of the community at large. In consequence of the North's responsibility for emancipation, there was also a recognition of obligation toward the Negro, and a sincere intention to offer him a helping hand in his newborn freedom. Elation over the victory of the Union arms induced a super-normal state of mind, among whose characteristics were a prevailing optimism and magnanimity, that included the Negro in their generous scope.

In Boston, these influences, of course, reached their maximum. Among the radical Abolitionist element, there was the utmost enthusiasm for the Negro. Among a much larger proportion of the community, which might be described as near-Abolitionist in its

views, there was genuine friendliness. In the case of
the rank and file, inherited antipathy was at least
softened to the extent that it did not express itself in
active resistance to endeavors in the Negro's behalf.

The Negroes themselves had, in the course of the
struggle against slavery, and in fact as its collateral
result, experienced a deep and general awakening.
This new impulse had taken on greater strength in
Boston than it had anywhere else. It had manifested
itself in a degree of individual and collective progress
much greater than would otherwise have taken place;
and, still more directly, in efforts to obtain larger
opportunities and a position of increased respect in the
community.[1] Exceptional men and women of the race,
to some of whom previous reference has been made,
had forced their way upward to places unheard of before. Several pioneer Negro lawyers had been admitted
to the bar, and several physicians to standard medical
practice. A group of noteworthy authors had emerged.
An artist had won a reputation. These attainments
by individuals were but the most conspicuous points,
moreover, in a notable advance by the Negro population as a whole. Above the level of menial and common labor, a sufficient number of skilled mechanics
to form the nucleus of a middle industrial class had
obtained a foothold. Business proprietorships had
undergone a marked growth as respects both number
and size. The leading catering establishment of the
city, and two of the best private gymnasiums, were

[1] For a fuller account of the advance of the Negroes during the
period 1830-65, with details of the matters briefly noted in the two
paragraphs following the above, see Appendix, pp. 446-53.

conducted by Negroes. The most remarkable case in
this field was that of a bootblack who became proprietor of a clothing shop and at his death left an estate of
$50,000. Ownership of homestead property had in-
creased from almost zero to a substantial total.[1] The
Negro churches had multiplied from one to five, and
half a dozen new lodges and beneficial societies had
been established.

Evidence of the Negroes' budding pride in their
part in the nation's history had appeared in a petition
submitted by them, which requested the erection of a
memorial to Crispus Attucks, the hero of the Boston
Massacre. An aroused purpose to take fuller advantage of the community's cultural opportunities had
been signified by the formation of a library association,
which served successfully the double function of encouraging the members of this race to take up reading
and study for self-improvement, while at the same time
gradually paving the way for their use of the Public
Library, and their attendance at lectures and entertainments, with immunity from openly contemptuous
treatment on the part of the whites. The point at
which the Negroes had shown their new spirit most
directly and plainly, however, was in a complete
change of attitude on the school question. In earlier
years, it will be recalled, they had themselves be-
sought and finally prevailed upon the city to establish
separate schools, on the ground that their children
were ridiculed and abused by the white children. But
early in the Abolitionist campaign, they had begun to
petition the municipal and state authorities to do

[1] Estimated in 1855 at $200,000.

away with those separate schools, on the ground that such segregation constituted objectionable and unfair discrimination. So persistently had they pressed their demand that in 1855 they had succeeded in obtaining the passage of a state law, forbidding thenceforth any distinction on account of race or color with respect to school attendance. That victory was the cause of great rejoicing.

To the Negroes in this aroused condition resulting from the Abolition Movement, the Emancipation Proclamation had appeared as the hand of Providence, extended to raise them from their depths. The war, to their vision, was a mighty struggle ordained for their deliverance. The valor of the soldiers of their own race had thrilled them with the consciousness of recognized manhood, courage, and patriotism. And at last the triumph of the North, bringing the certainty of their elevation to the estate of free men, was to them the Divine fulfillment of their entrance into the promised land. No wonder that when the war was over, the Negroes, especially in Boston, Anti-slavery's source and center, were in a state of accumulated emotion which bordered on spiritual exaltation.

The majority of Negro leaders of the Abolition period were still alive and active, with ardor and devotion magnified. Younger men and women, who had not taken so prominent a part before the war, now joined hands with the elders. Strong immediate reinforcement from without was provided in the persons of several capable veterans of the battlefield, who took up their abode in Boston as soon as peace returned. Subsequently, the ranks were augmented by other newcomers. The group thus constituted exercised leadership under the new order.[1]

The mass of the race were aglow with the first infusion of the spirit of freedom. Two purely local factors which contributed to their exhilaration were those of concentration in one district and rapid increase of numbers. The movement into the West End, the development of which as early as 1820 has already been noted, had gone on, till within a decade or two thereafter practically all the Negroes in the city were gathered in that section, in a single compact colony. The growth of consciousness of kind and sense of community was thereby greatly furthered. During the troublous times of the anti-slavery struggle and the war, the net increase in the Negro population was not large; — from 1875 persons in 1830, to 2348, in 1865. But immediately following the war, a veritable tidal wave of immigration set in. This sudden and sustained influx brought the mutual assurance which springs from numbers. The bulk of the newcomers, furthermore, were former slaves from the South, who were filled with wonder and unbounded hope in their new life.

Under these auspicious conditions, the Negroes in Boston joined with those of the other race who had their welfare at heart, for the common purpose of securing to the Negro people, in the South and throughout the nation, the full fruits of the Emancipation Proclamation and of the victory of the Union arms. The Proclamation, as a war measure, had been confined to the states or parts of states still in rebellion at the

[1] For names and other information concerning the most prominent members of this group of leaders, see Appendix, pp. 453–56.

time it was issued. It had not applied to the loyal
states of Maryland and Missouri, where slavery was
left undisturbed,[1] nor to certain Southern districts under military occupation by the Federal troops, where
the slave system continued to have a legal existence.
Neither had the Proclamation forbidden the reëstab-
lishment of slavery, or settled the question of the
Negro's future status. It remained, therefore, to complete slavery's eradication, and to bestow upon the
Negroes throughout the Union the rights of free citizenship, including the franchise. These results were to
be accomplished by federal legislation, in the form of
amendments to the Constitution so far as such fundamental enactments should prove necessary.

Boston continued to be the center of activity in the
Negro's behalf. The effort in this direction no longer
had to expend itself to any appreciable degree in converting local sentiment. It was now focused almost
entirely upon Congress, the National Administration,
and the inner councils of the fully empowered Republican party. There was little relaxation in the campaign of public meetings and addresses, petitions and
delegations. As for the Negroes themselves, though,
of course, their direct influence in determining the
action of the Government was subordinate, their zeal
surpassed even that which they had manifested during

[1] Both these states, however, abolished slavery by amendments
to their constitutions before the war ended. Maryland took this
action in October, 1864, and Missouri in January, 1865. One of the
chief factors in the remarkably speedy conversion of Maryland was
the perception by the poor whites that freeing the slaves and allowing them to enlist would aid wonderfully in filling the state's quota
of soldiers, and so would relieve these poor whites themselves from
entering the army. *William Lloyd Garrison*, vol. IV, p. 119, footnote.

the anti-slavery struggle. By still further enlisting public sympathy, and by demonstrating the reality and earnestness of their own desire for a higher place in the nation, they contributed very considerably to the results obtained.

The first proposed federal enactment was the Thirteenth Amendment, abolishing slavery throughout the nation and prohibiting it for all time. This amendment was looked upon as a matter of course, and encountered practically no opposition. Its passage through the House of Representatives was observed in Boston, that same day, by a salute of a hundred guns on the Common, and by the ringing of church bells all over the state.[1] The amendment was ratified by the requisite number of states and declared a part of the Constitution in December, 1865, eight and a half months after the close of the war. Its significance was thus expressed by Garrison in the next to the last number of the "Liberator": —

At last, the old "covenant with death" and "agreement with hell" no longer stands. Not a slave is left to clank his fetters, of the million that were lately held in seemingly hopeless bondage. Not a slaveholder may dare to present his claim of property in man, or assume the prerogative of trafficking in human flesh and blood. . . . It is not merely the abolition of slavery, with the old recognized right of each state to establish the system *ad libitum*, but it is the prohibition by "the Supreme law of the land," duly ratified, to enslave a human being in any part of our national domains, or to restore what has been overthrown. It is, consequently, the complete triumph of the anti-slavery struggle, as such.[2]

[1] January 31, 1865.
[2] *William Lloyd Garrison*, vol. IV, pp. 167–68.

On the point, however, of whether or not the time had arrived for the dissolution of the anti-slavery societies, a disagreement had meanwhile arisen in the Abolitionist ranks. The matter had come up first at the meeting of the Massachusetts society in Boston in the preceding January, and was carried over to the convention of the American Anti-Slavery Society at New York in May. Garrison was for disbandment, on the ground that the ratification of the Thirteenth Amendment being assured, the specific task of abolishing slavery was accomplished. He did not contemplate any abatement whatever of the endeavor in the Negro's behalf, but believed it more fitting that thenceforth the Abolitionists should "mingle with the millions of their fellow-countrymen in one common effort to establish justice and liberty throughout the land." Wendell Phillips took the opposed stand, contending that the existing organization should be kept up until the Negro was granted the franchise and the states were prohibited from enacting laws making any distinction among their citizens on account of race or color. The great majority of the members, as well as Douglass, Remond, and most of the other Negro leaders, proved to be of the latter conviction, evidently fearing that dissolution at that juncture might imperil the Negro's fortunes. Garrison, who was then in his sixtieth year and whose health had been broken by the long struggle, withdrew from formal connection with the anti-slavery societies, and brought the "Liberator" to a close the last week of that year.[1] Thenceforth, his service in the Negro's cause was rendered as

[1] 1865.

speaker and writer at large. The leadership within the Abolitionist ranks during the remaining period of organization passed over to Phillips.[1]

The question of giving the Negroes the franchise was the next one which demanded settlement. At first, there was some doubt about taking this action. It was not, like the abolition of slavery, a measure which had practical application only to the South; for outside of New England, and including Connecticut within that section, all the other Northern States still either withheld the ballot from the Negro entirely, or restricted its extension to him by educational and property qualifications. Indeed, Connecticut, in the autumn of 1865, refused to pass a law enfranchising Negroes, and the new State of Colorado excluded them from the suffrage. Discussion of the matter was brought to a head around the case of Louisiana, which was the first Confederate state to be put in readiness for admission to the Union, and which, in its proposed constitution, did not give the vote to the Negroes. President Lincoln was willing to readmit Louisiana on this basis, though he suggested extending the ballot to such Negroes as had borne arms for the Union or were sufficiently qualified by intelligence. For adopting this attitude he was severely rebuked by the Abolitionists, with the notable exception of Garrison. The latter, though he came out squarely for the adoption of a constitutional amendment enfranchising the Negroes,

---

[1] For a detailed account of the foregoing differences, see *William Lloyd Garrison*, vol. IV, pp. 153–62. The anti-slavery organization was continued till April, 1870, or until after the ratification of the Fifteenth Amendment. Phillips was born in Boston in 1811.

favored accomplishing this purpose in as regular and
conciliatory a manner as possible. He vividly foresaw,
moreover, the difficulties which the Negro's previous
status put in the way of making his right to the ballot
effective in fact, as well as obligatory in law, in the
South.[1] Though the majority of Northerners were

[1] In a letter to an English critic of the President, who condemned
the latter for not enfranchising the Negroes in Louisiana by exercise
of his war powers, Garrison expressed himself as follows: —

"By what political precedent or administrative policy, in any
country, could he have been justified if he had attempted to do this?
When was it ever known that liberation from bondage was accompanied by a recognition of political equality? . . . According to the
laws of development and progress, it is not practicable. . . . Nor,
if the freed blacks were admitted to the polls by presidential fiat,
do I see any permanent advantage likely to be secured from it; for
as soon as the state was organized and left to manage its own affairs,
the white population, with their superior intelligence, wealth, and
power, would unquestionably alter the franchise in accordance with
their prejudices, . . . Coercion would gain nothing. In other words
. . . universal suffrage will be hard to win and to hold without a
general preparation of feeling and sentiment. . . . It will come only
by a struggle *on the part of the disfranchised* and a growing conviction
of its justice. . . . With the abolition of slavery in the South, prejudice or 'colorphobia,' the natural product of the system, will gradually disappear, as in the case of your West India colonies, and black
men will win their way to wealth, distinction, eminence, and official
station." *William Lloyd Garrison*, vol. iv, pp. 123–24.

Referring to Garrison's position on this matter, another English-
man wrote to one of the former's sons, in later years: "I regarded
your father as a man of noble nature, but with concentrated views —
I do not say 'narrow,' because they were as wide as a race and included their emancipation. But in his reply to ——— there was that
largeness of view and recognition of outside difficulties which we call
the statesmanlike quality of mind." *Ibid.*, p. 120, footnote.

Accepting the foregoing expression on Garrison's part at its face
value, one might find some difficulty in reconciling it with his advocacy of enfranchisement of the Negroes by a constitutional amendment. Evidently he thought that the ratification of an amendment
would imply Southern acquiescence and believed that only a brief
time would be required for prejudice to disappear from the South.

rather loath to accept the general principle of Negro suffrage, the feeling steadily gained ground that it would be necessary to safeguard the rights of the freedmen before any of the Southern States were re-admitted. The Republican party, including even its most conservative elements, steadily gravitated toward this position as an obligation of political faith.

As a result, Congress passed in April, 1866, over President Johnson's veto, the Civil Rights Act, which provided that the Negroes were to be recognized as citizens of the United States, with all the privileges of citizenship, including the right to vote; and which made violation of these provisions a misdemeanor to be dealt with by the federal courts. Debate over the constitutionality of this act, however, led to the framing of the Fourteenth Amendment, which passed both branches of Congress on June 13, 1866, and by July 28, 1868, was ratified by the requisite two thirds of the states. This amendment bestowed citizenship, with all its privileges and immunities, upon the Negroes, provided that any state which denied or in any way abridged the right to vote should have its representation in Congress reduced, prohibited persons who had taken part in the rebellion from holding office, and repudiated the Southern debt.

Of course, this enactment had to be forced down the throat of the South. To accomplish that result was largely the purpose of the Reconstruction Act, passed in March, 1867, by Congress, which had by that time completely broken with the President.[1] The

[1] President Johnson, who had as Vice-President succeeded Lincoln after the latter's assassination on April 14, 1865, set out to follow his

former Confederate region was divided into five military districts, under the command of generals of the army, who were to direct a registration of voters which should include Negroes and shut out ex-Confederates. These voters were to elect conventions, in the former state areas, and the conventions in turn were to adopt constitutions, which, if acceptable to Congress, were to qualify the state for readmission as soon as it had agreed to the Fourteenth Amendment. This Act initiated the ill-fraught Reconstruction régime, under which the Southern State Governments passed into the hands of a sorry combination of unscrupulous white politicians from the North — the so-called "carpetbaggers"[1] — and the Negroes themselves.

The conditions which ensued proved so unbearable to the South as to incite the desperate retaliatory campaign of intimidation of the notorious "Ku-Klux Clan." For a time there was a veritable reign of terror, partly as a result of which the Southern whites succeeded in many sections in preventing the Negroes from voting, and in getting themselves back into control. A federal order aimed to destroy the Ku-Klux Clan was issued in 1869, and on May 31, 1870, and April 20, 1871, the two "force bills," designed to sup-

predecessor's policy of not insisting upon unrestricted suffrage for the Negro, but readmitting the Southern States with a minimum of delay and disturbance. Congress utterly opposed this plan, and took the situation into its own hands. The impeachment of the President followed in 1868, but ended with his acquittal.

[1] This epithet arose from the South's contemptuous report that the white politicians brought all their worldly belongings along with them in a Yankee carpetbag.

press this and all similar conspiracies against the civil rights of the Negroes, were passed. Though these measures were effective in breaking up the Ku-Klux organization, it proved to be too late, as will subsequently appear, to repress the uprising of the white South against Negro domination. Inasmuch as the Fourteenth Amendment, though imposing what was expected to be a prohibitive penalty, had not actually forbidden withholding the ballot from the Negroes, it was now deemed necessary to enact the Fifteenth Amendment, which declared that "the right of citizens of the United States to vote shall not be denied or abridged by the United States, or by any State, on account of race, color, or previous condition of servitude." That amendment was passed by Congress in February, 1869, and declared ratified in March, 1870.

Thus, so far as lay in the power of the Constitution, the Negro, who but a few years previous had been a slave, was now raised up not only to free citizenship, but to full political equality with his Caucasian fellow-countrymen. Never before in the history of the world, probably, had any people undergone such a transformation of its lot in so brief a space of time.

Meanwhile, the Negroes in Boston, with the encouragement and support of their white friends, had entered upon a campaign to secure an even larger measure of equality in their own state. In Massachusetts, where the Negro had been free since the days of the nation's birth, and where for many years, possessed of the ballot, he had stood on the same political plane as other members of the community, he now aspired to equal civil rights as well.

As a result of the Abolitionist propaganda and the other favorable influences which have been noted, Boston's Negro citizens were free in general, when peace returned, to come and go in the community as they chose, so far as availing themselves of public privileges was concerned. In certain respects, however, they were still subject to objectionable discrimination. This appeared principally in the refusal of some of the hotels, restaurants, theaters, and other places of recreation or amusement, to serve or admit Negroes.[1]

Immediately after the war, the Negro leaders petitioned for a law which should render illegal any denial to their race of privileges commonly accorded to all other citizens. The result was the adoption by the Legislature, in 1865, of an act forbidding discrimination, on account of color or race, in licensed inns, public places of amusement, public conveyances, or public meetings, under penalty of a fine not to exceed fifty dollars.[2] The following year another law was passed, specifying further that it should be unlawful to "exclude persons from, or restrict them in" any such places, "except for good cause."[3]

In October, 1866, was tried the only case involving the civil rights of the Negro which has ever reached the supreme court of the state. A certain Negro had been refused the privilege of playing billiards in a public billiard room kept by a white man. The ruling of the court was, that as the prohibitory statutes applied

---

[1] Brigham's restaurant on Court Street, and the Boston and old Globe Theaters, were complained of especially.

[2] Acts and Resolves, 1865, chap. 277.

[3] Ibid., 1866, chap. 252.

only to licensed places, and as the billiard room in question was not licensed, no offense had been committed, in law.[1] Ere long another complaint was brought up. A well-known Negro had been put out of a public skating-rink. The case was tried by two talented Negro lawyers, Archibald H. Grimké and Butler R. Wilson, both of whom were leaders in the equal rights agitation.[2] It was won in the municipal court, but in the superior court was dismissed. These adverse decisions, followed by considerable public indignation over the difficulty which a prominent Negro official from the South experienced in finding hotel accommodations in Boston,[3] led to a further extension of the provisions of the law in 1884. The broadening phrase, "licensed or unlicensed," was inserted, skating-rinks were included by name among the places in which any discrimination was forbidden, and the maximum fine was increased to one hundred dollars.[4]

In 1893, William H. Lewis, a young Negro then attending Harvard University Law School, and an ardent recruit to the ranks of the agitators for equality, was refused service in a barber shop in Cambridge.[5] He and Wilson went before the Legislature and asked that not only barber shops, but all places open to public patronage, be included in the scope of the law. The

[1] Commonwealth *v.* David Sylvester.

[2] For further information regarding Grimké and Wilson, see Appendix, pp. 455, 456.

[3] General Robert Smalls, who under the Reconstruction régime was head of the South Carolina militia, and later collector of the port at Beaufort in the same state. His experience in Boston to which reference is made above, took place in 1884.

[4] Acts and Resolves, 1885, chap. 316.

[5] For further information regarding Lewis, see Appendix, p. 456.

Act of 1885 was in consequence amended, and made to include "barber shops or other public places kept for hire, gain, or reward, whether licensed or not."[1] The last revision of the law was made two years later. It increased the maximum fine to three hundred dollars, made imprisonment of not more than one year an alternative or additional penalty, and provided also for the recovery of damages, of not less than twenty-five nor more than three hundred dollars, by the person subjected to discrimination.[2]

By 1895, therefore, the Negro's civil rights — that is, his share in all public privileges of whatever sort — had been made fully equal, in Boston and Massachusetts, to those of other elements of the community. So far as it was possible for the law to accomplish, all obstacles to the Negro's largest opportunity were removed, and he was placed abreast of his white fellow-citizens.

During the years in which this ground was being

[1] Acts and Resolves, 1893, chap. 436.

[2] Acts and Resolves, 1895, p. 519. The full text of the law, as it stands to-day, is as follows: "Whoever makes any distinction, discrimination, or restriction on account of color or race, or, except for good cause, applicable alike to all persons of every color and race, relative to the admission of any person to, or his treatment in a skating-rink or other public place of amusement, licensed or unlicensed, or in a public conveyance or public meeting, or in an inn, barber shop or other public place kept for hire, gain, or reward, licensed or unlicensed, or whoever aids or incites such distinction, discrimination, or restriction, shall, for such offense, be punished by a fine of not more than three hundred dollars or by imprisonment of not more than one year, or by both such fine and imprisonment, and shall forfeit to any person aggrieved thereby not less than twenty-five nor more than three hundred dollars; but such person so aggrieved shall not recover against more than one person by reason of any one act of distinction, discrimination, or restriction."

won, the Negroes were at the same time enjoying a
high degree of favor in the form of public offices. Prior
to the war, no recognition of this sort had been accorded them. Even in those of the Northern States
where they were allowed to vote, the attitude of the
community, in face of the fact that the mass of their
race were still held in slavery, was not indulgent to that
extent. Probably the one solitary case in the whole
country of a Negro being given a place of any kind,
however humble, before the war, was that of Lewis
Hayden, the escaped slave whose leadership among
his people in Boston has been remarked. In 1859, he
had been appointed messenger to the Massachusetts
secretary of state; — a post which he filled with ex-
emplary faithfulness until his death. Immediately
following the war, however, the sentiment which had
been aroused for the Negro began to manifest itself in
the bestowment upon him of public positions, both
appointive and elective.

This impulse found expression chiefly through the
medium of the Republican party, which represented
the great majority of the North, and which was now
fully established in power. The Negroes, on their side,
realizing their indebtedness to that party for their
freedom, as well as for their rights of citizenship and
the franchise, followed its banner with an almost religious devotion. But the friendliness toward the
emancipated race was too general to be entirely confined in its political aspects to the Republican ranks.
The Northern wing of the Democracy also was well disposed, and inclined toward an attitude of invitation
and promise. In local affairs, where party issues were

not involved, there were a scattering few Negroes, even at the beginning, who for one reason or another went with the Democrats; and the number of such gradually increased. Many years elapsed, however, before any considerable proportion of the race had the hardihood to deviate further than that from their Republican allegiance.

The Federal Administration took the lead in extending patronage to representatives of Boston's Negro inhabitants. The state followed immediately. In the city government, where even at that early date sentiment was held more closely in check by considerations of a more "practical" character, such recognition came less quickly, and was due in some measure to the claims which the Negroes themselves advanced. At first, a majority of the recipients of political favors were veterans of the anti-slavery struggle and the war. It is worthy of note, also, that most of them were from the class which had previously been referred to as "free persons of color." At the same time there was a considerable admixture of former slaves. Subsequently, younger men, many of them sons of freedmen, came in for an increasing share of the offices. For the reason that all were pioneers in the political history of their race, they have an interest which exceeds the actual consequence of the positions they held, — though for that matter, as will appear, some of these positions were noteworthy in themselves.[1]

In 1865, John Lenox Remond, of whose prominent part as one of the earliest Negro Abolitionists some-

[1] Information regarding some of these officeholders, in addition to that which follows, is given in the Appendix, Articles II and III.

thing has been related, was appointed a light inspector, and six years later promoted to be a clerk in the custom-house.[1] The next three federal appointees, curiously enough, were all former second lieutenants of the Fifty-fifth Massachusetts Regiment. James M. Trotter, who came from Ohio, was given a clerkship in the post-office, and soon rose to the head of the registered letter division. In 1887, he was appointed by President Cleveland to the high position of registrar of deeds for the District of Columbia. William H. Dupree, hailing from the same state, was started as a letter-carrier, but progressed steadily upward until he reached the post of superintendent of one of the post-office sub-stations.[2] In 1869, Charles L. Mitchell, who had come to Boston from Connecticut shortly before the war, was made a customs inspector, and was subsequently advanced to the rank of clerk, in which capacity he established an unusual record for length and efficiency of service.[3] That year, also, John M. Lenox, who had figured in anti-slavery activities, was given a messengership in the same federal department. In 1894, Archibald H. Grimké, previously mentioned in connection with civic rights legislation, was appointed United States Consul in the Republic of Santo Domingo.[4]

Far more striking, however, was the Negro's sudden elevation to state honors. In 1866, Boston elected two Negro members to the House of Representatives of

[1] He remained in this position till his death in 1873.

[2] Sub-station A in the South End. He still retains this position.

[3] He remained in the custom-house forty years, till his resignation in 1909, on the eve of his eightieth birthday. He has since died.

[4] Grimké occupied this position four years.

the Legislature. These men thereby won the distinction in history of being the first of their race to sit in
the legislature of any state in the Union. One of them
was Edwin G. Walker. He was the only child of David
Walker, who in the remarkable "Appeal," from which
previous quotation has been made, had described his
people as "the most degraded, wretched and abject
set of beings that ever lived since the world began."
Now, only a generation later, the son was raised to a
place among the chosen lawmakers of the very state
and in the very city where that cry had been uttered.
Elements scarcely less dramatic were present in the
case of Walker's colleague, Charles L. Mitchell, whose
subsequent federal appointments have just been noted.
For a time Mitchell had helped set the type for the
"Liberator's" denunciations of slavery. Then as a
soldier he had borne a valiant part in the final struggle
which insured his people's freedom. Now, he not only
beheld his own race transformed from chattels to free
citizens, but found himself elected by his white countrymen to represent the whole community in the decision of its public interests.

Both Walker and Mitchell sat in the legislature for a
single term of one year.[1] John J. Smith, previously
mentioned as proprietor in anti-slavery days of a
barber shop which was a favorite rendezvous of the
Abolitionists, served in the same capacity in 1868 and
1869; George L. Ruffin, who had come to Boston in

[1] Walker represented the district of Charlestown, which had not
at that time been annexed to Boston. It appears that his affiliations
in that town had been with the Democrats, and that his nomination
came from them.

1853, and was one of the first of his race admitted to practice as a lawyer, followed in 1870 and 1871; Smith was returned again in 1872; Lewis Hayden was elected in 1873; and Joshua B. Smith, another anti-slavery veteran, who had built up a large business as a caterer, came in for the same honor in 1873 — making for the second time two Negro members in the same year — and 1874.[1] Thenceforth, for a period of over twenty years longer, broken by brief intervals only, the Negroes continued to have their representatives in the legislature; those who were chosen, however, being later comers to the city.[2] Some of these men were elected from districts in which there were few of their own people, and all of them really owed their election to the generous good will of the other race.

Of state appointive positions given to Negroes, the most notable was that of judge of the city court for the Charlestown district, which, in 1883, Governor Benjamin F. Butler, a Democrat, conferred upon George L. Ruffin.[3] The latter was the first of his race to serve on the bench in the North. In 1893, William O. Armstrong was appointed a court officer.[4]

In city politics, as has been remarked, the recogni-

[1] Joshua B. Smith was elected from Cambridge. For further mention of him, see Appendix, pp. 449 and 454.

[2] The list of Negro members of the Legislature (strictly speaking, of its lower branch, the House of Representatives) for the remainder of the period covered in this chapter, is as follows: 1873–79, George W. Lowther; 1883–86, Julius B. Chappelle; 1887–88, William O. Armstrong; 1889–90, Andrew B. Leattimore; 1892–93, Charles E Harris; 1894–95, Robert T. Teamoh; 1896–97 William L. Reed. The only Negro subsequently sent to the Legislature was W. H. Lewis, who was elected from Cambridge in 1902.

[3] Ruffin retained this position till his death in 1886.

[4] He still holds this position..

tion which the Negroes received was due in part to
their own solicitations. So rapidly did they increase in
number in the West End colony, that by 1885 they
constituted more than half the Republican voters in
old Ward 9, which was of a strongly Republican cast.
They were therefore able to put forward, and if necessary to enforce, a strong claim to representation in
municipal affairs.[1] Each ward elected three members
of the Common Council, the lower branch of the city
government. Beginning in 1776 and continuing, with
brief lapses, till 1895, when the city was redistricted,
the Negroes had one — and for the last two years of
the period, two — of the councilmen from that ward.
The election in 1895 of another Negro, from former
Ward 10, in the South End, resulted in giving them
three members of the board in that year. Since 1773
they had also been represented, though not so continu-
ously, on the corresponding municipal body in the
suburb of Cambridge.[2] The first appointment of a

[1] It might be said that this was true also with respect to representatives in the legislature, of which each ward was entitled to two.
But though most of the Negro members of the latter body were
elected from old Ward 9, it nevertheless appears to have been the
fact that, with respect to that much higher honor, the friendliness
of the whites was really the determining factor.

[2] The following is a list of Negro members of the Common Council
in Boston, down to 1895: from old Ward 9, 1876–77, George L.
Ruffin; 1878, John J. Smith; 1881, James W. Pope; 1885–86,
William O. Armstrong; 1887–88, Andrew B. Leattimore; 1889–90,
Charles E. Harris; 1891, Nelson Gaskins; 1892–93, Walden Banks;
1894–95, Stanley Ruffin (son of George Ruffin) and J. Henderson
Allston; from old Ward 10, 1895, Charles H. Hall.

The list for the Cambridge Common Council, approximately, if
not exactly, correct as to dates, is as follows: 1873, J. Milton Clark;
1882–83, William Stevenson, 1883–84, W. C. Lane; 1891–95, Louis
E. Baldwin.

Negro to a city position appears to have been that of W. W. Bryant, whom in 1885 a Democratic mayor designated to be a deputy sealer of weights and measures.

Though none of this considerable array of Negro officeholders made what would be called a brilliant record, none, on the other hand, acted a discreditable part. All rendered at least ordinary, honest service. Though several were able to be of special use to their own people,[1] that phase of their accountability was subordinate in importance to their trusteeship in behalf of the community at large. Most pertinent of all, however, was the fact that the elevation of these members of the race to public office made the Negroes feel that they had a part of some consequence in the affairs of the community, and at the same time caused the community to form a higher opinion of them.

During these years, also, several Negro newspapers were published in Boston.[2] Besides serving the general function of expressing and stimulating the life of that element of the population, they had the particu-

[1] In the Legislature, Chappelle was instrumental in obtaining the passage in 1886 of the bill to erect the Crispus Attucks Monument. Harris was identified with the bill amending the civil rights statute in 1893, and Teamoh with the bill making the final amendment of this statute in 1895.

[2] The first of these was the Boston *Leader*, maintained from 1875 to 1883. The *Advocate* arose a little later and went out of existence about the same time. The *Hub*, edited by Archibald H. Grimké, ran from 1883 to 1885. The *Courant* appeared in 1883 and continued till 1899; Louis E. Baldwin, Butler R. Wilson, Mrs. George L. Ruffin, and George W. Forbes were among its editors. Baldwin and H. Gordon Street started the *Republican* in 1888 and kept it going till 1893. The foregoing dates are vouched for as approximate only.

lar purpose of furthering the equal rights propaganda. This was likewise the prevailing motive of a number of noteworthy books by Negro authors. William Wells Brown, to whose writings before the war allusion has already been made, continued his productivity in this respect. "The Black Man" was a collection of brief sketches of Negro leaders since the time of Crispus Attucks. "The Negro in the American Rebellion" was one of the first full accounts of the part taken by the Negro troops. "The Rising Son" traced the history of the race and confidently predicted for it a bright future. "My Southern Home" was a vivid portrayal of the conditions out of which Brown had himself come, and which were now gone forever.[1] From the pen of Frances Harper, of whose earlier writings there has also been previous mention, came "Moses, a Story of the Nile," and "Poems."[2] Under the title of "Music and Some Highly Musical People," James Munroe Trotter assembled much interesting material concerning members of his race who had won signal credit in that field.[3] Archibald H. Grimké was the author of two stirring biographies, the one of Garrison, and the other of Charles Sumner, Massachusetts' noted Abolitionist Senator.[4]

Altogether, these were for the Negroes years of rejoicing in their newly attained privileges, and of efflorescence in the first warm sunshine of their freedom. Before the law of the nation they were raised to a

[1] The dates at which these four books appeared were, in the above order, 1863, 1867, 1874, and 1880.

[2] Published in 1869 and 1871, respectively.

[3] Published in 1878.

[4] The former biography appeared in 1891, the latter in 1892.

place of political peerage with the white man. In the law of the state of Massachusetts they were endowed also with full civil equality. They were elevated to office and seated beside their white fellow-citizens in many positions of trust and esteem. In the midst of all this high fortune, their elation expressed itself in lyric and narrative celebration of their deliverance. On the side of the other race, popular sentiment with reference to the emancipated people was generous to the degree of indulgence. The fact of being a Negro actually counted as an element of advantage, as signifying a special claim upon the community and eliciting special sympathy and help. Such was the spirit of the period. The granting of equal rights to the Negro and the bestowal of public favor upon him were its dominant features.

CHAPTER IV

REACTION: THE NEGRO FORCED UPON HIS OWN RESOURCES

But while popular favor was going out to the Negro in the degree that has been described, and while the emancipated race was in the high state of exuberance attending its attainment of full equality before the law: — even then, down below the surface, the decisive conditions were passing through a change, and the public attitude was undergoing a reaction and radical readjustment. At the same time, the Negroes, on their part, in the face of the new situation by which they were confronted, were as a people moving toward the conscious discovery of a fundamental constructive power within themselves.

Northern sentiment for the Negro sustained its first check as a result of the wretched exhibition which that race gave in the South, during the period of Reconstruction. Passing reference has already been made to this dark chapter in the nation's history. Somewhat fuller note of it may advisedly be taken at this point.

The Reconstruction Acts, by enfranchising the Negroes and disqualifying large numbers of the more influential whites, made it possible for the blacks to get possession of the governments in most of the Southern States and to rule them in a most ignorant and extravagant manner. They were made use of by unprincipled adventurers from the North, who flocked to the South in considerable numbers after the close of the war. . . . A few native Southerners — "scalawags," they were called — also allied themselves politically with the Northern men and Negroes, for the purpose of sharing in the offices. . . . The carpet-baggers secured the nominations to the more important offices, and were easily elected by large black majorities. But the colored voters were not content to see all the offices held by their white allies, and their ambition was frequently too great to be ignored.

Consequently many of the important offices came to be held by ignorant blacks who but a few years previous were field hands on the plantations. In several states Negroes filled the offices of lieutenant-governor, secretary of state, superintendent of education. . . . In some instances they even sat upon the benches of the higher courts, while they filled many minor judicial positions. They occupied seats in the legislatures of all the Southern States, that of Mississippi in 1871 having as many as fifty-five colored members. A considerable proportion of these were ignorant, some of whom were unable to read or write, and all of whom were the pliant dupes of unscrupulous Northern men. With the state and local governments controlled by ignorant Negroes and designing white men, an era of extravagance, misrule, and corruption set in, which in some instances amounted to outright robbery and plunder.

Long and frequent sessions of the legislature were held, for service in which the members voted themselves large *per diem* allowances. Old laws were ruthlessly repealed, and replaced by bulky statutes, many of which bore the earmarks of animosity and oppression. . . . Laws favoring social equality were passed . . . offices were greatly multiplied . . . many of them mere sinecures. . . . Gigantic schemes of public improvement were undertaken, most of which were marked by frauds and extravagance. The rate of taxation was increased out of all proportion to the ability of the people to pay, in their then impoverished condition. . . . Large gratuities were voted state officials, the state capitol was furnished after the manner of a European palace, and vast sums were squandered.[1]

[1] Article "Reconstruction in the United States," in the *Encyclopædia Americana*, by James Wilford Garner, Professor of Political Science at the University of Illinois.

Such, stated in very moderate terms, were the intolerable conditions of misgovernment, pillage, and political debauchery which afflicted the South when the Negroes were endowed with the ballot and entrusted with power. These conditions could not be endured for long. They began with the passage of the Reconstruction Acts in 1867, and they were brought to an end in 1876, by which time the Southern whites, to some extent through Ku-Klux terrorism, but in the main by a determined political uprising on the part of the better element of the population, had succeeded in regaining control of the government of all the lately rebellious states.[1] This overturn was the beginning of that systematic political repression of the Negro in the South, which has not yet run its full course.

The effect of Reconstruction experience upon the North was decidedly to dampen the sentiment for the Negro which there prevailed. That element of the population, probably greatly in the majority, which had from the first been more or less dubious regarding the bestowal of equal rights upon the Negroes, pointed in justification of their misgivings to the ignorance, incompetence, and dishonesty which that race had displayed once the doors of equal privilege had been thrown wide open to it. People who had expected that the Negroes would become good citizens immediately the rights of citizenship were accorded them, were forced to qualify their views. Some — so deep was their

[1] North Carolina, Tennessee, Texas, Georgia, and Virginia were recovered by 1870; Alabama and Arkansas, in 1874; Mississippi, in 1875; and Louisiana and Florida, in 1876.

disappointment and disillusionment — completely abandoned their former faith, and joined the ranks of those who were at least skeptical regarding the Negro's capacity for progress.

Withal, there arose a growing belief that in forcing through the equal rights programme at all hazards the North had gone too far, and that in dealing with the Negro question in future it should follow a less precipitate and more cautious policy, based upon concrete facts rather than upon abstract doctrine. That section of the country had made such a dismal failure of its attempt to restore order and prosperity in the South that it was in a mood to be rid of the vexing task. The extremes to which the Southern whites went in regaining control, and the drastic manner in which they set out to prevent the Negroes from voting and to reduce them to a position of complete submission, were of course far from pleasant things for Northerners to stand by and observe. But inasmuch as there appeared to be no practicable alternative, events were allowed to take their new course. The action of President Hayes in 1878, in withdrawing the last of the Federal troops from the lately revolted districts, and thus removing the only remaining element of coercion, gave definite alignment to the changing attitude of the North and of the Republican Federal Administration.

Another influence now entered in to give the situation a further turn in the same reversed direction. Through the medium of an apparently half-spontaneous, half-deliberate, but at any rate very skillful campaign of public addresses, books, newspapers, and magazine writing, the South began to urge its own view of the Negro problem upon the North, and to solicit sympathy and support.

One of the Southerners who accomplished most in this respect was Henry W. Grady, the editor of the Atlanta "Constitution." On the evening of December 12, 1889, he made a notable address before the Merchants' Association in Boston.

"I thank God as heartily as you do," he said, "that human slavery is gone forever from American soil. But the free man remains. With him a problem without precedent or parallel. Note its appalling conditions. Two utterly dissimilar races on the same soil — with equal political and civil rights — almost equal in numbers, but terribly unequal in intelligence and responsibility — each pledged against fusion — one for a century in servitude to the other, and freed at last by a desolating war, the experiment sought by neither but approached by both with doubt — these are the conditions. Under these, adverse at every point, we are expected to carry these two races in peace and honor to the end. . . . In spite of these things, we are commanded to make good this change of American policy which has not perhaps changed American prejudice — to make certain here what has elsewhere been impossible between whites and blacks — and to reverse, under the very worst conditions, the universal verdict of racial history. And driven, sir, to this superhuman task with an impatience which brooks no delay — a rigor that accepts no excuse — and a suspicion that discourages frankness and sincerity, we do not shrink from the trial. It is so interwoven with our industrial fabric that we cannot disentangle it if we would — so bound up with our honorable obligation to the world that we would not if we could. Can we solve it? The God who gave it into our hands, He alone can know. But this the weakest and wisest of us do know: we cannot solve it with less than your tolerant and patient sympathy."

Grady was one of the foremost orators of the day, and in the impression that he made his eloquence doubtless played as large a part as did the substance of his argument. His address in Boston on this occasion was representative of the general character of the appeal which the South was making, with the object of persuading the North to its way of thinking.

That appeal was in fact successful in advancing the Northern change of attitude one stage farther. Though the North had withdrawn from Reconstruction, it had not done so without ranklings of resentment at the defeat of its efforts, feelings of chagrin at its own helplessness, and compunctions of conscience because of its apparent desertion of the constitutional rights of the Negroes in the Southern States. Now, however, the South's conciliatory professions largely overcame that resentment, while the inculcation of the peculiar character and exceeding difficulty of the problem which the Negro presented, at once assuaged chagrin and soothed the Northern conscience. Two convictions, furthermore, became firmly rooted. One was that the subordination of sectional differences on account of the Negro was essential to the peace and welfare of the nation. The other was that the question of how to deal with the emancipated race in the former slave states should be left to those states themselves to settle.

It was inevitable, however, that this change of belief should apply not only to conditions in the South, but also, though in different sort and degree, to the position of the Negro in the North. There, moreover, in addition to the effect of Reconstruction experience and Southern proselytizing, other kindred factors, closer at hand and of more immediate influence, were at work. Because sentiment for the Negro had mounted higher in Boston than anywhere else, the subsidence which was now taking place was, by contrast, most marked in that city.

In the first place, the Abolitionists gradually passed away. Garrison died in 1879, Phillips in 1884, and by the end of the third decade after the war most of the others were gone. With these zealots disappeared also that ardor for the Negro and that vehement championship of his cause which they embodied. The feeling that they cherished toward the Negro people grew out of the long and absorbing struggle through which they had gone in their behalf, and shoulder to shoulder with them. It was humanly impossible for that feeling to be shared in its fullness by others who had not also shared the same experience. To the sons and daughters of the Abolitionists, anti-slavery ideals did not and could not have the same transcendent significance. To the generation of the Abolitionists' grandchildren, emancipation and the war were things of the past, whose meaning was vague and pale beside the concrete living realities of the present.

Likewise, conditions among the Negroes themselves were taking a new aspect. The leaders of the "Old Guard" had been able, by virtue of the position of general respect and attention which they held, to act as middlemen between the whites and the rank and file of their race, and thus to exert a large influence toward mutual understanding. But the ranks of those old leaders were thinned by the years. Remond, the senior member of the group, died in 1873; Hayden, the most picturesque and forceful, in 1889. Soon thereafter only a scattering few, rendered comparatively inactive by age, still survived. The younger men who had come to Boston since the war were not able fully to assume the fallen mantles of the elders. They did not have the same stirring times to fire them with enthusiasm, nor were they subjected to such elemental incentives as would arouse in them an equal degree of devotion to the common cause of their people. Nor, finally, did they meet with the same close and real sympathy and support from the other race.

To complete the passing of the old order, there began immediately after the war, as has already been noted, a sudden and constantly increasing influx of Negro immigrants from the South. They came in thousands. Most of them were utterly uneducated and ignorant. Nearly all were more or less uncouth, many were ragged and dirty, and a large proportion were crude, dull, and indeed brutish, in appearance. These new arrivals became a common sight in the streets. They crowded into the cars, among the white passengers. They explored the shops, with mouths agape and eyes bulging at the marvels there displayed. They entered restaurants and took seats alongside the white patrons. They even invaded some of the most select Back Bay churches. In short, they were ubi-

quitous. Never before had Boston experienced the
Southern Negro en masse. Its previous acquaintance
had been chiefly with the Northern free persons of
color — a highly refined type in comparison. True,
most of the escaping slaves of Abolition days were sufficiently abject specimens; but the majority of the
latter had been kept out of sight, biding their flight
still farther north. As for the refugees who took up
their permanent abode in the city, the few exceptional
individuals among them, like William Wells Brown
or the others who have been mentioned, made such a
disproportionate impression upon the popular imagination as to cast a sheen of semi-illusion over the others,
who, moreover, were soon inclosed and somewhat
polished off by the Negro population of longer Boston
residence. But in the face of the black horde which
came pouring in after the war, the white inhabitants
of Boston involuntarily and at first unwillingly re-
coiled. Gradually, this recoil hardened into permanent
withdrawal.

The combined result, therefore, of the several influences which have been cited was to effect a pronounced
reaction in Boston's attitude toward the Negro.
Though during its formative period this reaction developed as an undercurrent, it made itself more and
more distinctly felt, as time went by, and constantly
rose nearer to the surface. Whatever expectation had
formerly been entertained that the Negro, endowed
with equal rights, would forthwith rise automatically
to the level of the other elements of the community
and be received by them into full association, was
now replaced by the conviction that the Negro was

different from these other elements and of a lower gradation. This change of view was in fact an approximation to the attitude held by the South. It was far more, however, than mere reconciliatory truckling to sectional opinion or prejudice. It amounted to an acceptance, in certain measure, of the South's anthropological theory with respect to the Negro, — the substance of which was, in the already quoted words of Grady, that he belonged to a "dissimilar" race, "unequal in intelligence and responsibility," thus constituting "a problem without precedent or parallel."

This conclusion, however, was not positive, but negative. It removed all doubt of the difficulty of the problem, but it did not supply any clear, concrete, and practicable plan of solution. It was an admission that the course previously followed with regard to the Negro had proved inadequate, but it was not a demarcation of any other course which could be pursued with the likelihood of proving adequate. It was destructive of former misconceptions, but it did not constructively replace them by practical understanding sufficient to the need. It compelled recognition of failure in the past, but it did not hold out any reasonable hope of success in the future.

At that juncture, however, the positive, constructive, hopeful note was clearly sounded. The way out was plainly indicated. And this was accomplished, not by a member of the white race, but by one of the Negro people — Booker T. Washington,[1] founder and work-

[1] Washington was born near Hale's Ford, Virginia, in 1858 or 1859, and received his education at the Hampton Institute, situated at Hampton in the same state. He founded the Tuskegee School in 1881. Prior to his Atlanta address he was already somewhat known

ing head of the Tuskegee Normal and Industrial Institute at Tuskegee, Alabama. On September 18, 1895, Washington delivered an address, not at Boston, but at the other end of the country, and, dramatically enough, in the very city — Atlanta, Georgia --- whence six years before Grady had gone forth to appeal to the white people of the North for sympathy and patience with the white South in its perplexities. This address brought its author into sudden and lasting fame. It proved a great landmark in the history of his race. Its effect has been so momentous as to render essential the citation at this point of some of its most important passages: —

Ignorant and inexperienced, it is not strange that in the first years of our new life we began at the top instead of at the bottom, that a seat in Congress or the state legislature was more sought than real estate or industrial skill; that the political convention or stump-speaking had more attractions than starting a dairy farm or truck garden. . . . Our greatest danger is that in the great leap from slavery to freedom we may overlook the fact that the masses of us are to live by the productions of our hands, and fail to keep in mind that we shall prosper in proportion as we learn to dignify and glorify common labor and put brains and skill into the common occupations of life; shall prosper in proportion as we learn to draw the line between the superficial and the substantial, the ornamental gewgaws of life and the useful. No race can prosper till it learns that there is as much dignity in tilling a field as in writing a poem. It is at the bottom of life we must begin, and not at the top. Nor should we permit our grievances to overshadow our opportunities. . . . In all things that are purely social we can be as separate as the fingers, yet one as the hand in all things essential to mutual progress. . . . The wisest among my race understand that

in Boston, whither he had journeyed, first in the later eighties, and after that at regular intervals, in the interests of his institution.

the agitation of questions of social equality is the extremest folly, and that progress in the enjoyment of all the privileges that will come to us must be the result of severe and constant struggle, rather than of artificial forcing. No race that has anything to contribute to the markets of the world is long in any degree ostracized. It is important and right that all privileges of the law be ours, but it is vastly more important that we be prepared for the exercise of these privileges. The opportunity to earn a dollar in a factory just now is worth infinitely more than the opportunity to spend a dollar in an opera house.

This was one "of the most notable speeches, both as to character and the warmth of its reception, ever delivered to a Southern audience," wrote the Honorable Clark Howell, who had succeeded Grady as editor of the Atlanta "Constitution." [1] "It was an epoch-making talk and marks distinctly a turning-point in the progress of the Negro race. . . . The whole speech is a platform on which the whites and blacks can stand with full justice to each race." Not only in the South, but in the North as well, — throughout the country, indeed, — the address made a profound impression.

The tremendous significance of what Washington said lay in the fact that he effectually shifted the emphasis in the Negro problem, placing chief stress not upon the question of the immediate endowment of the emancipated race with rights and privileges fully equal to those of the whites, — which had previously been regarded as the cardinal point, — but upon that of the Negro's substantial preparation for rising to a higher place in the nation through self-effort on his own part. The concrete means which Washington proposed, in or-

[1] This statement was made in a letter to the New York *Herald*, written soon after the address was delivered.

der to achieve that result, was the development by the
Negro of his own economic resources. Primary strategic importance was attached to agriculture — this with
a view especially to conditions in the South — and to
manual occupations requiring some degree of skill; for
the reason that these fields offered the race both the
readiest immediate foothold and at the same time the
surest stepping-stone to still further economic advance.
The most fundamental and practical education along
those lines, of the sort for which Tuskegee stood, was
— by implication — to be utilized to the fullest degree
in this industrial ascent. After this manner only, Washington declared, would the Negro eventually obtain,
through the actual demonstration of his own inherent
worth, such political and civil privileges and enjoy-
ments as were for the present withheld from him, on account of his obvious and indeed inevitable deficiencies.

As has already been suggested, the view thus taken,
in giving to the whole problem of the Negro this new
and radically altered orientation, was in fact the constructive complement of the change in the community's
attitude toward the Negro which was then, as has previously appeared, in progress. The truth of this statement will appear still more clearly, however, in the light
of a counter-movement which meanwhile had arisen
among the Negroes themselves, and which directed itself against both the reaction in Northern sentiment,
and against Washington's interpretation of conditions.

When, with the collapse of Reconstruction, the
Negroes realized that their rights under the Constitution were not to be maintained in the South, and when,
later on, they saw also that the tide of sentiment was

beginning to ebb in the North, the great mass of the race simply accepted and reconciled themselves to these reversals as to irrevocable matters of fact. But a certain element, consisting chiefly of the more highly educated Negroes, and of those who through long Northern residence had become saturated with Abolition doctrine, entered upon a movement of protest and agitation. This was, so to speak, a resumption of the earlier campaign for the passage of the Amendments and the Civil Rights Laws, — but it was a resumption on the defensive. As Boston had been the scene of the Negro's greatest activity in the anti-slavery struggle and the demand for equality, so now it became the principal center of his resistance to the current that was setting in against him.

This protest on the Negro's part first showed itself in murmurings of rebuke of the Republican party, for not standing by the race in the Southern States. For a long time such complaints remained almost entirely within the party lines, and did not grow so strong as to cause defections. Very early, however, there were a few who revolted outright. One of the first of these was James M. Trotter, to whose prominence among his people several previous references have been made. Shortly after President Hayes, in 1878, withdrew the Federal troops from the South, leaving the way open for the return of the Southern whites to power, Trotter declared he could no longer retain his Republican allegiance. His subsequent appointment by President Cleveland to the office of registrar of deeds for the District of Columbia, already mentioned, was at once a recognition of his going over to the Democrats — on the ground that he pre-

ferred no pledges at all to pledges broken! — and also
a bid from the Northern wing of that party for Negro
votes. But there was no considerable breaking-away
from the Republican ranks until General Benjamin F.
Butler ran independently for governor of Massachusetts in 1882. As major-general in eastern Virginia,
Butler had in 1861 issued a famous order which, by
proclaiming that escaped slaves who came within the
Union lines should be regarded as contraband of war,
in effect set the Negroes in that section at liberty. He
had also organized the Louisiana Native Guards from
free Negroes. For these reasons he obtained in the
state campaign in 1882 a large Negro vote, which contributed appreciably to his election.[1] From that time
the proportion among the Negroes of political inde-
pendents, who on occasion would support Democratic
or other candidates or policies, gradually increased.
The defection from the Republican standard, however,
was not based upon any disagreement with planks expressed in the party platform, but solely upon the failure of the Republicans to enforce the Fourteenth and
Fifteenth Amendments, and generally to accord the
Negro what he regarded as just treatment. In other
words, this revolt has been an integral part of the Negro's protest against the derogation of his rights and
immunities.

[1] Governor Butler's conferring of the judgeship of the Charlestown municipal court upon George L. Ruffin, to which previous allusion has been made, was an acknowledgment of his indebtedness
to the Negroes. He wished to appoint to this position Edwin G.
Walker, who, as has been mentioned, was a Democrat. But as the
Republican majority of his Council would not ratify Walker's selection, he appointed Ruffin, who was a Republican.

Two of the earliest organizations formed to voice this protest were the Wendell Phillips Club, started in 1876, and the Colored National League, formed about the same time and maintained till about 1900.[1] In 1899, the latter association sent to President McKinley an open letter, which began thus: "We, colored people of Massachusetts, in mass meeting assembled, to consider our oppressions and the state of the country relative to the same"; and, after reciting various grievances, went on to demand "the enjoyment of life, liberty, and the pursuit of happiness equally with other men."

Washington's Atlanta address at first bore practically all of his own people along in the general wave of commendation which it elicited. But after a time, as its underlying significance came to be more fully appreciated, and as those portions of it which deprecated insistence upon privileges, and appeared to relegate the Negro for the present mainly to an industrial rôle, were taken up and enlarged upon the country over, the address incurred the angry reprobation of the agitators for equality. Some of the author's subsequent utterances, of similar purport, were even more fiercely condemned. Thenceforth, one of the most prominent features of this agitation has been the vehement and bitter denunciation of Washington as recreant to the highest aspirations of his race, and the advocate of an unworthy and disastrous submissiveness.

The attack upon Washington was definitely initi-

[1] The former organization is still in existence, though comparatively inactive during recent years. It includes members of both races.

ated, in Boston, by William Munroe Trotter and
George W. Forbes. The latter, to whom there has been
previous reference, was a recruit to the equality propaganda in the third decade after the war.[1] Trotter is
the son of James M. Trotter, who died in 1892. In
view of the father's already mentioned declaration of
hostility against the Republican party, the son may be
said to have come into his fighting spirit by inheritance.[2] In 1901, these two men launched the "Guardian," a weekly newspaper devoted to agitation. The
following year they and several others engineered an
anti-Washington demonstration which, though in appearance at the time it was little more than a disorderly fracas, had in fact a real significance. Washington was to speak on the evening of July 30, in one of
the Negro churches,[3] under the auspices of the local
branch of the Negro Business League, an organization
which had recently come into being through his own efforts. When that occasion arrived, the hall was crowded
with an audience in part friendly and in part unfriendly
to him, but swelled withal by the rumor that something of an unusual nature was to occur. The introductory remarks of the presiding officer and those of

[1] See chapter III, and Appendix, article III.

[2] William Munroe Trotter was born in 1872. He grew up in a
white neighborhood, went to school with white children, and was
valedictorian of his class both in grammar and high school. In high
school he was also elected class president, and still holds this position since graduation in 1890. Entering Harvard College in 1891, he
stood among the first four in scholarship in his freshman year, was
elected to the Phi Beta Kappa in his junior year, and graduated
with the degree of A.B. and A.M., the latter *magna cum laude*. Prior
to starting the *Guardian*, he held various clerical and business
positions.

[3] The Zion African Methodist.

several preliminary speakers occasioned hissing and
other disturbance, and at one point led to the intervention of police officers. As soon as Washington began
his address, one of the hostile contingent jumped up
and started to put to him a number of questions that
had been prepared. The police removed the disturber.
An uproar ensued. Washington attempted to proceed,
but was again interrupted. This time it was Trotter
and another man, who shouted out the questions.
They, together with a companion who had joined in the
disorder, were arrested and taken to the police station.
After being bailed out by Trotter's mother, they hastened back to the church to renew the attack. By that
time, however, the meeting had broken up.

Shortly after this affair, Trotter and the two others
who had been taken into custody were brought to
trial, the plaintiff in the case being the church in which
the fracas had occurred, and the charge that of mali-
ciously disturbing a public meeting. The courtroom was
crowded with Negroes, and many white people also were
present. A white attorney acted for the prosecution,
but the defendants were represented by four lawyers
of their own race. The outcome was, that while one of
the defendants was let off with a fine of $25, Trotter
and the other were sentenced to a fine of $50 and thirty
days' imprisonment. An appeal was taken to the superior court, but the sentence was there confirmed.
Trotter and his companion went to jail, regarding themselves as martyrs, and held up as martyrs by those who
shared their general point of view on the Negro question.

What this point of view is may be gathered from the

five leading questions which at the meeting that has been described, Washington was called upon to answer: —

1. In your letter to the Montgomery "Advertiser," November 27, you said: "Every revised constitution throughout the Southern States has put a premium upon intelligence, ownership of property, thrift, and character." Did you not thereby indorse the disfranchising of our race?

2. In your speech before the Twentieth Century Club here in March you said: "Those are most truly free who have passed through the most discipline." Are you not actually upholding oppressing our race as a good thing for us, advocating peonage?

3. Again you say: "Black men must distinguish between freedom that is forced and the freedom that is the result of struggle and self-sacrifice." Do you mean that the Negro should expect less from his freedom than the white man from his?

4. When you said, "It was not so important whether the Negro was in the inferior car as whether there was in that car a superior man, not a beast," did you not minimize the outrage of the insulting jim-crow car discrimination and justify it by the "bestiality" of the Negro?

5. In an interview with the Washington "Post," June 25, as to whether the Negro should insist on his ballot, you were quoted as saying: "As is well known, I hold that no people in the same economic and educational condition as the masses of the black people of the South should make politics a matter of the first importance in connection with their development." Do you not know that the ballot is the only self-protection for any class of people in this country?

In an anniversary edition of the "Guardian" issued in 1904, the editors reviewed the so-called Zion Church affair.[1] They maintained that because of Washington's personal influence and the rapid dissemination of

[1] The exact date of this number of the *Guardian* was July 30.

his ideas, the Negroes who held diverse views had lost nearly all opportunity for a public hearing through the press, and that a prime object of the demonstration at the church had been to reach the public. This object they claimed to have accomplished, pointing in confirmation to the far larger amount of newspaper notice accorded their subsequent meetings and activities. They contended also that, by virtue of this setting forth of their principles, they had compelled Washington somewhat to modify his utterances, — which were still, however, sufficiently obnoxious.

Since these events occurred, Trotter has continued his agitation with unremitting vigor. He directs his protest against everything which can be even remotely suspected of drawing the color line or relegating the Negroes to an inferior place. One of the most signal local achievements in which he had a leading part, was the forcing from the Boston stage, in the winter of 1910, of the notorious play, "The Clansman," which portrays the Negro as essentially a brute. In his never-ceasing attack he is unyielding to the last degree, and has repudiated many a former friend for some deviation from what is to himself the true belief. The extreme to which he carries his pursuit of color discrimination is shown by the fact that he opposed a promising local effort on the part of a number of his race to carry on betterment work among newly arrived Southern immigrants, and attacked a social settlement established by whites for the benefit of Negroes, on the ground that both these enterprises furthered segregation and discrimination. His activity is not confined to Boston. He helped to launch the New Eng-

land Suffrage League in 1904, the Niagara Movement
in 1905, and the National Independent Political
League in 1908, and has become one of the leaders in
the larger movement to combat race prejudice which
these organizations represent.

Recently this movement has enlisted noteworthy
support from an element of the other race. In 1910 was
organized the National Association for the Advancement of Colored People. Its president is Moorfield
Storey, the well-known anti-imperialist, of Boston,
in which city it also has one of its most vigorous
branches. Jane Addams is a member of the executive
committee. This society, which draws no color line in
its membership, has secured W. E. B. DuBois, formerly
of Atlanta University, to direct its endeavors. Dr.
DuBois is regarded as probably the most intellectual
man of the Negro race to-day, as well as its foremost
present representative in the equal-rights agitation.
He is also one of the well-recognized sociologists of the
country. The line along which he will strive is indicated by the following statement which the association
sent out soon after its formation: —

The attitude of the American people toward our Negro
citizens has given rise to conditions, the spread of which
cannot fail seriously to imperil our democracy. . . . Race
prejudice is increasing, North and South. . . . On all sides we
hear of the grossest discrimination in the courts, in the public education system, and in industry. The remedy for this
state of affairs lies solely in a right attitude of the public
mind, and the endeavor to bring about such an attitude will
call for active, untiring work by our association. We must
leave no misstatement unanswered, no injustice unpro-
tested, and by a close, united organization must build up,
step by step, a public opinion that will make impossible our

present barbarities to a race which we have set aside, in its entirety, from normal citizenship.

Thus in recent years the agitation for equal rights has evidently made a certain amount of headway. It has enlisted new recruits. It has secured a hearing before the public. It has formed an organization through which it may the more effectively express itself.

But during the same period the change and readjustment of attitude toward the Negro, and the general indorsement of Washington's point of view and plan of operation, have made progress many times more extensive than that of the counter-movement which has been described. One of the most impressive and promising elements of this progress has been the turning to Washington's principles on the part of the great mass of his own race. In Boston, as has already been intimated and as will later be more amply shown, the rank and file of the Negro population is made up of recent immigrants from the South. These Southern Negroes grew up among their people in the "Black Belt," accustomed to regard the color line as a fact rather than a grievance. Their most immediate and vital concern is to earn a living. They instinctively recognize that a plan which will enable them to earn a better living will necessarily promote their general welfare. Except for a small and scattering minority, they have therefore accepted the gospel of salvation through work. This acceptance has not come about so much through a process of conscious reasoning as it has through the promptings of a native common sense. It finds expression not so much in words or declamation as in the ordinary acts of each day's routine. But therein

is it all the more real and substantial. As it is with
the rank and file, so it is with most of those who occupy positions of leadership, a majority of whom also
are to-day of Southern birth and rearing. They both
share and respond to the feeling of the mass of their
race. Especially noticeable is the extent to which the
younger leaders, as they arise, are planting their feet
squarely upon the solid ground of self-help.

More significant still is the fact that a majority of
the Negroes who were formerly in the forefront of the
equal-rights agitation have substantially modified their
views in the light of a fuller understanding of conditions. Most of the earlier leaders in that agitation no
longer take part in it with their pristine vehemence, and
have grown to be at least tolerant of the prevailing attitude. Some, while not abandoning their belief in the
importance of constant activity by the Negro to safeguard his rights, have become convinced that tactics
less precipitate and more conciliatory in character are
better adapted to that purpose, and have at the same
time openly committed themselves to the substance of
Washington's position. These latter are represented
most prominently in the Boston community by William H. Lewis, to whom reference has already been
made in connection with civil rights legislation, and
whose opinion should command special respect by
reason of the high posts in the public service which, as
will at a later point be mentioned specifically, he has
occupied.

For a time after leaving the Law School I was counted as
one of the radicals and agitators [said Mr. Lewis in a statement to the writer], but I found so many good people who

approved Dr. Washington's course and who were just as sincere in their advocacy of human rights and Negro rights as I myself, that I began to ask myself if they were wholly wrong and myself wholly right. I came to believe that they were more right than I, and so I decided that I should not make the business of my life the pulling down of some other men or slinging mud at a real worker.

In an address at Cleveland, Ohio, in August, 1909, he further defined his present attitude: —

Northern colored men — in their earnest zeal for better things — should be careful not to hinder, not to retard, not to jeopardize, the progress toward that happy consummation which both races are working out to-day. Mere indiscriminate denunciation, vituperation, recrimination, and abuse on our part, will accomplish nothing. . . . The race in the minority, like the individual in society, who is always in the minority, must advance, if at all, by the same line that the individual advances, by tact, ability, conduct, character, common sense, and diplomacy. . . . Our old-time methods of agitation, denunciation and exposition of our wrongs, to-day fall upon deaf ears and find little sympathy anywhere. . . . The educated colored men have not taken advantage of the human failing which will often grant a request when it will refuse to yield to a just demand. They have forgotten that, though man's heart may be apparently surcharged with the blackest hate and prejudice, somewhere from his inner consciousness flows the milk of human kindness. They have failed to realize that under present conditions the field of diplomacy has scarcely been touched in the solution of race problems.

Likewise by the vast majority of white people, in Boston as elsewhere, the principles enunciated by Washington have been accepted as the most practicable and normal course to be followed with respect to the emancipated race. There is a reason for this acceptance, moreover, which is far broader and deeper than any consideration peculiar to this particular prob-

lem. It is this: that while the dominant commercial
spirit which characterizes the present generation makes
less response than the humanitarian spirit of the preceding generation to abstract appeals regarding the
Negro's rights, this same commercial spirit responds
readily to the proposal to develop the latent productive
capacities of the Negro people and thus to enhance
their value to the community. This proposal, especially in its advocacy of industrial education, is, furthermore, in line with the rapidly evolving new
humanitarianism, which places less emphasis upon
the immediate relief of human distress and more
upon the eliciting of human powers.

By a chronological coincidence, which was, to say
the least, remarkable, Washington's epochal Atlanta
address was delivered in the very year that witnessed
the death of Frederick Douglass. The latter, who, as
previously remarked, had come to be looked upon as
the foremost representative of his race, may be said to
have embodied the old order, with uncompromising
Abolitionist doctrine as its dominant note.[1]   In
Boston the same year, curiously enough, saw the last
amendment which extended the scope of the state's

[1] In an address in Rochester, New York, March 13, 1848, Douglass
defined his position on equal rights as follows: "I look upon all complexion distinctions, such as Negro pews, Negro berths on steam-
boats, Negro cars, Sabbath or week-day schools or churches, etc.,
as direct obstacles to the progress of reform, and as the means of
continuing the slave in his chains." W. C. Nell, *Colored Patriots
of the Revolution*, p. 361.

After the war, Douglass was not much in Boston. He traveled
over the country as a lecturer, but spent most of his time in Washington, D.C., where he held a number of high federal offices. He died
in that city.

statute of civil rights. That year — 1895 — may, therefore, very aptly be taken as the dividing point between the old order and the new. This is not to say that the change was then complete. Indeed, it was still for the most part taking place beneath the surface. But it had by that time entered upon the decisive stage. Since then it has been fully consummated. In this new order the central motive is the belief that it is not so much the immediate possession of all political and civil rights and privileges, but rather the underlying equipment for the proper exercise of such rights and privileges, of which the mass of the Negroes now stand most vitally in need. The conviction has taken root that, if the Negro people are to achieve real and lasting progress, they must be made to depend primarily not upon the bestowal of favor from without, but upon their own independent effort from within. What is most significant of all, however, is that this fundamentally constructive principle has emanated from the emancipated race itself, finding its commanding expression through a member of that race who, as the son of a slave woman, himself born into slavery, symbolizes in his own life history the link between the chattel bondage that has been destroyed and the economic independence that must be achieved. Thus it is a fact that, as the Negro may warrantably be held to have insured his own deliverance from slavery by his crucial part in the Civil War, so now it is he himself who has discovered and entered upon what is generally believed to be the true course, which is to lead him up and out of the servitude that his own present backward conditions inevitably impose upon him.

Thus has it come about that even in Boston, where the Negro first attained to manhood's free estate, where his freedom throughout the nation had its birth, and where the sentiment in his favor reached its zenith, he has, as elsewhere, been forced back upon his own resources. And even in Boston, the historic stronghold of the Negro's agitation for equality, the place of all places where he might expect to accomplish most by adhering to a policy of agitation, he himself has come to recognize that in the last analysis his advance depends upon the cultivation of his own resources.

Judged now from the point of view of self-achievement, what verdict does the Negro merit? Do the actual facts reveal that, except in so far as he has been favored and bolstered up by the white race, he has either helplessly stood still, or fallen back? Or, on the contrary, do these facts afford ample proof that by his own powers and exertions he has forced his way upward and ahead? To-day, is he in a state of retrogression, stationariness, or advance? If he is found to be moving forward, then in what measure is this the case? These are the vital questions upon which conclusions as to the Negro's present and future position in the community must depend. To obtain clear and convincing answers to these questions is the task which now devolves upon us.

CHAPTER V

TAKING ROOT

FIRST of all, what of the physical basis upon which the well-being of the Negro community necessarily rests? It is sometimes asserted that this element of the population is gradually dying out. Is such in fact the case, so far as the situation in Boston is concerned? If the Negroes are found to be still growing in number, to what extent is this growth due to accessions from without, and from what localities do the newcomers hail? It might be assumed, offhand, that the Negro is relegated to the least desirable portions of the city. How far is that assumption correct? Are the members of this race cut off and practically isolated, with respect to residence at least, from the rest of the community, or are they in substantial measure intermingled and articulated with its other constituent elements? How is the Negro faring in his encounter with present-day urban conditions? Is he getting a firm physical grip and foothold, and is his situation in this basic respect favorable or unfavorable to his general progress?

The initial fact which these queries elicit is that a native Boston stock of Negroes has as yet barely begun to get established. From earliest times this race has been subject to a high death rate and a comparatively low birth rate. In 1860 the City Registrar reported that, for the five years preceding, "the number

of colored births was one less than the number of
marriages, and the deaths exceeded the births in the
proportion of two to one." For the eleven years from
1900 to 1910, the average Negro birth rate and death
rate were exactly the same, 25.4 per thousand persons,
as compared with a birth rate of 26.9 and a death rate
of 18.7 for the whites.[1] Under these conditions, it is
clear that, even assuming a complete absence of emigration, the Negro population would on its own base barely
maintain each year its numbers of the previous year.

This high mortality has been due to the combined
effect of a vitality less than that of the whites, the rigor
of the Northern climate, and economic and social hardships. The Negroes have always been particularly a
prey to tuberculosis and other affections of the respira-
tory organs. Deficient racial vitality is manifested also
in the greatly disproportionate number of deaths of
infants. Compared with the climate to which the Negro
race has for ages been accustomed in Africa, and that
to which the great mass of American Negroes have
been used in the South, the Boston climate is of course
severe. The peculiar vicissitudes and disturbances
which are a part of the Negro's lot add by so much to
the physical strain upon him.

The Negro birth rate in Boston is not strikingly small
when viewed locally and by itself. As has appeared,
it is only 1.5 per thousand less than that of the entire
white population, and it is undoubtedly above that of
the native-descended whites and the more highly cul-

[1] These rates for the white population are the average for the
period 1900–06, but would be practically the same if brought down
to 1910.

tured element. But it is low as compared with the birth rate of the Negro race in the rural South, and of course very low as set over against its companion death rate in Boston, — the high percentage of deaths not being counter-balanced, as is the case among some of the Southern-European and Asiatic peoples, by a still higher percentage of births. This shortage of births is not due to a lesser proportion of marriages. The local marriage rate for the Negroes is only slightly under that of the whites; for the years 1900–06, 18.5 as against 19.1 per thousand. But it is a fact that with Negroes of long Northern residence, and particularly with the more educated and refined, the proportion of childless marriages is large, and small families are the rule. There is considerable voluntary restriction of births, due sometimes to stern economic prohibitions, sometimes to an unwillingness to bring children into the midst of the difficulties which surround this race, and sometimes to merely selfish considerations of convenience. In the case of the upper gradations of the Negro community, and in appreciable degree even with the rank and file, the higher standard of living to which they become accustomed in Boston is also an important influence in reducing the number of births. But the low birth rate is accounted for in large part by the same factors which produce a high death rate: — inferior vitality, the stern climate, and the nervous-physical wear and tear of economic and social adversities to which the Northern environment renders the Negroes more sensitive.[1]

[1] For a comparison of the Negro and white population with respect to marital condition and proportion of children, see Appendix, table XI.

While the excessive mortality and the paucity of births have thus worked for the extinction of Boston's native Negro population, emigration has at the same time tended toward its dispersion. In the early period, there was doubtless little emigration of Negroes from Boston, inasmuch as oppressive "Black Laws" were in force in most of the Northern States.[1] The first emigration in large numbers was that of escaped slaves, who were again frightened into flight by the passage of the Fugitive Slave Law of 1850 and by the subsequent greatly increased activity of slave-hunters. The war made a further drain on the Negro population. Apparently more than half the Negro soldiers from Boston who survived the conflict cast their abode in other sections of the country, and especially in the South. Those who were married removed their families, and many drew away relatives and friends. Immediately following the war began a movement of young Negroes of both sexes into the South, to serve as teachers in the schools which were everywhere springing up in that section. This movement is still going on.[2] Such de-

[1] Indeed, prior to about 1840, refugees from those states constituted the bulk of the Negro immigration to Boston.

[2] One of the pioneers of these missionaries of education was Louise de Mortie (sister of Mark de Mortie, mentioned in Appendix, p. 454), who was known for her rare beauty and her charm as a public reader. She went to New Orleans to devote herself to the Negro children left orphans by the ravages of war, and there she met her death, in 1867, as a victim of yellow fever. Another was Charlotte L. Forten, who had come to Boston from Philadelphia in 1854, and who wrote for the *Atlantic Monthly* and other magazines. In later years Miss Forten became the wife of Francis James Grimké, of Washington, D.C., the brother of Archibald H. Grimké, previously referred to, and himself a minister and author. Richard Theodore Greener, of the class of 1870 of Harvard College, and the first Negro graduate from that institution, became profes-

partures, however, have constituted only a fractional part of the entire emigration, which has in the main been brought about by the same variety of influences which cause shifting among any element of the population. There have been two factors, however, of more particular character and greater effect than the rest. One of these is the economic and social stress which, as has appeared, bears such an important relation to Negro births and deaths; and which, especially since the change of attitude toward the Negroes in recent years, has compelled many of them to leave Boston and to seek a livelihood elsewhere. The second is an excessive migratoriness which is inherent in the Negro character. Obstacles in the environment are not opposed by a quality of rootedness, and so, many Negroes are continually leaving Boston, in the futile expectation of finding things easier somewhere else.

According to a careful calculation, based on figures from the national census, it appears that in the decade 1890–1900, from 835 to 1025 Massachusetts-born Negroes, and from 2141 to 2632 Negroes altogether,

sor of mental and moral philosophy in the University of South Carolina. Professor Greener was the United States consul at Vladivostock, during the recent Russian-Japanese War. About 1905 Georgiana Charleston, a graduate from the Boston Normal School and from a special course at the Institute of Technology, and in 1907 Marjorie Groves, a graduate of the New England Conservatory of Music, went as teachers to Livingstone College, South Carolina. Among the Negro graduates from local educational institutions in 1910, at least two, Edwin Kenmore, a student of the Massachusetts Normal Art School, and Esther L. Francis, who took a course at the New England Conservatory of Music, are turning their education to good account in the Southern field. These, moreover, are but a few instances of the large number of recruits for Southern schools who have gone out from Boston.

emigrated from the Boston district.[1] More went to New York than to any other state, and after New York came, in numerical order, Connecticut, Pennsylvania, New Jersey, Virginia, the District of Columbia, Illinois, and Rhode Island. But the diversity of destination is shown by the facts that only four states and territories, at most, did not receive Massachusetts-born Negroes in that decade; and that in all probability not a single state or territory failed to get Negroes who had been, for a longer or shorter period, residents of Massachusetts. Nor for that matter do the bounds of the United States limit the Negro's ranging afar.[2]

The tendencies toward both extinction and dispersion which have been pointed out are strikingly exemplified in the family histories of the group of Negro leaders who held sway in Boston during the first years after the war, whose names have already been mentioned. Some of those leaders died childless. Others had children who died in their youth. In the case of others, the children, most of whom have been females, have either not married or have not borne offspring. In still other cases, the children have moved away and scattered. Few, indeed, are the instances in which

[1] The figures on which this calculation is based were taken from the federal census of 1900. Similar data from the census of 1910 were not available when the present account was written. For detailed emigration figures, see Appendix, table VI.

[2] For instance, Joseph H. Lee, who comes of a Negro family of which more will be said at a later point, is trying his fortunes in Mexico. M. Hamilton Hodges went to Australia with a theatrical company and there won musical success. Walter F. Walker, who a few years ago was a printer's assistant in Boston and a student at Boston University, is now teaching in an industrial school in Liberia, of which country he is coming to be an influential citizen.

married progeny of those old leaders, with families, are still living in Boston to-day. And as it has gone with them, so it has gone with the rest of their generation and the generations before and after them.

Nevertheless, ever since the bringing of the first few slaves to Boston in 1638, the Negro population of this city has constantly increased. Prior to the war, the growth, in this respect, though steady, was slow. Mention has already been made of the figures of the early period. The first count, taken in 1742, — the one hundred and fourth year of the Negro's history in the city, — showed 1374 members of that race. By 1830, it had grown to 1875. In 1865, it was 2348. These figures have reference to Boston proper — that is, to the area included in the municipality of that name — and do not cover the outlying sections which are now comprised in the so-called Metropolitan or Greater Boston district. Not till after the war, as a matter of fact, did the number of Negroes living in these outlying sections become substantial. Subsequently, however, the whole metropolitan district has been practically a unit as regards the growth and intertexture of this element of the community, whose increase therein has been large and rapid. In 1865, there were 3495 Negroes in Greater Boston. By 1875, the number was 7400; by 1885, 9481; by 1895, 16,307; by 1905, 21,234; and by 1910, 23,115.[1]

With respect to the proportion of Negroes in the total population, a gradual decline before the war has

[1] For list of cities and towns included in the Greater Boston district, and for complete population figures for Boston proper, and Greater Boston, Negroes and whites, see Appendix, tables I to V.

been followed by a steady rise in the period since. The highest mark was attained in 1752, when the proportion of Negro inhabitants of Boston proper stood at 10 per cent. By 1865 this proportion had fallen to 1.2 per cent. Then it began to go up, till by 1895 it had become 2 per cent, at which point it still remains. In the Greater Boston district the ratio of Negroes to the entire number of inhabitants was, in 1865, .8 per cent. It has risen to 1.7 per cent to-day. During the forty-five years from 1865 to 1910 the Negro population of Greater Boston increased by 561 per cent, as against an increase of 225 per cent for the total population during the same period. Moreover, in every five-year period since the war, except that of 1880–85, and the decade 1900–10, the rate of growth of the metropolitan Negro population has outrun that of the population as a whole.

This growth of Greater Boston's Negro community has been due entirely, however, to immigration. Nor do these gains of the past four decades and a half, — 3905, 2341, 6466, 4929, and 1981, respectively, or 19,622 in the total — fully measure the influx, which has in fact exceeded these proportions by the number of immigrants who have simply gone to offset the losses sustained through deaths and emigration, and who are, therefore, not accounted for in the net increase.

A comparison of the nativity of the Negroes in Boston in earlier and later years shows clearly whence the immigrants have come, and how complete a change has taken place in the Negro community's nativity composition. In 1860, of the American-born

Negroes in Boston proper, nearly 70 per cent were of Northern birth. By 1870 the proportion had declined to 55 per cent, by 1890, to 44 per cent, by 1900, to 39 per cent, and to-day it must be down to about 36 per cent. Of these Northern-born Negroes approximately one quarter are immigrants from other Northern States. About the same percentage of the remainder are immigrants from points in Massachusetts outside the Greater Boston district. This makes the proportion of Negroes in Boston proper who were born within the limits of Greater Boston, about 20 per cent of the city's total Negro population. Recurring to the 36 per cent of Negroes of Northern birth, it appears that only one third of those are the offspring of parents who were also born in the North.[1] Of this one third, moreover, less than half are the offspring of parents who were born in Greater Boston. In other words, only about 5 per cent of the American-born Negroes in Boston are of Boston stock even one generation back.

On the other hand, the proportion of Negroes of Southern birth in the American-born Negro population of Boston was, in 1860, 29 per cent. By 1870, this proportion had risen to 43 per cent, by 1890, to 53 per cent, by 1900, to 57 per cent, and to-day it must be about 62 per cent. The great majority of these Negroes come from the upper seacoast districts of the South, chiefly from Virginia and North Carolina, and from the vicinity of the cities of Richmond and Charleston, in that region. It is clear, therefore, that for a Negro population predominantly of Northern

[1] That is, fully two thirds are the offspring of parents who were born in the South.

birth has been substituted, since the war, one predominantly of Southern birth. And inasmuch as each
year's quota of newcomers has been gradually reduced
by excessive mortality and emigration, it is clear also
that Boston's present Negro population is composed
for the most part of comparatively recent Southern immigrants — the majority probably having come in the
last fifteen years, approximately — and their offspring.

Besides the Negroes born in the United States,
Boston has a considerable number who are of foreign
birth. In 1860, the proportion of these in the city
proper was 14.9 per cent, in 1870, 10.8 per cent, in 1890,
14.2 per cent, and in 1900, 10.8 per cent. The two
largest groups of foreign immigrants are from the
British West Indies and Canada. A few hail from other
parts of the world.[1]

As to the effects of this constant immigration from
the South and elsewhere, — while, on the one hand, it
has added to the size of the Negro population, it has
meant, on the other hand, that the new material to be
absorbed and assimilated by the Negro community
has been continually increasing in quantity. At the
same time the constant emigration has meant that the
local base of assimilation has continually been sub-
tracted from, and that thus much of the ground
gained has been lost. Together, these incessant inward
and outward currents have kept the Negro community
in a permanent state of flux and unsettlement.

Under these in so far unfavorable conditions, the Negro has during the recent period been engaged in what

[1] For detailed figures applying to both American and foreign-
born Negroes, see Appendix, tables VIII to X.

is generally one of the most baffling of his urban problems, — namely, the location of his home. Notable developments under this motive have been the shifting of the principal Negro center from the West End to the upper South End and Roxbury; the rise of Negro colonies in the suburbs; and the increasing movement of Negroes into white neighborhoods.

From about 1830 till about 1892 more Negroes lived in the West End, beyond Joy Street and down along the northwesterly slope of Beacon Hill to several blocks below Cambridge Street, than in any other section of Greater Boston. But after the war and the beginning of the influx from the South, the proportion of the Negro population of the city proper residing in that locality steadily fell, from 80 per cent in 1865 to 36 per cent in 1890. Soon after 1890, and conspicuously after 1895, a movement to the South End and the suburbs began. It was started primarily by the prevalence of deteriorated housing conditions combined with rents comparatively high. Because the Negroes had lived in the West End quarter since the early days, the dwellings there had not been kept up to the standard for other parts of the city, but were old and rundown. Nevertheless, owing to more or less difficulty which Negroes experienced in locating in other sections, on account of the prevailing disinclination of white residents to have them as neighbors, landlords were still able to exact high rents in the old locality. The Negro residents in these other sections had, however, been increasing in number; thus, on the principle of the entering wedge, making access for newcomers easier.

The more well-to-do led the emigration from the West End, and many of this class, in the decade 1890–1900, bought homes in outlying districts. Their departure accelerated the general exodus. The increase of an objectionable element of both races in the vicinity made the better grade of Negroes, solicitous for the welfare of their children, the more desirous of getting away. By 1900, the proportion of the Negro population of Boston proper living in the West End had fallen to 22 per cent, and by 1905, to 17 per cent; their numbers meanwhile decreasing from 2935 in 1890 to 2603 in 1900, and to 2000 in 1905. To-day there are not more than 1500 Negroes, at most, in that district, and though they still reach to Joy Street on the east, at other points they are confined to a much more restricted area than formerly; not extending up Beacon Hill farther than Phillips Street to the south, nor beyond Cambridge and West Cedar Streets on the north and west. In the quality of its Negro residents the section is tending to deteriorate. It is true that some of the better type still live there, but this is usually for the reason that they are attached to the homes they have known for many years; and as the old folks die, their heirs will in all likelihood sell the property and move away. The newcomers of the Negro race are predominantly of the illiterate, shiftless, semi-vicious sort. The Jews, who since the late nineties have been coming in rapidly, buying up the old houses and building cheap though showy tenements, some of which they rent to Negroes, now form the great majority of the population. The racial change which has thus come about is further evidenced by the fact that two former Negro churches have been transformed into Jewish synagogues.

During the first part of the decline of the West End Negro colony, that of the lower South End, from Pleasant Street south to Castle Street, and from Washington Street west to Columbus Avenue, rose to first place numerically. As early as 1875 there were about 700 Negroes in this locality, and by 1898 the number had increased fourfold. In the decade 1880–90, there was no other section where Negroes and whites of good quality were so closely intermingled as next-door neighbors. Then traffic and small shop trade began to encroach, bringing noise, dirt, and unsightliness. A vicious element of blacks and whites increased rapidly, and ere long gave the section an unsavory reputation. The better whites and Negroes moved away, the latter chiefly to the suburbs. A deterioration, similar to that which has occurred in the West End, has subsequently taken place, and to-day some of the lowest Negro resorts are to be found in this section. At present there are only about 800 Negroes in the locality, and the number is growing smaller. The dwellings, chiefly tenements and lodging-houses, are now if anything inferior to those of the West End. The white population is Irish, Jewish, and nondescript.

Such emigrants from the West End and the lower South End as did not move outside the city, took up their abode in the upper South End and lower Roxbury district. The early nuclei of this colony were Northampton and Lenox Streets at the north, Kendall Street in the center, and Sussex and Warwick Streets at the south. Between these points a gradual filling-in has taken place. A noticeable increase of the Negro residents was evident by 1875, and by the middle nineties the number had grown to over 1000. But the great increase has come since 1895. By 1900, close to 3500, or 30 per cent of the Negroes in the city, lived in this section, as compared with 10 per cent in 1890. At present, between Northampton Street on the north and Ruggles Street on the south, Washington Street on the east and Tremont Street on the west, an area about one and a quarter miles long by a mile wide, are living approximately 5000 Negroes, or 40 per cent of the entire Negro population of Boston proper. If the boundaries be extended a little to the north, north-west, and east, to include several localities where the Negroes are less numerously colonized, the total would be close to 7000. The movement of the Negroes to this district led to the transfer thither of their churches and organization headquarters; which, in turn, especially in the case of the churches, only one of which still remains in the West End section, greatly accelerated and in fact gave the final impetus to the migration.

To-day this is the principal Negro center of Greater Boston. Within the smaller area, the boundaries of which have been given, the Negroes constitute about a third of the population. The Irish form a somewhat larger proportion. Americans ("Yankees") occupy third place, but are closely pressed for this position by the Jews. There is an appreciable admixture of Swedes, and small scatterings of half a dozen other races. The Negroes and the Jews are the incoming and increasing elements, and in many localities these two races, so diverse in their qualities but whose struggles upward have much in common, are both close neighbors and close competitors for the dwellings and the small trade. As in the West End the Jews now worship in two former Negro churches, so here the Negroes have returned the compliment by taking over a former synagogue for their own devotions. The distribution of the Negroes over this district is in part compact, in part dispersed. Only a few streets, of which the longest are Windsor, Camden, Kendall, and Sawyer, are almost wholly occupied by Negroes. On the other hand, there are twice as many streets which contain hardly any Negroes at all. A half-dozen streets and sections of streets are preponderantly Negro. For the rest, the two races are intermingled, sometimes one end of a street, or even one side, being white and the other Negro, and sometimes Negroes and whites alternating almost evenly. Thus far, therefore, the district is far from being a solid Negro quarter, like that which used to exist in the West End, and like the city's present Jewish and Italian quarters. Competition for cheap rents, on the part of the Jews and the Irish, and the movement of many of the most well-to-do Negroes to the suburbs, will probably keep this neighborhood a mixed one. It remains to be seen, moreover, whether eventually West End history will repeat itself in the Jews getting control. But to-day the Negro population is rapidly increasing from without, and promises to be, for some years at least, the largest racial element. Washington Street, the eastern boundary of this section, is a crowded business thoroughfare of stores and tenements, and on Tremont Street, at the west, the ground floors are generally occupied by shops. Not many of the Negroes live on these main avenues, however; and elsewhere the locality is for the most part light, open, and airy. As respects housing, Boston has in fact done the Negroes a good turn. Their being forced out of the deteriorated districts in the West End and lower South End, after the manner which has been related, made it possible for them to combine and take possession of this new outlying neighborhood, which was at that time being built up with an exceptionally good type of tenement house, wide and quiet streets, and considerable free space with trees and grass. The section is not characterized by the congestion and general unsightliness which prevail in the Jewish and Italian, and some of the poorer Irish, quarters, to which it is indeed distinctly superior. Probably in no other large city is the chief Negro colony so fortunately located. Not only does this mean much from the point of view of the inner standards of living and of life of this element of the population; it means also that the colony is not fringed with that deadly penumbra of the degenerate outcasts of all nationalities which usually besets a downtown Negro quarter.

Within the city only one other Negro community stands out conspicuously. That is the one about Dartmouth Street, from the Back Bay Station to Columbus Avenue, extending through Buckingham Street to the north, and through Harwich, Truro, Yarmouth, Holyoke, and Carlton Streets to the south. Negroes of the better class took up their residence on Buckingham Street soon after that area was taken from the water and made into land, in the later sixties. Before very long they got into the adjacent part of Dartmouth Street. The inclusion of the other streets mentioned, which were formerly given up to white lodging-houses, is a development of the last six or seven years. The building of the present Back Bay Station in 1897 involved the tearing-down of the buildings on Buckingham Street, nearly all of which were owned by Negroes, who in most cases subsequently bought homes in the suburbs. The erection of this station also brought to the locality many Pullman porters and other railway employees. Especially after the opening in 1906 of the only full-fledged Negro hotel in the city,[1] this section has been transformed from one of quiet residence into the abode and rendezvous of a nomadic, boisterous, sporting set. It is the Negro "Lower Broadway" of Boston.

The rise of Negro communities in the suburbs since the war has been marked. Of the 3495 Negroes in the metropolitan district in 1865, about 67 per cent were inside the present boundaries of Boston proper. In the decade 1865–75, the rates of increase within and without the city limits were nearly the same, but from 1875 to 1895 the rate of suburban growth was twice that for the city proper. Though since 1895 the suburban rate has been above 4 per cent less than the urban, the proportion of Negroes living in the suburbs is to-day 42 per cent, as compared with 33 per cent in 1865.[2]

[1] This hotel was closed in 1912 by the Licensing Board, on account of disorderliness.

[2] For detailed figures, see Appendix, tables II and III.

It is probable that in the earlier period one of the principal considerations which led the Negroes to settle in the suburbs was that, coming direct from the rural districts and small towns of the South, they found suburban conditions somewhat less strange and perplexing than those of the city. In the last twenty years or so, however, since the marked development of an urban movement of Negroes in the South, most of the Negro immigrants to Boston have, as previously noted, come from the cities; and as shown by the lesser rate of increase of the Negro population in the suburbs, a larger proportion of the newcomers have preferred to take up their abode in Boston proper, where they find larger numbers of their own kind, and greater novelty and excitement. But this tendency has been more than offset by a continuous secondary movement of Negroes away from the in-town sections of Boston into the outlying districts.[1] Among the reasons for this outward migration have been the prevalence of lower rents in the suburbs, and, in the case of the more well-to-do class, the opportunity to buy homes at a lower price and in localities of higher grade. A further potent influence, among the better element, is the desire of the latter to get their children into cleaner, more healthful, and morally safer surroundings. It is also a pertinent fact that, generally speaking, the Negroes encounter less antipathy in the suburbs and find the various avenues of self-improvement more accessible to them.

In point of numbers, the growth of these suburban communities did not become conspicuous — except in

[1] See Appendix, notes to table III.

the case of Cambridge, the Negro population of which
jumped in the first decade after the war from 377 to
1103 — till 1890. Between 1890 and 1895, a number of
other good-sized colonies arose. Cambridge still leads,
having to-day about 5000 Negro inhabitants. Most of
these live in Cambridgeport, between Hampshire Street
on the north, and the Charles River, in the vicinity of
Howard Street, on the south. Within these points are
several major, and a number of minor, groups. There
are also some small clusters scattered in other parts
of Cambridge. With the exception of a broken-down
shanty quarter about Hastings Street, the housing
conditions are good. Tenements are uncommon; medium-sized, one or two family dwellings are the rule.
Some of the streets where the more well-to-do Negroes
live are fully up to the standard of streets occupied by
the lower middle class of whites. The other principal
suburban colonies, with their numbers as reported in
the 1910 census, are as follows: Everett, 795; Malden,
486; Newton, 467; Medford, 431; Woburn, 242; Chelsea, 242; Brookline, 221; Somerville, 217. The conditions in these communities are essentially the same as
those in Cambridge.

Instances of Negroes living outside of distinctively
Negro neighborhoods were exceedingly rare till from
twenty to thirty years after the war. Then the number of such cases began gradually to increase, and to-
day from 5 per cent to 10 per cent of the Negroes in
Greater Boston live in neighborhoods predominantly
white. Sometimes a single street or section of a street,
or sections of several adjacent streets, are occupied
by Negroes, with no others of that race on any of the

other streets within a wide radius. More frequently
a small contingent of Negro families will be interspersed
among the white residents in a neighborhood. Both
these conditions may be found in Boston proper,
through the middle South End from Dover Street south
to Massachusetts Avenue and between Columbus Avenue and the railroad, and in the Charlestown, East
Boston, Roxbury, West Roxbury, Dorchester, and
Brighton districts. Such is still more noticeably the
case in most of the suburbs.

Racial intermixture in the matter of residence has,
however, progressed still further. It is by no means
uncommon to find two or three Negro families, or
even a solitary one, entirely surrounded by white
neighbors, with no others of their own race in the locality. In fact, a section half a mile square which does
not contain at least one Negro home is exceptional in
any but the most select parts of the metropolitan district. The geographical points of contact between the
Negro and white population have thus been multiplied
many-fold, and, so far as concerns conditions of residence, the process of racial inter-articulation has
reached an advanced stage.

In this connection, passing allusion has already been
made to the more or less difficulty which Negroes experience in getting into sections outside their own
compact colonies, on account of the unwillingness of the
other race to have them as neighbors. Such an attitude on the part of the whites is undoubtedly a serious
factor against which the Negroes have had to contend.
In general the degree of difficulty which they have encountered has been in proportion to the social grade

of the locality in view. Frequently the only way in
which a Negro family can obtain entry in a given neighborhood is by buying a home there, at a price which is
usually somewhat above the market value. Even in
the case of such purchase, the transaction is often made
through second parties, without the seller's knowledge
of the buyer's racial identity. Now and then efforts
are made to keep Negroes out of given localities by
some process of law. Thus far, however, such attempts
have been almost wholly unsuccessful, and have turned
out rather to the Negro's advantage; as, for example,
in the most recent case of this kind, which resulted in a
pronouncement by the State Supreme Judicial Court
upholding the right of a Negro to acquire property
and to make his home wherever he chooses.[1] It is true

[1] This decision was handed down March 5, 1913. The details
are covered in the following account taken from the Boston *Transcript* of that date: —

"That a Negro may purchase a house in a section where expen-
sive houses have been built by white people if the owner desires to
sell, regardless of whether it annoys the neighbors, is decided by the
Supreme Court in an opinion handed down to-day.

"The question arose in a bill in equity brought by Wellington
Holbrook and others against Mrs. Mamie C. Morrison. The plain-
tiffs asked for an injunction restraining Mrs. Morrison from displaying a large sign on her premises headed 'For Sale,' and concluding
with the words, 'Best offer from Colored Family,' all in large letters,
and also from advertising in the newspapers that her property was
for sale to Negro people.

"In the opinion of the court, Judge Morton says: 'There can be
no doubt that the respondent had the right to advertise her property for sale by signs or otherwise in the ordinary way and to sell it
if she saw fit to a Negro family, even though the effect may be to
impair the business of the complainants; just as, for instance, the
owner of land on a hillside may cultivate it in the usual way, even
though the effect of the surface drainage may be to fill up his neighbors' mill-pond below. If she had put up the sign and had caused
advertisements to be inserted without any intention of selling her

that the coming of Negroes into a white neighborhood of good quality usually has somewhat of a tendency to lower the selling value of property in the immediate vicinity. But this result is not marked unless more than a few families of that race enter the locality, and live near enough together to attract notice to their number.

When all is said, the objection to the presence of Negroes in districts predominantly white has come nowhere near amounting to outright prohibition or ostracism. It has, as previously stated, been a serious factor against which they have had to contend. It has forced them to exert themselves in locating their homes. It has often compelled them to try a long time before they have succeeded in establishing their abodes in the locality of their preference, and sometimes it has obliged them to fall back upon their second, third, or fourth choice. It has necessitated considerable resort to strategy on their part. But that is all. On the other hand, the degree to which they have succeeded in overcoming this adverse influence has appeared in the facts which have been given with regard to their increasingly wide and scattered distribution. On the principle of the entering wedge, as has previously been pointed out,

property, but solely with the purpose of injuring the business and property of the complainants, then there can be no doubt that such conduct on her part would have been actionable. She has a right to ask for bids from white people or colored people, or both. She is not limited to bidders of any particular race or class or creed. And if one of her purposes in asking for bids from colored families is to injure and annoy the complainants, and she succeeds in doing so, her conduct is not rendered unlawful so long as her object is to procure a purchaser for and to sell her house and lot.'

"The Court ordered the bill of the complainants to be dismissed."

each Negro who locates his home in a new neighborhood makes entry less difficult for others of his race. Such being the case, the actual detrimental effect of this factor upon the Negro may be expected to diminish rather than to increase.

Looking into the future, it appears practically certain that for the next generation, at least, the Negro community will still consist mainly of immigrants from the South and their immediate offspring, working out their destiny in Boston. But that at the same time substantial progress will be made toward the establishment of a native Boston stock also appears highly probable. Among the principal influences contributing toward this result will be less emigration, on the one hand, and less immigration, on the other; the former factor working positively, the latter negatively, to increase the proportion of the native-descended element. With reference to emigration, though definite figures are not available at this writing for the period since 1900, general report, together with the author's own inquiries and observation, are to the effect that, owing largely to the already noted improvement in the Negro's residential and living conditions in Boston, a considerable diminution is taking place in the outward movement to other localities. In the matter of immigration, the facts are definitely at hand. While from 1890 to 1900 the yearly immigration of Negroes to the Greater Boston district was about 1000, from 1900 to 1910 it declined to about 500.[1] This falling off, which is partly a general tendency throughout the North, has been due, on the one hand, to the growth of the "Stick to the

[1] For detailed figures of immigration, see Appendix, table VII.

South" spirit, and, on the other hand, to the realization, at last, that it is not so easy to get along in the
North as has hitherto been supposed.

As to the birth rate among the Negroes in Boston,
there has been a decided gain since ante-bellum days.
Whereas in the period 1855–59, as previously stated,
the number of births was one less than the number of
marriages, to-day the births exceed the marriages by
nearly seven in every thousand of the population.
Recently, however, the birth rate has on the whole
declined somewhat, and it is reasonable to believe that
a rising standard of living will at least work against substantial increase. But, as already remarked, the birth
rate of the Negroes is at present only slightly below
that of the population as a whole, and is no doubt above
that of the native-descended whites, so that, comparatively speaking at least, the Negro is not on this score
very badly off. The crucial factor which has hitherto
made it impossible for the Negro population of Boston to
grow upon its own native base, has been the extremely
high death rate. At this most essential point, however,
a great amelioration has taken place during the last
twenty-five years. Since 1885, the Negro death rate
has undergone a continued and marked decline. For
the period 1885–90, it was 36.2 per thousand; for 1890–
95, 32.1; for 1895–1900, 27.9; for 1900–05, 26.5; and
for 1905–10, 24.3.[1] Whereas for the years 1855–59 the
deaths were double the births in number, to-day the
deaths do not exceed the births at all,[2] and the ten-

[1] For detailed birth and death figures, see Appendix, tables
XII and XIII.

[2] This is on the basis of the average birth and death rates from
1900 to 1910, previously given.

dency, as shown by the figures just cited, is distinctly toward further decrease. This reduction in the death rate has been due chiefly to the steady betterment of both exterior residential environment and interior housing and living conditions among the Negroes. The constantly improving sanitation of the community at large, especially as respects preventive hygiene, has of course affected and will continue to affect this race along with other elements of the population. Thus a still further gradual diminution in the death rate among the Negroes, eventually leaving a substantial excess of births, may reasonably be expected.

As a net result, therefore, of these several favorable tendencies, operating in conjunction, it appears to be a fact that now at last, after two hundred and seventy-five years, the Negro is taking root amidst the Northern city conditions of Boston.

CHAPTER VI

SOCIAL CONSTRUCTION AND ETHICAL GROWTH

NECESSARILY prerequisite to an adequate understanding of the more distinctly religious, political, and economic aspects of the life of the Negro in Boston, is an appreciation of those less definable features which can only be designated as social-ethical in a broad and fundamental sense, but which both overspread and underlie the others. What, then, are the general characteristics and conditions of this nature which pertain to this element of the population, and what are the resulting tendencies? It having already appeared that the local Negro colony is in a fair way to become soundly established on a physical basis, is now any similar foundational process discernible in the higher sphere of the social order? Do the Negro people give evidence that they are drawing together, through some centripetal impulse, for purposes of closer and more effective organization as a social body? Are they laying a groundwork, along essentially constructive lines, for durable social progress? And — what is of the most central and vital importance — are the ethical motives, conceptions, and standards, which both arise from and intimately react upon social relations, growing constantly stronger, more clearly defined, and of more extensive and practical application and effect, in the well-being of the Negro community?

Section 1. Characteristics that Retard

In any capacity for such fundamental social coöperation as is essential to a strong and closely woven social
fabric, the Negroes are, as a matter of fact, conspicuously deficient. No other racial group in the city is so
much given to petty dissension, and so obviously lacking in unity and the spirit of unity.

The members of this race are excessively disposed to
circulating gossip and slander about one another and
generally to depreciating one another's conduct and
character. Apparently they cannot help doing this; —
at least, not unless they exercise unwonted self-control.
A white woman who has very close acquaintance with
the Negroes in Boston, who has lived and worked among
them a long time, expressed herself thus: " What
things they say about each other! What lies they tell!
Why, if I were to believe half I hear, I should have to
conclude that all the Negroes I know are libertines,
liars, and thieves." Few, indeed, are the fortunate
ones whose characters are not besmirched by some of
their fellows. The gossip-mongers let their fancies
wander as their tongue wags. Yet one cannot avoid
surmising that down underneath so much dirty smoke
there must be some smudgy fuel.

Likewise, the Negroes are jealous of one another,
and prone to weaken one another's hands. Let one of
them make a proposal or initiate an enterprise appealing for general support, and immediately detractors
arise, to cast aspersions on his motives and to propose
something different. There is continual pulling apart,
constant discord, a pitiable lack of coöperation. In

illustration of this failing may be cited a story which is related of an old Negro deacon in the South, who had the reputation of being mighty in prayer, and able to pray longer, louder, and more fervently than any one else in all the region roundabout. On a certain special occasion he was expected to make one of his very best efforts. First he offered up thanks for everything he could think of. Then he prayed for the bestowal of all possible blessings. It seemed as though nothing had been omitted, but that, on the contrary, mention had been made of a great number of items which might possibly, in a general dispensation, have escaped attention. But finally, at the end, after the "amen" had been said, the suppliant added a sort of apologetic postscript, to this effect: "Lord, there was one other thing that I was thinking of asking you to do, but, Lord, I concluded that would be seeking too much: — I was going to ask you to make the colored folks stop talking about one another and fighting one another, and get together."

This shortcoming is sometimes explained as one of the evil effects of slavery. Slaveowners, to prevent idling and to thwart all attempts at concerted revolt, are said to have fostered suspicions, jealousies, and quarrels, and to have encouraged the slaves to spy and bear tales on one another. Missionaries and others who have lived in Africa, however, testify that the natives there exhibit similar traits. Thus the truth appears to be that slavery helped to perpetuate, and perhaps exaggerated, a natural propensity.

But the conditions of slavery must be held in large degree accountable for another characteristic of the

Negroes; — namely, their extreme dependence on the whites. Was it not inevitable that two hundred and fifty years of servitude, during which the members of this race were completely under the direction and providence of the whites, experiencing no necessity for forethought, and having no rights, no property, no social organization of their own, should smother in them any quality of self-reliance? This weakness amounts, in its least modified form, to the servility which peculiarly fits Negroes for menial service. Among the more refined class, it often shows itself in an obsequiousness which detracts from respect. But the dependence of the Negroes is most of all evident in their hesitancy and frequent inability to take on their own initiative, without seeking the support of the whites, action departing from the accustomed routine or involving special responsibility. They are sadly distrustful of their own capacities.

Sometimes, however, this quality of servility is accompanied or replaced by a bumptious over-assertiveness. These two traits might appear to be mutually contradictory. But in fact the second is in a large degree a result of the first, by a natural enough process of reaction. In the same way that some extremely diffident persons, from more or less conscious motives of self-protection, assume an opposite bearing, so likewise many Negroes, as a sort of offset and antidote for their sense of humiliation, put on a lofty air, which, at first affected, tends gradually to become ingrained. More commonly, however, the process is less subtly introspective in character, and is produced by the exterior change from Southern to Northern conditions.

When a Negro comes from the South, where in nearly every way he has been subjected to discrimination and repression, into the North, where his liberties are in so many respects equal to those of the whites, what wonder that he is sometimes unable to hold himself in check, and that he frequently becomes no less overweening than he was formerly submissive! The more abrupt the break, the more extreme the reaction. Thus in the national capital, where the Negroes of Maryland and Virginia have but to step across the borders of those states to find themselves at once free from Southern restraint and under the protection of federal laws which forbid discriminatory treatment, considerable complaint is heard that they sometimes crowd white people off the sidewalks, make insolent remarks, and indulge generally in offensive conduct. In Boston, such behavior is not much in evidence, but in less glaring ways the same propensity is shown. It even crops out in a precocious touchiness among children; as in the case of a little tot of six or seven, who, when asked by his teacher if he would please to pick up a handkerchief she had dropped, declined to do so, with the pronunciamento, — " The days of slavery are over." It appears in the proverbial uppishness of Negro domestics, and in the patronizing officiousness of such exalted functionaries as, for example, head bell-boys. Pomposity of this kind, while far from being general among the Negro people, is nevertheless sufficiently common to make an unduly adverse impression on the other race, and thereby to arouse antipathy among many who would otherwise be inclined toward a more friendly and helpful attitude.

In any genuine and substantial pride of race, on the other hand, as distinguished from mere petty self-inflation, the Negroes are as yet woefully lacking. It is, of course, readily understandable that a people with two and a half centuries of servitude only fifty years in the past, could not yet have developed race pride in any high degree. Furthermore, the peculiarly humiliating conditions to which this element of the population have been subjected since their emancipation, have made the subsequent rise of racial dignity well-nigh impossible. Past influences might, indeed, be calculated to have imbued the Negroes with a consciousness of degradation as a people, and to have implanted in them an instinctive desire to get away from the fact of their racial identity. And such is, in truth, the case.

The want of race pride appears most plainly in a shrinking from acceptance of the racial name itself — the very word "Negro." Among the rank and file, predominantly of Southern birth or upbringing, such avoidance of this term is less noticeable, and amounts commonly to no more than a negative first impulse, easily overcome. But in the upper gradations of the Negro community, and generally speaking in measure proportioned to the elements of superior education, refinement, Northern rearing, lightness of complexion, and an admixture of white blood, objection to the word becomes deep-seated, positive, and even vehement. Members of the race who are marked by these characteristics look upon the designation "Negro" as merely the polite form of "nigger," and see in it mainly the suggestion of contempt. To escape using the word, they either resort to circumlocution or have recourse to substitutes. Some effort has been made to introduce the term "Afro-American," but with slight success, as it is too awkward to be convenient. "Colored people" — an expression doubtless tracing its origin from the "free persons of color" of the period preceding general emancipation — is the makeshift generally employed; without regard to the fact that this appellation utterly fails to distinguish the Negroes from the Chinese, the Indians, or, for that matter, from any of the non-Caucasian peoples. The fact that most white persons when speaking to Negroes likewise refer to members of that race as "colored," out of consideration for their sensitiveness regarding this matter, is naturally enough interpreted by the latter as confirming their own objection to the name "Negro" as a stigma of debasement. The lack of a real race pride, which is implied in this attempt to disavow what is in fact only a legitimate racial designation,[1] is still further revealed at practically every point in the life of the Negro community.

The foregoing characteristics and deficiencies, both severally and to a still greater degree when operating in conjunction, are in their influence and effect distinctly divisive. They constitute impediments to social progress which are, for the present at least, of a more or less inherent nature; and against which the Negroes must contend in their endeavors toward social coöperation and cohesion. Of all these hindrances, however, the want of a substantial increment of racial dignity is the one which most seriously retards the advance of the Negro people.

[1] "Negro" is the recognized ethnological name of the African race from which most of the American Negroes are descended.

Section 2. Nativity Groups and Social Gradations

No less pertinent, however, than these innate elements of character, in connection with the social development of the Negroes, are the conditions from which the members of this race have come, and those under which they are living to-day. An adequate understanding of these conditions will be promoted by some separate consideration first of the different nativity groups which, as has previously appeared, enter into the composition of Boston's Negro population; and then of the several social gradations into which this population may be divided.

With regard to circumstances arising from nativity, it must be said that the mass of immigrants from the South, who, as already pointed out, make up the main part of Boston's Negro colony, have always been but pitifully equipped for life's stern encounter. Those who came to the city in the first ten years after the war were for the most part former slaves and children of slaves, and the majority of those who are coming to-day are but the grandchildren of slaves. Nor, in the less than fifty years since bond slavery was declared abolished, has the lot of the great majority of the Negroes in the Southern States ceased to be slavish still. Though it is true that in that section the race is making remarkable headway in specific respects, and producing many capable individuals, nevertheless as yet the conditions which there prevail can in general hardly be said to have become such as to develop any considerable degree of intelligence, ability, and strength of character, in the average Negro.

During the first thirty years following the war, however, a larger proportion of the Southern immigrants
who took·up their abode in Boston were possessed of
rough native ability than has been the case during the
last fifteen to twenty years. Many of those who came
in the earlier period did so not primarily because they
found it too hard to make a living in the South, but
because they hoped to do still better in the North, the
great Land of Freedom, and especially in Boston, the
Mecca of the Negro people. There were more in those
days who had trades or could do work above the common labor grade, and who were therefore in a position
to earn better wages and to live better. In recent years,
one of the most striking developments in the South
itself has been the flocking of Negroes to the large cities,
where most of them have been able to get only menial
employment, where they have been herded together
in the poorest districts, and where disease, a high death
rate, crime, and immorality have wrought constant
havoc among them. Since 1895 most of the immigrants
to Boston have come directly from these Southern
cities, and, furthermore, have been of the poorer
classes. The majority of those who come to Boston
to-day do so no more in the hope of faring better than
in the belief that they cannot fare worse.

Of the Northern-born Negroes in Boston, those who
come from other Northern States and from other
points in Massachusetts are generally better educated than the Southern and foreign-born types. But
at the same time many of them are of the sort who are
not deeply rooted anywhere; who if occasion arises
can easily pull up stakes and move away; and whose

interest in the local community of their race is on the whole of a transient character.

The Negroes born and reared in the Greater Boston district have the best education, and, as a class, are indeed generally superior. Their worth is obscured to the general view, however, by the overshadowing proportion of Negroes of non-Boston and principally Southern birth. As has already appeared from the nativity figures previously given, the Boston-born element constitute about twenty per cent of the entire Negro population. Approximately two thirds of this element, however, are still under fifteen years of age, and of the remaining one third the great majority are still under thirty. This means that out of every hundred Negroes in the city, only three or four are at once of Boston birth and of an age at which they may be expected to have obtained a fair start in life. Nevertheless if a complete list could be made of the members of the race who occupy good positions, and who have good homes and good characters, it would, in the writer's opinion, prove conclusively that the Boston-born element has at least double that quota of successful individuals. Such partial evidence as is at hand tends to confirm this belief.[1]

If such is the fact, it would seem to refute the oft-made assertion that Northern conditions spoil the Negroes. It does disprove it in part, but not entirely. Conditions in Boston are so much more favorable to the Negro than they are in the South, especially with

[1] For example, out of 46 Negro clerks and carriers in the post-office of the Boston postal district, 8, or 17 per cent, were born in Greater Boston, and 17, or 37 per cent, are of Northern birth.

respect to facilities for education and opportunities
for entering superior occupations, that Negroes of
Boston birth should produce a percentage of successful men and women not only twice but five times as
large as their proportion of the total Negro population.[1]
This, however, is probably not the case. Northern
city conditions have their negative side for the Negroes
in general by tempting them to sacrifice substance to
appearance. Since they may come and go freely in the
community, they have naturally taken for themselves
the community's general standards. So far as they
have tried to live up to these standards in solid achievement and genuine merit, they have thereby been bene-
fited. Undoubtedly this spur accounts for many suc-
cesses. Many Negroes, however, have been carried
away by mere superficialities, particularly dress and
display, and have devoted far more attention to such
things than to the cultivation of character and efficiency. But, when all is said, those who have been
spoiled in this way are distinctly in the minority.

Within certain limits, — which are, however, not
very extensive, — it holds true that the Negroes of
Boston descent hold themselves rather apart and
aloof from the others, and are in fact somewhat distinguished by special characteristics. In this connection, it must of course be borne in mind that, as already pointed out, the number of those in the Negro
community who can go back to more than one generation of Boston ancestry is exceedingly small. But with
regard to the few such that there are, the writer has
been struck by certain points of comparison and re-

[1] That is, having regard to the factor of age, as above indicated.

semblance as between them and many of the present representatives of some of Boston's farthest descended families of the other race. Types of the latter may be seen about the select clubs on Beacon Hill, in the Athenæum Library, or at highly intellectual lectures or gatherings. They are often characterized by spareness of body and a thin, pointed, and distinctively mental cast of features. Everything about them suggests thought and introspection and a long-sustained process of inward self-consumption. Now some of the Negroes, claiming two or three generations of ancestors who have lived and died in Boston's intellectually rarified atmosphere, have impressed the writer as presenting an appearance similar to this, in kind if not in degree. Whether this likeness would hold good under further examination is a question. The observation is submitted suggestively, rather than scientifically.

The nativity group which is made up of Negroes of foreign birth possesses a special interest, in that it is as yet comparatively little known to the general public. The British West Indians, who form somewhat its largest element, differ noticeably from the American Negroes in appearance, usually having higher cheek bones and a firmer cast of features, and their dialect is often so different that at first it cannot readily be understood. They are clannish in their associations. Most of them are not naturalized, the plea of such as are not completely indifferent being that they expect to return to the Islands, as indeed many of them do. The fact that the majority are Roman Catholics and Episcopalians draws something further of a dividing line between them and their predominantly Baptist

and Methodist cousins. They pride themselves on their
longer possession of freedom, which dates practically
from the passage of the British Emancipation Act in
1833. Conditions in the West Indies have, besides,
been more favorable in many ways to the Negro's
development. There the members of this race have
formed not so much an ostracized class without any
recognized standing, as one of the horizontal layers
in the social strata. As a result, the higher avenues of
accomplishment have been less difficult of access to
them. The immigrants who come to Boston from that
quarter appear to hold their heads higher, and to
have more independence, stamina, progressiveness,
and — better side of their clannish tendency — coöp-
erativeness, than is the case with those from the
South. A large proportion of them are marked by a
general sturdiness and worth of character, and their
upper ranks include a number of exceptionally capable
individuals.[1] On the other hand, there is a rowdyish
and disorderly contingent, composed for the most part

[1] A good example of the middle grade is Peter Burke, of Chelsea.
From the Islands he went to England as a sailor, remained there a
little while, then, about twenty years ago, came to Boston. For six
years thereafter he served in the navy, and since that time, having
married, he has worked as a teamster, fireman, and watchman, and
has managed to support his family comfortably. He has three children, the eldest a girl of thirteen, and intends to give them as good an
education as his means will permit.

Among the West Indians who are well known in the Negro community are George W. Latimer, the lawyer (though, strictly speaking,
he is from the Danish island of St. Croix), who came to Boston
about 1886, and obtained his legal education at the Y.M.C.A. law
school; E. I. Wright, T. E. A. McCurdy, and A. H. Hunt, physicians; A. C. Dunning and Don J. Pinheiro, dentists; and the Rev.
M. A. N. Shaw, pastor of the Twelfth Baptist Church.

of sailors and porters who come and go on the fruit steamers.

Withal, the West Indians constitute for the Negroes of the United States the representatively American problem of the assimilation of the foreigner. Among them are several beneficial and relief organizations, as well as a literary society and a cricket club, which, however, do not aim to Americanize their members, but rather to have them retain their British citizenship and their distinct affiliations. Deeper factors are nevertheless working for amalgamation. One of these is the intermarriage of West Indian and American Negroes. Another is the increasing attention which the politicians of the race are giving to the naturalization of this group of potential voters.

A majority of the Negro immigrants from Nova Scotia and New Brunswick, who rank a close second to the West Indians in number, are the progeny of slaves who during Abolition days escaped into Canada by the Underground Railway. Others are the offspring of West Indian Negroes who migrated to the Provinces. A few are descendants of those of their race whom the English troops carried away when driven out of Boston by the Revolutionists. From another part of Canada, namely, Ontario and Quebec, come a small number of Negroes, most of whom are the issue of refugees who fled thither in the ante-slavery period.[1] In education the Canadian immigrants are superior to those from the South, for they have grown up under

---

[1] Not a few of the fugitive slaves who settled in these two provinces married white women, for the natural reason that women of their own race were almost an absent quantity in that region.

a system of compulsory school attendance. In other
respects, they are on approximately the same level.
They manifest no special affinity among themselves,
and mix readily with their American cousins.

Boston's Negro population also includes a hundred
or two persons whom the census designates as "Africans." Most of these are natives of the Portuguese
Islands of Cape Verde, which lie off the West Coast of
Africa. They are of mixed blood, being descended on
the one hand from the slaves who were originally
taken to these islands, and on the other from the
Portuguese colonists who have intermarried with the
Negroes since slavery was abolished. In appearance,
they range from individuals who at first glance would
be set down as Negroes, to such as would at once be
taken for Portuguese or Spaniards. The majority are
sailors, who tarry only between voyages, but some
have taken up their permanent abode in Boston. In
religious faith, they are Roman Catholics.[1] They
keep by themselves and do not affiliate much with
the American Negroes, though as a rule they live
in Negro districts. The police say that these African-
Portuguese give them next to no trouble, and that as a
class they are intelligent and self-respecting. Besides
this rather ambiguous element, there is among the
African immigrants a very small proportion who come
from Liberia or other parts of the Dark Continent.[2]

[1] Attending the Church of St. John the Baptist, in the North
End.

[2] The writer has been impressed by the marked intelligence and
capacity of the several native Africans whom he has met in Boston.
It must be borne in mind, of course, that only the most promising
or enterprising individuals could make their way from that continent

Finally, besides those from the West Indies, Canada and Africa, a few Negroes may be found who hail from still other quarters of the globe.[1]

Such, then, is the human material, differentiated as respects nativity, of which Boston's Negro community is composed. This material, it appears, instead of being of a single monotonous character, as those of the other race who are not closely acquainted with the facts are wont to assume, is, on the contrary, by no

to America. Most frequently they are sent here to be educated at the expense of churches and missionary societies. One such the writer came upon the day following his arrival; he could not speak a word of English, and bore upon his body the sign of his tribe, which had been branded into the flesh. His way was being paid, in part, by one of the Negro churches in Boston, and he was going to Tuskegee Institute, thence to carry back to his people the seeds of industrial progress. Tuskegee and other institutions have in the total a considerable number of African students. Recently a native Zulu won high honors in oratory at Columbia University, and subsequently delivered a series of public lectures.

One of the most interesting native Africans who has ever appeared in Boston is Dihdwo Twe, a member of the native Kroo tribe of the Liberian hinterland. He is a young man, who came to this city several years ago to attend the Burdett Business College, with the object of returning to Liberia and going into business with his father, who is an exporter of mahogany. That he will make his mark no one who has met him doubts. In appearance he is most pleasing; of a dark brown complexion, features broad but refined, and expression alert. His voice is soft and musical, his manners irreproachable, his dress immaculate. Most remarkable of all, however, is his use of the English language, especially in writing, where he is not hampered by the alien accent. His style is so imbued with an understanding of the inner meaning of words as to make it delightful to read. In the *American Journal of Religious Psychology and Education* for June, 1907, this young man had an article on African religions, and he has been engaged by the *Independent* to contribute some further articles on this and related subjects. He returned to his native land in November, 1909.

[1] As, for instance, Dr. Cornelius McKane, a Negro physician, recently deceased, who was born in British Guiana, South America.

means lacking in variety. The several large natal groups of which mention has been made have their more or less peculiar precedent conditions and distinguishing characteristics. Thereby is derived, on the one hand, such social invigoration and stimulus as come from diversification and the contact of different elements. Evidently an active process of abrasion and fusion is going on within the Negro community itself, concurrently with the moulding and unifying effect of the exterior environment. On the other hand, there is also manifest within this race, though on a smaller scale and in a narrowed field, the same general problem of assimilation by which the American nation as a whole is confronted.

Passing on now to the general social conditions, irrespective of differences of nativity, under which the Negro inhabitants of Boston are living at present, it becomes necessary to undertake some further analysis of this element of the population, from the point of view, this time, of its social gradations. For while here again most white people think of the Negroes en masse, as a matter of fact there are clearly defined economic-social distinctions of class among them, with each class subject to somewhat different circumstances and having its particular rank and place in the total scheme of the Negro community.

At the bottom of the scale is a deposit of those whose coming and going and mode of livelihood are obscure and ofttimes devious. This element is composed of the vicious, the utterly shiftless, and the hopelessly incapable. It includes a large quota of chronic rovers, many of whom work their way to Boston on the coastwise steamers. Its proportion of unmarried men and women is far greater than in the case of the Negro population as a whole. The members of this class live generally in questionable lodging-house sections in the downtown parts of the city. They supply most of the loafers in the open squares, about the streets, and in the saloons and so-called clubs. The bad impression which they make upon the public, by reason of their character and conduct, is out of all correspondence with their actual numbers. As a matter of fact, this contingent does not form, at most, more than ten per cent of the entire body of the city's Negro residents.

Next come the rank and file, the common people. They are the men and women who want to advance, and who in the mass are advancing, slowly but surely. Their occupations are mostly those with which Negroes are usually associated — hotel and janitor work, domestic service, and rough labor — with some of higher grade. Their earnings ascend from less than the minimum requisite for bare subsistence, in which case resort must be had to the assistance of friends or to charity, to an amount sufficient to provide the common comforts and pleasures. The poorer element among them, mostly young unmarried immigrants of both sexes, are lodgers, usually confined to one small room, picking up their meals here and there, and finding it next to impossible to live in a homelike manner. These lodgers are characterized by transiency of residence, lack of responsible neighborhood ties and community interests, and much aimless gadding about. Of the majority of the rank and file, who do not have to live quite in this manner, all but a small percentage are struggling tenants. Many, in spite of honest endeavor, are unable to keep the rent paid promptly. On this account, and still more frequently through the search for employment, coupled with the desire to eliminate street-car fares, they are forced to move every little while, oftentimes to a section far distant from that of their previous abode. This shifting about hinders the growth of both home and neighborhood life. Even those who are able to remain in one place have not the means, even when they have the latent capacity, to furnish their quarters attractively. Necessity compels a large proportion of the women, wives and mothers, to go to work, which imposes a further obstacle to home-building.

With the parents much away, what wonder that the children take to the streets? This undevelopment of home life among the Negroes, together with their need of relief from the daily round of toil and uncertainty, are factors which account negatively for the incessant visiting, going to parties and joining societies, of which later mention will be made from the point of view of their positive significance. Such social diversions, however, have to be of the most casual sort, as these Negroes in general have little assured leisure in which to cultivate life's amenities and acquire the substantial accomplishments. Their homes, however, are as a rule clean and tidy, and their children neatly clad.[1] The Negroes of this class are in their bearing and conduct at once self-respecting and unobtrusive. They are well aware of the disabilities under which they and

[1] The tidiness of Negro women is usually traced to their domestic training under slavery.

their race labor in the community, but without any involved reasoning they accept these things as facts and go on with their day's work, — industrious, patient, serious of purpose, and withal cheerful in their outlook.

The rank and file, thus characterized in a general way, is of course a large class, which emerges from the previously described lowest element at a point whose exact location must of necessity be arbitrary, and then gradually ascends till again, at the top, it shades imperceptibly into the class above, from which, indeed, it can be divided only by another arbitrary line. It comprises a number of successive gradations within itself, each of which is roughly determined by the economic status of the individuals included. So far as any more specific measure is adducible, it probably consists of the intermittent or regular character of the industry of the men, combined with the degree of pressure to go out to work which rests upon the women — matters which will be more fully taken up later in their more immediate connection with other economic conditions. Viewed as a whole, however, this class may be estimated to form approximately seventy per cent of the entire Negro population. Such being the case, and with the hampering conditions which have been described in mind, it is evident that the circumstances under which the great majority of the Negroes are living in Boston to-day, are such as greatly to retard the formation of a strong and healthy Negro community. Whatever social progress the Negro people are making, they are accomplishing in the face of tremendous obstacles.

The most well-to-do of the Negro rank and file pass, as has already been said, into a middle class, which itself gains in distinctness as its own gradations ascend. This middle class forms approximately eighteen per cent of the Negro population. Its lower ranks are made up of waiters, Pullman porters, janitors, and artisans, who, however, by dint of economy and good sense, have advanced to a point where they are assured of a comfortable living, and have a little fund laid up against the contingencies of the future. Next come clerical and lesser salaried employees, the smaller business proprietors, and the minor professional element. At the top, constituting as near an approach to a moneyed constituency as has yet evolved among the Negroes, stand the higher salaried employees, the more important business proprietors, some of the leading professional people, and the larger property owners. A goodly proportion of the members of this middle class own their homes. The number who are acquiring homes in superior outlying residential districts, oftentimes among white neighbors, is constantly increasing. A special motive which leads them to move into these better localities is the desire to get their children away from the moral dangers of the city streets. They are also influenced, however, by a willingness thus to publish concrete evidence of a rise in the economic-social scale.

Residence apart from the mass of their race, combined with their own attainment of a position somewhat above the general struggle for livelihood, are factors which frequently have the effect of causing Negroes of this class to lose close touch and sympathy with the common run of their fellows. Especially in the case of the second generation, who are usually better educated, there is a tendency to gravitate toward what may be called the Negro upper class. The majority of the middle element, however, still reside in predominantly Negro districts, and will probably for many years continue to do so, as in these districts Negroes may acquire homes more readily and at less cost. These men and women, living in the midst of their race, fully conscious of its trials, its hopes, its achievements, are in fact the mainstay of the Negro community, and slowly but surely are developing sound leadership. Most of them are Southern born and bred, and so have grown up with an inner understanding of the intrinsic reasons which account for conditions affecting their race. In education and refinement they are not too far above the majority of their people to make common cause with them and to be accepted by them. Though a great many have an admixture of Caucasian blood, the circumstances of their life have been such as to keep them from being in any appreciable measure deracialized. Their own accomplishment has shown them that, in spite of the Negro's peculiar adversities, success can be won. And their personal experience has freed them, for the most part, from bitterness. They are beginning to see the way ahead, and are commencing to preach, as they have themselves practiced, the gospel of salvation by solid achievement.

Finally, there is the Negro upper class. Justice demands, however, that this element be distinguished from a sort of "smart set," which may be described as an excrescence growing out of the several classes which have been noted. There are a host of Negroes who labor to create an impression of superiority by dressing far beyond their means and by attempting to assume the ways of culture. The members of this race — so far as they have opportunity — naturally seek to attain polished manners. Such aspirations are entirely in their favor so long as they are kept within appropriate limits. It is when they are perverted that they become objectionable. Many a Negro, who sports a silk hat and stick on Sunday, "totes" quarters of beef in the market on Monday. Time was when one was amazed at seeing on the street so many Negroes who had all the earmarks of the idle rich. But ere long one discovered that most of these persons were Pullman porters and hotel waiters. Once when the writer was having his shoes polished by a Negro bootblack, a typical representative of the class passed by; indicating him with a jerk of the head, the bootblack remarked: "If I could buy that fellow for what he's worth and sell him for what he thinks he's worth, I'd be able to retire from business." The propensity to display runs all through the Negro society and ascends from loudness of dress and extravagance of manner to an imitation of gentility so clever as to pass for real, till one catches a glimpse below the surface. These finished mimics constitute the "smart set" proper. They devote most of their time and money to aping the ways of white "society." They have many clubs with fancy and foreign names, and give *bals masqués*, *tableaux vivants*, and tournaments at bridge. Their daughters "study" music, art, or dramatics just long enough to make a

show of being "accomplished." Their sons endeavor
to look and act like college students or men-about-
town. Lightness of complexion is almost indispensable
to a place in this set, whose members taboo the word
"Negro," always refer to themselves as "colored" "ladies" and "gentlemen," and talk much of the slights
to which they are subjected. So conspicuous do these
characteristics make them that they greatly injure
their race in the eyes of the public.

The real Negro upper class — using this term, of
course, in a suggestive sense — is an element little
known and even less understood by the average white
person, but one whose position is exceedingly interesting. It is made up of lawyers, physicians, salaried
employees, business proprietors, literary and musical
people, and the like, who are distinguished by superior
education and refinement. This class comprises the
remaining small quota — two per cent — of the Negro
population. Not all, but the larger number of its
members, are of Northern birth or long Northern residence, have a considerable strain of white blood, and
are of light complexion. Their attractive homes bear
witness to their genuine good taste. The majority of
this class live in superior residential districts, among
white neighbors. In the practice of their vocations
they not infrequently come into contact with the other
race more than they do with Negroes. Further acquaintance with white people results from attendance
at white churches and from membership in various
white organizations. And, indeed, by virtue of their
actually superior qualities and usually attractive personalities, these men and women have many substan-

tial friendships with men and women of the other race.
Their natural endowments, education, and conditions
of life tend to divide them from the mass of the Negroes, and, in fact, most of them have comparatively
little close association with the Negro rank and file.
They are disposed, furthermore, as will later be shown
in more detail, to cast aspersion on most forms of
separate union among the Negro people along lines of
voluntary racial segregation. They tend to keep within
a small social circle of their own kind, while at the same
time cultivating affiliation with the whites. Nevertheless, they are wont to assume before the public the
position of understanding intimately the conditions
and needs of the Negro race, and of being its best accredited representatives. But the mass of the Negroes
are well aware of their attitude of aloofness, and even
while recognizing their superior attainments with mingled feelings of envy and pride, retaliate by accusing
them of wanting to deracialize themselves, and also by
opposing their attempted leadership.

It is among the members of this class that most
deep-seated and vehement objection is made to the
application of the name "Negro." And as applied to
many of them, this term is, strictly speaking, a mis-
nomer. Not a few are by blood and appearance more
white than Negro. For that matter, between a third
and a half of the Negroes in Boston have an admixture
of white blood; but in the case of the upper class now in
question, refinement and association with white people
combine with their Caucasian strain to make them
feel that they are not wholly of the one race. To this
element, as their life is lived to-day, the "tragedy of

color" is an ever-present one of heart and soul. And a great part, if not indeed the greater part, of the tragedy lies in the fact that this is a class which has not yet found itself. "When you write of the Negroes in Boston," one of them appealed, "tell about us who are neither Negroes nor whites, but an ambiguous something-between; — a people not yet known or named. While our sympathies tend to unite us with the Negroes and their destiny, all our aspirations lead us toward the whites." The intense insistence upon equal rights, and the relentless opposition to Washington's advocacy of giving first place to economic progress, emanate from — though they are not confined to — this class. That such is the case sheds light on the psychology of the agitation for equality, and suggests that it is animated not solely by reasoned conviction as to abstract principles, but also, in many instances, by unreasoned and very personal emotions.

The divergence between the so-called upper class and the rest of the Negroes means that the Negro community is subject at once to two tendencies which, at least on the surface, are mutually antagonistic. The one is a conscious and extremely sensitive effort to get away from racial lines, and indeed from the very fact of race. The other is an instinctive and largely unconscious adhesion to racial lines, and seeking after race coherence. Here are two points of view which are certainly, to some extent, opposed; two inner impulses which are, in some degree, set over against each other. The Negroes who hold to the non-racial attitude are able, by reason of their superiorities of education and position, to exert an influence out of proportion to their meager numbers. Friction, dissidence, and counter-action thereby result. The natural process of social integration is continually interfered with by cross-currents of disintegration. A similar hampering effect, though only in comparatively small measure, is involved in the emergence of the other horizontal social lines to which attention has been called. For the very reason that the Negroes are engaged in a severe economic-social struggle upward, class distinctions have an abnormal importance in their minds. They guard jealously anything which seems to set them even in slight degree above their fellows. They can draw distinctions, moreover, with a nicety that would do credit to the most punctilious arbiter of the most exclusive social circles. Persons of the other race who have attempted, for one purpose or another, to assemble or combine the Negroes of a given neighborhood, without knowledge or in disregard of their own inner class differences, have speedily found trouble on their hands. This condition of things detracts, of course, from the solidarity of the Negro community, and in so far retards its advance.

Nevertheless, the formation of the foregoing social classes, each of which is constantly increasing in distinctness, is an integral and inevitable part of the process of differentiation which accompanies, and which indeed is, in itself, an essential element of social progress. Especially does the evolution of the middle and upper classes signalize a growth in material means, education, and refinement, which are assets of indispensable advantage to the Negro community as a whole. The Negro society has become more complex, but at the same time more finely inter-constructed and resourceful. Its underlying, as distinguished from its superficial, power of unity has thus in fact not been impaired, but enhanced. Even in the case of the non-conformist position of the upper class, the net and legitimate effect thereof may, in the light of more ample understanding of the situation, prove to be not that of disturbance and disruption, but, on the contrary, that of requisite balance and counterpoise.

Section 3. The Actual Advance

When now, turning from the examination of the Negro community in its dissected parts, so to speak, account is taken of the positive advances and achievements of this community viewed in its entirety, the social progress which the Negroes are making in spite of all obstacles becomes clearly evident.

The free public school system is one of the chief permanent and fundamental factors in this progress. Ever since the Negroes succeeded in erasing the color line in public education, they have had unrestricted access to the Boston schools, which are among the very best in the country; and they are deriving from them benefits identical in kind with those derived by other elements of the population. Some of the better quality of immigrants from the South come to Boston especially to take advantage of the superior opportunities for the education of their children.[1] School attendance

[1] A typical instance is that of Mr. and Mrs. John T. Jackson. Here is Mr. Jackson's own statement: —

"I, John T. Jackson, tailor, of Athens, Georgia, came to Boston, Massachusetts, in the year of 1897, for the purpose of educating my

between the ages of seven and fourteen is compulsory. Though a large proportion of Negro children are taken out of school to go to work at the minimum legal age, before finishing the grammar course, the great majority of them complete the course. As white children in the proportion of four out of five do not go beyond grammar school, the Negroes who grow up in Boston thus have an opportunity of common school training at least equal to that of the rank and file of the whites. On account of the special economic stress under which the Negroes live, the proportion of Negro boys and girls who go through high school is, of course, far smaller than the corresponding proportion of white boys and girls; but nevertheless in the total the former constitute a substantial number. A great many young

children. In November, 1899, my wife and six children joined me, and since then there have been four additions to the family.

"The oldest, Mabel S. Jackson, was graduated from West Grammar School in the class of '01, Malden High School, '05, and Boston University, College of Liberal Arts (A.B.) '09. Now she is in her third year as teacher in the Academic Department of the State Normal School, Elizabeth City, North Carolina.

"John T., Jr., left grammar school after completing eight grades and entered into the business profession in Lowell, Massachusetts.

"Ella J. was graduated from Faulkner Grammar School, '05, High School, '09, Malden Commercial School, '10, and is now a teacher at Durham, North Carolina.

"Sallie H. was graduated from Faulkner Grammar School, '06, High School, '10, and is now preparing to enter Pratt University in New York.

"Lucy D. was graduated from Faulkner Grammar School, '06, High School, '10, and is now a stenographer at Malden, Massachusetts.

"Althea I. was graduated from the Maplewood Grammar School, '11.

"Louie R., fifth grade Faulkner Grammar School.

"Cecile H., third grade Faulkner Grammar School.

Negroes, whom the necessity of working prevents from going to school in the daytime, attend the evening grammar and high schools. In these evening classes are enrolled, too, many adult Negroes of all ages, even old men and women, all eagerly taking advantage of the instruction offered, from learning to read and write up to mastering higher mathematics. A few Negroes profit by the special opportunities held out by the Young Men's Christian Association,[1] the Young Men's Christian Union, the Wells Memorial, the Prospect Union in Cambridge, and other similar institutions. A very few carry their education into colleges, and into normal, technical, and professional schools.

Principals and teachers as a rule report that Negro children are not noticeably below the level of the others in alertness, application, deportment, and neatness. Cases of Negro pupils, who in competition with their white school-fellows receive distinguished recognition, are of frequent occurrence. In 1911, a Negro girl was valedictorian of her class at the Brighton High School.[2] By making an average of 95 in her four years' course, she also won a place near the head of the 1291 pupils who received diplomas from the Boston high schools that year. The year before, another girl of the same race stood third in her class in one of the Boston grammar schools, won first place in a competition in verse-writing, and was elected class prophet and poet. In a grammar school in Cambridge, two Negro boys ranked

[1] The central Association at Boston has about seventy-five Negro members, and nearly all the suburban branches include some of this race.

[2] Miss F. Marion Reed.

high in scholarship, and one of them was adjudged
second in a speaking contest, with a declamation on
the character and mission of Charles Sumner, the
Abolitionist. In another school of the same grade in
Boston, a Negro boy was elected class president and
captain of the football, baseball, and relay teams.

Such competitive achievements not only give the
Negroes themselves confidence in their own capacity,
but make upon the white boys and girls, and upon
their parents and the community, a lasting impression
of the Negro's latent capabilities.

The relation of the Negroes to the Boston schools is,
moreover, not confined to receiving benefits. They
also have a part in the direction of these schools,
through a number of teachers and other school officers.[1] The fact that all of the Negro teachers are
graduates of the Boston Normal School shows strikingly how members of the race are repaying the community, with ample interest, for the opportunities
it provides. In Cambridge, Miss Maria L. Baldwin,
who was born and educated in that suburb, has for
twenty-three years been principal of the Agassiz
Grammar School, in which she had previously served as
a teacher. Her position is the more remarkable in that
there are no other teachers of her race, and only a few
Negro children, in the school. But by sheer ability,
combined with a high degree of tact, Miss Baldwin has
not only performed her exacting duties satisfactorily,

[1] The teachers are Misses Harriet L. Smith (daughter of John J.
Smith, already mentioned in connection with anti-slavery events
and as a leader among his people), Eleanora A. Smith, Blanche V.
Smith, Mary E. Smith, Jacqueline Carroll and Iola D. Yates, in Boston proper; and Miss Gertrude M. Baker, in Cambridge.

but has commanded the respect and ready support of all who know her. Dr. Samuel E. Courtney served on the Boston School Board for several years in the latter nineties, and more recently James A. Lew, a descendant of the family of that name which, as previously mentioned, rendered valiant service in the Revolution, was a member of the School Committee of Cambridge. W. Clarence Matthews, of the class of 1905 of Harvard College, and one of the brilliant baseball stars in the annals of that seat of learning, is an assistant athletic director in the Boston schools.

In Boston all public institutions, not only libraries and museums, but hospitals, homes, baths, parks, playgrounds, and the rest, are in law as fully accessible to the Negroes as to any other element of the citizenship. Undoubtedly, owing to the prevailing attitude toward this race, which has already been described at some length, more or less discrimination enters into the actual administration of these institutions. But such prejudice is shown only by individuals, has nowhere received even tacit official sanction, and has not attained formidable proportions. And in nearly all the places of whatever sort which are open to the public, Negroes may be found among those who are profiting by the facilities afforded.

Not only through the schools, which in the main affect only the rising generation, are the Negroes educating themselves. Young and old, men and women, are also pushing forward earnestly along all the different avenues of self-development. Almost never has the writer been to the Public Library without seeing at least one Negro — and usually several — intently reading or industriously taking notes. In the Art Museum he has seen them studying the paintings, at concerts listening to the music with unfeigned enjoyment, and at lectures of all kinds and in all places; — living witnesses to the multiplicity and diversity of the outreachings of the Negro mind. The contribution thus made by such institutions to the progress of the Negro people is very great.

Of semi-public institutions not specifically devoted to work for Negroes, such as settlements, clubs and classes of a social service nature, homes supported by private contributions, and the like, there are many which make it a hard-and-fast rule to have nothing to do with this element of the population. The majority avoid accepting Negroes or extending their work among them, so far as they can do this without openly drawing the color line. Nevertheless, not a few Negroes slip through the loophole between what the officers of these places would like to do if they dared, and what they feel they have to put up with to escape criticism on account of too overt discrimination.

Five institutions, however, to the writer's knowledge, include a considerable number of Negroes in their activities. Cambridge Neighborhood House, which grew out of a day nursery and kindergarten started in 1881 and which is now the principal settlement in the University City, is situated in a locality where the Negro population has increased rapidly in the last decade. Mrs. Quincy A. Shaw, one of Boston's foremost philanthropists, who supports this settlement, has insisted from the outset that no racial discrimination should be shown, but that all elements of the neighborhood should be received with equal welcome.[1] In consequence, the proportion of Negroes enrolled in the various clubs and classes has come to be approximately 10 per cent of a total of about 750 (which includes thirteen other nationalities) and more are constantly coming in. In the trade-school department, two thirds of the girls are of the Negro race. No separation whatever is made, but throughout, Negroes and whites, both children and adults, are intermingled. Though there has been occasional friction in the past, thus far, owing to the genuine determination of those in charge not to countenance segregation, and the constant exercise of tact, this friction has not resulted in serious trouble. At present the most pleasant relations prevail. The women's club affords a striking example of how amicably and effectively it is possible for Negroes and whites to work together. About a third of its forty-odd members are of the former race. Recently a Negro woman served as president, with general satisfaction. This club has been the means of bringing about some substantial neighborhood association between families of the two races. Recently the secretary of the men's society was a Negro. Two of the club leaders are Negroes and one of these has charge of a group of white children.

At Emmanuel Memorial Parish House, a settlement connected with the Church of the Ascension, built in

[1] Mrs. Shaw is a member by marriage of the same family from which came Colonel Robert Gould Shaw, who, as already related, met his death in the Civil War while leading a charge of his Negro troops.

1905, and located near the northeast corner of the principal Negro district, there are from 50 to 60 Negroes in an enrollment of 600; — again a percentage of 10 per cent. No separation is made, and pleasant relations have been maintained. Only at the dances does some embarrassment arise, owing to the fact that the whites are averse to taking Negroes as partners. In the Pleasant Street section, in the lower South End, Morgan Memorial, a semi-settlement conducted under Methodist auspices, has about 300 Negro boys and girls among its 1000 children. In the children's church and Sunday school, 100 out of a total of 350, and in the evening children's church 125 out of 400, are Negroes. Here, too, the Negroes and their white associates of many races have got on pleasantly. In Hope Chapel, a mission situated near the Morgan Memorial and conducted by the Old South Congregational Church, the entire enrollment is around 800, and the number of Negroes about 162. Here, however, Negroes and whites are separated except in the kindergarten. At Parker Memorial, conducted by Hale House, a social settlement, and located near the Dartmouth Street Negro section, there are only a few Negroes in the general classes, but the use of the rooms has been granted very freely to Negro organizations for lectures, concerts, conventions, lodge meetings, and dances.

Though in the five institutions which have been mentioned, such racial friction as has resulted has not been serious, nevertheless the possibility of more serious trouble, to some extent the suggestion of it, and to a far greater extent the imagination of it, have been present as disquieting elements. A determined outbreak of latent racial antipathy in any of these institutions, with the possible exception of Neighborhood House, would probably have as an outcome the exclusion of the Negroes. The policy of receiving Negroes into the same building with whites, but grouping them separately, as in the case of Hope Chapel just mentioned, represents a transition stage between intermingling Negroes with whites, on the one hand, and completely segregating them in distinct institutions, on the other. The segregation plan, however, is very plainly the one which is gaining favor in Boston, not necessarily to the abandonment of the others, but to their comparative disregard. Some of the most radical equal rights agitators among the Negroes see in this tendency only the desire of the whites to get their race off out of the way. Undeniably this motive enters in. But in the main the policy of segregation is based on the belief that it is more practicable under actual existing conditions, with reference especially to the general backwardness of the Negroes, and the prevailing disinclination of the whites to be thrown into close association with them. Those who advocate this policy believe also that in the long run it is more likely to yield results satisfactory to the majority of the Negroes themselves, in that, while the dangers of friction are avoided, the coherence and self-dependability of the Negro community are promoted.

There is one institution that occupies a position between those in which Negroes form but a minor proportion and those which are set aside for that race exclusively. This is the Robert Gould Shaw House, a settlement established in 1908, and situated on Hammond Street, in the heart of the principal Negro center. It is an outgrowth of work which had been carried on for several years by the South End House. Miss Augusta P. Eaton, who had been in charge of that work, was put at the head of the new settlement, which was founded with the particular moral support of the Episcopal Diocese, though no religious services were held and the financial support was to be derived from general contributions. The managing board includes several leading Negroes.[1] There are twenty-six white and twenty-seven Negro workers, most of whom are unpaid. All the opportunities provided are open to children and adults of both races. In the summer-time outdoor classes and picnics, for the little ones, are a considerable number of white children. But the great majority of those who take advantage of the institution are Negroes.

The activities carried on are many. There is a kindergarten group of 25 or more. For women, there are classes in cooking, sewing, dressmaking, millinery, embroidery, and basketry, containing altogether about fifty members, and a mother's club of more than that number, which has weekly meetings of a social and civic nature, with lectures on hygiene, the care of children, and similar topics. For girls, there are 3 classes in cooking, 3 in sewing, 2 in embroidery, a group called "Little Housekeepers," and classes in basketry, brass-work, clay modeling, dancing and folk-dancing, with a membership, inclusive, of about 160. There are also an orchestra and several clubs composed of girls. For

[1] Among them Miss Baldwin, the school principal previously mentioned.

boys, there are classes in brass, bent iron, clay modeling, wood-burning, chair-caning, rug-weaving, gym-
nastics, and singing, with about 100 members; 3 boys'
clubs; and a troop of Boy Scouts of about 20 members.
Two clubs of young men, numbering from 75 to 100
members, are connected with the house. For a time an
employment bureau was conducted by a Negro woman
prominent in social service, on an independent business
basis, and once a week there were social evenings for
girls in domestic service. Over 300 families are regularly visited and assisted in various friendly ways.

After carrying the settlement through its period of
infancy, the original director was compelled by considerations of health to resign, and was succeeded in
the autumn of 1910 by Miss Isabel Eaton, formerly of
the College Settlement, New York, and Hull House, in
Chicago, who is the present head worker. The latter
defines the position of the Robert Gould Shaw House
thus: "It is a neighborhood house located in a section
largely settled by colored people, and therefore it concerns itself chiefly with the activities desired by the
people who are its chief constituents. It stands for
justice and equal opportunity for all, irrespective of
race, color, or other arbitrary distinctions, for the removal of civil, political, and industrial disabilities and
the promotion of a just and amicable relation between
the white and colored people." Certainly not only is a
work of great value to that section and to the whole city
being carried on at present, but a broad and strong
foundation for further development and greatly enlarged usefulness is being laid.

Of the social betterment institutions devoted solely

to the Negroes, two are homes for the sick and aged.
St. Monica's Home, founded in 1888 and occupying a
house in the Roxbury district in which Garrison at one
time lived, cares for sixty or seventy sick Negro women
and children every year. It is conducted under the
auspices of the St. Margaret Sisters, an Episcopalian
order, and is fostered particularly by Trinity Church.
Two groups of Negro women, the Relief Association
and the Sewing Circle, contribute toward its support,
as do also Negro churches and societies and not a few
individuals of that race. The Home for Aged Colored
Women, located on Hancock Street in the West End,
has about twenty inmates and gives some assistance
outside. Here also the Negro people help somewhat in
the institution's maintenance.

In November, 1908, the Mission Priests of St. John
the Evangelist [1] completed the erection of a large
building called St. Augustine's and St. Martin's Mission, which is situated on Lenox Street, in the principal
Negro district and which is designed for the double
use of a church and a center for social service. Clubs
and classes for both sexes, children and adults, including about 200 persons, are conducted, and a programme of physical, moral, domestic, and manual
training is carried out.[2] In connection with this mission there is a farm of 130 acres at Foxboro, not far

[1] This is an English Church order which has been carrying on
religious proselytizing among the Negroes in Boston for twenty-five
years or more, under the direction mainly of the now venerable
Father Field.

[2] Prior to 1908, social service activities of a character similar to
the present ones, but on a smaller scale, had been carried on at the
old St. Augustine's Mission in the West End, and in a branch on
Bradford Street, in the Lower South End.

from Boston, where young Negro girls are taken for a vacation in summer and where a number of them are cared for all the year through, instructed in housekeeping, and later assisted in obtaining positions as domestics.

Several years ago the Roman Catholics rented a hall, where work for Negroes, of the same general kind as that carried on by the Mission Priests, has been started.

All these outside agencies are assisting vitally in the Negro's progress. They represent the good-will and the helping hand of the other race. But even more important than their activity is the collective endeavor which is going on within the Negro community itself, and which, with the general conditions to which attention has already been called as a background, may now be presented.

Note has previously been taken of the deficiency of this race in the ability for social coöperation of the most fundamental sort. But, on the other hand, it must be said that in at least such sociability as makes immediate appeal to the ear and to the eye, and in such spontaneous association as springs from this outflow of the feeling of fellowship, the Negroes easily excel the whites. Any but the most obstinate attack of melancholy would be cured by a saunter through one of the city's Negro districts.[1] The people accost one another as they pass with hearty banter. On every side vociferous groups are loitering. Women are exchanging gossip from neighboring windows. The barber-shops and

[1] Along Shawmut Avenue above Northampton Street, for instance, or through Dartmouth Street and up Columbus Avenue.

pool-rooms are loafing-places for noisy gatherings of men. Bright-eyed children, of ripe-olive skin, romp and play with charming abandon and absence of self-consciousness. If perchance some have hands and faces besoiled, their complexions happily obscure the fact. Depression and taciturnity, so evident in the Ghetto, for instance, are here found hardly at all. But still rarer are disagreeable hurry and overexertion.

The Negroes are instinctively companionable folk, with whom all the ordinary relations of life are free and easy. They are no seekers after solitude. They love laughter and noise. They are warm-hearted, and search their souls for language to convey their emotions. Their appearance harmonizes with their nature. Their features are soft, rounded, ample. Often their skins have a bronze richness of hue that might well make a "pale-face" envious. Their eyes and teeth gleam lustrously from their dark setting. Their voices are melodious. Their manners are of the comfortable sort, and they are naturally courteous. Travellers who have penetrated into Africa say that, on emerging from a long sojourn among the natives, they have been shocked by the first returning sight of the sharper, harder features of the white race, and the initial contact with their brusquer ways. The American Negroes invite a similar comparison with their Caucasian fellow-countrymen. They are irresistibly likable. They have, too, an innate drollery of speech, look, and demeanor, and an infectious humor, which are all their own. They cannot help feeling good, and one cannot help feeling good with them.

Their passion for sociability finds expression in no

end of visiting. Distance and car-fares cannot keep them apart. They are incessantly going to parties, concerts, dances, and all kinds of jollifications. Accounts and announcements of these festive gatherings, which in pretentiousness ascend from small home affairs to full-dress or masquerade balls, crowd the columns of the two Negro newspapers. Nor do such occasional gatherings satisfy the members of this race. They eagerly promote consecutive, continuous association. No racial type has a stronger craving to "belong." They have clubs and societies without number and of every description. They eagerly seize upon the slightest warrant for banding together, with a name, officers, and numerous committees. It does not take the observer long to discover that with the majority of these organizations the actual if not the professed object, as well as the chief result accomplished, is the furtherance of a general good time. Many societies, as, for instance, the "Fleur-de-lis," "Longworth," "Waverley Outing," and "Blue Ribbon" clubs, make no claim whatever to soberer ends.

The innate sociability and associativeness of the Negro people give them a great advantage, at the very start, in the developing of that far deeper and more durable kind of coöperation which is essential to social advance. The various societies of lighter vein have, moreover, an underlying value greater than might at first thought appear. They are primary schools, so to speak, where thousands of Negroes, nearly all of the rising generation, are being educated in the rudiments of combination, which elsewhere they may turn to sterner account. But of more immediate importance are a great many organizations of serious purpose, some of them of an artistic and literary nature, and others of a more specifically cöoperative and benevolent character, which are already at work.

With reference to the former, many people believe that, as the Negroes advance, they are going to contribute to the composite life of the nation much of distinct value in music and the various fields of art. There can be no doubt that the Negroes are by nature musical. They love to hear music and to make music, have a strong sense of rhythm and a marked capacity for rudimentary melody. When a large group of them sing in unison, the rhythmical and emotional vehemence of their singing is compelling. Generally, too, their voices are soft and pleasant to the ear. But finished musical performances are rare among them, and wretched ones are common. The fundamental explanation of this fact is that the great majority of the race are still deficient in the qualities of fine perception and unflagging application which are essential to musical excellence. In addition, comparatively few have the material means to provide themselves with a sufficiently long and thorough course of instruction in this department. However, the number of Negroes who are possessed of musical ability of a grade to entitle them to creditable recognition, even when measured by the standards of the community at large, is constantly increasing, and the frequent musical honors won by Negro children in the public schools is evidence that some measure of substantial education along this line is being acquired.[1]

[1] In 1910, for example, a Negro girl acted as pianist for the Lynn

Of musical organizations, there are many which are undoubtedly sowing good seed for future harvests, but only a few whose present accomplishments are noteworthy.[1] The most ambitious musical undertaking in which the Negroes have engaged has been the presentation of grand opera. The initiative, inspiration, and persistence in this undertaking were supplied chiefly by Theodore Drury, who had previously, from 1900 to 1906, presented a series of operas in New York City, with a Negro company which he organized. Then he came to Boston, and working against disheartening inertia, he contrived to prepare for the same purpose a group of about fifty men and women, few of whom had trained voices, and most of whom had little time to spare from their day's work. In 1907, the opera "Aida" and a scene from "Carmen" were given. The next year "Faust" was presented, and the year after that, "Cavalleria Rusticana." In these presentations, a creditable proportion of the principals carried out their singing parts well, and a few showed dramatic ability.

In painting, sculpture, and the decorative arts there are hardly any of this race in Boston who have done

High School in her senior year, and composed the music for the class hymn. In a Boston grammar school, a Negro boy was selected to play the graduation march. The same honor fell to another girl in a Cambridge school; and still another was the only soloist out of a class of a hundred in the graduation exercises of a school in Winchester.

[1] These latter are Wolff's, Matthews', White's, and Portuondo's orchestras, and Ransom's Choral Union. This chorus, organized by Mr. John Ransom, a Negro music teacher, and numbering about fifty voices, gives many good concerts in the Negro churches and societies.

superior work, though a Negro of Boston birth is said to be winning success as a painter in Paris.[1] There is, however, an interesting and worthy organization in this field — the Boston Negro Art Club, formed in 1907. The fact that its officers are waiters and kitchen-workers shows against what odds the Negroes are striving for some of the finer things. This club gave its first exhibition, consisting of one hundred and twenty paintings and drawings, in the autumn of 1907, and has had other exhibitions since. All the work has shown promising endeavor and some has indicated real capacity.

With regard to acting, while little local talent has yet attained recognition, there is much which is latent. In an entertainment at the South End House, for instance, two Negro boys of the neighborhood gave an imitation of Chinese laundrymen engaged in an argument. It was altogether their own concoction, and, besides being side-splitting, was amazingly true to life. Not a few Boston Negroes are scattered here and there throughout the country as vaudeville performers or members of troupes. For drolly humorous, and withal intensely human, portrayals, the Negroes undoubtedly display a special faculty, probably because this is for them only slightly modified self-expression.[2]

In the domain of oratory, the Negroes easily excel

[1] Robert Hemings.

[2] As a comic actor, no one on the American stage surpasses Bert Williams. Whenever he and his partner Walker, or Ernest Hogan, or Cole and Johnson, have come to Boston, they have packed the theater with crowds in which the color line has been forgotten in the fellowship of laughter. The recent deaths of Walker, Hogan, and Cole are a distinct loss to the forces of good cheer.

their Caucasian fellow-countrymen. If a hundred Negroes and a hundred whites were to be taken at random, it is safe to say that the former would yield at least twice as many stirring speakers as the latter. The presence of Negroes on school and college debating teams, and among the prize-winners in declamatory contests, is not infrequent.[1] When infused with close reasoning and clothed with the impregnable armor of facts, this inborn eloquence of the Negro will prove a powerful instrument to his advantage.

Boston abounds with Negro literary societies. The majority are small, the most competent of this class being the Booklovers and the Menticulturists. Half a dozen are larger, and the two that stand out most prominently in point of size and importance are the Boston Literary and Historical Society and the St. Mark Musical and Literary Union. The Boston Literary was organized in 1901. It inclines somewhat toward the equal rights point of view.[2] It meets alternate Monday evenings at one of the Negro churches. The St. Mark Union, which is controlled by a younger element and inclines rather toward the Washington attitude, had its inception in 1902. Its meetings are held every Sunday afternoon in the St. Mark Congregational Church. At the sessions of these societies the usual attendance, drawn not only from the imme-

[1] Roscoe Conkling Bruce, who was elected orator of the class of 1902, was one of the most eloquent debaters Harvard ever had. For many years there has been no more moving public speaker in Boston than the Rev. Reverdy C. Ransom, recently pastor of the Charles Street African Methodist Church.

[2] As is implied by the fact that among its presidents have been Messrs. Grimké, Wilson, and Trotter, to whom previous reference has been made in connection with equal rights agitation.

diate district, but from the whole Greater Boston area, is from two hundred to two hundred and fifty, but not infrequently the Literary attracts three times that number, and the Union would get as many, provided only it had the necessary seating capacity. The programmes are strong, consisting of addresses by locally well-known men and women of both races. More noteworthy than the prepared talks, however, is the extemporaneous speaking from the floor, in which the Negroes exhibit a mental grasp and ability in debate calculated to surprise uninformed white visitors. Indeed, hardly any more persuasive argument in the Negro's favor can be brought to bear on skeptics than the lasting impression, which they cannot help carrying away from one of these meetings, of the courtesy and cordiality, the tasteful dress, the close and intelligent attentiveness of the audience, and the efficient management of the programme on the part of the presiding officers.

One member of Boston's Negro community has achieved literary distinction of a high rank. This is William Stanley Braithwaite, who is generally reckoned, since Paul Lawrence Dunbar's death, the leading poet of his race; though, unlike Dunbar, his poetry has practically no direct reference to the life of the Negro people. Braithwaite has also risen to be one of the accredited younger literary men of America to-day. There now stand to his account two volumes of collected lyric poems, as well as many still scattered verses, of his own composition, and a scholarly series of four English anthologies. It is as a literary critic, however, distinguished in unusual degree by the qualities of sympathetic insight, broad comprehension, and choiceness of style, that he is attracting most notice.[1]

[1] The following brief biographical statement was supplied by Mr. Braithwaite at the writer's request: —

"My paternal grandfather, John Braithwaite, was a man of distinction and influence in Demerara, British Guiana, the proprietor and editor of a newspaper, through which he advocated, and won for the colony, the establishment of a Local Assembly from the English Colonial Office. His eldest son, my father, William Smith Braithwaite, was educated at Queen's College, his native place, afterwards studying medicine in London, England. He came to America in the early eighteen-seventies, settling in Boston, where he married Emma De Wolfe, who was born in North Carolina, but whose life has been spent in Boston since she was six years old. My father was a man of remarkable intellectual ability; of a sensitive, haughty, and highly nervous temperament, but who apparently lacked the will to concentrate his energies in a determined purpose to achieve success in some one particular vocation. Consequently his life was one of erratic talent, distilled through a lovable personality which drew men under its influence, directing and shaping their energies, but achieving nothing substantial toward its own development and acquirement.

"I was the second child and eldest son of these parents, born at Boston, December 6, 1878. At my father's death in 1886, he left his widow the asset of a brilliant but ineffectual memory, and the liability of some domestic indebtedness and a family of four children to maintain and rear. I remained at school until the middle of my twelfth year, when an overwhelming sense of duty sent me into the world to assist my mother in her struggle to provide for the family. I have not been back to school since. My effort to earn wages placed me in various occupations such as a competent youth might pursue (also in many against which my pride and competency rebelled), and such as a colored youth had some difficulty in obtaining. At fifteen, like a revelation, there broke out in me a great passion for poetry, an intense love for literature, and a yearning for that ideal life which fosters the creation of things that come out of dreams and visions and symbols. I dedicated my future to literature, though the altar upon which I was to lay my sacrificial life seemed beyond all likelihood of opportunity and strength and equipment to reach. I set about it, however, with a fortitude, hope, and patience, which now seem to me most amazing in one whose chance was one against a thou-

A promising writer of verse is George Reginald Margetson, of Cambridge, who recently had published a volume entitled "Songs of Life." For the most part his compositions, too, contain little of racial character, but occasionally, as in the stanzas entitled "Ethiopia's Flight," he attacks the Negro question with striking boldness and directness.[1]

sand in surviving the ruthless obstacles which attend even the most favorable literary career, and succeeded in having recognized the quality of my efforts, which were attained through a sheer determined personal cultivation. I am the more satisfied in all this, since I never made a special appeal either in my work or my person; I neither expressed nor interpreted racial characteristics, but always attempted to speak the universal language of human nature; and if I ever carry any distinction to the grave, it will be in proving that art, and especially art as it has developed and been perfected under the influence of American civilization, with all its peculiar paradoxes, knows no distinction of race.

"My first book, *Lyrics of Life and Love*, was published in 1904. It won for me the immediate recognition of the critics, the personal friendship of eminent literary persons, and introduced me to a market for my other literary wares. Practical difficulties were not banished, but this book gave me the power of, and hope in, battling them, and I am now doing so with increasing success. My other books are: *The Book of Elizabethan Verse*, 1906; *The House of Falling Leaves*, 1908; *The Book of Georgian Verse*, 1908; *The Book of Restoration Verse*, 1909; *The Book of Victorian Verse*, 1910. I have contributed a large number of uncollected critical essays to various publications, and am the literary correspondent of the Los Angeles *Times*.

"My personal experience with color prejudice has been slight, hardly recognizable in my career as a whole; I encountered it once in seeking a dwelling-place. As an author it has never touched my life — certainly not in any concrete or personal experience. And I venture to say that my dealings with publishers and editors have been without a thought of it."

[1] It is from *Ethiopia's Flight* that the lines quoted at the end of the closing chapter of this volume are taken. Those two lines impress the writer as prophetically encompassing the Negro's whole past and future in the American nation. The immediate context, of which they form the conclusion, is as follows: —

The Negro organizations which are more specifically concerned with activities of a benevolent and ameliorative nature show in a still more direct way the social progress which the Negroes are making. As might be presumed, the advance in this respect has barely begun to take form in institutions of the larger importance implied by possession of a domicile and a generally recognized place in the community scheme. The two nearest approximations thereto are the Young Men's Educational Aid Association and the Harriet Tubman W.C.T.U. Home; the work of both of which, however, is of very modest proportions. But short of such an institutional development there are a good many Negro organizations which have more or less of a social service character.

Of these the most important from a numerical point of view are the various lodges of secret and semi-secret fraternities, of national ramification, which have mutual aid features. These Negro orders have no official

"America, O mighty government!
Thou matchless star in Earth's vast firmament!
Beneath thy banners in thy heaven-kissed land,
Ethiopia stretches forth to thee her hand.

"Extend to her the aid her cause requires,
Incline her way to where kind Hope inspires.
.   .   .   .
"She seeks no claim but what is hers by right,
The same as thou dost give unto the white.
.   .   .   .
"For thy care were both by Nature lent,
And both alike should feel thy moral bent,
Both formed thy bulwark since thy life began,
And both together still must work thy plan."

Margetson's method of composition is interesting. He works as a stationary engineer and composes most of his verses in the midst of his daily tasks, often singing them, and seldom committing them to paper till he is fully satisfied with them.

connection with any of the corresponding ones among the other race. There are six lodges of Odd Fellows in Greater Boston, with a membership of about 600. Two of those in the city proper own, subject to a small mortgage, a hall which has been assessed at $25,000, and several of those in Cambridge hold joint title to a building valued at $7000. The six together have in their treasuries funds amounting to $20,000 or more. The auxiliary women's order has four lodges, with a membership of about 500.[1] The Masons also have six lodges, with a membership of approximately 450; which, with the customary higher-degree organizations drawn from them, have on hand savings close to $15,000. The rapidity with which this fund has grown in recent years is shown by the fact that, whereas a decade ago one lodge had next to nothing in its treasury, to-day it has about $4000.[2] The National Grand United Order of Brothers and Sisters of Love and Charity has six lodges, with a membership of about 600. There are seven or eight small lodges of the Independent Order of St. Luke, with a total membership of about 200. In this order, every cent taken in goes to the national headquarters at Richmond, while all the money dispensed comes from that central source. Whenever a member in any part of the country dies, all the members are taxed half a penny. There are two lodges in Boston, with about 75 members, of the fraternity known as the True Reformers, which also has headquarters at Richmond, and which is one of the

---

[1] The Household of Ruth.

[2] The women's auxiliaries of the Masons are the Heroines of Jericho and the Order of the Eastern Star.

most successful national organizations among the Negro people. The Improved Benevolent Order of Elks (white Elks please take notice of the word "Improved"!) have three lodges, with a membership of about 250. The Knights of Pythias have four societies. The Foresters have a strong association. All these organizations, as well as a few other similar ones of lesser importance, bestow sick relief ascending from $4 to $7 a week for the first six weeks, and from $2.50 to $5 a week thereafter, and death benefits of from $50 to $150. In view of the facts that their collective membership is approximately 3500, and that a majority of the members represent family groups consisting of several persons, it is evident that, in their relief of distress caused by sickness and death, they must reach a large percentage of Boston's Negro population.[1]

Of the societies which have as their chief object social service of broader scope than mutual aid, and extending beyond their own membership, the great majority are composed of women. The work which these local organizations are doing is, moreover, part of a large national movement of Negro women for the betterment of the conditions of their race, of which Boston was the source and is to-day one of the most active centers.

In 1892, the Woman's Era Club was founded in Boston by Mrs. Josephine St. Pierre Ruffin, the widow of Judge George L. Ruffin, to whom previous reference

[1] There are also many purely local organizations of a combined social and beneficial character, such as the Fraternals, the Unity Club, the Benevolent Fraternity of Coachmen, the Head and Side Waiters' Association, and the Sons of North Carolina.

has been made as a man of prominence among his
people in the period following the war.[1] This club,
which is still in existence, adopted as its stated purpose
the furtherance of the welfare of the Negro race generally and of Negro women in particular. Its meetings
have been held twice a month, and its membership is
about 60, including nearly all the leading Negro
women of Boston and vicinity. Its prestige was recognized by its being received into both the state and
national federations of women's clubs of the other
race. It very soon succeeded in arousing a wide interest in practical measures of betterment, and in 1895,
a national convention of Negro women was called to
assemble in Boston. On August of that year, in the
Charles Street African Methodist Church, the National
Federation of Afro-American Women was organized,
with Mrs. Ruffin as president. In July, 1896, this body
united with the Washington National League to form
the present National Association of Colored Women.
In June, 1896, was launched the New England Federation of Women, which within two months outgrew its
New England bounds and became the Northeastern
Federation of Women's Clubs, which to-day has a
membership of over 2000. The Federation has departments devoted to work among children, mothers'
meetings, education, philanthropy, arts and crafts,
temperance, the prevention of lynching, and other
similar matters. It publishes the "Northeastern," a
quarterly in which the work being carried on in various
localities is recorded. The National Association has

[1] For reference to Mrs. Ruffin's own part in affairs both before and
after the war, see Appendix, Article III.

similar departments, and both bodies are rapidly uniting the Negro women of the country in a correlated programme of amelioration.

In the Greater Boston district, there are to-day about twenty women's clubs of a social service nature, with a total membership of about 750. The general character of their activities is indicated by extracts from several typical reports published in the "Northeastern."

The Women's Protective League of Malden writes: —

We have been able to place in the bank more money this year than in any of the previous years. Twelve new members have been installed; we have given ten dollars to Rev. Carrington's church; smaller donations have been given to the sick, and we have aided St. Monica's Home. The young ladies of the league have opened an industrial department.

The Cambridge Charity Club reports: —

The membership has been increased from twenty-five to fifty. [Three months later an increase of ninety-six was recorded.] A committee was appointed whose duty it was to locate the needy poor and assist them as far as our means would allow. Thirty dollars has been expended in this manner. We have had a flower committee, which has done excellent work. We have donated five dollars toward defraying expenses for defending the soldiers in the Brownsville affair; five dollars toward the ice chest in St. Monica's home, and eight dollars toward the educational fund to be used for the benefit of Miss Davis. Juvenile Circle No. 1, consisting of thirty children, has been organized, and our committee hopes to report great success in this new line of work.

The Sojourner Truth Club of Boston makes this statement: —

We have conducted a very successful class of boys and girls in sewing, knitting, and millinery. At Christmas-time, we had a very heavily laden tree for our children and distributed clothing, material for useful garments, and other things. During Old Home Week we worked with the General Committee in doing honor to this occasion, and distributed two thousand flags and post-cards through the hospitals of the city, and in children's homes.

As the funds of these societies are derived from dues, which generally do not exceed twenty-five cents a month, and from occasional entertainments, it is apparent that the work carried on must of necessity be of humble proportions. But the spirit which animates it is the simplest, truest, and best; each club is a center of good influence and an example inviting emulation, and the members are disciples of the gospel of social helpfulness. For several years there has been a movement looking toward the ownership of a building, to serve as a common meeting-place for the Negro women's clubs of greater Boston and a center for their philanthropic and educational activity.[1]

With the Negroes there is a closer approximation to equality between the sexes than is yet the case among those of the other race. That this is so is, in the writer's opinion, due mainly to special economic conditions. In the stern struggle for a foothold in which the Negroes have been engaged since their emancipation, and especially since the recent hardening of public sentiment toward them, the women have perforce become bread-winners to a very large degree. Thus they have made a relatively greater economic contribution within their race than have white women in theirs,

[1] Among the women at present most actively devoted to this work are Miss Eliza Gardner and Mesdames Hannah C. Smith, Charlotte E. France, Agnes Adams, Olivia Ward Bush, and Minnie T. Wright.

and so they have attained to a place of relatively greater importance in the social order of their own community. Negro women manifest a marked independence, coupled with a sober realization of the extent to which the welfare of the race is in their hands. Negro men recognize and respect their position. The women take and are given a very important share in race affairs. More fully than the men, if anything, they exemplify the qualities of patience, hope, and determination. The writer has in fact heard many Negro men declare that to-day it is the women who are leading the race in its struggle for better things. Here is surely fertile soil for cultivation by the equal suffragists: — on the one hand, a special need for the leavening and uplifting influence of the suffrage movement; and on the other, the certainty of a ready response.

With regard now to the general results to which the various ameliorative factors and activities which have already been described have contributed, one of the most noticeable of these is the marked development of the Negro community in self-support. The substantial progress which has been made in this respect is shown by the small and constantly decreasing extent to which the Negroes fall into the hands of public and private charity. According to the National Census, in the decade 1870–80, while the Negro population of Massachusetts increased from 13,947 to 18,697, the Negro paupers in state institutions increased only from 73 to 78; and in the decade 1880–90, while the Negro population increased to 22,144, the number of Negro paupers in institutions did not increase at all. The Massachusetts Census of 1895 showed that in that year, when the Negroes formed 1.1 per cent of the population of the state, of the 11,054 paupers in institutions or cared for by private families, only 164, or 1.5 per cent, were of this race. In view of the special adversities under which the Negroes live, this showing was remarkably favorable. The extent to which the Negroes take care of themselves appears still more clearly in the light of a table compiled by the Associated Charities of Boston in the early nineties, giving causes of poverty, on the basis of 7225 specific individual cases, with reference to the various racial elements. Of poverty due to personal misconduct, the percentage was lowest in the case of the Negroes; whereas with poverty caused by misfortune, the percentage was highest among them; and still higher, relatively, as regards the particular misfortunes of sickness or death in the family.[1] It is a fact that seldom does one find a Negro begging on the streets. The members of this race possess in high degree the quality of human kindness, and are ever ready to help their fellows in time of need. One outward sign of this is had in the numerous socials and entertainments which are constantly being given for the benefit of some household that has suffered affliction. The increasing ability of the Negroes to provide for their own needs in ways material, goes to counterbalance, in some measure, their previously noted dependence on the other race, and is, moreover, but one of many evidences of their growth in general self-reliance.

One of the central elements of the social progress which has already been made, and one of the surest

[1] For the table in full, see Appendix, table xv.

guarantees that this progress will continue, is the marked improvement which has been affected in home conditions. As will later appear, a constantly increasing number and proportion of Negroes are acquiring the ownership of homes; and a still larger proportion are becoming able, though still tenants, to live in a comfortable and homelike way. Though these facts do not take long in the telling, they signify much. Ownership and permanency of residence are, in fact, developing the qualities of responsibility and stability of character in the individual, and at the same time promoting sound conditions in the neighborhood and the community.

All through the social life of the Negro, as overtone and undertone, runs the never-ceasing discussion of the future destiny of the race. Among white people this is one of the questions which arouses much interest; but with the Negroes it is the all-absorbing and all-dominating theme. Even those who profess a desire to minimize and ignore race distinctions, nevertheless, by the vehement assertion of their doctrine on the slightest provocation, do as much or more than others to keep alive the perpetual query, which will not down. In all the talk "about it and about" there is much uncertainty, much discouragement, and some despair. But there is vastly more hope and trust and confidence. The conviction has constantly grown upon the writer that the Negroes themselves understand their own conditions far better, when all is said, than do the whites. Their deepening comprehension of these conditions is accompanied by a growing determination and an increasing power successfully to cope with them.

Every day the will to advance is taking on greater strength.

At the same time the Negro people are becoming ever more fully conscious of themselves as a fellowship and of their collective potentialities; and what is most significant and promising of all, are acquiring a deeper and stronger race consciousness and the rudiments of a genuine race pride. The two Negro newspapers, the "Guardian" in Boston and the "Advocate" in Cambridge, are, by their weekly recording of local activities among this element of the population, continually making the Negroes in the Greater Boston district better acquainted with one another and thus binding them more closely together as a single community. At the same time, by their discussion of public affairs which especially concern the race, they, together with over two hundred other Negro newspapers and periodicals published in the United States, are furthering the national unity of the Negro people. The many organizations of which examples have been cited, with their membership drawn from diverse parts of the Boston district, are having a similar effect. The most discerning of the leaders are instilling the "get together" spirit. A particularly important factor, moreover, which is working to enhance national race consciousness, is the celebration of events vitally related to the Negro's history in America. The birth anniversaries of Lincoln, Whittier, and Douglass, the issuing of the Emancipation Proclamation, and many other events of similar significance, are appropriately commemorated. The most important recent celebration was that of the hundredth anniversary of the birth of Garrison, to which two entire days, December 10 and 11, 1905, were devoted. Thus a groundwork for the eliciting and instilling of a real pride of race, which, as has already been emphasized, is one of the most indispensable elements to the Negro's advance, is being laid; and almost unconsciously, such a pride in racial history and attainment is beginning to take form. This is all that can as yet be said, but this much is fundamental and pregnant with possibility.

The independent advance of the Negroes is both accompanied and still further evidenced by their increasing participation in the affairs of the community at large. For instance, James H. Wolff, a veteran of the war and a man of prominence among his people, was in 1906 elected head of the Massachusetts Commandery of the Grand Army of the Republic, in which all but a slight proportion of the members are white; and in 1910, he was appointed by the mayor to deliver the city's official Fourth of July oration.[1] William H. Lewis, to whom there have been several earlier allusions, was a charter member of the recently established City Club, and was one of the speakers at the great memorial mass meeting held at Symphony Hall on the occasion of the death of Julia Ward Howe. Probably the most striking example in this connection, however, is that of the civic prominence of Theodore H. Raymond in Cambridge.[2] The latter is one of the directors of the local Y.M.C.A., recently served as

[1] This appointment was conferred by Mayor John F. Fitzgerald, a Democrat. For further reference to Wolff, see Appendix, Article III.

[2] Mr. Raymond is a grandson of the Rev. John T. Raymond of Abolition days, for further reference to whom see Appendix, Article II.

chairman of the special committee in charge of the
erection of a new building, and also acted as treasurer
of the building fund of the Y.W.C.A. He is treasurer
of the Prospect Union, — a sort of people's forum with
class and club features, — is a leading member of all
the principal civic organizations, and president of the
corporation organized last October which publishes the
only daily paper in that suburb. In short, he is a living
refutation of the complaint that color prejudice is an
insuperable obstacle to a Negro's success. He is a
flesh-and-blood demonstration of the fact that, at any
rate when ability, attractive personality, refinement,
and tact are present, the color of a man's skin will not
and cannot keep him from rising to his proper level.

These, moreover, are but a few of the most striking
instances of general influence exercised by persons of
the Negro race. Cases which approximate to them
could be multiplied indefinitely. The sum of them all,
however, is that the Negroes are forging ahead not
only among themselves, as a people bound together by
ineradicable racial ties, but also as a determining
factor, individual and collective, in the whole community.

Nothing could be more unquestionable than that the
inherent weaknesses, and the adverse past and present
conditions, which have retarded the Negroes in their
social advance, must have kept them back in their
ethical progress as well, and have entered with serious
directness into their everyday standards of morality.
When it is considered that the ancestors of the American Negroes of to-day were taken from a state of primi-

tive savagery, and were then for two and a half centuries subjected to a condition of slavery which kept them in ignorance, treated them as mere beasts of burden, disregarded their personal chastity and marital allegiance, fostered bestiality, and utterly deprived them of all opportunity for independent endeavor and achievement; when it is considered also that these conditions passed away less than fifty years ago, and that during the period which has since elapsed the great mass of the race have continued in their benighted lot; — when these things are taken duly into account, it would surely be a miracle, contrary to the natural and accustomed workings of the laws of cause and effect, if the Negroes of to-day were not morally backward. Close acquaintance with the facts makes it plain beyond a doubt that such a miracle has not taken place. To go into any extended citation of figures to prove that there is a more pronounced tendency to immorality and criminality among the Negroes than among the whites would be superfluous. That such is the case may be, and indeed must be, presumed.

According to some recent statistics, 203 out of 6041, or 3.3 per cent, of the convicts in Massachusetts were Negroes, while members of this race formed but 1.1 per cent of the state's inhabitants:[1] that is, the proportion of Negro convicts was three times the proportion of Negroes in the population. In view, however, of the past and present forces inimical to the Negro's moral welfare, this record of crime is far less unfavorable than would be expected, and should not in fact be taken as bearing witness to any abnormal criminal propen-

[1] Massachusetts Census, 1895.

sity. If the Negroes were of an exceptionally criminal bent, such an innate proclivity, combined with the social and economic adversities with which they have had to cope, would make their percentage of convicts much more than three times as large as their percentage of the population.[1]

As regards crimes against the person, in general, the Negro's inborn good nature acts as a preventive

[1] Most discussions of this subject leave out of account altogether the peculiar conditions to which the Negroes have been subject and those under which they are living to-day. Many simply enlarge on the extent of immorality and criminality among the Negroes without making any comparison whatever with the extent of the same evils among the whites. Some are nothing more than lurid recitations of particular acts of immorality and crime, lacking even the suggestion of general proportion. It is very easy by the narration of such particular acts or crimes, especially if uncommonly brutal ones are selected, to make upon the hearer's imagination an utterly false impression. Not only in the case of the Negroes, but in the case of any element of the population, would this be an easy thing to accomplish. Indeed, a Negro need only clip from the newspapers, for a week or two, the accounts of atrocious crimes committed by individuals of the white race, to be able to go among his ignorant brethren in the Southern black belt and make them believe the whites to be fiends incarnate. When particular acts of immorality and crime committed by Negroes are exploited, each one should properly be balanced by the citation of similar acts committed by members of the white race. When what purport to be general figures of the extent of immorality and crime among Negroes are given, these figures should be carefully compared with corresponding figures for the whites. It will usually prove that the proportion is much less excessive among the Negroes than might at first sight seem to be the case. And finally, after such a comparison has been made, the conditions which have retarded the ethical development of the Negroes should be given due weight. It will then become evident, as in the case of the Massachusetts figures already referred to, that the proportionate extent of immorality and criminality among the Negroes is far less than might be presumed. In other words, the outcome of the comparison will be rather to the Negro's credit than to his discredit.

influence. His lesser degree of the trait of economic acquisitiveness operates to reduce his temptation to theft. Neither of these characteristics, however, is such as to have any appreciable restraining effect with reference to illicit sexual relations, but, on the contrary, especially in the case of the former, tends if anything to make such relations easier. And the Negro's shortcoming in point of morality in fact shows itself most flagrantly in proneness to extreme sexual laxity. This is inherently a matter concerning which it would be next to impossible to gather statistical data at once trustworthy and of any value for purposes of comparing conditions among the Negroes with those among the whites. But it is a matter with respect to which common report, though considerably exaggerated, is nevertheless confirmed in substance by scrupulous observation. The laxity in question, however, does not appear so much in the form of any outright sexual viciousness or confirmed depravity, as it does simply in that of an innate weakness or failing. The impression made upon the observer is not that the Negroes, proceeding with at least ordinary appreciation of what is right and what is wrong in this respect, nevertheless willfully and pervertedly do the wrong; but, on the contrary, that with very inchoate and undefined conceptions of sexual rectitude, and mostly as the result of ignorance coupled with a deficient power of resistance, they simply follow their animal-human instincts. This view of the matter is borne out, on the one hand, by the rarity among the Negroes of houses of prostitution; and on the other, by the comparative yieldingness of the common bars to intimacy between

the sexes, which in itself constitutes a lesser motive for
the maintenance of such resorts. This lax condition of
things applies not alone to the unmarried element.
There is also a want of rigidity within the marital state.
It is a fact that a considerable number of Negro men
and women are living together, as husband and wife,
without legal sanction. In a large proportion of such
cases, however, the relationship is practically equivalent to marriage, so far as its permanence and assumption of family responsibilities are concerned, and the
individuals are only in minor degree conscious of serious transgression on their part.

Thus it is not out-and-out immorality, but rather
the want of any positive morality, which characterizes
the Negro. This lack, showing itself most flagrantly
in connection with relations between the sexes, where
the term "moral" has come to be more narrowly applied, amounts in its broader manifestation to a general ethical undevelopment. Though after the present
survey of the Negro's situation on all sides has been
completed, more will be said with regard to the deep-
reaching significance of this deficiency, enough has
already been said to make plain its inter-relation with
all the Negro's past and present social conditions.

Out of the social the ethical naturally rises. The
whole ethical code consists in fact of a definition of the
mutual relations and common standards which are
indispensable to a sound social order. If, then, as previously stated, the factors which have been adverse
to the Negro's social well-being have at the same time
retarded his ethical development, it is, on the other
hand, equally true that the Negro's social progress

implies, and must indeed involve, his ethical advance. So close is this inter-relation that many of the gains which have been described as social might no less properly be set down as ethical. Such is particularly the case with the inner strengthening of the Negro home, the work of neighborhood amelioration undertaken by some of the Negro societies, and all efforts toward the subordination of personal and factional interests to organized collective endeavor for the common good. Furthermore, in view of what has already been stated concerning the betterment which is being accomplished in these vital respects, it almost goes without saying that the laxity in moral conduct to which allusion has been made does not apply indiscriminately to the entire Negro population. On the contrary, just as gradations have been distinguished with reference to economic-social conditions, so likewise may be perceived roughly corresponding ethical layers. And in proportion as the whole Negro community builds itself up in the one regard, so it must surely rise to a higher level in the other. A double, and still inherently single, process of social construction and ethical growth is now under way.

CHAPTER VII

THE UPWARD STRUGGLE OF THE NEGRO CHURCH

SOME of the other humiliated peoples find both a source and bulwark of racial coherence and dignity in their religion. Such is the case with certain of the foreign groups who take up their abode in America. The Polish immigrants, for instance, seeking escape from oppression in their native land at the hands of alien governments, make their immemorial church of the Roman Catholic faith the starting-point and center of their life in the new world. The almost indispensable nucleus of every Polish colony in this country consists of a priest and a meeting-place for religious devotion. Clustering about the church edifice the settlement gradually extends, till ere long there is need for other churches, which in their turn bring still further growth. In the course of years there stretches out a close-packed, monotonous expanse of humble wooden cottages; from among which, however, stand forth great stone church-temples, with towers high rising toward the heavens, as though indeed to symbolize the aspiration and potentialities of the people from whose individual mites, collectively amassed, these splendid structures are erected. The preëminent example of religious unity is, of course, that of the Jews. In their synagogues the descendants of Israel find solace for their tribulations, strength for their daily encounters, and hope and inspiration for the future.

What might such religious solidarity do for the Negro; and in what measure is it, in fact, manifest? Is the religious life of the Negro people subject to such cross-currents and undertows as those which, it has appeared, retard his social progress? If such be the case, is a similar centripetal forward movement nevertheless discernible? Beyond this, and more specifically, how far are religious forces and activities being organized in practical ways and for practical ends, with reference to their strengthening effect in the Negro's concrete problems?

Turning now to these inquiries, it appears that the religious life of the Negroes has three avenues of expression. The first is through attendance at white churches. The second is through missions established and supervised by whites, but set aside exclusively for Negroes. The third is through their own separate churches.

As has already been noted, the Negroes in Boston attended white churches for a long time before they had any of their own. In the earliest days, while slavery was still in existence, they were restricted to a gallery, like the one which may still be seen in the Old North Church. After slavery died out, this restriction also passed away, and the Negroes sat among the whites, generally as servants in the family pews; but to some extent, particularly in the case of those following independent callings, on a basis of apparent equality.[1]

Then, after one hundred and sixty-eight years, the first independent Negro church was founded. Its estab-

[1] Phillis Wheatly, for instance, to whom earlier reference has been made, was a member of the Old South Meeting-House.

lishment was due not primarily to any positive movement toward a policy of exclusion on the part of the
whites, but rather to the increase in the number of the
city's Negro inhabitants and the gradual rise of a
community of interest among them. Since that time,
the great majority of this element of the population,
partly of their own accord and partly because of the
prevailing attitude of the other race, — of which more
will presently be said, — have gone to these separate
churches of their own.

Nevertheless a considerable minority, for one of
several reasons, or a combination of them all, attend
white churches instead. Among these, the group
which stands out with chief distinctness is composed of
some of the most uncompromising of those members of
the race who insist on the importance of equal privilege, and who profess to be opposed to all racial segregation. This group has its historical origin in the
Abolitionist propaganda. Garrison himself advised
the Negroes against forming separate churches, and
Frederick Douglass exhorted his people to intermingle
with the other race in religious activity.[1] To-day, most

[1] In 1874, Garrison deprecated the attempt of the Negroes in a
town near Boston to start a church of their own, as establishing "a
precedent which logically ends in indorsing the old pro-slavery doctrine that there should be no fraternization between the two races
on account of color." *William Lloyd Garrison*, vol. IV, p. 239.

In the same address at Rochester, New York, in 1848, from which
previous quotation has been made (see chapter IV), Douglass
said: "I am well aware of the anti-Christian prejudices which have
excluded many colored persons from white churches, and the consequent necessity for erecting their own places of worship. This evil I
would charge upon its originators, and not upon the colored people.
But such necessity does not exist to the extent of former years.
There are societies where color is not regarded as a test of membership.

of the Negroes who adhere to this doctrine in practice
are members of what has already been designated as
the upper class, who are generally characterized by a
considerable strain of Caucasian blood and by lightness
of complexion. Probably a majority of this class, indeed,
attend white churches, so far as they go to church at
all. They contend that in religious worship, surely,
racial prejudice should not be tolerated, and maintain
that drawing the color line here has the effect, identical
with that of the emphasis of color difference at other
points, of encouraging general segregation and perpetuating race hostility. Negroes who desire to contribute to the solution of the "problem" should, in their
opinion, regard it as a matter of duty to attend white
churches. Many go so far as to advocate doing away
altogether with the separate Negro churches. An additional argument which they advance is that individuals
of whatever race must seek and find their proper intellectual level — which they themselves cannot do
among their own people. It should be noted, however,
that this group is considerably overlapped by another,
made up of members of the "smart set" to which
reference has been made in an earlier context, and who,
notwithstanding any professed loyalty to principle, as
a matter of fact frequent white churches chiefly because of the higher position which they think to gain
thereby in — "society."

Many Negroes become connected with white
churches themselves, but to a larger extent send their
children to them, on account of the actual superior

And such places I deem more appropriate for colored persons than
exclusive or isolated organizations."

advantages which they believe white churches afford, in the cultivation of good manners, intelligence, and character. Still others go to white churches either because they have a particular admiration for the pastor, or especially friendly relations with some of the members, or because they live in neighborhoods where there are few or none of their own race, or, at any rate, no Negro church in the vicinity. Finally, a certain number of Negroes are obliged to resort to white churches for the simple and sufficient reason that the religious creeds which they profess are not represented by separate Negro churches. The more recent and less common denominations, such as Christian Science, Swedenborgianism, Spiritualism, and the various brands of New Thought, fall in this category. Because such religious fellowships are still in the zealous propagandist stage, they are more disposed to accept conversion to their tenets as the essential thing, and to pay less regard to race or color distinctions. The Negroes who enter these faiths are as a rule received on a cordial and substantial basis.

Most of the white churches in Boston are attended, at least occasionally, by a few Negroes belonging to one or another of these groups which have been described; but the number in which the regular Negro attendance amounts to more than a slight percentage is very small. Usually a congregation of ordinary size includes only two or three of this race. In not more than a score of churches in the entire metropolitan district may a dozen Negroes be counted regularly. There are only five or six in which the regular Negro attendance attains really considerable proportions. Among these few exceptional cases, the Roman Catholic Cathedral and two Episcopal churches stand out most prominently.

It is a fact not generally known that the Roman Catholics lay claim to about one thousand members of the Negro race in Greater Boston. The majority of these are immigrants or children of immigrants from the West Indies; others became of this faith through receiving their education in Catholic schools; still others are descendants of slaves of Catholic masters; and the remainder are converts in the ordinary course. Till recently, all the Negro Catholics have attended the same services as the whites, without distinction, and the largest single group of them have gone to the Cathedral in the lower South End. In 1903, at the request of many of the Negroes themselves, the experiment was begun of holding at the Cathedral some separate masses. In 1907, this plan was given up, chiefly because the attendance at the separate masses remained small. Late in the following year another departure, which has proved more successful, and of which more will subsequently be said, was undertaken. It consisted in holding certain separate masses in a church set aside for the use of the Negroes. The latter still have unqualified access, however, to the general services elsewhere, which most of them continue to attend, at least occasionally. No serious friction has developed, though in several churches, in addition to the Cathedral, the Negro attendance is of considerable size. It is, of course, natural that less difficulty should arise in churches of the Roman Catholic faith. The priests stand in a position of greater authority and influence over the lay members than do the ministers of Protestant denominations, and are thereby able more effectually to curb any expression of prejudice. The Negroes on their side appreciate the more equitable treatment thus received. Moreover, the Catholic doctrine, in its strongly personal embodiment of religion and its definite and tangible dogmas; the direct challenge of the confessional; and the impressive church buildings and rituals, — all make a powerful appeal to the Negro's emotional and out-flowing nature. In Boston, as throughout the country, the number of Negro Catholics is increasing. That further accessions from this source are desired is shown by the fact that in the autumn of 1908 the Roman Catholic Church in the United States organized a special department to deal with the extension of work among the Negro people.

Emmanuel (Episcopal) Church is situated in the heart of the aristocratic Back Bay, and has one of the largest and richest congregations in the city. Of late years Negroes have been attending in increasing numbers. There are two distinct church organizations, one for members of the parish and the other for the public at large. The Sunday services are open to the general public, but at these the Negro attendance has somehow not become large enough to be conspicuous. Two Sunday-school groups are maintained, however, and for all week-day services the parish and public organizations meet separately. In the parish organizations, only a scattering few Negroes are found. But in the public organizations about one third of the adults are Negroes, as are also nearly two thirds of the children in the public Sunday school. The whites with whom they are intermingled are members of the lower middle class; and thus far they have raised no serious objection to the presence of the Negroes. Doubtless the fact that these white people are not members and supporters of the church, but are themselves, like the Negroes, beneficiaries of it, tends to restrain them from expressing any antipathy which they may feel. The Negroes, who come from far and wide, not only from all sections of the city but from the suburbs, are, furthermore, very well dressed and good mannered, and are thus less likely to cause objection than others of lower grade would be.

The Church of the Ascension, a mission of Emmanuel, whose social service activities have already been mentioned, was established in 1886 in the Pleasant Street locality, but in 1890 moved to its present location at the corner of Washington and Newcomb Streets in the upper South End, near the northeast corner of what is now the principal Negro district. At that time this particular neighborhood was almost entirely white. But soon Negroes from the West End and elsewhere started to come into the vicinity, and it was not long before some of them began to attend this church. To-day, of about five hundred and fifty communicants, approximately fifty are of the Negro race. The proportionate attendance of Negroes at the services is sometimes greater than this, sometimes less. Occasionally, when the Negroes have been more conspicuous than usual on account of sitting together in clusters, or at times when the proportion of this element has appeared to be increasing, murmurings have arisen among the whites, but on the whole there has been little trouble. In the Sunday school, a quarter of the children are Negroes. Those in charge say the number would have been much larger, and that friction would have resulted, had not a rule been made that children whose parents are connected with other churches should not be admitted.

There is probably a larger number of Episcopal churches which have some Negroes on their rolls than is the case with any other denomination. The Episcopalians, in fact, report nearly fifteen hundred Negro adherents, — of which, however, about half belong to the Mission of the Society of St. John the Evangelist, previously mentioned in connection with social service, and to whose religious work separate reference will presently be made. A great many, though not the majority, have antecedents in the Church of England, being from the West Indies and Canada; others have come under influences similar to those mentioned in the case of Negro Roman Catholics; while a large proportion go to Episcopal churches for the same non-religious reason that many whites do, — because they think it savors of distinction. By 1904 the Negro attendance at Episcopal churches had increased to such an extent that complaints began to be made by the whites, and in certain churches serious friction threatened. In May of that year the Convention of the Diocese of Massachusetts appointed a commission to investigate the desirability of instituting separate missions for the Negroes. The most important parts of that commission's report, made in May, 1905, are as follows: —

The commission finds that there are over thirty churches in the Diocese having colored people on their list of communicants. In most cases the numbers are small, but several report from fifty to one hundred and fifty in attendance.

Bearing in mind that God hath made of one blood all nations of men to dwell on the face of the whole earth, and that the Christian Church stands for universal brotherhood in Jesus Christ, the commission believes that the Church should extend its already effective work among the colored people of this Diocese. It is unanimously of the opinion that, though they are sometimes peculiarly isolated because of surviving racial prejudices, they should be reached through the same moral and spiritual agencies as other people.

It recommends that the clergy and laity of all parishes and missions in the Diocese make special efforts to reach their colored neighbors.

The Convention showed its agreement with the commission by adopting the following Resolutions: —

That the clergy and laity of all parishes and missions in the Diocese should make special efforts to reach their colored neighbors. That both clergy and laity should make a firm and aggressive stand for the principle of a fair chance for every individual.

This remains the official Episcopal attitude. But though it is true that as a rule churches of this denomination accord the Negro better treatment than do those of other Protestant creeds, the writer is, however, aware of no Episcopal church, with the possible exceptions of Emmanuel and Ascension, already mentioned, the members of which actually "make special efforts to reach their colored neighbors," and to bring them in on the same basis with the whites. Episcopal rectors do not hold the same position of immediate authority over the lay members of the church as do Catholic priests, and so, in the matter of the attitude

toward Negroes, prejudice on the part of the whites has
less difficulty in asserting itself. As a matter of fact,
this prejudice is asserting itself, and in a number of
churches serious embarrassment has arisen.

In the case of one of the latter, St. Peter's in Cambridge, affairs reached a crisis. Since 1900, the increase
of Negroes in this church had been rapid. As there is
only the single parish organization, the Negroes had to
be accorded privileges in common with the whites. In
the Sunday school there were no separate classes, and
some of the mixed classes had Negro teachers. In 1906,
some of the white parents began to object to this condition of things. As a result, a new rector who came in
at that time separated the Negro and white children
in most of the classes, putting each under teachers of
their own race. This action offended the Negroes, who
raised the cry of "Jim-crowism," and refused to be
conciliated by the assurance that they still enjoyed
benefits identical in kind with those of the whites, and
that, besides, there were still a few mixed classes. Soon
afterwards a Negro boy was expelled from the church
for mischief-making. The Negroes took this as an
affront, and manifested their indignation by remaining
away from the services. A meeting of the church, including the Negro members, was then called to discuss
what action should be taken. At this meeting the
assistant rector — inadvertently, it is said — made the
remark that he thought the white church members
would be glad if the Negroes should withdraw altogether and form a separate church of their own. This
gave still further offense. Though the vote of the
meeting was to continue as before, every one expected

that "something would happen" soon. What did happen a few months later was a request from the Negro contingent that they might have a church by themselves. No objection being made by the whites, St. Bartholomew's Church, previously a mission, was turned over to them. This was in 1908. Only a few Negroes still continue to be members of the parent body.

This case has been related in some detail because, in a representative sense, it is significant of a general tendency toward the effectual, if not the open and avowed, exclusion of this race from white churches. White ministers say that the objection to the presence of Negroes comes from the laymen. It does, in fact, usually originate with the latter, but the clergymen appear to give at least tacit sanction. It is, indeed, a fact, that Negro ministers make far more effort to preserve and inculcate in their people a Christian attitude toward the white man, than white ministers do to inspire a like attitude toward the Negro. Pastors of the Negro race could make themselves most dangerous incendiaries, were they so minded; but nearly all of them choose instead to preach endless patience and unbounded charity. On the other hand, it is seldom that a white minister refers from the pulpit to the question of the Negro's welfare, and when one does it is usually to some far-off phase of the "problem," rather than to the immediately pertinent consideration of how the white people in Boston should conduct themselves toward the Negro people who are right in their midst. In this city, as elsewhere, the church is making comparatively little effort to contribute to the bringing about of better relations between the two races. The people who make up the churches are, of course, members of the general community and subject to its shortcomings. It therefore follows that, as a prejudice against the Negroes exists in the community at large, the same prejudice enters into the churches, and affects even the pastors — the assumed leaders in holding up the ideals of church brotherhood.

It is interesting, in this connection, to set in contrast the treatment accorded white visitors in the Negro churches, and that which is meted out to Negroes in most white churches. In the one case, as soon as the white visitor enters the door of the Negro church, several ushers hurry up to him with a pleasant welcome and conduct him to one of the best seats. The faces all about him are friendly and smiling. At the close of the service many cordial nods are given him; the leaders come up to tell him that they are glad he dropped in, and that they hope he will do so again. The chances are the minister will shake hands with him and repeat the invitation. Such complaisance may, of course, run over into obsequiousness. But, withal, the visitor must surely be thick-skinned if he does not feel the glow of human fellowship. Perhaps he may reflect that these people could readily enough find justification for treating him otherwise. And he may be led to conclude that this race affords rather good material for genuine Christianity, a Christianity of the heart as well as the head. When, however, the tables are turned, what usually happens? A Negro, as soon as he steps inside the door of a white church, must be impervious if he does not become aware of a decided chilliness in the atmosphere, dim-eyed if he does not see glances far from friendly turned upon him, and dull-eared if he does not detect in any words which may be addressed to him the notes of perfunctoriness and displeasure. He is given a seat in the least conspicuous place. Then he is still embarrassed by having people pass by the pew where he has been put, and he finds himself left with abundance of elbow room unless the church is closely packed. As he goes out after the services, members of the congregation do not greet him cordially and shake hands with him. He is not asked to stay to any after-meeting, or to come again.

Because of this prevailingly inhospitable attitude toward the Negroes, on the one hand, and on the other, the fact, of which more will subsequently be said, that the independent Negro churches are gradually getting a stronger hold on the race, the general tendency at present is toward a distinct decrease in Negro attendance at white churches. A contributory element in this result, however, is the further fact that comparatively few of the Negroes who have been going to white churches have made any decided effort to become active, helpful members, and to contribute to the advancement of church work according to their ability. Most of them have taken a merely passive part. They have, therefore, laid themselves open to the criticism of being of no effect from the point of view of practical religious endeavor. This rebuke has been the more justifiable in that a large proportion — probably the majority, indeed — of the Negroes who have dropped out of white churches have not then become connected with churches among their own people, but simply have not gone to church at all.

Underneath this main tendency, however, is a sub-current, which, though of very minor volume, is nevertheless too real and important to be left out of account. There are a considerable number of Negroes, each one constituting an exception to the general rule, who after what may be considered a period of probation are received into white churches cordially. Such individuals come to be liked and respected, and, on their side, manifest an earnest desire to be of use, and do in fact render valuable service in aiding to conduct the various church activities and in contributing generously from their usually slender means. Those of whom this is true may be considered as constituting the really substantial and durable element in the connection of Negroes with churches of the other race. Their number, though still comparatively slight, is slowly but surely increasing.

Occupying a position midway between resort of Negroes to white churches, on the one hand, and maintenance of their own independent churches, on the other, stand missions established and directed by the whites, but set aside exclusively for the Negro race.

Reference has already been made to the action of the Roman Catholics, in 1908, in instituting separate masses for Negroes. These are held in a church formerly vacant, St. Patrick's on Northampton Street, at the northern boundary of the principal Negro district. A white priest is in charge.[1] Inasmuch as thus far only

[1] There are at present only two or three Negro Catholic priests in the United States, but a small number are now in training. In Africa, where many successive generations of the race have grown up under the Roman Catholic Church, native priests are gradually being installed as subordinates.

certain services are observed in this separate meeting-
place, it can as yet hardly be called a full-fledged
mission church for Negro Catholics, but it will probably become such provided the latter give evidence of
their ability to maintain it. This they have already
done to the extent of undertaking to acquire ownership
of the land and edifice.

The most fully developed Negro missions, however,
are those conducted by the Episcopalians. The establishment of St. Augustine's Mission in the West End
in 1885 by the previously mentioned Order of St. John
the Evangelist, more commonly known as the Cowley
Fathers, marked the beginning in Boston of such religious work among the Negro population on the part of
the other race. Following the migration of the Negroes
to the South End, in the latter nineties, two additional
missions were established; — St. Michael's in the
lower South End, and St. Martin's on Lenox Street in
the upper South End, in the principal Negro district.
St. Michael's was abandoned in 1907, and in 1909, St.
Augustine's and St. Martin's were united in the present
large building erected on the latter site. About eight
hundred Negroes are connected with this institution.
The teaching is intense and stringent, and the attitude
of the Fathers toward the Negro people is one of
paternal character. The work is supported mainly by
local contributions, the Negroes themselves contributing a large if not a major part. Though the mission is
independent of the jurisdiction of the Diocese, the
Cowley Fathers have close relations with the Diocese
and take part in its conventions. The commission
appointed by the Diocesan Convention in 1904 to look

into the question of establishing Negro missions, from whose report earlier quotation has been made, recommended also "that generous moral and material support be given the missions under the Society of St. John the Evangelist by the churchmen of the Diocese," and the Convention itself adopted an identical resolution. An arrangement has been made whereby the Diocese has agreed to institute no other Negro missions within a wide radius of St. Augustine's and of St. Martin's. That agreement gives the Cowley Fathers a right of way which will materially help them in the extension of their own work; but, considering the location of the chief Negro quarter, it is a distinct obstacle to the promotion of other similar work by the Diocese.

St. Bartholomew's, the offshoot of St. Peter's in Cambridge whose origin has already been related, stands on the border-line between a Negro mission and an independent Negro church. Strictly speaking, it is an autonomous mission ultimately subject to the control of the Diocese. The use of the church building and the parish house is contributed by the Diocese, and a part of the rector's salary is paid by the Archdeaconry. But as respects immediate control and assumption of the greater part of its running expenses, St. Bartholomew's is essentially a Negro church. Its enrolled membership has grown to several hundred, and the average attendance reaches two hundred or more. The majority of members are of the better element of the Negroes and appear to be earnest in their desire to build up a strong church. The present rector is a young Negro of good education, who has had some previous experience with missions among his people.[1]

[1] The Rev. Walter D. McClane.

If St. Bartholomew's proves a permanent success, as it now bids fair to do, it will no doubt be referred to by the other race, and in some measure by the Negroes themselves, as an argument in favor of the establishment of similar churches for Negroes by other denominations, as well as by the Episcopalians.[1]

Coming now to the principal, and by far the most important, avenue of religious expression which the Negroes have, we find the separate and independent churches which they themselves maintain.

The first Negro church in Boston was founded in 1805, as has been related, under the name originally of the African Meeting-House, and was of the Baptist confession. Not many years afterwards, a Methodist church was established. The fact that the latter was included within the general (i.e., the white) Methodist organization, perhaps furnished the occasion for the elder church to take the name of the First Independent Baptist; while in the course of time it became popularly known as the old Joy Street Church, and later still its name was changed to that of St. Paul's Baptist, which is its present form. During the Abolition period, an African Methodist Zion church was founded by Negroes who withdrew from the Methodist body, an African Methodist church was set up by another group of secessionists, and a schism in the old Joy Street congregation resulted in the formation of the Twelfth Baptist

[1] A step in this direction has in fact been taken in the recent opening of a Negro Unitarian society under the fostering care of the general Unitarian organization. The meeting-place is Parker Memorial, and a Negro minister, the Rev. Powhattan Bagnall, has been installed. This undertaking is still, however, in a very experimental stage.

Church.[1] Since the war, owing to the growth of the Negro population, the moving of Negroes into new localities, and the rise of suburban communities, many other independent churches have been created. At present there are twenty-five in the Greater Boston district, of which eleven are in Boston proper, five in Cambridge, two in West Newton, two in Malden, and the others in Woburn, West Medford, Winchester, Everett, and Chelsea. Of these twenty-five, seventeen are Baptist, three African Methodist, one African Methodist Zion, one Methodist, one Congregationalist, one Seventh Day Adventist, and one of a sect which styles itself the Church of God.[2]

The local order of precedence of these denominations may be said to correspond with that in the country at large; the Baptists almost equaling in number the combined total of all the others. The proportion of Negroes of Southern birth is at its highest in this confession. The Baptists and Congregationalists, like their white confrères, have complete local self-government, the ministers being elected and dismissed by the church members. The several divisions of Methodists have limited self-government, to the extent that their min-

[1] For exact dates of the founding of these churches, and references to their early ministers, see Appendix, Article ii.

[2] The names of these churches are as follows: In Boston proper: — Calvary, Morning Star, and Ebenezer (Baptist); St. Mark's (Congregational); Seventh Day Adventist; and Church of God. In Cambridge: — Union, Mt. Olive, and St. Stephen's (Baptist); Rush, and St. Paul (African Methodist Episcopal). In West Newton: — Mt. Zion, and Myrtle Avenue (Baptist). In Malden: — Union, and Ebenezer (Baptist). In Woburn: — St. John's (Baptist). In West Medford: — Shiloh (Baptist). And Baptist churches in Everett, Chelsea, and Winchester.

isters, whose regular term of service is but two years, are appointed and removed by a district conference of the denomination. The African Methodists and the African Methodists Zion are, as has been noted, off-shoots of the Methodists, but are entirely discon-nected from the latter, as well as from each other, in their organization. The Methodists among the Negro people, though having their separate congregation, are, as has been said, a part of the general Methodist body, and so have no independent organization.

As to the balance pro and con with respect to the Negro Church, the factors on the debit side consist partly of certain inherent elements of weakness in the Negro character, and partly of certain phases of the conditions from which the Negroes have come and those under which they are living in Boston to-day.

With reference to the innate characteristics in ques-tion, the one of most distinctive influence, and in fact the only one to which previous reference has not been made in connection with more broadly social ten-dencies, is a propensity toward uncontrolled emotional-ism. The other traits whose effect in religious activity is most obvious, are the already noted general ethical undevelopment of this race, and its deficiencies in point of self-reliance and the ability for organized social coöperation. Regarding the conditions involved, it ap-pears that the proportion of Negroes who have come to Boston from the South is even larger within the churches than it is in the city's Negro population as a whole, amounting to nearly four-fifths of the church membership. These Southern immigrants are, there-fore, mainly responsible for church management and support. They are, however, as has previously been stated, poorly equipped in education, and generally backward. Their earnings are usually not much above the amount needed for subsistence, and their work consumes the greater part of their time and energy. They are almost entirely lacking in business experience; though a church, on the material side, is virtually a business enterprise. All these adverse factors, it is clear, must severely limit the progress which the Negro churches are able to make. Specific reference to the local situation will show in what ways and to what extent such is actually the case.

In most of the Negro churches in Boston, the propensity to emotionalism appears only in a form much modified by the Northern environment, but there is one in which it has free rein. This is the congregation of the "Church of God, Saints of Christ," which meets on the corner of Shawmut Avenue and Woodbury Street, in the principal Negro district. It is one of a score or more in the United States belonging to the same sect, all founded by a self-announced Negro "prophet," by the name of William Crowdy. "Prophet" Crowdy, who died a few years ago of paralysis, had been a cook; but, according to his own testimony, he had revealed unto him his special divine mission, and thereupon proclaimed that he had come to save the world, beginning with the Negroes. His followers refer to a passage purporting to be from the Scriptures, and predicting that when the true prophet appeared, he would come "out of the pots." Crowdy, by virtue of his previous culinary occupation, therefore fulfilled the requirements. The writer had the honor

of meeting the prophet, who proved to be a very black
Negro, with white hair and mustache, something wrong
with one eye, and corpulent. He established the Boston church about ten years ago. "Elder" Plummer, a
gaunt, tall Negro, known in the faith as "Father
Abraham," is in charge. The congregation is composed
of about fifty individuals who are drawn from the most
ignorant class and who lead a sort of communistic life.

Services of one sort or another are going on at the
church — which is a room over a grocery store — most
of the time, but especially on Saturday, the "seventh
day," and Sunday. The writer has attended several
services. The procedure of one Sunday morning may be
given as typical. As soon as four or five of the members had arrived they fell to singing, without books,
their peculiar, long-drawn-out, monotonous hymns.
These are most rudimentary in phraseology and ideas,
the stanzas often differing only in a single line, and
an identical refrain usually recurring at regular intervals. One of these refrains, so far as it was possible
to catch the words, was as follows: —

> "God was a man,
> God was a man,
> God was a man,
> And the Lord God was his name."

Another appeared to run thus: —

> "Teach all the nations Thy commands,
> Teach all the nations Thy commands,
> Teach all the nations Thy commands,
> For the coming of the Judgment Day."

Each newcomer at once joined in the singing. The
songs were started in moderate tones; after a time would
rise, sometimes by degrees and at other times with

startling suddenness, to a full shout, and then, toward
the end, — an indeterminate point finally arrived at
when every one was fully satisfied, — would subside
to a hum or a hoarse whisper. When one song was
finished, another would immediately be started, without any prearrangement, by some one of the congregation. The singing continually grew in volume and
intensity. Soon the singers were marking the beat by
the clapping of hands. Then feet as well as hands were
brought into action. The rhythm became almost irresistible, even to an outsider. Ere long the members began, one by one, to stand up, in order to secure greater
freedom of motion. At length all were on their feet,
beating their hands, stamping, turning, and twisting,
and going through all sorts of fancy movements, each
according to his preference and capacity. Off in one
corner, a row of little tots, their heads scarcely rising
above the seats, were bobbing up and down in perfect
time. One old fellow, the most powerful-throated of
the company, kept yelling, "Sing it! Sing it!" At
length a young woman, good-looking and well-dressed,
emerged from the others and began a violent dance,
bending her knees, throwing up her arms, and bringing
one foot down with great force at alternate beats in
the singing. She continued this until completely ex-
hausted. Then the singing gradually ceased.

Next came "testifying," by the members. As each
one got up he would say something like this, to the
accompaniment of a sympathetic running comment
from the others: "Members er der Church er God and
Saints er Christ — I wants ter say I's glad to be here
on dis first day er der week. Bless der Lawd, befo' I

heared der Prophet's voice I didn' know dis was der first day er der week — I done thought it was der las' day. Doncher know, I's sho now dat I's saved. Der Prophet done tol' us so — Bless der Lawd"; and so on. After the giving of testimony was completed, "Father Abraham" arose to preach. At first he was hesitating, dull, even cold, but soon he began to speak faster and louder, and to stamp about on the platform, till by the time he was well under way he left nothing to be desired in point of vehemence. His discourse was entirely without any semblance of reasoned order, being a hodge-podge of laudation of the prophet and exposition of his teachings. Every other sentence contained a quotation from the Bible, located with extraordinary accuracy by chapter and verse. The apostles were referred to familiarly as "Ole John," "Ole Peter." Incidentally, the preacher demonstrated by scriptural quotations that Christ was a Negro. After he finished, the singing started up once more, and when the writer finally left, a little before one o'clock, the end was still in the distance.

This is an extreme example — for Boston — of the Negro's exhibition of uncontrolled religious emotionalism. Yet even in this case, the underlying religious energy is accomplishing some good results. The material progress of this particular church has been rather remarkable, considering the fact that all of its members are by occupation odd-jobbers with meager earnings. The church owns, subject to a mortgage, a large frame building which is used as a home for widows and orphans, and in rented quarters profitably conducts a grocery store, a dry goods shop, and a restaurant.

Apart, moreover, from what may be their own peculiar mode of life and moral standards, as among themselves, the members of this sect in Boston have the reputation of being law-abiding, industrious, and honest in their relations with the rest of the community.

The second element which has been mentioned as handicapping the Negro in his practical religious endeavors, namely, his moral and ethical undevelopment, rises up to face him in the personal character of the men who occupy the pulpits of his churches. A considerable proportion of these Negro ministers — at least one quarter of them — are patently lax in their morals, and the good name of the majority is not free from more or less suspicion. The most unsavory recent case in point was that of the pastor of a suburban group of Baptists, who was proved to have had illicit relations wholesale with women, especially young girls, both within and without his congregation. This man was brought to justice and sentenced to the House of Correction. There are others like him, whose evil-doing is equally well known, but who have thus far escaped the penalty. Most of them are ignorant and incompetent floaters and hangers-on, hailing from parts none too certain with credentials none too reassuring, and getting along prosperously with so little visible means of support as to warrant grave question as to their mode of living — which, according to report, consists largely in exploiting the pocketbooks of weak "sisters." Many of these fellows start so-called "missions." Some of them find a chance to preach in regular Negro churches now and then, and sometimes they succeed in imposing themselves upon such a congregation permanently. Other culprits, of a higher grade so far as intelligence and outwardly respectable standing are concerned, combine with their corruption, as weapons of offense and defense, education, ability, and suavity of speech, and are intrenched behind the pulpits of some of the larger churches. One of this sort — a fat, sleek individual, at present connected with one of the leading Negro congregations in the city — makes a special practice of approaching white candidates for office and offering, in return for a substantial consideration, to deliver over Negro votes.

Far more serious, however, than the immorality of these pulpit reprobates themselves is the tolerance of it and of them by the members of their churches. "Like priest, like people," is the obvious implication, and while the facts are not quite so bad as that, it is at least a case of living in glass houses. The ethical undevelopment of the race shows itself nowhere more obviously than at this point. Their moral perception is dull; they do not fully realize the obliquity of having a minister of easy morals as their accredited leader. This is especially the case if the man in question be a stirring preacher, and popular. And when they do realize, they still lack the moral backbone to come out openly against the offender. One suave individual whose gross immorality was a matter of common knowledge, nevertheless kept himself for many years in one of the large city churches. It would have required only some courage to convict him before the public. Now and then half-hearted and cautious protests were made, but there was no determined effort to dislodge him. This man has now passed to his reward. Two other ministers brought upon themselves charges which, though not entirely proved, were so damaging that the good name of the churches involved should have made their resignation imperative. Both these men, however, continue to occupy two of the most important pulpits among their people. The members of these congregations murmured, it is true, but they did not rebel. Neither have the better Negro ministers nor the better element of the Negro community risen in revolt against this state of affairs.

The further hampering characteristics of lack of self-reliance and incapacity in social organization, operating in conjunction with the comparative absence of business experience, to which also reference has been made, are reflected in the financial condition of the Negro churches. Only one of them is entirely free from debt. Several are not seriously encumbered. But the majority are beset by debts which, in proportion to the material means of the church body, are simply enormous. In most instances this indebtedness was incurred within the last fifteen years, when the present church edifices were bought. Previously, most of the churches in the city proper occupied land and buildings in the West End, which they had purchased in the early days at small cost; but when these congregations moved to the South End, they either sold their former buildings or turned them over in part payment for the new ones. Whether they sold or traded, however, they were usually worsted. For the new buildings they paid much more than their value in the open market — sometimes twice as much. In addition they bound themselves to pay interest far in excess of the prevailing rate. These damaging transactions were, in a few cases, due partly to a conspiracy for personal profit; between the minister or some of the members, or both together, on the one side, and the white sellers and mortgagees, on the other. In recent years, there have been several exposures of such diversion of church funds to private use by ministers and church officers, and undoubtedly much further dishonesty has escaped detection. But for the most part, the great financial difficulty which the Negro churches have experienced, even in meeting interest payments, has been due simply to business incapacity on the part of both the church members and the ministers. Want of business initiative and aggressiveness has kept the Negroes from obtaining, to the extent which otherwise they might have, a reduction in the exorbitant interest rate, while lack of foresight and of a carefully worked-out application of available funds has proved a terrible obstacle to the cutting-down of the debt. The keeping of systematic records of receipts and expenditures is exceptional, and in consequence a considerable leakage of church moneys is more than possible. One of the Negro pastors who worked hardest, while he was in Boston, to improve the financial situation of his church, acknowledged to the writer that at the outset the meetings of his business committee well-nigh took all the heart out of him, they were so unbusinesslike.

As a result of all these adverse elements combined, no Negro minister or Negro church has in recent years won in the community at large a commanding position of respect and influence for good. While such a position would be harder to attain to-day than it would have been prior to the change of attitude toward the Negro race, yet the essential reason why it has not been attained is that the requisite merit has not made itself manifest. A recent pastor of one of the larger Negro churches was on the way to acquiring such a standing, when he left the city under somewhat of a cloud. With eloquence, this man united rare charm of personality, education, and intellectual ability. He was invited to speak at important meetings in the community, and was consulted by the whites on matters affecting his people.

So much for the debit side of the account. Passing now to the credit column of the balance-sheet, it is a fact that notwithstanding the weaknesses which have been pointed out, and which are so glaring as to obscure the more favorable features, the Negro church has already attained many fundamental elements of strength, and is at present making still further underlying progress.

To begin with, the Negro's propensity to emotionalism has another and deeper side, which is altogether in his favor. This was forcibly expressed by one of the speakers at a recent convention of the American Missionary Association, himself of African descent, who declared that "the Negro has religiousness enough to save America." [1] Doubtless the tropical African habitat bred in the Negro race a warmth of religious feeling. The natives of that continent, how-

[1] This statement was made by Professor William Pickens, a graduate of Yale, now teaching in the South.

ever, do not stand out so conspicuously in this respect, as compared with other primitive peoples, as do the members of this race in America, when compared with other elements of our country's population. The high degree of development of this quality in the American Negro is largely an outgrowth of the conditions which prevailed under slavery. Rigidly limited in all other directions, the slaves found full self-expression only in their religion. Their bondage, their ignorance, and their superstition, on the one hand, combined with their hope of freedom and their sturdy sense of innate manhood, on the other, united in impelling them to seek fulfillment in the religious outlet. At night, when they were supposed to be in bed, they used to slip away to some secluded rendezvous, and there pray and sing and give themselves over without restraint to their pent-up feelings. In such secret congregation they found solace for their sufferings, comfort in their sorrows, hope for deliverance, and patience for endless endurance. During the period of slavery, at least, religion was the Negro's "mighty fortress." The religious experience which the slaves underwent was, in spirit and in kind, like that undergone centuries ago by the early Christians in the Roman Empire. To-day religious fervor, of which such uncontrolled emotionalism as that exhibited by the "Church of God" is but the ignorant outpouring, still remains one of the most impressive characteristics of the Negro people. This fervor, rightly directed, cannot but prove an asset of the greatest strength to the race. It is itself, indeed, the central motive power of religious endeavor and achievement.

That the aberrant display of emotion is in fact held
well in check in nearly all the Negro churches in
Boston has already been remarked. The advance
which has been made in this respect is especially pronounced. At present Negro congregations are in the
main noticeably self-restrained. In former years, what
may be termed the dress-parade collection was regarded as an indispensable feature. This was a procedure in which, to the accompaniment of lusty music
from the choir, the members, as the spirit moved
them, went forward and deposited their offering on
a table placed before the pulpit. This gave the fem-
inine portion of the congregation an excellent opportunity to display new gowns. It was also effectual in
swelling the size of the collection. In a majority of
the Negro churches, nevertheless, this custom is now
being abolished.

Paralleling the ascendancy of higher forms of religious expression among the church members, thus
indicated, is a decided improvement in point of education and intellectual standards on the part of Negro
ministers. To-day there is comparatively little of the
"shouting" and "exhorting" of days gone by; on the
contrary, there is a far larger measure of intelligent
appeal to reason and common sense. There are more
and better Negro theological schools than there were
fifteen or twenty years ago. Most of the ministers of
this race in Boston have received their education either
at such schools or, in some cases, at white institutions
of recognized standing.

The progress which is most difficult to discern in
the Negro churches is that pertaining to standards of

morality. The scandals to which reference has been made have a very discouraging effect, not only upon white people who want to help the Negroes, but still more noticeably upon the Negro people themselves. A minister whose character is above reproach remarked to the writer, "Why! I almost feel ashamed to appear on the streets in my clerical garb and to be recognized as a Negro clergyman." The very fact, however, that the Negroes are conscious of the disgrace thus brought upon them is one of the most hopeful elements in the situation. In spite of the recent unsavory record in this respect, moreover, it is a fact that the Negro community is to-day more sensitive to moral delinquency on the part of its ministers than it has been in the past, and that in general the moral standards which it applies to the churches are higher. Though it is true that most of the delinquent pastors have continued to hold their pulpits, it is also true that to-day there is more open discussion of this bad state of affairs, more protest against it, and more determination to remedy it, than there has ever been before. A fact the significance of which does not appear on the surface is that the scandals have occurred chiefly in Baptist churches. Now it must be taken into consideration that, as stated at an earlier point, each Baptist church is completely independent and subject to no control from without. For this reason, it is sometimes extremely difficult for the members to dislodge a bad minister, even when a majority of them genuinely desire to do so. In various ways the culprit, with a few trusty allies to lend assistance, is able to obstruct measures aimed against him, while at the same time gathering in new members pledged to his support. This is, indeed, the method that has usually been followed. In one church, the opposition to the pastor became so strong that finally a vote was passed calling upon him to resign. But by cunning manipulation he and his adherents actually obtained a subsequent vote declining to accept his resignation. There have been two recent cases, however, in which guilty ministers have actually been forced out. One of these was that of the suburban Baptist church, previously mentioned, where the commitment of the offender to the House of Correction was the final result of charges lodged against him by members of his own race. The other case occurred in a Zion African Methodist church, protest on the part of the better element among the members being carried into effect by the denominational district conference. These two instances of effective protest against pulpit corruption afford hope for a more general demonstration to the same end on the part of the better element of the Negro people.

It is unfortunate in this connection that the average white person's impression of Negro ministers is formed from occasional contact with, or, still more commonly, rumors and newspaper reports about, those of the worst sort. A white clergyman once said to the writer, with reference to one of the Negro pastors of the better type, "It is a pity that white people do not come into contact with Negroes like him. He is one for whom I have as deep a respect as for any white man — a fine, clean, intelligent Christian gentleman." At least a quarter of the Negro ministers merit equal commendation. These men are pastors in the original simple

sense of that term. They live in the midst of the
"common people" of their race. Their salaries have
not yet reached a point which permits them to view
the struggle for existence impersonally and compla-
cently. Not only their sympathies, but the facts of
their own daily life, render them keenly alive to the
hardships of their fellows. Their churches are not so
large, prosperous, and well organized as to allow them
to dispense funds and give orders from a comfortable
desk chair. They verily do their work and earn their
bread in the sweat of their brows. As the needs of their
people are simple but real, the help which they give is
homely but true. One Sunday morning the writer
chanced to attend the church of a minister of this
sturdy mould. A deacon was speaking from the pulpit, bewailing the "terrible conditions" of the Negroes,
calling them "a people without a home, a race without
a country," and urging colonization in Africa. When
he had concluded, the pastor himself rose and thus
quietly expressed his own attitude: "Our brother's
heart is full this morning. He has given us much to
think about. But I do not agree with all he has said.
I think the United States is the home of the Negro.
He has been here nearly three hundred years, and is no
longer a foreigner. He has become a taxpayer and a
voter. He is in the professions and in business thousands strong. His situation is, indeed, bad in many
ways, but it is far better than it might be, and it is
improving every day. I did not intend this morning
to speak about our conditions, but I cannot let you
leave this service without giving you a hopeful view of
the future. For many years I have watched the prog-

ress of my people, and I want you to know I am
optimistic." Negro ministers of the stamp of this man
are receiving increasing support from the better class
of the Negro community, and are being held up as
examples with growing respect. They are coming to
be accorded a position of relatively greater influence
among their people than used to be the case in the
past, when the minister's personal character was in
fact given far less thought than his capacity to exhort,
and on occasion to quote Latin or some other language
which the congregation could not comprehend. All of
which surely bears witness to the development of
higher religious-moral standards.

Viewing the situation on the more material side, the
mere increase in the number of Negro churches in Boston, from five at the close of the war to twenty-five
to-day, — the simple fact that these churches have
been organized and maintained, — is in itself significant of religious progress in the rough. The Negroes
have held to their churches with remarkable tenacity.
Though there have been instances of churches going
unused for a time on account of internal dissension,
financial inabilities, or other causes, there have been
but few cases of permanent abandonment. In addition, the church buildings are to-day larger, more
attractive, and more comfortably furnished than ever
before. In most of the churches the membership has
been steadily growing. The Charles Street African
Methodist, for example, added, in the three years
1908–10, 369 new members, which, allowing for those
who dropped out, meant a net gain of about 250. In
approximately the same period, the Sunday school

grew from 162 to 548. As this is next to the largest Negro church in point of membership, its recent gains are somewhat above the average. That similar growth is general, however, is shown by the record of the Calvary Baptist Church, one of the smaller ones, which in 1903 had only 95 members, while in 1910 it had over 300.

Though, as has been said, the majority of the churches are still heavily in debt, it is at the same time true that a majority are making progress in reducing their debts. The Zion African Methodist Church, for instance, assumed a debt of $59,500 in 1903 when it purchased its present edifice. Since then it has paid off $28,500 of this debt, which as a result stands to-day at $31,000. What a highly creditable achievement this has been appears when the material means of the church members, on the one hand, and, on the other, the regular yearly expenses of merely keeping the church going, are taken into account. This congregation includes about 635 members, of whom more than ninety per cent are of the laboring class, and not far from two thirds women. The present annual expenses, exclusive of any payments on the principal of the debt but including interest, amount to about $6000. This has meant an average contribution of at least $9.40 from each member. When allowance is also made for frequent extra collections taken up in behalf of Southern schools, for money expended in the relief of distress, and for disbursements in other directions, as well as for miscellaneous individual contributions for special cases of which no stated account is kept, the yearly expenditure per capita must be set at well above $10. That the members, in spite of the meagerness of their earnings, give this much on the average each year to their church, is a performance which merits high praise in itself — not to mention paying $28,500 in eight years on the accumulated debt besides. The pastor states that there have, indeed, been occasions when each man and woman has had to sacrifice the wages of an entire week. Nor is this particular church exceptional in this regard; in most of the others equal sacrifices are being made and similar results are being accomplished. The members of Negro churches undoubtedly contribute several times more money, in proportion to their means, than church members of the other race.

So long as the Negro churches continue to be debt-ridden, it is hardly to be expected that charitable and social betterment work, of the character to which white churches are devoting such marked attention and for which there is the utmost need in the Negro community, will exceed very modest proportions. For the most part the church activities do not extend beyond the narrower religious limits. Yet the progress which is being made in the new direction is substantial. The church which is doing most along these lines, and whose example may be cited as indicating what an increasing proportion of the others are in lesser degree attempting, is the Charles Street African Methodist, already referred to in another connection. The fact that its debt amounts only to $7000 at five per cent interest puts this church in a favorable position to extend its usefulness. There are senior and junior boards of stewardesses, and also a board of deaconesses, which

have as their special function assistance of the poor
and needy. The collections of the first Sunday in each
month are turned over to the senior stewardesses, who
expend about $500 a year in relief and help. The
junior stewardesses, besides paying all the interest on
the debt, make charitable use of over $200 a year, and
the deaconesses of about $300. In this church are also
a number of well-to-do individuals who assist generously in cases of need which cannot be met with the
collective funds. Still more important than the money
expenditure, however, is the genuine, earnest personal
thought and service which are devoted to these hopeful out-reachings in directions of community uplift.

The sociability and associativeness which are inherent in the Negro nature are fundamental assets for
organized religious progress. White ministers find
themselves obliged to keep up an unremitting effort to
popularize their churches, and those who succeed are
regarded as having accomplished something remarkable. Negro ministers are generally free from this
burden, for with this race going to church is popular
beyond any possible doubt. The majority of the Negro people, kept hard at work through the week, find
the church the best place at which to meet their
friends and exchange the latest news. The Negroes,
too, even as others, like on Sunday to show their
best clothes and to inspect those of their neighbors.
Moreover, the music, especially the congregational
singing, together with all the emotional stimulation
connected with the services, appeals strongly to their
responsive natures.

While these various attractions help to swell church

attendance, a deeper element of strength consists in the traditional place of primacy which the Negro church has occupied in the life of this race since its emancipation. The churches were the Negro's first, and in the South for many years their only, institutions. They were the centers of organization, not only for religious objects, but for all purposes. To-day they still retain the major part of this unique significance. Previous remark has been made of the fact that in Boston the social progress of the Negroes has not yet reached the point of producing full-fledged institutions, with domiciles of their own. This statement should, however, be amended by the qualifying clause, "outside of the churches"; for the latter constitute a most important exception to the rule. They provide the largest, most comfortable, and best equipped gathering-places of their own which the Negroes have. Meetings of many different kinds are held in them. Consequently they fulfill relatively a far larger general function in the Negro community than do white churches in the white community. This explains why, as previously noted, the Negro churches both followed and furthered the migration of this race from the old West End colony to the South End. So far as concerns a certain unquestioning acceptance of spiritual authority, the attitude of the mass of Negroes toward their ministers approximates, moreover, to that of the mass of Roman Catholics toward their priests. The substance of the whole situation was compressed in a remark which one of the Negro pastors made to the writer: "Take their churches away from the Negro people," said he, "and you pull down the mainstay of their social order."

That there is a distinct and well-grounded movement among the Negroes toward a deeper realization of the central and vital importance of the Negro church, not only in its religious but also in its social and ethical value, is the fact which holds out fullest promise for the future. Though some small gradual increase may be expected in what has been called the substantial and exceptional part of Negro attendance at white churches, the unsubstantial major part of that attendance will in all likelihood continue to diminish, for the reason, principally, that these Negroes themselves will come to see that their position in white churches is lacking in dignity and practical effectiveness, and that they are not deriving therefrom a sufficient increment of solid satisfaction. Missions for Negroes, under the direction of the other race, will doubtless hold their own and may considerably increase their following. These serve a useful intermediary function between the white church, on the one hand, and the Negro church, on the other; at once relieving the former of possible embarrassment and friction, while exerting an influence along educational, disciplinary, and generally preparatory lines, among certain elements of the Negro race not yet arrived at a point qualifying them for independent organization. But when all is said, the fact that such missions inherently suggest racial dependence will limit their acceptability to the Negroes in general. The independent Negro church, in spite of all its present shortcomings, is nevertheless the natural and logical medium of religious expression for the Negro people. And the Negroes are in fact rallying around their church. As yet this movement is most clearly observable among the sturdy rank and file, as should and indeed must be the case if the church is to get its essential grip on the mass of the race. At the same time it is also true that, to a very appreciable extent, the middle and upper classes are either being aroused from hitherto complete indifference to religious forces, and brought into active connection with the churches of their own people; or, in the case of others, converted from their previous futile efforts to gain standing in white churches. The Negroes of these higher gradations in the economic-social scale are bringing to the service of the Negro church not only the increased material means and some degree of the practical business experience which are almost indispensable factors in its progress, but also superior education and refinement, and generally more advanced standards. They are the element who should be the natural church leaders, and they are now in fact entering upon the exercise of such leadership. They are helping to put the churches on a sounder financial basis, are strengthening their moral tone, and gradually are building up a more efficient religious organization.

When, then, full account is taken of these innate elements of strength and this underlying progress, it is evident that an affirmative and favorable answer must be given to the broadly fundamental questions which were proposed at the outset, with reference to the religious factors in the life of the Negro people. It appears that the Negroes are, indeed, applying their religious resources in more practical ways and to better purpose; and that, furthermore, a fundamental tendency toward religious coherence and solidarity, in and about the Negro church, is clearly manifest among them. The Negro community is, in short, bringing religion more effectually to bear in the betterment of its conditions and in the solution of its problems.

CHAPTER VIII

THE LEVERAGE OF THE BALLOT

THE Negro's most direct means of safeguarding and promoting his well-being, so far as these ends can be accomplished through law and public action, is had in his possession of the ballot, with its accompanying privileges and powers. In the use which he makes of the ballot, moreover, is to be found the most immediate and specific test of his interest in the welfare of the community at large, and of the character and tendency of his own contribution thereto. Such being the case, certain general inquiries suggest themselves as having pertinence and importance in this connection.

First, from the broader point of view of the whole community: Does the Negro take advantage of the right to vote, and does he manifest an active concern in political affairs? In other words, is he of merely negative, or of positive, political effect? If positive, then does his influence count on the side of ignorance or of intelligence, venality or honesty, degraded politics or good government? Is there any marked tendency, either downward or upward, in these respects? Secondly, from the point of view of the more or less distinct interests of the Negro himself: Have the Negroes turned the ballot to good account in their own behalf? Have they come to have a fuller and more intelligent appreciation of its potential value as a practical means for achieving desired ends? Have they profited by their numbers to combine and organize for political purposes? Have they manifested any measure of political self-reliance and independence as a racial group? Have they, finally, as a total result, succeeded in obtaining a substantial political footing in the community, and in making themselves a recognized factor in the affairs of the body politic?

Previous note has been made, in connection with the general narrative, of the outstanding features of the Negro's political history, from early days down to the time of the recent change of front toward this race on the part of the whites, the crucial stage of which was roughly marked by the year 1895. Before proceeding to take account of the subsequent period, however, it will be serviceable, as affording historical background and perspective, briefly to review the salient points of the preceding political development.

The right to vote has apparently been possessed by the Negro in Boston ever since the test case of the Cuffes which arose in 1764; and, at any rate, has clearly been his since the adoption of the Body of Liberties of 1790. But prior to the Abolitionist agitation, the proportion of Negroes who exercised this right was practically negligible. That campaign of propaganda, however, maintained for over thirty years, awakened the majority of the Negroes to a realizing sense of their citizenship; while in the endeavor to put strong anti-slavery men in office they found a sufficient inducement to make their votes count. Yet before the war the Negro's participation in political affairs went no further than voting or petitioning. With a single exception, to which reference has previously been made, they held no public positions, either elective or appointive; for the reason, mainly, that nine tenths of their race in the country at large being still held as slaves, friendly sentiment had not, even in Boston, reached the point of elevating them to office.[1]

Through the conventions and committees of Abolition days, however, the Negroes gained considerable experience in methods akin to those of politics, which subsequently gave them greater confidence in advancing their claims. After the war they of course expected to be of more political consequence. But whatever effort they exerted on their own behalf was of secondary importance and effect, for they were immediately made the protégés of white friends and enthusiasts, at whose hands they forthwith became recipients of bountiful patronage. During a period of twenty years at least, the outflowing favor of the other race was the potent factor in the appointment of Negroes to many respectable posts and in their election to the City Council and the State Legislature. Not till about 1885 did they themselves reach the point where, by virtue of having become so numerous in the West End as to comprise over half the voters in the Republican majority of old Ward 9, they were in a position effectually to demand representation. But though thereafter their numbers constituted the most apparent reason for their political prosperity, the continued though diminishing favor of the whites was still its underlying cause.

In 1895, as has also been previously stated, the city

[1] The single exception referred to was that of Lewis Hayden's messengership in the office of the Massachusetts secretary of state.

underwent a political redistricting.[1] Ward lines were altered to the form which they have to-day. As a result the Negro colony in the West End was split in two. A small portion of it was put into the present Ward 8, the rest into the present Ward 11. In Ward 8, which from the beginning has been controlled by the Democrats, the Negroes became, politically speaking, a negligible quantity. Though in Ward 11, which was even more strongly Republican than former Ward 9, they formed a large and, for a few years, increasing element, their proportion among the voters of that party was reduced from the fifty per cent or more of former Ward 9, to less than fifteen per cent. Thus was undermined whatever political strength they had acquired or were on the way to acquiring through mere force of numbers in that section. This mischance was coincident, in point of time, with the decisive formation of the new attitude toward the Negro, one of the principal elements of which has been the withdrawal from this race of that special favor and indulgence which prevailed during the earlier post-bellum period. Though in political affairs this reaction of public opinion with respect to the Negro did not at once become fully manifest, it was by that time, nevertheless, predetermined and under way. As, therefore, the year 1895 marked a general realignment of conditions, by which the Negro has been forced back upon his own resources, it ushered in an order under which he has been compelled to look out for himself in a political way. Thus it is from that year, and not before,

[1] Such redistrictings are made from time to time on account of increase and shifting of population, and annexation of new territory.

that the political record of the Negro, on his own feet and in his own right, really dates.

What has that record been, and what are the elements which have entered into and determined it?

The most obvious index to the political standing of any particular group in the community consists of the number and importance of elective offices obtained by members of that group. In the absence of special sentiment, election to office implies either public approval on a basis of substantial merit, effective political organization, or, as usually holds true, a combination of both these elements. The application of this test to the case of the Negroes will, therefore, afford some introductory evidence, at least, as to how the latter have fared, on the political side, during the recent period.

Immediately preceding the redistricting to which reference has been made, and in line with the previous long-standing policy, a Negro, William L. Reed, had been elected as a representative in the Legislature from old Ward 9, for the year 1896. He was reëlected from the present Ward 11 for the year following, out of regard for the custom of allowing each man to serve two terms. But the next year both the representatives from that ward were white. Reed was the last of his race to be elected to the Legislature from Boston proper, terminating the long line which had begun in 1866. In the case of the Common Council the Negro vote was still reckoned of sufficient importance to let the Negroes continue to have one of the ward's three members of that body.[1] Meanwhile, however, the

[1] For list of Negro common councilmen down to 1895, see chapter III. Just before the redistricting of that year, Stanley L. Ruffin

emigration of the Negroes away from the West End had been going on rapidly, with the result of still further reducing their proportion of the voters in that section. That decided the matter. Thereafter, it was only the influence of long custom, and the good-will of the white Republicans of the ward, which kept a Negro in the Council; and in 1908, the representation previously accorded this race was finally discontinued.

When the Negro colony in the West End was beginning to diminish, the colony in the lower South End, about Pleasant Street and in the adjoining district, included in present Ward 10, was, as previously noted, in the ascendant. That ward, too, has always been preponderantly Republican. By 1898, the Negroes formed over fifteen per cent of the Republican voters. Five years earlier, as already mentioned, they had first been given one of the councilmen. From that time, with brief lapses, this representation was continued.[1] About 1900, the proprietor of a so-called

had been reëlected for a third term from former Ward 9, and thus served through 1896. A lapse of a year intervened; then from the present Ward 11, Edward H. Armistead was elected, and served for the three years 1898–1900. He was succeeded by S. William Simms, who served for the four years 1901–04. The latter, a janitor by occupation, was an interesting character and a favorite among his white colleagues. He was of a pious turn of mind, and used to take it upon himself to rebuke any of his fellow-members who indulged in profane or irreverent language. When the meetings were opened with prayer, he was frequently called upon. He was followed by Dr. Isaac L. Roberts, one of the leading Negro physicians, who served for the four years 1905–08.

[1] The pioneer, as mentioned at an earlier point (cf. chapter III), was Charles H. Hall, who served for the four years 1893–96. His successors were: 1898, David R. Robinson; 1900–01, Osborn A. Newton; 1903–06, Charles W. M. Williams; 1908–09, J. Henderson Allston.

"club," which holds a license to sell liquor, became the Negro "boss" in the ward, being recognized as such by the white "boss." Whatever this man's alleged shortcomings in other respects may be, he must at least be given credit for much more political sagacity and ability than most of the Negro aspirants for leadership. Largely through his exertions the Negro voters in the ward were so well organized, and made to contribute so substantially to Republican intrench-ment in that quarter, that there appeared to be a prospect of having a member of the race elected to the Legislature. A semi-agreement was formed with the local white politicians that the Negro councilman from the ward, whose fourth consecutive term expired in 1906, and who had shown marked capacity, should be selected for this promotion. But for various reasons, among them the lack of sufficient insistence on the part of the Negroes, this result was not brought about at that time; while the previously mentioned tend-ency toward a decline in the Negro population of that section has forestalled its subsequent realization.

In 1909, the Common Council was abolished by the adoption of the present city charter. It so happened that Ward 10's Negro representative in the Coun-cil that year, J. Henderson Allston, was the senior member of that body, by virtue of his former election from old Ward 9 in 1894. In that capacity it fell to him to preside at the opening session. This was the first time that a Negro had performed that function. Allston's brief remarks to his colleagues were the sub-ject of favorable comment. "Allow me to felicitate you," he said, "upon your election to a seat in the

Common Council in the great city of Boston. It is, indeed, a very high privilege to be entrusted thus in part with the preservation and destiny of a city so rich in the traditions of all that mankind loves to honor and revere. And need I add that it is my sincere desire that this year shall prove to each and all of us a period of boundless happiness and prosperity? That we shall honorably demean ourselves here, so as to show our gratitude and to merit the approval of those whom we have the honor to serve, will be only in keeping with the exalted traditions of our predecessors in these seats. And surely the most earnest hope of every member-elect must be one in this, that 'as God was with our fathers, so may He be with us.'" These were creditable words to be spoken by the last Negro member of Boston's Common Council in the last year of its existence.

Deferring, for the present, reference to the political, situation in Boston's principal Negro colony in the upper South End and lower Roxbury section, and passing outward to the suburbs included in the metropolitan district, chief interest attaches to Cambridge. There the Negroes form a large element of the voters in three wards, and in one of these they poll approximately fifty per cent of the Republican strength.[1] Political conditions in Cambridge, as they particularly affect the Negroes, have differed from those of Boston proper in two important respects. There has been more departure in municipal elections from national party lines, — that is, more division upon strictly municipal issues. This state of affairs has, on

[1] The wards referred to are 6, 7, and 4, the latter being the one with the largest Negro population.

the one hand, worked against the fostering of the Negroes by the Republicans for purposes of city politics, to the extent that they are so cultivated in Boston, and in so far has tended to keep them from getting as many offices as they otherwise might. In the ward where the Negroes are most numerous, indeed, a Negro has never been elected to office. But, on the other hand, the members of this race in Cambridge have gained a special increment of political importance from the very fact that their vote has been more largely sought by both sides, in divisions on municipal matters irrespective of party. Furthermore, the change of attitude on the part of the whites toward this element of the population has not gone quite so far in suburban Cambridge as it has in Boston proper, and politically as well as otherwise the Negroes are there ranked somewhat higher in the community.

Those who have been put in public positions in Cambridge have usually been chosen with more regard to their individual merits. Such has been the case with the only two Negroes who have held elective offices in that suburb during the recent period. Clement G. Morgan was elected to the local Common Council from a ward where the proportion of Negro voters is slight, and served in that body for the two years 1895–96. He was then elected alderman, which place he filled for the two years following. In 1899 and again in 1900, he was one of the ward's Republican nominees for the Legislature, but failed of election. For a long time he has been chairman of his party's ward committee, notwithstanding that he is its only Negro member.[1]

[1] For mention of Morgan in connection with the equal rights agitation, see Appendix, article III.

W. H. Lewis, to whom several important references
have already been made, was chosen as a councilman
from another ward where the Negro vote is small,
and served in that capacity for the three years 1899–
01. He was then elected a representative in the Legislature, which position he filled during the year 1902.
He holds the double distinction of having been the last
Negro member of the Common Council of Cambridge,
and the last Negro member of the Legislature of the
State of Massachusetts.

In only two other suburbs have Negroes held elective offices. In Chelsea a member of this race, who has
taken a considerable part in local civic affairs, was
elected, entirely on his individual worth, to the position of alderman, and served in that rôle five years.[1]
Not long ago there was a Negro member on the Common Council of Everett.

So far, therefore, as election to public office is indi-
cative of the Negro's political standing, two facts
become evident. The first is that this race has received
a measure of recognition of this kind in the body politic which is altogether substantial, especially when
viewed in the light of the Negro's small proportion of
the population.[2] Set over against this fact, however, is
another, which relates to the tendency involved. It
appears that since 1897, with the exception of the
single year 1902, there have been no Negroes in the
Legislature; that since 1901 there have been no

[1] William J. Williams, the lawyer, who is also captain of the
Negro company (Company L) of the State Militia. His term as
alderman was 1902–06.

[2] As previously stated, only 1.7 per cent in the Greater Boston
district.

Negroes in either branch of the Cambridge City Council; and that when the Common Council of Boston proper was abolished in 1909, there was but one Negro member in that body, as compared with three for the earlier years 1894–95. In other words, the Negroes have in this respect suffered a gradual subsidence, till the number of elective offices held by them has at last declined to zero. In part, this falling-off has been due to causes for which the Negroes themselves were not in any way to blame. The redistricting of the city, and the abolition of the Common Council, were general events over which they had no control. Likewise the migration of this race, away from the West End colony and more recently from that in the lower South End, which has had the effect of terminating its political representation in the former section and of preventing the election of one of its members to the Legislature from the latter, is a movement which cannot be held to the Negro's political discredit. Down below these fortuitous and transient elements, however, are others which must be charged in part against the Negro himself, and in part against his past and present conditions. Of these, which are more determinate and continuous in their operation, and which have tended to produce, and in fact have entered very largely into, the final outcome in the matter of elective offices, account may now appropriately be taken.

Among the Negro's inherent characteristics, two especially, to both of which attention has already been called in other connections, count seriously to his disadvantage in the political field. These are, — first, the lack of self-reliance; and second, the deficiency in the capacity for social coöperation. The former short-coming tends to perpetuate the political dependence of the Negroes upon the whites, and to keep them from displaying initiative and generally asserting themselves. The latter shows itself in an inability to subordinate personal and minor differences to an inclusive and effective organization and a general fixed policy. The propensities of the Negroes to "backbite" one another, to be jealous and envious of each other's success, to quarrel and to split into continually changing factions, crop out conspicuously and damagingly in their political conduct.

As to the conditions from which the great mass of the Negroes in Boston have come and those under which they are living at present, it can hardly be questioned that these have been and are still, in the main, adverse to political progress. The great majority of immigrants from the South, no less because of their own ignorance and lack of interest in political affairs than because of their previous exclusion from politics by the Southern whites, have acquired next to no political experience and understanding. Even after taking up their abode in Boston they tend, through their own inertia, to remain in a benighted state. A large proportion of the newcomers from other parts of the North are, as has been said, of the migratory sort, here one day and gone the next. A great many of them are not sufficiently interested in the local situation to take the trouble of registering as voters. Most of the immigrants from Canada and the West Indies are not even naturalized, the former merely through indifference, the latter because they expect to return to the Islands.

In Boston, the great mass of the Negroes are immersed in the ever-present problem of earning their daily bread, and are, besides, peculiarly subject to many irregularities of working conditions, so that they have but little time to inform themselves with respect to political questions or to attend to political duties. Many of those who work as porters and waiters on the cars and boats, or who are employed at summer hotels, are often away from Boston on voting days.

By 1895, moreover, as has previously been noted, the Negroes had lost, either through death or retirement from activity, nearly all of the capable leaders to whom they owed a great part of their political good fortune up to that time. These men had gained the attention and the respect of the whites, and commanded the following of their own race. Neither the junior recruits who have been mentioned as reinforcing the Old Guard in its fight for equal rights, nor those of the race whose election to office in recent years has implied some degree of influence, have been able to take the place of the leaders who passed away. This has not been owing to inferior ability on the part of these younger men, for in education and mentality most of them are on a higher level. It has been due to a number of concurrent conditions. The fact that the Negroes of the upper class have in large part assumed a position aloof from the mass of the race has disqualified the majority of this element for political directorship. The division which has arisen between the agitators for equality, on the one hand, and the supporters of Washington's economic policy, on the other, has worked against harmony of effort; many of those who might otherwise take command being so at variance among themselves that they cannot act as a group, and are continually blocking one another's efforts. The quarrels of the aspirants for control have set a bad example to the rank and file, with endless squabblings as a result. The increasing stress upon material success and the growth of the commercial spirit, which are characteristic of the present day and which affect the Negroes along with the rest of the community, have worked against close interest and active participation in political affairs on the part of the more substantial element of this race, and have tended especially to keep Negroes of such standing from assuming the responsibilities and making the sacrifices incumbent upon worthy political leadership. Finally, the prevailing tendency on the side of the other race, with relation to the political claims of the Negro, has been, as already suggested, toward a replacement of the generous sentiment which formerly held sway by considerations of a more dispassionate character. The general disposition has been to accord the Negro no more recognition, in the way of positions, than that for which he could render back at least the full equivalent, usually in the form of votes, of value received. It is true that the Republicans have shown themselves desirous of retaining the Negro's allegiance, and that at the same time the Democrats have extended him a welcoming hand. But in harmony with present-day methods in American cities, "practical" politicians of both parties have shown themselves less generous in the bestowment of offices and more liberal in the use of funds. Thus the political appeal made to the Negro, and the inducements held out to him, have tended to fall to the lowest plane.

Such are the obstacles, as they arise from certain incapacitating elements of character and certain phases of the previous and present conditions of the Negroes themselves, on the one hand, and from the attitude of the whites toward the Negroes, on the other, against which the people of this race have had to contend in the political field. The manner and, more roughly, the measure, in which these obstacles have actually hampered and retarded the Negroes in a political way throughout the Greater Boston district, may be judged by concrete example taken from the principal Negro center, in the upper South End and lower Roxbury section. The major part of this colony is included within the limits of Ward 18. There, in what should be to-day the Negro's political stronghold, may be seen the sorry workings, in combination, of the various adverse factors which have now been pointed out.

Till within a few years, at least, there has never been in Ward 18 any Negro who has succeeded, even measurably, in making himself a capable political leader, with the interests of his race clearly at heart. On the contrary, the proprietors of a couple of liquor-selling and gambling "clubs," which are situated just outside the ward, have exercised much influence in local politics. With them, white politicians who have been desirous of getting the Negro vote have negotiated. Because there has been no able, disinterested leader, there has never been among the Negroes in this section any general movement toward political organization. As newcomers, for the most part immigrants from the South, the West Indies and Canada, have swarmed into the district, no systematic steps have been taken to inform them and interest them as to political affairs and to get them naturalized and registered as voters. With regard to the attitude of the other race, the Irish, who, as earlier noted, hold first place among the racial elements in this locality, are solidly Democratic in their political alignment, and have always had such an easy time in carrying the ward as to feel no special inducement for attempting to promote Negro support. The white Republican politicians have confined their attention chiefly to feathering their own individual nests. They are well aware that the Negro Republicans greatly outnumber the white ones, and that if the full potential Negro vote could be got out, it would easily dominate the ward's party organization. Though four of the nine members of the Republican ward committee have usually been Negroes, they have obediently taken their orders from the white boss and have probably done more to injure their race in a political way than to help it.

The Negroes have failed dismally in this ward to realize their political opportunities. By 1905, the Negro males of voting age formed over 25 per cent, and to-day they form close to 35 per cent, of all the males of voting age in the ward. The white Republican males of voting age constitute a proportion of about 20 per cent of the total. By enterprising registration of their own and the white Republican vote, and by taking advantage of factional quarrels among the Democrats, the Negroes could probably have obtained control of the ward and have elected members of their race to the Common Council and to the Legislature.[1] But whenever the better element have nominated a ward committee, as a first step in this direction, the Negro members of the regular "machine" committee have forthwith sown seeds of dissension, while a certain irrepressible member of the race has usually insisted on putting a committee with himself as chairman in the field, thereby causing still further division, — with the result that the "machine" has always won. Any one who has wanted to give himself the appearance of some consequence has run for the Republican nomination for the Common Council; and as the white Republican politicians have exercised slight supervision over the candidates, some of them have necessarily been nominated. With few exceptions, these Negro nominees have been so completely lacking in qualification that they have not obtained even the more intelligent Negro vote, let alone that of the white element. Likewise most of the Negroes nominated for the Legislature have been egregiously unfitted for such public trust. Nor has enough effort been made to unite the white and the Negro Republican voters by selecting one of the two legislative nominees from each race. As regards the election of an alderman, prior to the recent adoption of the present city charter Ward 18 was combined with Ward 21 as the 10th aldermanic district, and the elections were always very closely contested. It would not

---

[1] This and the following reference to the Common Council of course apply to the period prior to 1909, the year in which that body was abolished by the adoption of the new charter.

have been impossible for the Negroes to have secured the balance of power in this district and thus to have forced either the selection of one of their own number or some compensating political recognition.

In 1890, prior to the city's redistricting and while this section was mostly included in former Ward 20, it happened that a stray individual of the Negro race was given a place in the Common Council by the Democrats.[1] In 1896, another Negro was chosen to the Governor's Council, but only through a misunderstanding which had its elements of humor. Many voters, not aware of this candidate's racial identity and seeing in his name, Isaac B. Allen, that of some good old Yankee family, complimented him with their ballots, — with an outcome mutually surprising, and on one side highly pleasurable. Except for these two windfalls, however, the Negroes have as yet failed to elect any of their race to public positions from this district where they are to-day most numerous.

So much for the political count against the Negro people. What now of the evidence in their favor?

First of all, the Negro has an inborn predilection for politics. Its boundless opportunity for talking and speechifying gratifies his volubility and provides an outlet which vies with the religious for his emotional eloquence. Its schemings, concealments, reckonings with chances, and suggestion of deep-laid plot, stir his imaginative nature. Its air of consequence inflates him, and is to some extent a solace for his humiliated position in the community. Its numberless

[1] This man was Paul C. Brooks, to whom previous footnote reference was made in chapter III.

conferences, committees, and conventions, appeal to
his sociable instincts. This quality of sociability, moreover, combined with the Negro's disposition toward
lasting forms of association, affords a good basis for
political development. The spontaneous social sense,
with which the Negro appears to be endowed in high
potential degree, is in fact the most potent animating
force of political endeavor and achievement. With
this sense cultivated and educated, the race will find
itself possessed of a powerful asset in the promotion of
its welfare by political means.

With respect now to such actual progress as has already been accomplished, the most obvious political
gain the Negroes have registered, and one which is by all
means of primary and fundamental importance, is that
of their mere increase in numbers. In Boston proper,
as has already been stated, the growth has been from
2348 in 1865 to 12,500 to-day; while in the Greater
Boston district, during the same period, it has been
from 3495 to 23,000. Concurrently, the number of
Negro males of voting age has increased in Boston
from approximately 900 to 4750; and in the metropolitan district from 1500 to 8750. As to the proportion of those who actually go to the polls and vote, it
may be said that this appears to be not far below the
corresponding proportion in the case of the white
population, and that in a similar way it varies greatly
from time to time and in accordance with the occasion.
Though the proportion of Negroes in the total population is now only slightly larger than was the case in
1865, it nevertheless holds true that the great increase
in the actual number of Negro inhabitants and poten-

tial Negro voters has been of much political advantage
to this race. Their numbers have caused them to stand
out conspicuously as a distinct group in the community, which must be reckoned with politically, as well as
otherwise. Though in the past, as has been previously
emphasized, this leverage has not in any large measure
been brought to bear directly, it is nevertheless true
that indirectly the Negroes have had the outstanding
fact of their numbers to thank for the major part of
such political recognition as they have received. In
other words, had it not been for the substantial size of
Boston's Negro colony, very few members of this element of the community would have been given public
positions, no matter how friendly the attitude of the
other race. Mere numbers may thus be considered a
foundation for the future effectiveness of the Negro
people as a distinct political group.

Qualitative gain has accompanied quantitative. The
second basic element of the advance which the Negroes
have made has been that pertaining to their competency for performing the functions of citizenship and
for taking part in political matters. Though as has
been said, the majority of the Negro immigrants to
Boston during recent years have been of an inferior
grade in many respects, yet so far as relates to education they have been better equipped than those who
came before. With this better education they have
developed, through the Boston environment in general, but more particularly through the medium of the
many local organizations among their own people, a
higher degree of what may be called practical or applied intelligence. The rising generation has had the

further advantage of Boston's public schools. As the boys grow to voting age, they are far better qualified to vote competently, and with an appreciation of the best interests of both their own race and the community at large, than has been the case with preceding generations of Southern birth and rearing. The manifold opportunities which Boston affords have stimulated natural capacity and developed an increasing number of capable individuals among the Negro people. This has meant, in the present context, a deeply grounded movement toward two essential and closely interrelated results: on the one hand, the ability of the Negroes to appreciate, and in political ways to further, their own special interests, has been constantly growing; at the same time their qualification for acquitting themselves creditably of their civic duties and their political responsibility toward the community at large, has been continually enhanced.

A specific part of the improvement which has taken place in the latter respect is the decrease of political venality. Reference has already been made to the recourse politicians of the other race have had to the money appeal in enlisting Negro support. Thus has been held out the temptation. When the ignorance of the great mass of Negroes, their poverty, and the lowly place to which they are relegated in the community are taken into account, is it to be wondered at that to some extent this temptation may have been invited, and that to a much greater extent it should have been yielded to? The willingness of large numbers of Negroes to part with their vote for a substantial consideration has in fact become proverbial. But there is

little doubt, first, that in the matter of this short-
coming the Negro has been made the butt of much
semi-humorous exaggeration, and second, that with
improving education, growing intelligence, and general progress, the prevalence of such venality has
greatly diminished. To-day, in Boston, Negro voters
are probably on the whole no more mercenary than the
lower gradations of white voters, — with whom only,
of course, as in a measure approximating the economic and general conditions of life of the Negro people, a comparison of any fairness is possible. This is by
no means giving the Negroes an entirely clean bill of
character, but it is relieving them from an unde-
served excess of stigma. A well-known and highly
respected political leader of the other race, who for
many years has had an exceptional opportunity to
observe the Negro on the political side, puts the situation thus: —

I do not think that the Negro vote is any more purchasable than any other kind of vote of the same degree of intelligence. We have in Cambridge many very respectable colored
people who vote at every election just as intelligently and
conscientiously as any of our voters; — on the other hand, we
do have colored men who are in politics for what money they
can get out of it, — just as we have men of other races, including many of the Anglo-Saxon origin, who are in politics
for the same mercenary purpose. My experience has been
that many of the more ignorant colored people are apt to
view with suspicion a man of their own race, like my dear
friend, Mr. ——, for instance, who is a college graduate and
of the very highest character and integrity. Instead of taking
such men for leaders they are apt to give their confidence
and support to men of less education and very much less reliability. It is easy to see how these inferior leaders, who
themselves are actuated solely by mercenary motives, give

the impression to the casual observer that the whole Negro vote is purchasable. The same hasty judgment might be passed upon many other classes of our voters. If the individual Negro voter, like the average member of our trade unions, would only do a little more thinking for himself and look to men of ability and character as leaders, he would soon rid himself of the unenviable reputation which he now bears.

With higher standards of political honesty are coming also fuller understanding of, and more active interest in, the principles and measures of good government. Particularly striking evidence that such is the case was afforded in the autumn of 1909, when the campaign for a new city charter was being waged. Many of the leading Negroes were at that time invited to attend a special meeting for the discussion and furtherance of the so-called Plan 2, which, in intention at least, was the reform plan, as opposed to Plan 1, which was regarded as that of the self-interested politicians. Both schemes involved the abolition of the Common Council, thereby incidentally putting an end to the representation which the Negroes had long enjoyed on that body. Plan 1, however, proposed that the majority of the members of a single chamber city council should be chosen by wards. This held out to the Negroes the possibility that sooner or later they might elect one of their own number as a councilman from Ward 18, where their proportion of the voters is, as already stated, steadily increasing; and the probability that in several wards they could barter their support for appointments and jobs. Plan 2, on the contrary, by proposing a small council of nine members only, chosen by the city at large, made it highly improbable that any Negro candidate, unless he should be a man of very remarkable ability combined with prominence, could be elected thereto; while at the same time it reduced to a minimum the possible gain open to the Negroes by trading their votes. At the meeting referred to, the Negro leaders were nevertheless urged to support the latter plan, on the ground that it would tend to do away with the régime of dubious ward politics, in which the Negroes were at the mercy of politicians and got the least in return for what they gave, and to substitute a new order of things under which, with the better element of citizens in control, the members of this race would be able to ally themselves with the forces of clean government and would stand a better chance of having their actual deserts recognized, by appointments and otherwise. Before the meeting came to an end, those present, both Democrats and Republicans, had almost unanimously indorsed this view of the situation; and when, not long afterwards, the two plans were submitted to the city electorate for decision, more than a third of the Negro voters appear to have supported Plan 2, which was adopted by the narrow majority of 3894. Surely this was a practical demonstration of the fact that the Negro is disposed to help in pushing forward the intrenchments of civic righteousness, and is coming to realize that in the long run his own higher interests are thereby best promoted.

Beyond and largely in consequence of the Negro people's increase in number and their improvement in point of citizenship, there is also discernible among them some progress along lines of political organization and leadership. The headway in this direction has not yet become marked, being still of a rather rudimentary and preliminary character. But nevertheless it is real. Though it is true that for immediate purposes the Negroes appear to have been more effectively marshaled in old Ward 9 in the West End, and for a time in present Ward 11 in the same section, than they are to-day in any part of the Greater Boston district, it is also a fact that now a much larger number and proportion of the race have had some personal contact with political organization than was the case in the earlier period. The participation in party activity of the Negro rank and file, as compared with the dictation of the old group of leaders who in former days largely managed the affairs of their people, is increasing, and this means wider political experience and a more intelligent conception of civic matters. There are four Negroes, for example, on the Republican committee of Ward 18, two on the committees of Wards 10 and 11, one on that of Ward 12, half a dozen on similar committees in Cambridge, and a few more in Chelsea, Everett, and other suburbs. Inasmuch as these various ward groups compose the inclusive city committee of the party, the Negroes are thus appreciably represented in the direction of Republican city politics. Till very recently one of their number was messenger and general factotum at the headquarters of the Republican State Committee, in which capacity he exercised considerable discretion as to the minor affairs of that body.[1] Almost always there are Negro delegates at Republican city, county, and state conventions, and,

[1] Julius Goddard. He now occupies a position at the State House.

among the spectators, men of that race are much in evidence.

The many and various Negro societies are incidentally providing a training in methods of organization which later will surely be turned to political account. There are, besides, six or eight specifically political clubs among the members of this race in Greater Boston, which, though with one exception they have not as yet accomplished a great deal in immediate results, are tending still further to develop the ability to combine for political ends. One — the exception referred to — has in addition already succeeded in making itself an important factor in the politics of its locality. This is the Young Men's Republican Club of Ward 10, which has maintained its existence for nearly twenty years, with a retention of the same officers and a continuity of purpose which are, for the Negroes, rather remarkable. The present secretary, for instance, has occupied that position for thirteen years or more, while the president has been reëlected for seven or eight consecutive terms. This club has organized and united the Negro vote in that ward to a larger extent than has been accomplished in any other section. The petty factionalism, which as already described has been so flagrantly in evidence in Ward 18, has in Ward 10 been reduced to a minimum. The Negro candidates whom the club used to recommend for the Common Council were usually indorsed by the white Republican politicians. Previous allusion has been made to the rise of a sagacious Negro "boss" in this ward. The results obtained have been due largely to the exertions of this man and several of his lieutenants. Without reference to personalities, this fact may be pointed to as showing what some degree of leadership among the Negroes can bring about.

Even in Ward 18 signs of improvement with respect to both leadership and organization have begun to appear in the last few years. The principal candidate for open and accredited recognition as the political leader of his people in that quarter is a young man who, besides having a pleasant personality, good education, level-headedness, and marked capacity for conciliation, also gives evidence of having a genuine interest in the welfare of his race. He belongs to all the leading Negro organizations and takes a prominent part in the affairs of the Negro community. He has of late done a good deal in the way of registering and solidifying the Negro vote in that locality. Because he has stood out for clean politics, he has usually encountered the hostility of the "machine's" ward committee, together with that of a club which this committee fosters. The fact that, notwithstanding the opposition from these sources, he has several times been nominated for the Legislature, is testimony not only to his own personal hold upon the members of his race, but also to the willingness of the latter to rally around a leader of the better type.[1]

One of the most striking and important elements in the Negro's political advance is a manifest growth of that self-reliant attitude as a racial group, to the

[1] The candidate for leadership here referred to is Joshua A. Crawford. His earnestness and natural ability are shown by the fact that he recently applied himself to a law course at the Y.M.C.A. Evening School, and subsequently passed the state examination for admission to practice as a lawyer.

fundamental need for which attention has already been called. Historically, the rise of the spirit of independence, as previously related, dates from the protest against the Republican party's withdrawal from its programme of Southern Reconstruction and its failure to uphold the Negro's constitutional rights in the former slave states. In recent years, not only in Boston but throughout the country, the expression of this spirit has reached its maximum strength in the censure of certain acts and policies of the Roosevelt and Taft administrations. The discharge by President Roosevelt in 1904, on evidence that is still subject to question, of part of the 25th United States Infantry,[1] a Negro regiment, for the alleged "shooting-up" of the town of Brownsville, Texas, was the event which brought on this ill feeling. Taft, who as Secretary of War carried out the obnoxious Brownsville order, was blamed along with his chief. Roosevelt was condemned also on account of his alleged policy of sacrificing the interests of the Negroes in the South for the sake of conciliating the Southern whites. In Boston, the protest against Roosevelt's acts was started by Editor Trotter in the "Guardian," and in other parts of the country it was initiated by Negroes who hold the same general attitude that he does on race matters. But the attack was soon joined in by members of the race not usually allied with the agitators. The hostile sentiment aroused by this affair has in fact penetrated, and in greater or lesser degree affected, the Negro population of the entire country.

[1] Specifically, Companies B, C, and D, forming a battalion of the regiment.

In the spring of 1908 this hostility focused itself in opposition to Taft's nomination for the Presidency, on the ground that he was Roosevelt's candidate and would carry out the latter's policies. A mass meeting held at Faneuil Hall adopted condemnatory resolutions, which in their catalogue of grievances quoted Taft's alleged remark that the Negro people were "political children, not having the mental stature of manhood." The attitude of the Negroes in Massachusetts proved in some localities a considerable factor in the election to the State Republican Convention of delegates unpledged to any particular presidential candidate. At this convention, the Negro contingent made a strong effort to elect as an alternate delegate to the party's national convention one of their own number who had been emphatic in his criticism of Roosevelt. This candidate actually received 340 votes, as against 35 for the pro-Taft nominee of the same race; but with the Negroes thus divided, neither of the two was successful. When the national convention assembled, a large proportion of the Negro delegates who presented themselves were opposed to Taft's nomination, but most of these were shut out by "steam-roller" methods and contesting pro-Taft delegates admitted in their stead. After the latter's nomination, Trotter and many of the agitators in other parts of the country went to the extreme of advising the Negroes to vote for Bryan, the Democratic nominee. To the great mass of the Negroes, however, this, of course, appeared like jumping from the frying-pan into the fire; and even in Ohio, which, on account of the championship of the discharged Negro soldiers by Senator Foraker, was the storm center of the opposition to Taft, all but a small minority of the Negroes nevertheless voted for him. After he became President his alleged failure to make full restitution for the Brownsville "outrage," and his carrying even further than Roosevelt the policy of Southern conciliation, — as shown particularly by his announced purpose not to appoint Negroes to office in localities where whites objected, — were bitterly assailed.[1]

So strong is the influence of tradition in the Negro's party allegiance, however, and so unpromising any alternative political alignment which has thus far presented itself, that the actual proportion of this race in Boston who in national elections vote otherwise than as Republicans, is slight, while the proportion of those who regularly vote otherwise, even in local and state contests, is not large. But the percentage of those who on occasion vote for independent and Democratic candidates in city, county, and state elections, has steadily increased to formidable size. A substantial Negro vote was given to the "People's" candidate for mayor in 1905,[2] while fully half this element of the population cast its ballots for the man who was elected district attorney on a "citizen's" label in 1905, and as a "nonpartisan" and "Independence League" nominee in 1907.[3] The first steps to organize a dependable Negro Democratic vote in Boston city politics were taken in 1895, with the formation of a Ward 11 Democratic

[1] This in spite of his high appointment of W. H. Lewis (to be mentioned), and his bestowal of a number of other offices upon Negroes in the North. The objectors rejoined that they could not be silenced by these "sops."

[2] Henry S. Dewey.

[3] John B. Moran.

Club. In 1901, a similar club was formed among the
Negroes in Ward 18, and a transient proselytizing campaign undertaken in the interest of the Democratic
nominee for the mayoralty.[1] In 1905, a goodly number
of Negro votes went to the same party's candidate for
the same place, largely because of a speech com-
mendatory of the race which he had made in Congress.[2] The latter after his election made several
Negro appointments, which went far to secure him still
further favor among this element when he repeated his
candidature in 1907. But that year the great majority
of the Negroes were working hard for the Republican
nominee,[3] and did what they had never done before
by raising among themselves a contribution for the
local Republican campaign fund. The subsequent
failure, however, of the official whom they thus helped
to put into office, to reward them with appointments or
in any other substantial way, led to much disaffection
among them, not only with the mayor himself but with
the Republican city organization. Consequently, in
1909 a large Negro vote contributed to the election of
the present incumbent of the mayoralty — the same
man whom they had supported in 1905 — when he
again entered the arena and defeated the candidate
nominated by the reform element,[4] in one of the hardest fought contests of many years. In state issues, the
largest Negro vote cast for a Democratic candidate
was that of the autumn of 1910, when from a fourth to

[1] Patrick A. Collins.

[2] Reference is had here to John F. Fitzgerald, who occupies the
mayor's chair at the present time.

[3] The late George A. Hibbard.

[4] The reform nominee was James J. Storrow.

a third of the Negroes of Boston voted for the present governor,[1] the reason given for their action being their desire to register effective protest, particularly against the alleged unfriendly influence of Roosevelt and Senator Lodge in Massachusetts politics, and in a more general way against recent Republican lukewarmness toward the Negro race.

In the foregoing instances the Negro Democratic vote, though it counted substantially in the results, was not decisive. There has been one case, however, where the vote of this element did play a crucial part. In 1908, the Republican who was appointed district attorney to fill an unexpired term removed a Negro from a clerkship in that department.[2] Somewhat later, in trying a case, he inadvertently made a remark which was interpreted as reflecting discreditably upon the character of the Negro people. These two acts aroused widespread hostility to him among the Negroes, and when the following year he became a candidate for election to the same office, a majority of the Negro voters supported his Democratic opponent, who was successful.[3] As the latter's majority, however, was only 3211, it is probable that if the Negroes had not voted for him the Republican incumbent would have been returned.

No doubt a secondary motive which has influenced many of the Negroes to support Democratic or other non-Republican candidates or measures, and one

---

[1] Eugene N. Foss.

[2] The official who made this removal was Arthur D. Hill; the Negro clerk James G. Wolff, to whose appointment later reference is made.

[3] Joseph C. Pelletier.

which by reason of its practical character tends to become constantly more potent, is to be found in the bid, in the appealing form of appointments, which the Democrats and various temporary political aggregations have made for the Negro's vote, conjoined with the understandable willingness on the part of the Negroes themselves to partake of such substantial favors. As a matter of fact, most of the appointments of Negroes to city positions of late have been made by the Democrats, who thus appear to be resorting to this method of persuasion in somewhat larger measure than the Republicans. But after all is said, whenever any considerable percentage of the Negro rank and file have turned their ballots against that party to which they are indebted for the franchise itself, they have been impelled to this radical action by what they take to be some form of recreancy with regard to their fundamental rights and their higher interests. And as has appeared, they have in fact succeeded in making increasingly effective use of this means of protest and self-protection.[1]

[1] The most recent development in this general connection has been that growing out of the advent of the Progressive party. On the one hand, the already mentioned hostility to Roosevelt, and more immediately the action of the Progressives in excluding from their convention at Chicago two Negro delegations from Southern States, together with this party's announced purpose of keeping the Southern Negro in a distinctly subordinate place in their ranks, — these elements have disposed the great majority of the Negro people adversely. On the other hand, the declared intention of the Progressives not to discriminate against the Negro in the North has brought some accessions from this race in the Northern States. In Boston a State Progressive Club has been organized among the Negroes. It is too early as yet, however, to predict whether any large gains will be made by this movement.

Probably the most concrete and convincing evidence
of the better political standing to which, as a joint
result of the foregoing advantageous factors, the Negroes are to-day attaining, is afforded by the marked
increase of appointive positions held by members of
this race. In the case of election to office, where, as
has appeared, the Negroes have lost ground, the
responsibility for the successful candidate's satisfactory performance of his duties rests in an indeterminate
way upon the entire electorate involved, and the resulting tendency is to exercise less care as to a candidate's
individual qualifications. Thus the election of a given
Negro might signify, and in fact sometimes has signified, nothing more than personal popularity, effective
backing, or mere luck. In the case of appointments,
however, the responsibility for the appointee's record
narrows down to a particular body, or still oftener to
a single official. On this account, the individual's
actual suitability for the place in view is somewhat
more likely to receive proper attention. In the case
of Negro appointments, at any rate, the peculiar
necessity which has existed in recent years for their
justification in the eyes of a more or less antipathetic
public, argues special motive why the requisite merit
should be present; while the fact that, even when the
ability has been there, these Negro appointments
should be made, bears witness that this race has come
to be regarded as an element to be reckoned with in the
body politic.

The city positions which have been conferred upon
Negroes, during the period since 1895, include, in
Boston proper, one as deputy health commissioner,

three as deputy tax collectors, two as deputy sealers of weights and measures, one clerkship, and a number of lesser places, such as those of messengers, janitors, elevator attendants, and workmen. In Cambridge, the range of Negro appointees has comprised a member of the Highway Commission, a member of the Board of Licenses, an assistant sealer of weights and measures, an inspector in the health department, a district physician, a clerk, and a scattering of smaller positions. The other suburbs furnish a few similar cases.[1]

Among state appointments recently awarded to members of this race, one of the most important has been that of Charles W. M. Williams, who in 1906 was made clerk of the juvenile court established in that year. This appointee who, as already incidentally mentioned, had previously served on the Common

[1] Details of the foregoing appointments are as follows: In Boston proper, William L. Reed was in 1900 appointed deputy tax collector, and filled this position for two years. Napoleon Bonaparte Marshall succeeded him, and served for four years, till he resigned to take up the practice of law in Washington, D.C. Julius B. Goddard and Joseph Hendricks were deputy sealers of weights and measures in 1900 and 1901. Edward Everett Brown was deputy health commissioner in 1907, and is now a deputy tax collector. Stewart Hoyt was appointed a clerk in the tax collector's office in 1906, and still retains this position, being regarded as one of the most efficient employees in that department.

In Cambridge the most important appointments have been those of Clement G. Morgan as a member of the Highway Commission; the Rev. Henry Duckery as a member of the Board of Public Licenses; Emery Morris as assistant sealer of weights and measures, which position he still occupies; Dr. W. C. Lane as district city physician and as inspector of milk and vinegar; and Arthur Jewell as a clerk in the Wire and Lamps Department, where he has made an exceptional record of good service.

In Melrose, a Negro dentist is one of the teeth examiners in connection with the public schools.

Council, has performed his duties with exceptional fidelity; and in obligingness, politeness, and good cheer, sets an example which many public officials of the other race might with advantage follow. The state positions also include, beside minor places, those of a clerk in the district attorney's office, a public administrator, a member of the Board of Veterinary Physicians, and seven messengers and clerks in various departments of the State House. Of the latter, the so-called messengers perform duties which as a matter of fact entitle them practically to the rank of clerks. William L. Reed, to whose earlier service in the Legislature reference has been made, stands out especially by reason of his ability as messenger in the office of the governor and Council, which position he has filled since 1902. The holder of this post must have exceptional tact. He must receive courteously all persons who call to see the governor, lieutenant-governor, and members of the Council, and must frequently reconcile some of them, politely and without offense, to going away with their errand unsatisfied. In point of courtesy which is altogether free from obsequiousness, the present incumbent leaves nothing to be desired. He is well educated and endowed with attractive personality, natural refinement, and a high degree of the moral qualities of dependability, accuracy, and constancy of purpose, in which generally the Negroes are lacking. His qualifications fit him for public service of a responsible order.[1]

[1] With reference to the other state appointments beside those of Williams and Reed, names and dates are as follows: James G. Wolff, a son of James H. Wolff to whose noteworthy part in affairs there has

Outside the field of the civil service, only two federal
appointments have come to the Negroes since 1895,
but these two have been very important. Both of
them have been conferred upon the same man, William
H. Lewis, previous references to whom will be recalled.
In 1907, Lewis was made Assistant United States District Attorney, at Boston, and in that capacity was
placed at the head of the Naturalization Bureau for
New England. The fact that one of this race should
thus be put in charge of the naturalization of aliens is
surely suggestive of considerable progress on the part
of the Negro people in the way of becoming an inner
element of the community. In 1911, he was appointed
an Assistant United States Attorney-General at Washington; which was the highest political position ever
bestowed upon a member of his race.[1] This appoint-

been previous allusion, was in 1907 made a clerk in the office of the district attorney. The resentment aroused over his removal by the succeeding incumbent of that office has been mentioned. William J. Williams, already alluded to in a footnote as having been elected an
alderman in Chelsea, is one of five public administrators in Boston
proper, where he has his law office. Dr. Henry Lewis, of Chelsea,
was made a member of the Board of Veterinary Physicians in 1903.
Alexander Robinson was appointed messenger in the attorney-
general's office at the State House in 1895; John W. Schenck, messenger in the treasurer's office in 1898; Clarence J. Smith, clerk in the
office of the clerk of the House of Representatives in 1900; Julian
Stubbs, messenger in the office of the secretary of state (the position
held by Lewis Hayden and later by Sergeant Carney) in 1908. Two
women appointees during recent years are Miss Eva Lewis, as clerk
in the office of the secretary of state, and Miss Ruth Woods, as
clerk in the Bureau of Labor.

[1] This appointment aroused much protest from Southern and
anti-Negro sources, but the President and Attorney-General stood
firmly by it. By virtue of his position, Mr. Lewis took precedence at
formal functions over many high officials of the other race. An episode was the unsuccessful attempt to exclude him from the national

ment was thus not only a remarkable tribute to the appointee's individual ability, but from a representative and therefore far more significant point of view, it was a signal recognition of the standing to which the Negro people have risen in the political life of the nation.

The most conclusive proof of all of the Negro's growing qualification for efficient public service is found in the automatic, race-regardless operation of the civil service. The number of Negroes holding appointments in this field has steadily increased. To-day there are 2 official stenographers at the court-house; 2 clerks, an assistant weigher and 3 laborers in the custom house; a superintendent of a sub-station, 48 clerks, 7 letter-carriers, and 10 laborers in the post-office of the Boston postal district: — making a total of 72 Negro occupants of civil-service posts.[1] These individuals won their places in equal competition with members of the other race, and to retain them they must, day in and day out, do work at least equal in quality to that of their white associates. Not a few of them have done better work, and have gained promotion or special recognition by reason of superior ability at their tasks. In the Boston post-office, for instance, the postmaster's personal clerk, whose duties call for exceptional trustworthiness and efficiency, is a young Negro, Joseph W. Houston, who was born in that city and educated in its schools. In the custom-house,

lawyers' association. With the incoming of the present Democratic administration, Mr. Lewis's occupancy of this position came to an end.

[1] Some of these appointments were made prior to the civil service régime, but all are now under its regulations.

William H. Batum, another young man of the same
race and of Boston rearing, is one of eight entry clerks
who have the special responsibility of seeing that all
papers are made out in correct form, and that the
immense amount of detail involved in the recording
of merchandise is accurately carried out.[2] Many other
similar individual examples could be cited. But the
essential and promising point is that the Negroes, when
given an opportunity to be judged solely on their actual
merits and upon an even plane with members of the
other race, should have succeeded, in such substantial
and constantly increasing numbers, in winning these
creditable positions in the service of the Government.

In the light of the facts which have now been set
forth, it is possible to reach conclusions with regard to
the essential features of the Negro's political situation
at the present time. In the first place, it cannot be

[2] The case of Mr. Batum well illustrates the way in which many
a young Negro succeeds, in spite of obstacles, in working his way
upward. He was born in Providence, Rhode Island, in 1876, but his
parents came to Boston when he was two years old. He graduated
from a high school in Boston in three years, and took a fourth year
at the Cambridge High School, finishing with the rank of twelfth
in his class and with special honors in certain subjects. Notwithstanding some manifestations of prejudice, he then completed a course
at a business school, as a result of which he obtained a position as
stenographer and office assistant with a wholesale house, which he
retained till the firm dissolved. For a year thereafter he was unable
to secure steady employment, and had to do such odd jobs as came
along. Eventually he obtained a place as messenger at the Museum
of Fine Arts, which he kept for four years. Realizing by that time
that this position offered slight chance for advancement, he prepared
for the civil-service examination, and passed with a percentage of
90.4, only 1.8 per cent below the leader. He received his present
appointment in 1903. In 1909, he was enabled to buy a comfortable
home.

denied that, since the withdrawal of special favor from
the Negro after the critical year 1895, this element of
the population has in some ways lost political ground.
It was inevitable that such should be the case, when a
group of people which had previously stood in a pro-
tégé relation to the other race was thrown upon its own
resources. The most conspicuous political respect in
which the Negroes have suffered appears to have been
in a falling-off as regards the holding of elective positions. But this loss was in large part due, as has been
already pointed out, to the redistricting of the city, the
abolition of the Common Council, and the shifting of
the Negro population to new localities; — all factors
which can in no way be set down to the Negro's discredit. Furthermore, though on its face the fact that
the Negro people to-day hold no elective offices suggests a reversal of their political fortunes since the
period of public favor which followed the war; yet, after
all, this is only one, and by no means the most vital,
index to their political standing. The losses in point of
such political leadership and close coherence as used to
exist in the West End, before that old stronghold was
broken up, have really been more serious, in that they
strike deeper, and are in themselves not only effects,
but causes tending toward further detriment. But even
in the case of these underlying losses, it cannot be
denied that they were in large measure necessarily
incidental to the transition from the old order of
things affecting this race. The passing away of the
old group of Negro leaders, the sudden and continued
influx of raw immigrants from the South, the movement of the Negro population to new districts, where

it has required time to become adjusted and established, — these things especially, which have for the
time operated to the Negro's political disadvantage,
were essential elements in the general change which
has taken place. In this light, their effects on the
political side appear rather as set-backs, of a contingent and temporary nature only, than as essentially
political losses of a permanent character.

That such is in truth the case appears more clearly
when account is taken of the fundamental and durable
gains that are being made to-day, under the new
conditions which have come into existence and which
must serve as the basis of all substantial progress on the
Negro's part. Judged from the point of view, first, of
the requirements of the community at large, the great
majority of Negro voters are to-day better educated,
more intelligent regarding political matters, more sensitive to the higher standards of political honesty, and
more interested in and disposed to uphold the principles
of good government, than was the case in years past.
The Negro's asset value as a citizen and as a political
unit has, in short, been much enhanced. At the same
time, the Negro people are making good strides forward
from the point of view of their own more or less distinct interests. In their mere quantitative increase,
with which their political strength must of necessity be
roughly commensurate, they have become possessed
of a solid substructure upon which they can build.
Growing numbers have been accompanied by fuller
understanding of their own interests, and wider experience in the political field. On this triple basis, the
promising beginnings of organization and leadership,

adapted to the situation as it stands to-day, are now being reared. As contrasted with their former political dependence on the whites, and their rather slavish following of the Republican party, the Negroes are at present drawing together among themselves as a self-reliant racial group, and have already in considerable measure brought their independent political leverage to bear in the protection and advancement of their own collective welfare. As the combined result of their progress in these several respects, they have succeeded in making themselves a reckonable factor in the body politic, and in obtaining substantial political recognition in the form of an increasing number of appointments to public positions of trust and credit. And finally, in the field of the civil service, they have convincingly demonstrated that they no longer stand in need of special indulgence, but are able to hold their own on a strictly competitive basis.

CHAPTER IX

ECONOMIC ACHIEVEMENT; THE SOLID FOUNDATION

THE physical, social, ethical, religious, and political aspects of the life of the Negro in Boston have now been considered. The one other large phase of his conditions of which account still remains to be taken is the economic. That his situation in this regard is of fundamental import cannot be gainsaid. Next, at least, to the question of the mere physical survival of the race, certainly this one, which has to do with the obtaining of an independent livelihood, bears most vitally of all upon the welfare of the Negro people. The case may, indeed, be put still more strongly. Upon the Negro's capacity to earn his daily bread depends, in the long run, the very perpetuation of his racial stock; while unless his ability proves equal to providing somewhat more than enough to meet the minimum needs of bare subsistence, all hope of any real and permanent progress on his part, in other respects, must be abandoned. In the absence of an economic surplus, no strong social order can be built up, nor can the social amenities and ameliorations be cultivated in any substantial measure; for neither the necessary respite from incessant toil nor the requisite material means will be present. Under such circumstances, also, the bitterness of the struggle for economic self-preservation would prevent the rise of altruistic ethical standards and ideals. With respect to religion, though each individual's most essential altar may be contained solely within himself, nevertheless collective religious activity, if it is to have practical effect, must needs be materially supported. On the political side, finally, any element of the population, which is compelled to expend its entire energy in the dire necessity of maintaining life, is hardly in a position either to acquire an adequate understanding of political affairs or to use the ballot and its accompanying privileges to intelligent and advantageous purpose. In last analysis, therefore, the Negro's progress at every point must hinge upon his economic well-being; and as he cannot move forward in other directions except upon a sound economic basis, so, reversely, it follows that with such a foundation he stands in the way of advancing all along the line.

Such being the case, it is of the utmost importance that this aspect of the Negro's situation be subjected to the most careful scrutiny and interrogation. First, what is the present general industrial and economic level of the Negro, as compared with that of the white race? In the event that the Negro is found to be occupying a lower plane than the other race, what are the essential factors which account therefor; and in what measure do these factors consist of inherent deficiencies in the Negro himself, on the one hand, and of adverse influences from without, on the other? More specifically, — is it true that, as is usually taken for granted, the great mass of the Negroes are engaged in the menial or lowest forms of labor? If such be the fact, are there at the same time, however, any circumstances, arising out of the peculiar position of this race, which somewhat qualify this fact's signification? Passing on to work of intermediate grade, what is the situation in the Negro's case; is he to any considerable extent forcing his way upward into the substantial middle class of occupations, which must constitute the industrial bulwark of any element in the community? In general, is the tendency toward a contraction or an expansion of his industrial opportunities, as respects the number, grade, and variety of callings in which he is able to find employment? Ascending a stage higher still, to the professions and business proprietorships, does it appear that here, too, at the top of the industrial scale, where the qualities of initiative, independence, and responsibility come most fully into operation, the Negro is making any promising headway? With regard to the Negro population as a whole, how far are the members of this race taking advantage of the most important avenues of industrial and economic betterment which — though perhaps not in equal degree — lie open to them, as well as to other classes in the community at large? Are they, in particular, deriving whatever benefits accrue from participation in the labor-union movement? Are they increasing their own efficiency and earning power through the medium of industrial education? Are they establishing themselves on the solid rock-bottom of property ownership, thus throwing up powerful intrenchments against the future? Finally, are the Negroes displaying any capacity for, and in any promising degree actually putting into practice, business combination and coöperation, of a sort calculated to promote race coherence, and to apply to their own economic problem the axiom that in union there is strength?

Section 1. Unfitness and Discrimination

The Negro's present economic standing, relatively to that of the white man, appears most plainly when a comparison is drawn between the proportion of the members of each race who are found to be engaged in work of the lowest grade. For purposes of such a comparison, certain occupations, of a character, chiefly, to which the term "menial" is commonly applied, may be regarded as at the bottom of the industrial scale.[1] Now while the latest available census returns showed, on the one hand, that only 13 per cent of the white males and 30 per cent of the white females at work in Boston proper were employed in these specific occupations; they revealed, on the other hand, that 61 per cent of the Negro males and 76 per cent of the Negro females at work were employed in identically the same occupations.[2] In other words, the proportion of Negro males engaged in work of the lowest grade was five times larger, and that of Negro females two and a half times larger, than the proportion of white males and females,

[1] In the case of men and boys, the occupations here referred to are those of bootblacks (except those having stands of their own); servants and waiters; porters and helpers in stores; and laborers not attached to any particular industry. In the case of women and girls, the corresponding occupations are those of servants, laundresses (except those having laundries of their own); and others classifiable only as laborers of nondescript type.

[2] Inasmuch as the State Census of 1905 did not tabulate its findings according to color, and as the tabulations of the 1910 Federal Census, as respects occupation by color for Boston, are not as yet available, the Federal Census of 1900, therefore, contains the most recent authoritative figures upon which a detailed comparison of the situation of the Negroes in this regard with that of the whites may be based. It is from this census that the foregoing and also subsequent computations are made.

respectively, engaged in similar work. It thus becomes strikingly and authoritatively evident that the great mass of the Negroes are to-day on an industrial level far below that of the mass of the other race. This is the first outstanding and significant fact which pertains to the economic situation of the Negro people.

Still further testimony to this condition of economic depression is afforded by a second comparison, this time as between the total proportions of each race reported as being, to use the technical phrase, "gainfully employed," — or, in plain terms, at work for pay. In the case of the white population this proportion was 65 per cent for men and boys, and 24 per cent for women and girls; while among the Negroes the corresponding proportions were respectively 76 per cent and 40 per cent. That is, the proportion of men and boys at work was greater by 11 per cent, and that of women and girls by 16 per cent, in the Negro's case. This means simply that the degree of economic pressure to which the Negro people are subjected is much more severe than that which affects the other race. The high employment rate for Negro males is no doubt accounted for in some measure by the more urgent necessity for putting the boys to work as soon as they have completed the legal requirements of school attendance. The more significant figure is that pertaining to the employment of women and girls, which is even higher among the Negroes than among the city's foreign immigrants.[1] That such is the fact bears witness not only to a larger contingent of unmarried working-women, but also to the excessive proportion

[1] Forty per cent as compared with twenty-nine per cent.

of wives, mothers, and daughters in Negro homes who, by the rigor of the demand for family support, are forced into labor beyond their own domestic responsibilities. In the case of the white population, the great majority of the men who are not at work are either living on their incomes, or tiding along on savings until employment is again obtained. But with the Negroes the voluntary or enforced idleness of the men has to be offset by the labor of the women. The mass of this race, in short, are at present on an economic plane so low that the struggle for livelihood must be kept up incessantly.

The two principal factors by which the foregoing conditions are accounted for are: — first, the industrial unfitness of the Negroes themselves; and second, the discrimination against the latter on the part of the other race. Of these elements, both separately and in their combination, it will now be profitable to take further note.

Both the conditions out of which the great mass of Negroes in Boston have come, and those to which they are still subject in this city, have been adverse to the development of industrial efficiency. Under slavery, the great majority of the Negroes in the South were agricultural laborers, while the remainder were either artisans or domestic servants. Nearly all were specialized and in greater or less degree skilled in their various occupations. But as a result of the breaking-down of this old order of things, consequent upon the abolition of slavery and the ravages of war, a large number of the race were thrown out of their customary employment. These Negroes soon began to betake themselves to the Southern towns and cities. The cityward movement has gone on at a constantly increasing rate, and has conspicuously gained momentum in the last fifteen years. A majority of these Negroes who have gone to the cities have been forced to make their living as they could, and have formed a class dependent upon odds and ends of occupations, and leading a precarious hand-to-mouth existence. It is from this class that a major part of the Southern immigrants to Boston have always come; while in recent years, since the more intelligent of the race have realized that the North is not all it was supposed to be, the proportion drawn from this element has been even larger than before. Increasingly, Southern Negroes possessed of some degree of specialized skill have chosen to remain in the South. Most of those who have come to Boston have been ignorant, deficient in practical ability, and almost entirely lacking in any training which would fit them for work above the level of the least responsible unskilled labor and menial service. The number of those capable of taking their place in the intermediate industrial ranks, as artisans and skilled workmen, has been small. Only a very few have had the experience or understanding to qualify them for commercial employment or for any sort of independent professional or business initiative. With reference to industrial education, through the medium of which the members of this race might qualify themselves for work of higher grade, more will be said at a later point. Here it is sufficient to observe that in Boston there is no special provision for the Negroes in this regard; and that while most of the facilities along this line are open to them along with other elements of the community, nearly all of such facilities call for some capacity, at least a completed grammar-school course, and sufficient freedom from the immediate necessity of earning a livelihood to be able to apply one's self for a substantial period to the instruction offered. The very industrial and educational unpreparedness of the Negroes, however, combined with the constant economic pressure to which they are peculiarly subject, puts them at a severe disadvantage in availing themselves of such general opportunities for vocational betterment.

But the industrial unfitness of the Negroes goes deeper than lack of training. Owing in part to the effects of the conditions from which they have come, and in part to their own inherent traits of nature, the mass of the race are deficient in some of the qualities which are essential to the satisfactory filling of even a common-labor position; and in nearly all of the qualities which are indispensable for advancement into the higher grades. That such is the fact will appear more clearly in the light of further specification.

The majority of Negroes are characterized by an easy-going manner of life which borders closely on indolence. This is not to say that out-and-out laziness and idleness are typical Negro failings; — the common belief to this effect being, in the writer's opinion, erroneous. That such is the case is at least the suggestion, if not the necessary implication, of the fact, already noted, that the proportion of Negroes at work is much above that of the white population. Notwithstanding the dire necessity for labor on the part of the former, this necessity could to some extent be escaped by resort to charity; whereas such dependence or pauperism, as has also been remarked, is not excessively in evidence. Confirmed Negro loafers, on the street corners, about saloons, or in the Common, appear to be rare. Usually, Negroes who seem to be merely loafing in loquacious groups, prove on inquiry to be waiters, or other employees of irregular hours, off duty. The easygoingness of the members of this race is rather a distaste for monotonous and long-continued labor and a preference for varied and intermittent employment. It is a common thing for Negroes to give up good positions because they find the hours too exacting or the routine too dull to suit them. They are also prone to quit working when they have earned enough money to tide them along a little while, and to return to work only when their money is gone. Odd-jobbing, maybe requiring strenuous exertion for the time being but with frequent intervals of leisure, is much more to their liking than tasks that go on without relaxation. While the intermittent laborer is somewhat above the merely casual one, he is of course on a lower character plane than the workman of regular and steady application.

To a considerable extent the notion is prevalent among the Negroes that hard manual labor, and especially such as is dirty also, savors of servility and degradation. This misconception is a natural product of the reaction from the old order, when hard and begriming work was the lot of the slave, while ease and good clothes pertained to the privileged freeman. So it results that to-day, even though the wages and prospects of advancement may be better in occupations which necessitate rough labor, a great many Negroes nevertheless prefer employment which, though really inferior, enables them to put on an appearance of gentility and circumstance. This is in fact one of the reasons why comparatively few of this race are found among the common laborers who perform the heavy, dirty tasks in manufacturing, and why, on the other hand, so many are counted in the ranks of waiters, bell-boys, Pullman porters, and other brass-buttoned and impressive functionaries. Such highly ornamental positions as that of a handsome black giant, till recently stationed in front of one of Boston's leading confectionery shops, and who, helmeted and furred, looked the Emperor of all the Africas, while performing the unimperial duty of opening and closing carriage doors for patrons, are after the very heart of many of this race.

Closely related to the easy-going quality of the majority of Negroes and their aversion for steady work, are their traits of irresponsibility, instability, and untrustworthiness. The propensity which they show to leave a position whenever they feel like it illustrates all three of these shortcomings. The chances are against a Negro's continuing to be satisfied long in any given place. Lack of permanency of purpose with respect to occupation is accompanied by failure to realize and assume the responsibilities of punctuality, regularity, and conscientious performance of duties; — a failure which practically amounts to untrustworthiness. The Negroes are unreliable, furthermore, in that dependence cannot be placed upon their statements. Though not addicted to outright and premeditated lying, they do not appreciate the vital

importance of sticking closely to the actual facts and
of abiding strictly by their word. The fertile imagination which is part of their nature often gets the better
of them. The mass of this race are wanting also in
point of thoroughness, pertinacity, and providence.
They are inclined to rest content with doing just well
enough to meet superficial and immediate requirements. The painstakingness and exactness, which will
not permit a good workman to rest content till he has
done the work before him as well as it can be done, are
much rarer among the Negroes than they are among
the whites, even in comparable industrial strata. The
Negroes also become discouraged more easily when
they encounter obstacles in their work, or when it does
not bring them higher wages and advancement as
quickly as they wish. They are lacking in the strength
of purpose which would enable them to stick to their
tasks till they accomplished the desired results by
sheer determination. Improvidence is a characteristic
which may be inferred from these others. As a rule the
Negroes do not take the future sufficiently into
account, and so constantly exhaust their resources and
fail to provide a surplus to assist them in bettering
their economic conditions.

There are other deficiencies in the Negro make-up
whose hampering effect is more marked in connection
with employment of higher grade and with independent industrial enterprise. The lack of independence and
initiative, first of all, shows itself in the failure of the
great majority of Negroes to seek occupation outside
and above the beaten path. Because of the fact that
the mass of the race have always been in menial and

low-grade labor, most Negroes are wont to assume that they can obtain only employment of that character. At their tasks, moreover, they seldom display the quality of originality, rare among any class, but sure wherever found to carry its possessor forward. These incapacities also keep the Negro people from striking out more largely for themselves along professional and business lines, while their deficient ability for coöperation is an additional obstacle to the organizing of companies, and to the undertaking of any other kind of industrial or commercial combination.

The foregoing statements regarding these adverse elements in the Negro character are based neither upon *a priori* reasoning as to what ought logically to be so, nor upon common report; but are the expression of convictions gradually forced in upon the writer as a joint result of his own personal experience in trying to find employment for Negroes, his inquiry among employers, and his general observation. Among the considerable number of Negroes who have sought his assistance in obtaining work, there have been few, indeed, — not more than one in ten, — who were qualified for any form of industry above the grade of menial service or the commonest sort of labor. A large proportion of those for whom work was secured kept their positions but a short time, either because they did not fill them satisfactorily or because they themselves became discontented. Some even failed to present themselves at the places where employment had been promised, while the great majority were extremely remiss in keeping appointments. Few displayed initiative, resourcefulness, and persistence. The testimony of most employers who have had experience with Negroes is to the same effect. While admitting that there are many individuals of this race who have exceptional qualifications, they declare that as a class they are unreliable and incompetent. Though the bad traits which have been indicated are most glaringly exhibited by Negroes in the lower industrial grades, they are also clearly in evidence at points further up in the economic scale. Moreover, while these failings are all too common in the inferior industrial strata of the other race, especially among domestic servants, they are prevalent to an appreciably larger extent and degree in the case of the Negroes.

Besides the industrial unfitness of the Negroes themselves, the second general factor which accounts for their economic backwardness is, as previously stated, the discrimination against them on the part of the whites. To make a statement at once comprehensive and accurate, respecting the manner and degree in which this discrimination affects the Negroes industrially, is very difficult. It cannot be said that there is a point in the industrial scale above which Negroes are barred; for, as will presently appear, members of this race are found in every industrial gradation from common labor to substantial business and professional proprietorship. Nor can it even be said that those occupations of the various grades which are accessible to Negroes are but a few in number; for, as will also appear, Negroes are likewise to be found in the great majority of all the occupations which the census enumerates.

Nevertheless, the discrimination in question is very

real, and its effects are very plain. It shows itself first in a prejudice against Negro applicants for employment. Except in the case of the menial occupations in which Negroes are most numerously engaged, it is much harder for a Negro to get employment than it is for a white person. Even in the case of these menial occupations, moreover, it is difficult for a Negro to obtain work if the particular employer to whom he applies has not been accustomed to employing Negroes. As a rule this prejudice increases in strength as the grade of work ascends. Speaking very broadly, one may say that in low-grade work a Negro finds it twice as hard to obtain employment; in work of intermediary grade, such as the trades and lesser clerical lines, from ten to fifty times harder; and in work of high grade, such as that of bank clerks, salaried officials of business houses, and the like, a hundred times harder than is the case with applicants of the other race; and that furthermore there are some occupations from which Negroes are practically shut out. With respect, secondly, to advancement after employment is once secured, the Negro is likewise, though in lesser degree, the object of prejudice. In order to gain promotion he must as a rule do work which is not only equal in quality to that of white employees of the same sort, but better. Even so, his promotion is at best slow and uncertain. The prospects of advancement diminish as the grade of work ascends, and after a certain point they sink to zero.

Examples of how the discrimination in question operates may be had in the case of several forms of employment from which Negroes are practically

excluded. The occupations of salesmen and saleswomen in department stores, conductors and motormen on street-cars, and trainmen, conductors, firemen,
and engineers on railway trains, fall within this category. In smaller stores and shops in Boston there are a
few Negro salesmen and saleswomen, while there is at
least one case of a Negro in the superior position of
buyer in a large establishment. The reason given for
the non-employment of members of this race in department stores is that both the white employees and the
white patrons would object. But as against this assertion it may be submitted that, in the first place, the
white employees are not organized in unions, through
which they could voice any such collective protest effectively; that in the absence of union organization, and
in view of the abundant outside supply of labor of this
sort upon which the stores may draw, they would not
be likely to carry their resistance so far as to lose their
positions; and finally, that in the smaller stores above
mentioned neither the white employees nor the patrons
have registered any objections of pronounced character. It would appear, therefore, that in this case the
eventual and real responsibility must rest upon the employers, even though the latter may in good faith hold
an opinion to the contrary. In the case of railway
train employees, immediate responsibility rests chiefly
upon the labor unions, which in practice, if not in their
public utterances, bar Negroes. But as respects conductors, at least, the public enters in as a potential
factor, in that it is very questionable whether white
passengers and Negro conductors would get on satisfactorily. In the case of conductors on street-cars,

inasmuch as there have been no unions till very recently, the probable attitude of white passengers is the decisive element. When account is taken of the frequent squabbles between passengers and conductors over fares, transfers, stops, and what-not, as well as the occasions which arise for conductors to eject passengers because of disorder or intoxication, it is easy to foresee that serious trouble might ensue if Negro conductors were employed. This would not be true, however, with regard to motormen, and as they, too, were not unionized till within a short time, the employers again appear to have been mainly accountable for the non-employment of Negroes in this capacity.

The three parties to the industrial prejudice against the Negro are thus seen to be employers, white employees, — especially some of those who are organized in unions, — and the public. But wherever the immediate responsibility may rest, it is, of course, in every case the employers who are ultimately and in the most tangible way accountable.

This very discrimination to which the Negro is subject, however, is in major part the product not of any inherent hostility to him on the part of the other race, but of the actual industrial unfitness of the Negro himself. When a Negro applies for a position, he labors under a heavy burden to prove his ability to fill that position satisfactorily; or, in other words, to show that he is an exception to the general rule applying to his race. Either the particular employer's own previous experience with Negroes, or his knowledge of the experience of other employers, causes him to assume, in the absence of the strongest evidence to the contrary, that any given Negro applicant is in all likelihood incompetent. The employer, therefore, sees no sufficient reason for going into the qualifications of each individual. He simply adopts as the safest general policy that of refusing employment to all Negroes. On the surface this appears to be a drawing of the color line. But, in fact, it is primarily a rough-and-ready application of the competency test. The situation is similar with respect to the advancement of Negroes after they are employed. Though the prejudice becomes less pronounced, for the reason that each Negro has more of a chance to demonstrate his own personal ability, the burden of proof is still against him and he must fight his way against great odds.

In recent years the Negroes have lost ground in some of the menial occupations where their hold has supposedly been strongest. In this respect they have suffered especially from competition on the part of some of the immigrant groups from southern Europe and elsewhere. Many hotels and restaurants, for instance, have replaced Negro waiters by white ones of various nationalities. Negro barbers with a white patronage have practically disappeared, having been displaced largely by Italians. Negro coachmen are not nearly so much in evidence as they were twenty-five years ago. Even Negro bootblacks have declined markedly in number, ousted by the enterprising Greeks. Several years ago Japanese bell-boys were substituted for Negro bell-boys at the American House. The manager of this hotel stated that he had found the Negro boys unreliable, given to petty thievery, lazy, and deficient in personal cleanliness; and that this was why he was making the change. In domestic service, also, Negro girls are usually a second choice to those of Swedish, German, and other nationalities. The majority of the Negroes themselves say that it is the increase of prejudice which is blamable for these losses. But the underlying explanation is that even in such menial occupations Negroes have been found wanting when weighed in the scale with other races.

If by some miracle the present industrial prejudice against the Negroes could be made to disappear overnight, no doubt the immediate effect would be that the latter would suddenly rise many degrees in the industrial scale. But they would not retain their higher position long. As their actual industrial unfitness made itself evident anew, discrimination based on this unfitness would again come into being, would operate as it operates to-day, and soon the mass of this race would drop back, — not, it is true, to the same point as previously, for the temporary absence of prejudice would have enabled many to demonstrate individual ability, while fuller opportunity would have enhanced the capacity of many more, — but certainly to a point not so very far above that which they had occupied before. That is to say, the present industrial standing of the Negro people is roughly commensurate with their present actual industrial worth.

But while thus, on the one hand, the Negro's unfitness is the underlying reason for the discrimination against him, it is also true, on the other hand, that this very discrimination itself operates to perpetuate his unfitness, by limiting his industrial opportunities. If he is practically barred from certain occupations, confronted with great difficulty in entering others, and in general relegated to those of inferior grade, the result must inevitably be that his prospects for eliciting and cultivating any latent industrial capacity he may possess are minimized. He is thus caught within an entangling mesh of cause and effect: finding himself through his own shortcomings, in last analysis, brought hard up against an adverse discriminatory force from without; which in turn tends to keep him from rising above his present inferior place in the industrial scale, or to push him still further down. Such is the crux of the economic problem with which the Negro is to-day face to face.

Section 2. Getting a Foothold

When now one turns from the negative to the positive aspect of this situation, and seeks to find whether the problem which has been pointed out is in process of solution, by any distinct economic advance on the Negro's part, what are the facts which here align themselves?

A comparison of the conditions of to-day with those of the past, as the latter have already been indicated, will show whether, on the whole, the general movement which has taken place in this regard has been of a backward or forward trend. In the beginning, the Negroes in Boston were slaves, and as such had no independent industrial status whatever. Gradually, and owing largely to the endeavor and industry of the Negroes themselves, slavery was undermined and by 1780 eradicated. Its abolition marked the starting-point of the semi-independent economic history of this element of the population. The status of slave was succeeded, however, by that of traditional servant, which in the case of the great majority of the Negroes in the Boston community lasted until after the general emancipation of the race. Then the full economic liberty and responsibility of the Negro people began. Though even before that a few Negroes had entered the professions and become business proprietors in a small way, yet, as between this handful at the top and the rank and file still engaged in menial labor at the bottom, the proportion who had made their way into the manual and clerical intermediate occupations remained slight for fifteen or twenty years following the war. The change which has subsequently come about, however, is shown by the fact that to-day approximately thirty-five per cent, or more than a third of the city's Negro inhabitants, are found to be in occupations above the lowest or menial plane, and mostly in those belonging to the intermediate gradation.[1] Thus it becomes manifest that a great improvement has taken place; and one which, moreover, does not have to do only with a small minority composed of exceptional individuals, but with a very large proportion of the entire Negro population.

The progress in this respect which has been accomplished during the recent period, appears when the latest available census findings are compared with those of ten years previous. In order to appreciate the real significance of the figures involved in this com-

---

[1] This figure is simply the complement of that given at the beginning of the chapter with reference to the proportion of the Negroes employed in occupations of lowest grade.

parison, however, it is necessary to take account of the fact that during the decade in question, that of 1890–1900, the Negro colony of Boston proper grew from 8125 to 11,591, — an increase of 3466, or over 42 per cent. Inasmuch, too, as the deaths during the decade exceeded the births, and as there was much emigration, the total immigration of Negroes must have been considerably in excess of the net gain in numbers; and in fact probably amounted to at least 50 per cent of the Negro population at the beginning of the decade. The great mass of the individuals who made up this immigrant tide were unfitted for anything above common and menial labor. Under these conditions it might reasonably have been expected that, while the absolute number of Negroes in occupations of higher grade would have increased somewhat by the decade's close, the ratio of such to the total of Negroes at work would have decreased in no small measure. Indeed, it might have been regarded as not unlikely that this influx of ignorant blacks would have intensified the industrial prejudice to such a degree, that the proportion of the Negroes in occupations of higher grade would have declined by as much as the Negro population had increased.

But here is what actually took place: In 1890, the proportion of Negro males in Boston proper engaged in occupations above those of servants, waiters, porters, helpers, and nondescript laborers was 43 per cent, and the proportion of Negro females in occupations above the grade of servants and laundresses was 21 per cent. In 1900, the corresponding proportions were 40 per cent and 25 per cent. In the case of men there had been only a slight decline of 3 per cent, and in the case of women there had been a net gain of 4 per cent. Viewed in the light of the foregoing analysis of the situation, these figures show that in the course of the decade the Negroes made enough headway in moving up the industrial scale to offset fully the depressing effect of the flood of raw immigrants from the South. The actual advance which was accomplished stands out still more clearly when expressed in terms of numbers instead of in percentages. Whereas, in 1890, the number of Negroes of both sexes in occupations above the level of those cited as the lowest was 1674, in 1900 it was 2326, — an increase of 652. This means that by the end of the decade the Negro people had succeeded in establishing that many more individual advance guards — or, perhaps better said, scouts — to assist in pushing its industrial intrenchments still further forward.

A second form of evidence of the Negro's economic progress is afforded by the increase in the number and variety of occupations in which members of this race are found. In the latest census to which reference has been made, not only were substantial numbers of Negroes listed in each of the five general industrial classifications, — agriculture, the professions, domestic and personal service, trade and transportation, manufacturing and mechanical pursuits, — but also, in the case of the 123 secondary classifications into which the entire working male population of Boston was distributed, Negroes were reported in 96; while of the 57 similar classifications for women, members of this race were reported in 34.[1] Though it is impossible to enter

[1] The occupations of males in which no Negroes were reported

into an item-by-item comparison of these findings with those of preceding censuses, for the reason that, previously, occupation statistics by color were not given in such detail for Boston, it is nevertheless practically certain, in the light of general information and observation, that the industrial distribution of the Negroes is wider and more varied to-day than it ever has been before.[1]

Still another index to the improvement in the Negro's economic conditions is had in the decrease of

were: farmers, planters, agricultural overseers; nurses; street railway employees; broom- and brush-makers; cabinet-makers; carpet-factory operatives; clock- and watch-makers and repairers; copper-workers; dressmakers; electroplaters; engravers; furniture-manufactory employees; gas-works employees; glass-workers; hat- and cap-makers; model- and pattern-makers; paper- and pulp-mill operatives; rope- and cordage-manufactory employees; rubber-factory employees; sail-, awning-, and tent-makers; steam-boiler-makers; sugar-makers; textile-mill operatives; tool- and cutlery-makers; trunk- and leather-case manufactory employees; woolen-mill operatives.

The occupations of females from which Negroes were absent were: agriculture; hucksters and peddlers; packers and shippers; bakers; broom- and brush-makers; button-makers; carpet-factory operatives; confectioners; cotton-mill operatives; glove-makers; hosiery- and knitting-mill operatives; iron- and steel-workers; lace- and embroidery-workers; manufacturers and officials, photographers, rope- and cordage-manufactory operatives, rubber-factory operatives; sewing-machine operatives; shirt-, collar-, and cuff-makers; textile-mill operatives; tobacco- and cigar-factory operatives; upholsterers.

It will be seen that in many cases these occupations are so slightly different from those in which Negroes were found, and are withal of such a wide variety, as in general to carry little suggestion of the exclusion of members of this race on account of prejudice. In other words, the list appears to be on the whole of a merely casual nature, and at another time might be very differently made up.

[1] Further discussion of this point is deferred till later in the present chapter.

the percentage of Negro women at work. While the proportion of men employed remained at the same point — 76 per cent — during the decade 1890–1900, that of women declined from 40 per cent to 36 per cent. This reduction in the proportion of wives, mothers, and girls who are compelled to labor outside the home implies a lessened economic stress upon Negro families, owing largely, no doubt, to more fruitful industry on the part of the men. In positive terms, this means a better economic situation.

Conclusive as are the foregoing evidences of industrial advance, however, they are still of a rather general character and significance. The progress to which they bear witness will be much more fully and vividly understood when the particular kinds and grades of work in which the Negroes are engaged are taken up specifically, and the concrete facts thus scrutinized at close range. To this end, while aiming so far as possible to summon one's first-hand observation of the more humanly interesting features, and to avoid forbidding statistics, it will at the same time prove advisable to have recourse again to the findings of the census, in order to insure the desirable and essential element of comprehensiveness. But inasmuch as the most important consideration in the present inquiry is that of the rise of Negroes into superior occupations, the purpose in view will not be met by the census returns as they stand tabulated in the Government volumes; the five general classifications there given, and most of the secondary ones, including not only employees of different grades, but proprietors as well. In the light of one's own acquaintance with the facts, however, it is possible to estimate with approximate accuracy the number of proprietors in most of the cases, — as, for instance, that of "barbers," — where they are comprised under the same heading with employees, and thus to separate the proprietors from the rest. Even with this separation effected, however, the further question arises as to how to classify the various employees. Grouping them merely according to variety or character of occupation gives no idea of their rank. A possible basis for grading would be the prevailing wage or salary of each occupation. But even if the practical impossibility of obtaining this information in accurate form and on a sufficiently extensive scale could be overcome, it would still remain true that stipend is not by any means always commensurate with an occupation's grade. The amount of special preparation or ability required in the case of any given work, and the degree of intelligence combined with skill or expertness for which its performance calls, constitute together another test which strikes somewhat nearer the mark. But probably the best criterion of all is that of the general esteem in the community at large, which attaches to the various occupations in question. This is a standard which, besides taking account in a composite way of the factors that have been suggested, includes also the additional psychological element, which, though of somewhat intangible character and effect, is none the less real. For purposes of the present inquiry, at any rate, which is economic-social in a broad sense rather than narrowly and strictly industrial, the test of public esteem appears to be the most satisfactory one in determining the rank of different kinds of work. On this basis it is possible to arrange the occupations in which Negroes are found, as these are reported by the census, into three general gradation groups; consisting, respectively, of those which are lowest in the industrial scale, those which occupy an intermediate position, and those which take rank at the top.

The first group, thus made up, includes the employees of those occupations to which specific reference has already been made as the least esteemed, and of a few others which are on substantially the same plane in this respect. The composition of this group, in 1900, was as follows: [1] —

FIRST GENERAL INDUSTRIAL GROUP

Menial and Common Labor Occupations — Employees
Boston Proper

MEN

Bootblacks (employees)	27
Newsboys	4
Errand and office boys, and messengers . . .	48
Hostlers	61
Agricultural laborers	11
Steam-railway employees	34
Laborers (not attached to any particular industry) .	665
Porters and helpers in stores, etc.	404
Servants and waiters	1676
Total	2930

65 per cent of all men at work.

[1] It should, of course, be borne in mind that as the above figures are from the Census of 1900, the number of Negroes in the majority of the occupations given would be appreciably larger to-day; and that it is only as indicating relative proportions, in an approximate way, that these figures, which as previously stated are in this particular connection the most recent ones available, are to be understood.

WOMEN

Laborers (not attached to any particular industry) .	25
Laundresses (employees)	492
Servants	1222
Total	1739

76 per cent of all women at work.

Most of the Negroes employed as bootblacks are boys who are getting a start in this way, and who later go into other occupations, or, in the case of a small proportion, become proprietors of bootblacking stands. The same is true of the newsboys, who are a common sight on streets situated in or near Negro districts. The errand and office boys and messengers occupy a somewhat higher position, from the point of view of possibilities of advancement. Not infrequently these boys gradually work their way up into semi-clerical and clerical positions, and a few eventually become business proprietors or enter the professions. Some of the messengers are full-grown men, who, while getting more in wages than the boys, tend, on the other hand, to remain permanently in positions of this sort. A small number of messengers of higher grade, connected with Government offices and banks, are included in the next industrial group.

A little above the foregoing occupations, in point of earnings, come those of hostlers, and agricultural and railway laborers. Of the hostlers, the majority are to be found in private stables. The agricultural laborers are employed by nurseries, truck farms, or large estates. The railway employees are mostly coal shovelers, polishers, and the like, in the shops, or common laborers on the tracks. The subdivision made up of laborers not attached to any particular industry comprises a wide variety of more or less nondescript occupations. A great many, though probably not the majority, of those who fall under this heading, can be described by no more definite term than "odd-jobbers" or "men-of-any-work." Mainly from inability to obtain permanent employment, but partly also from preference for intermittent exertion, they make shift with whatever they can get to do — washing windows, cutting lawns, shoveling snow, helping unload coal, or what-not. A corresponding class is, of course, to be found among the other race, but the fact that it is not nearly so large as in the case of the Negroes further witnesses to the lower economic status of the latter. Because of the uncertainty in the occurrence and duration of their employment, the earnings of these odd-jobbers are likewise extremely uncertain and variable. Another contingent in this subdivision consists of elevator tenders. A large number of Negro men and boys are employed in running elevators in business buildings, apartment houses, and hotels. Their earnings are increased by tips, especially in the holiday season. Still another quota is made up of street and construction laborers, of whom there are several score on the rolls of the city and those of private contractors. The members of this subdivision who earn the most are the longshoremen, who load and unload cargoes of all sorts along the water front. Some of them do not have assured steady work, but are taken on intermittently at certain docks where no regular force is kept, or elsewhere as extra hands. By circulating about, however, these men usually keep

busy most of the time. The majority of those who are
regularly employed receive $12 a week. For overtime
work they get 30 cents and for Sunday work 45 cents
an hour. Thus many of them manage to bring their
weekly earnings up to $15 or $20.

The subdivision "porters and helpers" also comprises
many more particular occupations. It takes in all sorts
of attendants and factotums in stores and other business places. Though there is little dignity attaching to
such employment, — except when decorated with
brass buttons! — and though the wages which it
yields are low, still not a few of these humble lend-a-
hands come gradually to occupy positions of trust and
good pay, thus rising into the industrial group next
higher up. In this subdivision are also included the
porters about the railway depots and the elevated
railway stations, and the meat-carriers in the markets.
These meat-carriers earn as much or more than the
longshoremen. Their usual wage is $12 a week, but
after regular hours many of them work at loading and
unloading cars, and because special skill is required
in the handling of meat, the pay per hour is higher
than that of miscellaneous dock labor. Occasionally
a very rapid worker makes as much as $5 in a single
night, while earnings of $20 a week are not rare.

By far the largest subdivision in this first industrial
group is that of servants and waiters. Between twenty-
five and thirty hotels, restaurants, clubs, and apartment
houses, in Boston proper, employ Negroes as waiters.
This is the case in nine leading hotels, while several of
the same grade have Negro waiters in some of their
dining-rooms, and white waiters in the others. The

wages paid range from $22.50 to $33 a month, that of most usual occurrence being $25, plus meals in working hours. Captains and head waiters receive more, the former from $30 to $40 and the latter usually about $75. In addition to the regular wages, however, there are the tips. In nineteen hotels and restaurants which the writer investigated, the lowest reported monthly income from tips was $12, while the majority of waiters took in about $25 a month, thus bringing their gross earnings up to $50 a month, or approximately $11.50 a week. Frequently the yield from tips is much larger. One waiter reported $185 during a lucky month. This is very exceptional, but cases of $50 a month are not uncommon, especially in so-called bohemian cafés. The gross earnings of captains is usually about the same as that of ordinary waiters, the higher wage being offset by a smaller amount in tips, owing to the less direct contact with patrons. For the same reason head waiters are not tipped to any large extent, except in one or two of the best hotels and several resorts of the sporting element. In these places the amount thus received depends mainly on the head waiter's popularity, but on the average is about $50 a month, making the gross earnings $125 a month, or close to $29 a week. An especially coveted position under the heading of servants is that of Pullman porter. The usual wage is $25 a month. The income from tips, though very variable, and ranging from next to nothing on poor "runs" to $100 a month and even more on the best ones, averages about $50. Thus the combined income is $75 a month, or something over $17 a week.

Of the women included in the first industrial group

now under consideration, the majority of those set down as laborers are scrubwomen and the like. The servants consist for the most part of general house-work girls, nursemaids, ladies' maids, and cooks. The cooks get the best pay, sometimes making as much as $10 a week. Also included among the servants are a considerable number of helpers and attendants in manicure and hairdressing parlors, and millinery, dressmaking, and other similar establishments. These positions are often especially attractive because they have more or less of an appearance of smartness or gentility. Of the laundresses, the majority go out to work by the day. The usual day's wage is $1.50, plus carfare. This means $4.50 a week if a woman has only three days taken, $7.50 or $9, if she works five or six days, as many do, the demand being far in excess of the supply. A smaller proportion of the laundresses take in work at their homes. These women might well be considered as belonging to the proprietor class, and a few who have home or shop laundries open to public patronage will be so graded. The laundresses who take in work, as a rule make more than those who go out by the day.

By way of general characterization and summary applying to this first large industrial group, the examination of which in detail has now been completed, it should be noted that in the case of both sexes the specific occupations comprised are of two kinds: common labor, such as that of longshoremen; and menial work, such as that of servants and waiters. In the case of common labor, the suggestion of inferiority is less, and attaches rather to the labor alone than to the laborer also. The menial occupations, however, in which a much larger number of Negroes are found, are customarily looked upon as not only inferior in themselves, but as stamping the persons employed in them with inferiority. The underlying explanation of this fact is doubtless to be had in the intimately physical nature of the service rendered, such as serving food and blacking boots. The way of referring to the employees in such kinds of work as "boys," and of addressing them by their first names, suggests their lack of dignity. A particular reason which partly accounts for the low esteem in which some of these occupations are held is that they are subject to the practice of "tipping." Whenever a tip is offered and taken, not only the giver's respect for the taker, but also the taker's respect for himself, are impaired, and the inferiority of the latter's position is not only implied, but, in tendency at least, produced. The better element of the Negroes are conscious of the deteriorating influence to which so many of their race are thus continually subjected. Tipping is not the sole element, however, in the disregard which attaches to labor of this sort, as is shown by the fact that domestic servants, who usually are not tipped at all, are nevertheless the most distinctly menial of all. The conditions which surround most forms of menial employment are, furthermore, not such as to bring out the best traits of character. Waiters and bell-boys, especially, are constant witnesses to over-display, extravagance, vulgarity, heavy drinking, and immorality; — with more or less lowering of their own standards as an almost inevitable result. In so far, therefore, as the foregoing unfavorable features are concerned, the fact that so large a proportion of the Negroes are employed at menial labor is undoubtedly one of the most serious obstacles in the way of general progress by this race.

But, on the other hand, it would be a mistake to attach any necessary stigma to work of this kind. Any task done honestly and well is creditable, and the worthiness of one's employment really depends upon the character of one's own fulfillment of it. Some of the better educated and more sensitive Negroes are beginning to urge their people to keep out of menial service. That is well enough, provided employment of higher grade is procurable. But if the choice rests between menial occupation, and enforced idleness or dependence, which is often the case, the former is certainly to be preferred. So long as large numbers of the race must earn their livelihood in this field, they should strive to enhance the dignity of their employment by self-respecting and efficient performance of their duties. Under actual existing conditions, moreover, the case is far from being one-sidedly against work of this character. There are some very substantial considerations, in fact, which must be set down to its credit. The first is, that the earnings in some of these occupations, as has already appeared, reach a point far above those of common labor, and for that matter considerably above those of some of the semi-skilled manual and clerical lines of employment which are usually regarded as superior. Positions as Pullman porters and as head waiters, which not infrequently yield an income of $125 a month, are by no means to be despised. In point of skill required, moreover, the work of a good hotel waiter is something of an accomplishment; and an efficient head waiter, who sees to it that his men are properly drilled, marshaled, and kept at attention to their duties, is veritably — to borrow a term from the economists — a "captain of industry."

Earnings above those of common labor imply better living conditions, better education for the children, and enhanced social worth. As will be shown when ownership of property is considered, many of the Negroes in menial positions in Boston have by thrift and saving set aside enough to buy a home, and provide their families with the comforts and some of the luxuries of life. Some have invested in additional property, and a few have accumulated snug little fortunes. The majority of these men and women are respected and serviceable members of the community.

Any handicapped group, of course, as, for example, some of the foreign immigrants to whom reference has been made as displacing the Negroes in certain occupations, have to resort to menial employment more or less, at least while they are getting a foothold. In the case of the white population, however, it holds true that the great majority of persons engaged in work of this grade are of a generally humbler standing. But with the Negroes this is not the case to nearly such a degree. On account of the difficulties experienced by members of this race in obtaining work of higher grade, it results that Negroes of every degree of ability, education, and standing among their own people, are found in menial occupations. For some this is simply their first employment, through which they hope to get a start that will enable them to move higher. And many do move higher. It is safe to estimate that two thirds of the Negroes who occupy the best positions to-day have at some time in their life worked as waiters or as menials of some other sort. A second contingent, while remaining in menial occupations permanently, nevertheless rise, through saving and the purchase of property, to an economic level equal to that of workers in superior lines. Others, students especially, take this readiest way of supporting themselves till they can enter upon their chosen work. Still others, who have through various exigencies lost better positions or whose abilities are of a sort — as literary or artistic — which is not sufficiently remunerative, take up menial work as either a temporary or permanent mode of making both ends meet. An aspiring verse-writer known to the writer earned his daily bread for a time by working as an elevator boy. The minister of a suburban church is employed during the week as a porter in a city store. These instances are typical of many more which could be cited, and which, as already suggested, are far more common among the Negro people than they are among any other element of the population.

It is evident, therefore, in the light of the foregoing concrete facts, that there is much in connection with the occupations in this first industrial group which bears witness not to industrial inferiority, but to very substantial economic progress. These occupations cannot justly be dismissed as "lowest," except in a purely comparative and underogative sense. An unmodified comparison, moreover, between the percentage of the Negroes engaged in work of this sort with the percentage of the whites in work of the same kind, does not constitute a true and adequate measurement of the relative economic levels of the two races; the reason being that in the case of the Negroes the proportion who in their living conditions have risen above their employment is so much larger than it is among the other race. In short, the Negro people, in considerable degree making a virtue of their necessity, have turned occupations reckoned as lowly into the means of substantial economic intrenchment.

The second industrial group is made up of employees in two general kinds of occupations, the one higher grade manual, the other clerical, which from the point of view of their esteem in the community belong in approximately the same intermediate gradation. This group was in 1900 constituted as follows: —

SECOND GENERAL INDUSTRIAL GROUP

Higher Grade Manual and Clerical Work — Employees
Boston Proper

MEN

Barbers	81
Bartenders	16
Stewards	29
Janitors and sextons	319
Watchmen and policemen	24
Boatmen, fishermen, and sailors	22
Soldiers, sailors, and marines (U.S.)	16
Teamsters	150
Packers and shippers	27
Iron and steel, wire, brass, tin, brick, and leather workers; quarrymen; meat-packing, electric-light, and brewery employees; telegraph and telephone linemen	36
Marble- and stonecutters	8

Blacksmiths and wheelwrights 9
Machinists 7
Boot- and shoemakers and harness-makers . . . 2
Carpenters, coopers, painters, paperhangers, plasterers,
and roofers 75
Plumbers, gas- and steamfitters 9
Upholsterers 9
Tobacco-workers 6
Piano-makers 3
Masons 30
Butchers 6
Bakers 5
Tailors 11
Photographers 2
Gold- and silver-workers 3
Engineers and firemen (stationary) 53
Engineers and surveyors 2
Electricians 4
Bookbinders 2
Printers 19
Foremen 3

Stenographers and typewriters 7
Messengers (high grade) 16
Clerks and copyists 83
Bookkeepers and accountants 4
Architects and draughtsmen 3
Agents and commercial travelers 26
Salesmen 23
Officials of companies 3
Total 1153

25.5 per cent of all men at work.

WOMEN

Hairdressers 5
Stewardesses 88
Janitors and sextons 34
Nurses and midwives 30
Box-makers 1

Boot- and shoemakers	7
Seamstresses	38
Shirtmakers	1
Tailoresses	9
Dressmakers	114
Milliners	4
Bookbinders	1
Printers	1
Telephone operators	1
Stenographers	8
Clerks and copyists	9
Bookkeepers	4
Agents	5
Saleswomen	7
Total	367

16 per cent of all women at work.

This group includes a much more extensive gradation of occupations than the first one, with respect to
skill, earnings, and public regard. Though, as above
set down, these occupations have been arranged
roughly in an ascending scale according to their estimation in the community, no hard-and-fast arrangement, on this or any other basis, is possible. While it
will not be necessary to consider each occupation
separately, still, before generalizing, some observation
of a more specific character will prove profitable.

At the beginning of the group, forming the transition from the one preceding, come the semi-menial
occupations of barbers, stewards, bartenders, janitors,
and sextons. The barbers are employed in places pa-
tronized exclusively by this race. There is to-day only
one Negro shop which has a white patronage — this
one being in the State House, where it remains as a sort
of inheritance from earlier years. Some of the bar-

tenders are in the Negro "clubs" to which previous
reference has been made, while the remainder are in
white cafés and hotels. Most of the stewards are to be
found in white clubs; a few in hotels and restaurants.
The janitors, who are employed mainly in apartment
houses, business blocks, and public buildings, are as a
class characterized by thrift and sturdy moral qualities. The position of janitor is, of course, one which
calls for trustworthiness, industry, and practical
ability, while the consciousness of being placed in such
a situation of responsibility tends further to develop
the better elements of character. Having to take care
of property gives rise to an understanding of the value
of property and an ambition for ownership. Probably
the Negro janitors include a larger proportion of
property owners than is the case with any other single
occupation. Several of the men whose real-estate
holdings are most substantial have this as their present
or past vocation.

Negro teamsters are much in evidence. Most of
them are employed by coal companies, who testify
that in general they are as satisfactory for such work as
any other race, while being more desirable in point of
good humor and humane treatment of their horses.
Negro drivers of delivery wagons for many kinds of
business are also a common sight. In this context,
note may appropriately be made of an occupation in
which no Negroes at all were reported by the Census
of 1900, but in which to-day there must be at least a
hundred in Greater Boston. The occupation to which
reference is had is that of chauffeur. The rapid increase of Negroes in this calling within the last few

years reflects considerable credit on the members of this race, in that the work requires not only special preparation, but exceptional qualifications, including accuracy of observation, cool-headedness, quick-wittedness, mechanical skill and ingenuity, and trustworthiness of character. If Negroes are not found wanting at such work after a fair competitive trial, their fitness for employment as motormen, railway trainmen, firemen, engineers, and the like, may warrantably be taken for granted.

From teamsters to foremen, this second group is composed of what may be broadly termed skilled manual occupations, including the trades in the narrower sense. These may be considered collectively, inasmuch as the conditions pertaining to them are similar. The multiplicity and diversity of occupations of this character in which Negroes are found is what first impresses the observer, while the considerable number of members of this race in certain vocations, especially those of carpenters and allied branches, and masons, stationary engineers, and printers, is particularly striking. With respect to the Negroes reported in the building trades, it may be said that they are as a rule employed among the white workmen, with whom they appear to be approximately on a level in point of efficiency. A goodly proportion of the Negroes in the trades are not wholly in the employee class, strictly speaking, but are at least semi-proprietors, owning their implements and working more or less as their own masters. Such is the case especially with many of the carpenters, roofers, plasterers, and paperhangers.

The skilled manual occupations are the ones of

chief strategic importance for the Negroes to-day, as constituting the most practical avenue of industrial advance for the rank and file of the race. They are mostly occupations for which the necessary training may be acquired not only through a school course of industrial education, — though, to be sure, such special preparation is a great advantage, — but also, as is usually the case, by working one's way up through lower grades of related work. They are also occupations in which the demand for satisfactory workmen is generally in excess of the supply, and with regard to which, therefore, possession of the requisite skill is almost certainly a passport to employment, whatever may be the color of the applicant's skin. They command good wages. What is still more important, they compel recognition of and respect for practical ability. The conditions surrounding such work are furthermore conducive to the development of the qualities of responsibility, thrift, and definiteness of purpose, which are themselves both the prerequisites and the guarantees of substantial industrial progress.

The remaining occupations in this group, from stenographers to the end of the list, are of a clerical or semi-clerical character. Some of the Negroes in these lines of work are employed by Negro establishments, but such are distinctly in the minority. Besides two court stenographers, to whom previous reference has been made in connection with the civil service, there are several others who have won exceptional recognition in this calling; among them a young man holding a position in a well-known public stenographic office, with white associates, who has the reputation of being one of the best of this vocation in the city. The messengers listed at this point consist of those in the State House, post-office and custom-house, who, as previously stated, really perform the functions of clerks; and of a few others of the same grade in banks and business places. Several of these bank messengers would be promoted to full clerkships were it not for the alleged objection that their white associates would make.[1] A considerable proportion of the Negro clerks are also to be found in city, state, and federal offices. The rest are scattered about here and there in business establishments of various sorts, which is likewise true of the bookkeepers, salesmen, and architects.

In clerical employment, the proportion of Northern-born, or at least Northern-reared, Negroes is at its highest. Among this element especially, but also among the rest of the Negro population, work of this nature is at a premium. This, of course, holds true not only in the case of the Negroes, but also in that of the whites, with whom likewise clerical occupations are generally held in higher social esteem than manual ones, even though the latter be of skilled grade; the reason being, apparently, that clerical employment carries more of a suggestion of gentility. It is well and good that Negroes should enter these clerical occupations to an extent warranted by the real benefits thereby derived. These benefits are chiefly the gain in self-respect resulting from the consciousness of being

[1] There are only two full-fledged Negro bank clerks in Boston: — Louis Pasco, at the National Shawmut Bank, and Leigh Carter, with N. W. Harris & Co.

in work which is commonly regarded as superior, and the winning of enhanced respect from the whites through demonstration of assumedly superior capacities. For a small minority of exceptionally qualified Negroes, moreover, clerical work affords opportunity for exceptional advancement and earnings. But for the great majority of the race the clerical field is of much less practical and certain value than that of skilled manual work. In the first place, the supply of labor for clerical employment, much of which — as, for instance, that of ordinary store clerks — requires no special training beyond a common-school education, is far in excess of the demand. This means that the Negro must encounter more severe competition in obtaining such employment, and that in all except its upper grades the wages are much lower than in the case of manual work which calls for special skill. Of a piece with the superficial gentility of clerical employment, the prejudice against the Negro is more pronounced in it and the opportunity for advancement much less favorable. The nature and conditions of such work are as a rule not so likely to develop the more rugged and fundamental qualities of character. There is more temptation to squander earnings on dress, empty accomplishments, and the aping of "society." Unfortunately, many Negroes succumb to these temptations.

Considering together the higher grade manual and the clerical occupations now under discussion, what has been said regarding the men in their ranks applies also, in general, to the women. But there are several points of difference. The percentage of Negroes em-

ployed by members of their own race is larger in the
case of the women; as is also the proportion of those
who are semi-proprietors, as, for instance, many of the
hairdressers, seamstresses, dressmakers, and milliners.
The number of occupations of intermediate grade in
which Negro women are found is much smaller than
in the case of Negro men, owing largely to the fact that
racial prejudice is more pronounced on the part of
white women employees, thus making it more difficult
for Negro women to gain an entrance.

With respect to this intermediate industrial group as
a whole, men and women combined, there are certain
important observations to be made. The first of these
is, that whereas the great majority of the Negroes comprised in the first or lowest group, previously considered, carry on their work either in segregated gangs,
as in the case of hotel waiters, or under conditions
where their contact with the other race is as between
inferiors and superiors, a majority of those in this
second group work side by side with white employees
of the same kind, under circumstances of at least
industrial equality. This fact has vital consequences.
These individual Negroes are living arguments — the
most convincing ones possible — against the injustice
of an undiscriminating prejudice. Their presence and
example are the most persuasive appeal which could be
made for mutual amity and respect between the two
races. Every Negro who is performing work of this
grade is thus an asset of the utmost strategic value to
his people.

The general public sees or hears little of the Negroes
who occupy such superior positions. Most of these

Negroes are not making a noise over their good fortune. On the contrary, they are keeping quiet, minimizing the fact of their racial identity, and in all ways trying to avoid attracting to themselves an attention which they fear might arouse prejudice and endanger their employment. But the observer who goes about with his eyes open comes upon these individuals in unexpected places and in surprising numbers. The head milliner in one of the most fashionable of Boston's millinery establishments, for instance, is a Negro man, who not only carries on his work among white employees, but has charge of them. One of the salesmen in a well-known furniture store is a Negro, who has been with this particular establishment for many years, having gradually worked up from humble employment, in the beginning, to his present place, in which he is reckoned among the firm's most valuable men. There is nothing in the relations between his white fellow-salesmen and himself, or in the attitude of patrons, which intrudes the color line. Incidentally, this man attracts a considerable trade from members of his own race.[1] Another Negro is one of the buyers in a leading department store, and ranks among the foremost in this capacity. An especially noteworthy case is that of a member of this race who, starting as a bottle-washer, is now in charge of the laboratory of the company that manufactures the well-known Cuticura remedies.[2] Several score examples as striking as these

[1] The case referred to is that of William C. Lovett, in Eldridge & Peabody's.

[2] Reference is had to Philip J. Allston, who at the writer's request has contributed the following brief autobiographical sketch: —

"I was born in Edenton, North Carolina, August 12, over forty

could be given, as well as many more which approximate to them, but the ones which have been cited will serve as representative.

Though it is true, as previously noted, that a Negro encounters much more difficulty in getting work than does a white man, yet the writer, in his own range of

years ago, of slave parentage, my mother being the product of a Caucasian man. My father the result of like association from another plantation.

"I was left in the care of my mother when only a few years old, my father hastily leaving for the North, and I did not see him for eight years. I came to Boston, July, 1871, where my mother joined my father.

"Large opportunities for her children, and a desire to see her husband again, caused Mrs. Emily Allston, my mother, to leave her own home for Boston.

"She had instructed the children in the first steps of learning. As a seamstress she was considered above the average slave. She engaged a private tutor to advance the children. I attended the primary and grammar schools, but left the latter before reaching the graduating class that I might aid in the support of the home. With an intense desire for educational advancement, being forced to make a livelihood at an early age, I immediately, upon leaving day school, joined the Evening English High School, which I attended for eight years, and the Starr King Drawing School, where I remained for five years.

"My first position was as a helper to a janitor (a white man) of the National Shawmut Bank. Finding no chance here to advance on account of my color, I left after the first six months, to work at the Weeks & Potter Company, wholesale and retail druggists. Here as bottle-washer I remained until promoted to the laboratory of this concern.

"Mr. Warren B. Potter, one of the partners of this establishment, took a great interest in me, and offered me the position of foreman in their laboratory in their new quarters on Columbus Avenue some thirty years ago, with the privilege of attending the Massachusetts College of Pharmacy. I was the only student of the colored race at that time.

"The entire force of workers in the laboratory are of my race. A few years ago Mr. George R. White, the sole owner of the business, honored me by sending me to inspect the soap works which he had

experience, has encountered very few cases of Negroes, who were fitted for work of the superior grade now under consideration, who have not been able, at least through diligent effort, to obtain such work. He grants that he has come upon many instances of persons of this race who appeared at first to be the victims solely of racial prejudice. Nearly always, however, these individuals have proved in fact to be lacking either in the requisite skill or in some essential quality of character. Though the attitude of the majority of employers, as has already been stated, is that of assuming all Negroes to be incompetent, there is a substantial

purchased in Malden, and I offered suggestions and drew recommendations for many improvements. The works cost one million dollars.

"The products of the Potter Drug & Chemical Corporation are found in every country of the world, Cuticura being the chief laboratory product.

"I have found prejudice one of the best elements to my advancement, as I realized the great mistake made in the lack of good judgment in freeing the slaves in such an unbusinesslike and unreasonable way. The so-called problem to my mind is mainly with the Negro himself and depends on his knowing how to handle opposition and to grasp opportunities. One of the first duties of the Negro is to give this prejudice question a sane and Christianlike consideration.

"For centuries the white man of the South despised labor for himself and family. Habit is a tremendous force to upset; in land the betterment is only the result of years of toil and cultivation. So it is the duty of the Negro to educate the Caucasian race to a better Christian cultivation and to a nobler humanitarianism.

"If the Negro desires help from the Caucasian race, we must show them that we believe in their improvability in this practical way. The fact that the Negro has demonstrated his capacity to broaden in education and advance in the moral and social scale, together with his commercial achievements, no one knows better than the white friends of the Negro of the South; that Ephraim is not joined to his idol of ignorance, sensuality, and selfishness.

"Then Christian character is the great force wanted by both races.

"My personal property is assessed for $7500."

minority of whom this does not hold true. Officials of a number of concerns have said to the writer: "It makes no difference to me whether an employee be black or white. The man that I want, and that is worth most to me, is the man who can do the best work." Though still relatively small, the proportion of employers who take this view, and who, instead of following the policy of refusing employment to all Negroes indiscriminately, make it a rule to judge applicants on their actual merits as workmen, irrespective of race or color, is at the same time steadily increasing. The most convincing proofs of this, as well as the most impressive demonstration of the extent to which the Negro on his own side is forcing his way upward, are had in the fact that the number of Negroes employed in these occupations of higher rank is constantly growing. As has already been pointed out, an increase of six hundred and fifty-two individuals of this race took place during the decade 1890–1900, in work above the menial and common grade. For the most part, this gain was registered in the ranks of the specific occupations now under discussion, while it is in this quarter also that the greater variety of employment in which Negroes are found to-day, and of which previous note has been made, chiefly obtains.

Not only the community at large, but the Negro people themselves, are far from realizing the actual progress which the latter are making in climbing up the industrial ladder. Among both races, one hears considerable talk about the alleged narrowing of the Negro's industrial opportunities during the recent period. But in the light of the facts now before the

reader, the belief that such a narrowing has taken place
does not appear to be borne out by the concrete evidence which is available. On the whole, indeed, the
opposite has occurred. It is true, as already mentioned, that in certain kinds of lower-grade employment, such as that of waiters and domestic servants,
the Negroes have lost ground, owing especially to the
invasion of these fields by various foreign nationalities.
But the very fact that the Negroes have to some
extent been pushed out of such inferior work has practically forced them to exert themselves more successfully in getting into occupations of higher rank. As to
the net effect of foreign immigration in this respect, it
is a matter of common observation — to digress for the
moment — that frequently the latest group of newcomers, being as a rule the most heavily handicapped
by ignorance of the English language and otherwise,
has to take the poorest work at the lowest wages, thus
displacing the group just preceding; which forthwith,
both under the spur of necessity and also with the
advantage of its longer American experience, moves up
a peg in the industrial scale. Now there is good reason to believe that the lower ranks of the immigrant
legions are rendering the Negroes a similar service in
disguise; in that, while immediately ousting the latter
from some of the less desirable forms of employment in
which they have been most numerous, mediately, on
the other hand, they are actually helping to boost the
members of this race into work of better grade, where
till recently they have been comparatively few in
number. Certain it is, at any rate, that on this higher
level the Negroes have experienced not a narrowing,

but a widening, of their opportunities. Here lies their present chief field of industrial conquest. These manual occupations demanding a degree of skill, and these lines of clerical employment calling for a substantial measure of education and intelligence, constitute together, as between menial and common labor below, and the professions and independent business above, the great middle industrial group, which holds out most practical and ample promise to the Negro rank and file.

The group next in order — the third and last — consists, as has just been indicated, of Negroes in the professions and semi-professions, and those who are engaged in business on their own account. Though of course this group includes occupations of different standing, and individuals of various degrees of ability, in the large it represents the height of the Negroes' industrial achievement; — namely, their rise into positions of more or less complete proprietorship. The composition of this group in 1900 was as follows: —

THIRD GENERAL INDUSTRIAL GROUP

Professions and Business Proprietorships
Boston Proper

MEN

Actors and showmen	29
Artists and teachers of art	3
Musicians and teachers of music	31
Literary and scientific men	5
Teachers in schools	4
Clergymen	13
Dentists	10

Physicians and surgeons	12
Lawyers	12
Bootblacks	9
Barbers	25
Hucksters	8
Boot- and shoemakers	15
Teamsters	17
Laundry proprietors	4
Restaurant, saloon, boarding- and lodging-house and hotel keepers	47
Livery-stable keepers	3
Bakery proprietors	3
Confectioners	2
Bottlers and preservers	3
Butchers	6
Photographers	2
Tailors	15
Printers	4
Undertakers	2
Real-estate agents	6
Newspaper proprietors	2
Manufacturers and officials	7
Bankers	1
Merchants, retail	50
Merchants, wholesale	3
Total	353

7.8 per cent of all men at work.

WOMEN

Actresses	18
Artists and teachers of art	1
Musicians and teachers of music	15
Teachers in schools	9
Literary and scientific women	2
Ministers	1
Physicians	1
Hairdressers	5
Laundry proprietors	12
Milliners	2

Dressmakers 12
Restaurant-keepers 1
Boarding- and lodging-house keepers 55
Merchants 2
Total 136

5.9 per cent of all women at work.

Comment on these occupations may for the most part
be made without separate mention for each sex. Actors
and showmen are on the border-line between this and
the preceding group. They are mostly vaudeville performers or members of Negro troupes. The number of
Negro music teachers is constantly increasing, to keep
pace with the increasing demand for musical instruction among this race. At least one of the women
teachers has sung in a white church for many years,
and has had some white pupils. She is also the in-
ventor of the phoneterion, a device to assist persons
whose purity of tone is impaired because they cannot
keep the tongue in place while singing.[1] Among the
literary men and women are included a small number
of newspaper reporters, most of whom are employed
by local or outside publications of their own race, but
two of whom are on white newspapers of the city.[2] The
Negro men listed as teachers in schools, though having
their home in Boston or happening to be there when the
census was taken, are, with one exception, connected
with institutions in the South. The single exception

[1] Reference is had to Mrs. Nellie Brown Mitchell, widow of the
late Charles L. Mitchell, who will be recalled as one of the prominent
figures in the local history of his people since the war.
[2] Robert Teamoh, on the *Globe*, is well known among the report-
orial coterie. His special field is educational news, and only to a small
extent does his work fall among his own race.

referred to is that of the head and proprietor of a local school of pharmacy, in which all but a few of the pupils are white.[1] Mention has already been made in another context of the Negro women who are teaching in the public schools of Boston.

Of the Negro dentists, one who recently died had the most noteworthy record.[2] At one time this man was a member of the faculty of the Dental School of Harvard University. He made a reputation by exceptional skill in bridge work, and his patronage included a substantial proportion of white people. Among the physicians, of whom there are now about twenty, several have a considerable white practice.[3] One has rendered a special service to his race and to the community by establishing a hospital, managed on a semi-coöperative plan participated in by Negro churches and organizations, and providing better opportunity than has hitherto existed for clinical work by Negro physicians, and for the training of Negro nurses.[4] At this hospital some white patients have been treated. The lawyers, who now number close to twenty-five, show a larger proportion of men of ability than is the case in any other single occupation. Reference has already been made, in other connections, to some of the most prominent of these Negro attorneys; — William H. Lewis, Archibald H. Grimké, Butler R. Wilson, Clement G. Morgan, James H. Wolff, William J. Williams, and

[1] Dr. Thomas W. Patrick.

[2] Dr. George F. Grant.

[3] This is notably the case with Dr. S. E. Courtney, whose election to the former School Committee of Boston has been previously mentioned.

[4] Dr. C. N. Garland.

Edgar P. Benjamin.[1] All these men, by virtue of their part in affairs not only within but outside their own race, must be accounted influential members of the

[1] Though others are more active in public affairs, purely on the basis of professional success Benjamin ranks among the first. The following autobiographical statement, which he consented to write, is representative of the conditions from which a majority of Negro professional and business men have risen: —

"Within sight of Fort Sumter out in the bay and with a fragment of a Yankee shell still embedded in the eaves were the conditions under which I first saw the light, December 22, 1871, at Charleston, South Carolina.

"The youngest of five children, I, the child of a Negro mother and a Hebrew father, formed a link between the old and the newest acquisition to civilization. With self-complacency the dominant race claims the credit for any good qualities that a mulatto might develop and a disclaimer of any and all bad ones. Without attempting to point out the fallacies of such a view, I am convinced that the teachings and training of 'the best mother that ever lived' is the foundation stone upon which has been built all that may redound to my credit in a comparatively uneventful career.

"There is reason to believe that on the paternal side a near relationship might be shown to Judah P. Benjamin, the one-time Secretary of the Southern Confederacy and afterwards the foremost jurist of England and leading authority in the branch of the law called Sales; but tracing the branches of the genealogical tree must bide a time before it becomes an alluring avocation for the American Negro.

"My sojourn in the Southland, however, was not even a memory, as in 1872 the little mother with her brood of five started for what was already the Mecca of the Negro — Boston. And such a brave little mother it was, single-handed and alone to fight climate and privation so that her children might 'get a good schooling.' This was her chief thought and she well knew the value, for her own education was very nearly the equal of a Boston grammar-school graduate.

"We arrived just before the great fire, and with the exception of eighteen months spent in Charleston in 1882, after an attack of sickness, my adopted city has found me a constant worshiper.

"Attendance at the primary, grammar, then the English High School, and an advanced course there, entering Boston University and graduating from the Law school in 1894 was my preparation for my chosen calling, the practice of the law. Originally intending to do this in the West, the chance taking of the bar examination before

community, while as many more are close seconds to
them in this respect. The majority of the Negro
lawyers have some white clients, and in the case of half
a dozen the larger part of their practice, at least in

completing my course, and passing it successfully, determined me
upon staying in Boston.

"My desire was to enter the office of some first-class law firm for a
year or two, but I found that the supply for such positions far exceeded the demand, and further that such openings were entirely
without compensation. Both of these conditions compelled me to
strike out for and by myself, and, though I felt it a misfortune at the
time, I have since realized it to have been of the greatest value to me,
as there being no short cuts in solving knotty points the laborious
learning involved and the self-reliancy developed have often proven
their worth.

"With the loan of twenty dollars, and a desk and a couple of
chairs as an office equipment, I started out, and have remained in the
same building but in larger quarters to the present time.

"Perhaps others of the newly fledged have had the same experience, but much to my surprise I found that the many friends and
acquaintances from whom I had mentally calculated I might get a
stray bill or two to collect were apparently well satisfied with their
own attorneys, and that my clients, if they came at all, must come
from the ranks of strangers. One resolution, however, I made and
have proudly kept, — never to solicit any man's work or patronage,
but that it must come unsought on my part. Another was to give to
each man my best work and my best judgment even if the latter
meant turning him aside from his desire to litigate. These, with
loyalty to clients and the ethics of my profession, are the only
secrets to my success. My practice is general and includes both civil
and criminal. The latter, of course, is always more conspicuous
to the general public, but is nevertheless but a very small part of my
practice. About one third in number of my clients are colored, and
of course the pecuniary value of their work is much smaller. I am
sole counsel for many large firms and corporations and business
associations, many of which are white, and perhaps do work for the
larger portion of the piano concerns of the city. It might be of
interest to note that a large part of my business has come to me
through a Southern white man residing in Boston and whose friendship has been invaluable.

"Color prejudice undoubtedly exists and exists strongly in Boston,
as it does everywhere else in the United States; and as I observed on

terms of money value, is with members of the other race. Several share offices with white men. Most of the younger lawyers are graduates of schools of good standing.

The percentage of the Negroes of both sexes engaged in these semi-professional and professional occupations, though of course slight, is nevertheless gradually increasing and will continue to increase, in pace with the advance in education and intellectual ambition. The professions doubtless hold out to Negroes of exceptional ability the fullest opportunity for the exercise of their powers on a plane above racial lines, so far as this is possible. Individual achievement in this field has probably done more to break down the misconception that all Negroes are incompetent, and to compel respect for the potentialities of this race, than has any other single factor.

Passing on now to business proprietorships, it may be remarked that the typical Negro establishment, of which the others are to a large extent modifications or

two different visits to Europe there are a few signs of it in England. This, I presume, is because of the close intercourse with Americans, but which the difference in language prevents on the Continent.

"There is absolutely no 'Negro Problem,' so-called, in Boston, and which to my mind is only another name for the 'Problem of safely doing injustice to the Negro.' The Negro asks, insists, and only wants his Manhood Rights. He is content to have the same reward and the same punishment meted out to him as to a white man. This he substantially gets in Boston. True, there is prejudice, and he is debarred from most all employments, and yet is expected to be as law-abiding as a white man. The difficulties in meeting this requirement are great, but still the Boston Negro is making a creditable showing, is increasing and prospering. He has been purchasing real estate at an amazing rate for the past six or seven years, and in but few instances has made a bad investment."

outgrowths, is a grocery-fuel-dry-goods-hardware-china-stationery-tobacco-and-candy shop, and frequently a restaurant, real-estate agency, and moving-dray, all in one — and looking like the proverbial country store transplanted to the city. According as sometimes one feature predominates, sometimes another, the census enumerator lists these pot-pourris now under one term, and again under some other; but he would be sorely put to it to classify the majority did he not have the inclusive category "merchants" upon which to fall back. The undifferentiated character of these places affords further evidence of the rudimentary stage of the Negro people's economic development. Inasmuch as the Negro community has not yet produced many specialized business concerns which can compete with similar concerns under white management, Negro proprietors offer for sale a range of wares so wide as to enable them to pick up the petty trade of the vicinity, and thus to piece together a livelihood, — oftentimes a tolerably comfortable one.

The bootblacks included in this group are those having their own stands or shops; of which, however, none are large ones, like those so successfully operated by Greek immigrants. Among the barber shops are about a dozen of good size, having an average of three or more chairs. The hucksters usually have wagons, from which they peddle vegetables, fruit, fuel, or ice. The draymen, or proprietors of moving-wagons of various sorts, are rapidly increasing in number. In addition to the teams whose owners confine themselves to this business, there are an equal or larger number which, as already suggested, are run in connection with miscellaneous shops. The majority of Negro teams compare very favorably with those of white owners, as respects the appearance of both horses and wagons. These draymen do a thriving business among both races, and some of the most successful have two or three outfits. There are also several Negro cabmen.

Little lunch-rooms and restaurants abound. There are no separately conducted Negro saloons, but there is one connected with a large grocery and liquor store, and four or five with the so-called "clubs" to which previous reference has been made.[1] The only pretentious Negro hotel was the Upton, the recent closing of which, on account of disorderliness, has already been noted. Report has it that for a while one of the Upton's proprietors was of the white race, but that later the place passed entirely under Negro management. At one time the bartender was a white man. Apart from its bad character and judged purely as a business enterprise, this hotel appears to have proved successful. There are several smaller establishments which style themselves hotels, but which are really more like lodging-houses. The proprietor and manager of one of the city's well-spoken-of apartment hotels, however, the patronage of which is entirely white, is a Negro.[2] There are two good-sized livery-stables, one connected with a large undertaking business in the principal

[1] The fewness of Negro saloons is mainly accounted for by the fact that the Licensing Board makes it a general rule not to issue licenses for them.

[2] Probably the fact of the proprietor's race is known to few of the patrons, with whom his direct contact is slight, though he is in charge on the premises.

Negro section, and the other situated in the select
Fenway district and having mostly a white trade. A
downtown photographic studio owned by a Negro is
also largely frequented by white people. There are an
increasing number of Negro tailors with small but
busy shops, one of the most enterprising of whom
shares quarters with a white man, among which race
he is working up a considerable custom.

The majority of the Negro merchants are proprietors of those little-of-everything shops, with
groceries predominating, to which reference has
already been made. One out of every half-dozen of
these concerns, however, is of substantial proportions.
There are a smaller number of business places of more
distinct character. One man has built up a good-sized
trade in new and second-hand furniture. Another carries on a rather unique business in imported books.
Of the dozen or more stationery and news shops, the
longest established and probably best-paying one is
located on Howard Street in the West End, in the
midst of what has become Boston's nearest approach
to the Bowery; and enjoys a patronage drawn for the
most part from the bohemian white inhabitants of the
neighborhood. The proprietor says he has often
thought of writing a book giving his observations,
experiences, and reflections in connection with the
varied life of this section. His story would doubtless
be interesting, and might perhaps put an interrogation
point after the pretensions to superior morality on the
part of the white race. Another prosperous business is
that of Boston's only Negro cigar manufacturer. The
nearest approach to a banking business among the

Negro people is that conducted under the name of the Eureka Banking Company, but which is practically a real-estate investment enterprise.

Of the women proprietors, the great majority are boarding- and lodging-house keepers. Note has already been made of the large proportion of lodgers among this element in the population; although most of these find rooms in private homes, there are enough others to create a demand for a considerable number of regular lodging- or rooming-houses. The proprietor of one of the largest Negro restaurants is a woman. Several of the laundries which are operated by women, and of which previous mention has been made, have developed to the point where they maintain collection and delivery teams. Among the many dressmakers are at least two who have a large trade that includes fashionable white patrons.

The roll of medium-sized Negro business concerns could be much prolonged. But present purposes will be served by considering as representative those which have already been mentioned, and by taking account now in somewhat more detail of a few establishments which are important enough to stand out in the community at large, and which have proved successful in general competition with business enterprises of the same kind conducted by members of the other race.

Occupying such a position higher up in the scale, are three high-grade tailors. One of these, J. H. Lewis, should not, strictly speaking, be included, inasmuch as he recently went out of business, but the story of his rise is too interesting to be omitted. Twenty-five years ago, while still eking out a livelihood in a little back-street room, he suddenly gained a reputation in the making of the "bell" trousers then in vogue. With reputation came increased profits, and with increased profits removal to larger quarters on Washington Street, where he gradually built up an extensive trade, of which a minor part only was drawn from his own race. Most of his employees also were white. Following his retirement one of his sons has opened a shop and is emulating the father's example. The other two tailors to whom reference is made above, have select locations and command select prices. They are Ulysses S. Ridley, on Park Street, and W. S. Sparrow, on Tremont Street. Probably few of their patrons, most of whom are white, and still fewer of the general public, are aware of their racial identity. The late Joseph Lee built up a large catering business in Boston, and also established at Squantum, on the South Shore of Massachusetts, an inn which won a name for its excellent fish dinners. Since his death several years ago, his widow and children have carried on the inn, and have also conducted a successful restaurant in the downtown business section of the city. At both places, both the patrons and the majority of employees are white. The largest wig manufactory in New England is that of Gilbert C. Harris, on Washington Street. Harris came to Boston from Virginia in 1892, and found employment in the hair-working shop of a man whose surname, Gilbert, he later adopted as a prefix to his own. After his employer died, he took over the business himself. He now supplies all the wigs for the Castle Square and Bowdoin Square theatrical stock companies, and a large proportion of those used by the well-known producer, Henry W. Savage. He also has a large mail-order trade. He owns his home and several other pieces of property, contributes generously to the Negro church which he attends, and is a man of sterling character.

The Negro newspaper, the "Guardian," with the general printing-shop run as an adjunct to it, merits leading mention purely as a business enterprise. It has been going now for twelve years, which is much beyond the average length of life of the papers which spring up among this race. It is published regularly every week, has eight pages, is well set up and illustrated, and is lively and readable. More pretentious numbers, commemorating special events, are issued frequently. A good stock of advertisements, including white as well as Negro concerns, has been built up, and year by year the circulation has been extended, a considerable number of white people having been interested sufficiently to become subscribers. Independently of the question of his equal rights propaganda, which has previously been considered, the editor, William Munroe Trotter, is entitled to substantial credit for having made his paper a business success.

The retail and wholesale grocery and provision store of Goode, Dunson & Henry, situated on Shawmut Avenue near the center of the principal Negro colony, is a concern which has grown up to its present size gradually from small beginnings. It is an example of a specialized business, conducted by members of this race, which has attained proportions that enable it successfully to compete with white concerns of the same kind, not only for the Negro trade, but also for that of the white residents of that district. Through its wholesale department it supplies many of the smaller Negro grocery stores.

Probably the most noteworthy example, everything considered, of a Negro business which has been built up almost entirely within racial lines, is that of Basil F. Hutchins, the undertaker. The latter's main establishment is located in the midst of the principal Negro colony, while in addition he has a branch in Cambridge and agents in other sections. He has come nearer than any one else to acquiring a monopoly among his own people. He is also the proprietor of one of the livery-stables already mentioned, and is one of the leading Negro property owners.

The most remarkable record of all, however, but exactly the opposite of that just described, in having been achieved almost wholly outside of race bounds, is that of Theodore Raymond, in Cambridge, to whom previous reference has been made as respects his civic prominence in that suburb. Raymond has the largest real-estate business in the University City, having distanced all white competitors. His own property holdings are said to be worth upwards of $200,000. Comparatively little of his business is with Negroes, and his employees are white. A great many of those who engage him as agent know nothing of his racial identity. So high is his standing in the community that the fact of his race has been a negligible factor, at least so far as any adverse effect is concerned. This, indeed, is the most notable feature of the case.

The number of Negro business places is rapidly increasing. In the chief Negro district, where ten years ago there were not more than twenty-five of them, there are to-day, exclusive of lodging-houses, close to one hundred. In the lesser Negro sections of the city are approximately as many more, while tucked in here and there in predominately white neighborhoods are still others, probably half a hundred. The total for Boston proper is thus about two hundred and fifty. In Cambridge are at least fifty more, and in the other suburbs, combined, an equal number; which brings the entire number for Greater Boston up to three hundred and fifty or above. Though, as has been said, most of these concerns are still of humble proportions, it is also true that most of them are in process of growth; and the small number which have already attained considerable stature indicate the future toward which many of the others are developing. Even in the case of the humblest, however, the elements of ownership, management, and responsibility are present, as vital factors in instilling the Negroes with confidence in their self-reliant economic ability. Though probably these business places get only a small fraction of the entire trade of the Negro people as measured in terms of money, inasmuch as the members of this race appear to buy where they can obtain what they want, making no special effort to patronize their own concerns, they do secure most of the petty day-by-day purchases of the Negro rank and file, for the simple reason that they are nearest at hand. This trade within the race is surely tending to draw the Negroes more closely together, especially along economic lines. Every time a Negro makes a purchase in a Negro store, his respect for his race and for himself is enhanced. These Negro business places when taken together, moreover, provide work for from five hundred to a thousand Negro employees. For the proprietors, this means development of the sense of being responsible employers of labor, and as such contributing to the economic upbuilding of the Negro community; while for the employees, it means increased respect for and loyalty to their race, and the consciousness of having through their daily work a part in the Negro people's economic advance. Also, as has been mentioned, many of these Negro establishments receive a considerable measure of patronage from among the members of the other race. Every time a Negro proprietor sells goods to a white customer, his confidence in himself and his people is increased. Every time a white customer buys goods from a Negro merchant, his respect for the Negro rises. Furthermore, the total of white employees in Negro business places is much above what might be supposed, — probably between one and two hundred in Greater Boston. When a Negro becomes able to employ a white man, he naturally feels somewhat more hopeful regarding the future of his race. When a white man finds himself working for a Negro proprietor, he speedily gets rid of the notion that all Negroes are menials.

The survey of the three broad industrial groups or gradations, into which the Negroes at work in Boston have for present purposes been distributed, has now been completed. The special conditions which apply to each group, and to the specific occupations of which each is composed, have been taken up in sufficient concrete detail to give the reader at least a cursory acquaintance with the facts. It has appeared that in the case of all three groups there is a distinct trend upward toward industrial and economic betterment. This survey may now be supplemented by consideration of certain factors whose application is not limited to any particular occupation or to any one group, but which are of more general bearing, and which also involve in somewhat larger measure the connections which exist between the economic situation of the Negro people and certain forces operative in the community at large. The Negro's relation to the labor unions, the degree to which he is taking advantage of the opportunities for education along industrial lines, the extent of his ownership of property, and the manifestation of any movement on his part in the direction of combination and coöperation for the purpose of furthering his own economic welfare; — these are the principal factors of such wider scope to which reference is here intended.

With respect to the labor unions, it is a fact that the number of Negroes found in their ranks is not large. Probably not more than one union in twenty has any Negro members at all, and of those which have, probably not over one in ten counts half a dozen or more of this race on its rolls. The chief reason for this is not far to seek. As has been pointed out, the proportion of Negroes engaged in menial and common labor is far larger than the proportion of whites employed in similar labor; — in the case of men, 76 per cent as compared with 13 per cent. In work of this lowest grade, the supply of laborers is ordinarily much in excess of the demand for them. Unions, however, depend for their effectiveness on a shortage in the labor supply which enables them to enforce their demands upon employers. The unions are, therefore, fewest in number and weakest in strength in the field of menial and common occupations. This means that for the great mass of Negro laborers there are either no unions at all to join, or none that are much worth joining. At the same time, the number of Negroes engaged in work of higher grade, where unions are more numerous and stronger, is so small, as compared with the number of whites, that, even if the percentage of such Negro workmen belonging to unions should equal the percentage of unionized white workmen of the same grade, the former would still form but a very slight contingent of the union membership.

Beyond this, however, there are two further, though minor, reasons why the number of Negroes enrolled in the unions is smaller than otherwise it might be. One of these consists of a lack of understanding and to some extent a mistrust of unions on the part of the Negro people. A majority of those who by the nature of their work are qualified for union membership do not appreciate the union's purposes and functions. Individuals whom the writer has questioned have said to him that they see clearly enough the certainty of paying out hard-earned money in dues and special assessments, together with the danger of losing good positions through strikes; but not much in the way of sure and substantial benefits. The number of Negroes who hold this view, and who make no effort whatever to get into unions, is undoubtedly far larger than the number of those who do make such an effort but find themselves barred.

At the same time it is true that the attitude of some of the unions is unfavorable to the Negro, and that this is the remaining reason which accounts for the latter's limited enrollment in the ranks of organized labor. The effect of this element in the situation, however, is usually much exaggerated. On the basis of evidence at hand, in fact, the writer would be unable to point to more than half a dozen organized trades in which he feels sure the unions are opposed in any positive way to admitting members of the Negro race. Even in these cases, it would still be doubtful whether the non-admission of Negroes was a hard-and-fast rule applying to all local unions in the trade without exception; while the chances would favor finding in some quarter at least a few individuals whose personal popularity, exceptional skill, or other special circumstance had gained them entry. Even in some of the cases where Negroes are completely absent from the union membership, there would yet be a question as to whether the principal reason therefor does not lie in the fact that practically no Negroes are engaged in this kind of work, or at least none who have ever applied for admission to the union. Under such conditions any alleged opposition to the Negro within the unions is of rather an abstract character which has never been put to a concrete trial, and which if subjected to such a specific test might give way. But after making all such allowances, it nevertheless remains true that a considerable number of the unions are averse to admitting members of the Negro race. The Negroes themselves complain that such is the case, and the absence of persons of this race from the membership of the great majority of the unions may fairly be taken as implying a hostile attitude on the part of some of them. Furthermore, though the constitutions of most unions expressly forbid discrimination on the grounds of religion, race, or color, and though very few unions would openly and officially admit that they pursued an opposite policy, the writer has nevertheless heard representative individual members of various unions grant that it would be next to impossible for a Negro to get into those unions. What proportion of the unions are opposed to Negroes is a question to which only a broad answer can be given; but in all probability they are distinctly in the minority. To say that even a minority are thus prejudiced is going further than the report of a special inquiry into this matter conducted by the State Bureau of Statistics of Labor, which stated its conclusions on this point very briefly, as follows: "There appears to be no discrimination shown by the trades unions in regard to membership of the Negro. . . . Application was made to trades unions in the state as to their attitude, and the generally expressed opinion was that no discrimination was made." [1] But while the majority of unions are not positively hostile to the Negro, and while some of them, as will appear immediately, have a contingent of Negro members, it is at the same time a patent fact that few, if any, have shown any interest in the Negro's industrial welfare.

[1] *Annual Report of the Massachusetts Bureau of Statistics of Labor,* p. 285.

The unions have not yet undertaken any educational campaign among this element of the industrial community to provide it with a better understanding of their objects. They have made no special effort to enlist the Negroes in their ranks. In short, they have for the most part kept to a passive and neutral position.

The part which the Negroes have in the local labor-union movement to-day is by no means so small, however, that it may be left out of account. There is one separate Negro organization, the Boston Colored Waiters' Alliance, or Local 183 of the American Federation of Labor, which, however, appears to be more of an employment station and social club than a union in the full sense. It is composed mainly of so-called "public waiters," who are not regularly employed anywhere, but who work intermittently on catering jobs and as extra men. They hold their charter from the white waiters' alliance (Local 80) to which the Negroes used to belong, but from which they withdrew of their own desire to form a semi-independent group, this step apparently being taken because of the more or less distinct demand for Negro waiters and the more sociable time the members of this race could have by themselves. They are still closely affiliated with the white union, a joint committee conducting joint business, and there being an agreement that white and Negro waiters shall not attempt to compete with each other. Though this organization sometimes intercedes in difficulties with employers, strikes have never been resorted to and probably would accomplish little, on account of the plentiful supply of non-union waiters who may easily be had.

There used to be a union among the meat-loaders about the docks which included both Negroes and whites, but it was disrupted as a result of attempting strike tactics. At present there are several longshore-men's unions which have Negro members, but for the same reason of the excess of supply of such labor, these amount to little. A few Negroes belong to the freight handlers' unions, which are in a little better po-sition in that they have an agreement with the railway companies regarding conditions of employment. Of the Negroes engaged in work of better grade, a small number are scattered here and there through unions of the various vocations, while in one group, namely, that which is made up of the different kinds of team-sters and teamsters' helpers, they contribute a con-siderable quota, being reported to have several hun-dred union members. They are especially numerous among the coal drivers' unions, in at least one of which they constitute a majority. Negroes hold places on the executive committees of at least half a dozen of the separate unions of teamsters, and there are four mem-bers of this race on the joint council which repre-sents all these unions together. It is interesting to note in this connection that at the time of the general teamsters' strike in 1902, all but two or three of the Negro unionists remained loyal to the organization.

Summarizing the facts which have been set forth in this matter, the conclusions which the concrete evi-dence appears to warrant are, then, as follows: First, that the unions have not as yet been a factor of much importance, either pro or con, in the Negro's industrial welfare; second, that only in the case of a small minor-

ity of unions, however, has there been any positive opposition to receiving Negroes into membership; and,
third, that in the total a considerable number of
Negroes do actually belong to unions, and are sharing
in whatever benefits they may bestow.

Passing now to the question of whether any amelioration of the Negro's condition is being effected through
the medium of industrial education, it may be stated
that a substantial number of Negro young men and
young women are in fact equipping themselves thus to
do better work and to earn a better living. The 1909
Report of the Boston Trade School for Girls showed
that during the then ended five-year period following
the school's establishment, there had been 86 Negro
girls in a total enrollment of 961. This was a proportion of 9 per cent, or more than four times the proportion of Negroes in the population of Boston. In a table
giving the records of a representative number of
girls who had attended the school six months or more,
it appeared that out of 11 Negro girls who had attended
the dressmaking department from six to nineteen
months, only 2 showed no marked progress by the time
of leaving, while 2 advanced from "poor" to "good,"
4 from "fair" to "good," and 3 from "good" to "very
good" and "excellent"; that all subsequently obtained positions in the dressmaking trade, and at the
end of from six months to four years, all but one showed
wage increases averaging $2.15 a week, and in several
cases running as high as $4 a week. The presence of the
Negro girls at this school gave rise to no friction. Some
of the Negro girls who have attended this institution
carry their practical education still further in the

dressmaking, millinery, and handwork classes at the Women's Educational and Industrial Union. These girls are reported as doing well, as causing no embarrassment, and as being able to obtain good positions without much difficulty.

Negroes are found among the students enrolled in the special industrial classes of the Y.M.C.A., Wells Memorial, Franklin Union, and other similar institutions, and at private trade schools run on a commercial basis. The Y.M.C.A. had about forty members of this race last year, and Wells Memorial about a dozen. The great majority of these were in the classes for chauffeurs and automobile workers. Most of the private automobile schools also reported a few Negro pupils, the generally expressed opinion regarding whom was that they were substantially on a level with the whites in point of aptitude. The reference which has already been made to the rapid increase of Negro chauffeurs in the last few years suggests that the members of this race are turning the opportunities for education in this calling to very practical and immediate account. The recently established Franklin Union is limited to advanced technical instruction for men already engaged in the respective trades, but who are ambitious to better themselves. On account of this restriction, the number of Negroes in attendance would necessarily be slight. There were about half a dozen last year and also the year before. The instructors say that while the Negro pupils do not take hold quite so quickly and earnestly as the white ones, when they are once started they do fairly well, get on amiably enough with the others, and in most cases are enabled by the instruction given to obtain better positions. As regards the Negro boys and girls in such of the public schools as provide industrial and commercial courses, specific figures are not available, for the reason that no statistics by color are kept or given out by the school authorities. But unofficial information is to the effect that a substantial number of Negro youth are going to these schools, the proportion apparently being largest in the courses in stenography and bookkeeping. Many of the rising generation of this race are taking up similar subjects in the private business schools, a particular attraction in the case of the latter being the comparatively brief period of application that is required.

All in all, it is evident that the Negro people are coming to have a better understanding of the practical value of industrial training. They are talking about it more and more in their society meetings. Each Negro boy or girl who enters an industrial school brings in others by the influence of example. The most potent element of all, doubtless, in furthering this movement, is observation on the Negro's part of the fact that boys and girls who are equipped in this way do actually get more satisfactory positions and better pay. As a joint result of these factors, the number of Negroes who are thus preparing themselves to mount to a higher rung in the industrial ladder is year by year becoming larger. Such is the prevailing testimony. At the Trade School, for instance, to which reference has already been made, there were seven Negro girls the first year of the school's existence, and twenty-eight the fifth year. This particular rate of increase may be accepted as roughly representing the general rate at which the members of the race are moving to avail themselves of the opportunities in this direction.

It is when the test of ownership of property is applied, however, that the basic economic progress the Negroes are making becomes most strikingly manifest. Several references in general terms have previously been made to this matter, but some concrete figures may now be adduced. These figures have been gathered at no small pains and through the coöperation of many persons. The desired information could not be obtained from the land records alone, since these records contain no specifications as to race or color of owners, and since Negro owners could not be distinguished by characteristic name forms as would be the case with Polish or Italian immigrants. The only practicable method, and the one which has been followed, has been to ascertain the facts from individual Negroes who, by reason of being in the real-estate business or through other circumstances, have become accurately informed as to property ownership among their people, and who have also undertaken to verify and supplement their knowledge by consultation of the official records. In the case of the suburbs, where, with the exception chiefly of Cambridge, the number of Negroes is comparatively small, the facts could be more easily known or discovered, and substantially complete information has been procured. In Cambridge, where the Negro contingent is large and somewhat scattered, several persons were called upon for the desired facts pertaining to the several districts concerned, and in this way an approximation to completeness was obtained. In Boston proper, where this element of the

population is still larger and still more widely distributed, about a dozen persons supplied information, but
even so the approximation to the facts was necessarily
less close. As for the values given, these are in part the
assessed valuation, and in part the estimated selling
price; on the average they may be accepted as fair
market values.

The actual figures obtained, for Boston proper,
Cambridge, and 15 of the 27 other suburbs, but cover-
ing only ownership by individuals, were as follows:
In 15 suburbs, real property to the value of $693,085;
in Cambridge, to that of $869,000; and in Boston
proper, to that of $1,143,500; making the total for
Greater Boston, $2,705,585. These, however, are
minimum amounts. In the case of the suburbs, for
which as previously stated the returns were substantially complete so far as they went, there were, nevertheless, 12, including one (Lynn) with a good-sized
Negro population, for which no returns were made.
In the case of Cambridge, and to a still greater degree
in that of Boston proper, it was apparent that the returns were considerably below the facts, inasmuch as
each new informant was able to add appreciably to the
count. Nor do the above figures include property owned
by real estate companies, churches, and societies. Intelligent supplementary estimate, made on the basis
of collateral evidence at hand and general acquaintance with conditions among the Negro people, must
therefore be brought to bear to round out these figures.
Considerations no less important than the matter of
value, moreover, are the number and occupation of
property owners, and the number and character of the

properties owned. Though occupations were given for a quota sufficient to be regarded as representative, the number of owners reported (641) must be added to by estimate, while similar calculation must enter even more largely into the number of pieces of property owned, this information having been lacking in about twenty-five per cent of the returns. The question of what constitutes a "piece" of property is also open to difference. For example, there are many cases of two adjacent lots containing a so-called double house. It might be said that if a single lot and house is counted as one "piece," two lots and a double house should be counted as two "pieces." But for the reason that the most important element involved in this connection is probably the enterprise and responsibility contingent upon ownership of properties which require separate management, the writer has reckoned such double houses and also a few tracts of unimproved lots or gardening land, which are units so far as management is concerned, as single "pieces."

The figures finally arrived at, on this basis, and which may warrantably be regarded as near, and if anything below rather than above, the facts, are as follows:[1] —

PROPERTY (REAL) OWNED BY NEGROES

Individual Ownership.

	Number of owners	Number of pieces	Value
Suburbs (all except Cambridge) .	365	407	$ 900,000
Cambridge	200	300	950,000
Boston proper	215	265	1,250,000
Total, Greater Boston . .	780	972	$3,100,000

[1] For fuller details, see Appendix, table xvi.

Corporate ownership

Owned by real-estate companies	$150,000
Owned by churches and societies	250,000
Total, corporate ownership	$400,000

Summary

Owned by individuals	$3,100,000
Corporate ownership	400,000
Grand total	$3,500,000

Individuals owning more than one piece

87 individuals own	2 pieces
11	3
9	4
1	5
1	6
3	7
1	10
1	25 pieces or upwards.
Total 114	2 or more pieces.

Occupations

346 owners distributed through 80 specific occupations, and grouped as follows: —

Laborers, waiters, Pullman porters, and janitors .	148
Skilled workmen in various trades	62
Clerks, professional men, and business proprietors	136
Total	346

In the foregoing calculation the word "own" is used in a moral rather than a strict property sense. Probably not over ten per cent or fifteen per cent of this property is fully paid for and free of mortgage, and probably not over twenty per cent is more than half paid for. But in the case of all of it, purchase has been begun and full ownership is gradually being acquired. The responsibility for payment and management has been assumed. In a moral sense, these Negroes must be regarded as owners. And the first thing which the figures prove is that the Negro people own many times as much property as, in view of their industrial disabilities, would generally be presumed.

Nearly all this property consists of homes, business holdings forming a very small item. The great majority of these homes, probably eighty-five per cent, are occupied by the owners. At this stage of the Negroes' development, when the strengthening of their social and moral order is essential, the ownership of homes is far more important and holds out far more promise of substantial progress, than would be the case with ownership of business property on a basis of investment or speculation. It further appears that both the number and proportion of home-owners is larger in suburban Cambridge than in Boston proper, and still larger in the smaller suburbs. This means that the Negroes are acquiring homes under the best conditions, — that is, not principally in the more or less congested, noisy, and dirty sections of the city, but in the more open, quiet, and cleanly outlying districts. It also means a tendency toward the wider distribution of the Negroes and toward residence in white neighborhoods, which in turn implies progress toward interracial understanding and amity.

The number of real-estate holders shows that a surprisingly large proportion of the entire Negro population belong to the property-owning class. It is fair to assume that, on the average, each owner represents a

family group of at least four, — husband, wife and
children, widow or widower with children or relatives,
brothers and sisters, or other combinations, — and
that the total of 780 owners, therefore, represent at
least 3120 people, or about one eighth of the entire
Negro population. In other words, approximately one
Negro out of every eight is either a property owner
himself or an immediate member of a property-owning
family group. A people with so substantial an experience as this in the possession of land and home may
look into the future with no small degree of justifiable
confidence.

The information respecting occupations of owners is
significant in several ways. It fully confirms the statement made at an earlier point that a goodly proportion of those Negroes who must nominally be set
down as belonging to the lowest industrial group, have
in fact acquired property and thus become entitled to
a higher ranking in the economic scale. It shows at the
same time, however, that the members of this race who
are engaged in what may be regarded as skilled manual
occupations have possessed themselves of property to
a still larger extent, in proportion to their numbers;
while the clerical, professional, and business class
have done better still. The number of persons owning
two or more pieces of property evidences the evolution
of a landlord and investor class, and the accumulation
of a surplus capital fund. The writer knows personally
of a dozen people who hold from four to ten pieces of
property each.[1] One of these, who, starting with innate

[1] The largest owner of all is Theodore Raymond, of Cambridge,
to whose holdings previous reference has been made. He is credited

common sense and an appreciation of what thrift can
do as almost his sole assets, has been most successful
in increasing his holdings, is Robert F. Coursey; all of
whose time is now required in giving proper attention to his responsibilities of ownership.[1] It is sig-

in the Cambridge tax records with real property to the assessed value
of $190,000. This total is said to be made up of twenty-five or more
pieces of real estate which he has gradually acquired in the course of
his business career. No doubt he owns additional property in other
suburbs and in Boston proper. His particular case, however, is in all
respects very exceptional.

[1] The following little autobiography shows how Coursey's success has been attained, and is typical of the way in which many
others of the race are accomplishing similar results: —

"In offering to the public this brief sketch of my life, I dare not
hope that it will make the strong and lasting impression that I would
wish, but I trust that it will be productive of some partial benefit. I
hope it will give inspiration to build character, also to strengthen
ambition, and generally to assist in encouraging those who have
decided to make their mark in life. They should remember that
diligence is the mother of all good luck and that God gives all things
to industry.

"I was born May 19, 1861, on a farm in Canada, my father having
escaped from slavery to Canada in the early forties. My mother was
a Canadian by birth; her father was also a fugitive slave, having
escaped from servitude when a lad of about sixteen years of age. By
industry and frugality, he accumulated sufficient means to purchase
a farm of two hundred acres, but lost it all, and all that he possessed,
by indorsing notes for farmers of the Anglo-Saxon race.

"When I was a boy, I attended the country school until about
sixteen years old. I then worked on a farm for a year or so longer
and then determined to try for a fortune in the city. At the age of
seventeen, I went to Toronto, a distance of about twenty miles, and
remained there about a year, after which I went to Cincinnati,
Ohio, and from the latter place came to Boston. I readily found
employment in the hotels there, and two years later went to Montreal, Canada, where I was employed in the Pullman Car service.
This work I liked very much, as it offered me an excellent opportunity of seeing the different large cities throughout the United
States and Canada. My headquarters being in Montreal, I ran to
Quebec, Halifax, Toronto, Detroit, and Chicago, and at the end of

nificant that as a rule Negro landlords give preference
to Negro tenants. Thus, while making it easier for
their own people to find suitable homes, they are at
the same time encouraging and furthering racial cohesion and mutual help.

every trip I invariably deposited the entire proceeds of my trip in
the Molson Bank in Montreal, minus fifty cents that I kept in my
pocket to begin my next run. It was not long before I had accumulated the neat little sum of $420; but alas, the tide changed. Misfor-
tune overtook me. I found myself in the middle of winter, out of
employment. I was bewildered. Here I was in a French-Canadian
city, out of employment, with $420 capital. What was I to do? I
drew my cash from the bank, packed my personal belongings, and
hastily left for Toronto, a distance of three hundred miles, where I
invested a portion of it in a marriage certificate. After all the little
details were arranged and the ceremony performed, I returned to
Boston, and when I found myself fairly comfortably settled in three
rooms, I counted up my cash and found to my surprise that I could
only strike a balance of $50.

" I soon obtained employment with a drug firm and for my service
received $8 per week. From this I paid rent and provided for my
wife and self. A year or so later I took up janitor work, and when
about thirty years of age, I again went over my accounts and found
that I had a balance to my credit in the bank of $1250. This was
Capital No. 2. Capital No. 1 having escaped from me so easily, I
determined to put this where it would be more secure. I decided
to invest it in real estate. I was somewhat timid in venturing alone.
I looked around for company and found a friend whose capital was
about the size of my own. He, like myself, was also a little afraid,
so we decided to make the leap together, purchasing the property on
Irving Street, giving us an equity of $2500. About a year later, I had
saved sufficient to purchase my friend's share, and from then I began
on my own account. I had contracted the real-estate fever. I longed
for capital to carry on the business on a large scale. Through the
purchase of my first property I became acquainted with a gentleman
who was going to be absent from the country for eighteen months
and who had some property here which he wanted some one to care
for. I persuaded him to lease me three houses in the West End.
These I sublet and made a fair profit, working during the day and
collecting my rents at night. I would be at my work in the morning
as early as four o'clock, often not returning at night until eight. I

The fact of perhaps greatest import of all, in this connection, is that the bulk of the property owned by Negroes, probably two thirds of it, has been acquired during the last ten years. Testimony is unanimous on this point. The implication is that within the past decade the Negroes have at last got far enough ahead of the daily necessities to be able to lay something aside for the purchase of homes for themselves; and,

soon found myself with capital sufficient to purchase another house which, after keeping about a year, I sold at a fair profit. A few years later I drifted into politics, joining the ranks of the Democracy, and in 1895 organized the Ward 11 Democratic Club, a local organization composed of colored voters of the ward. Two years later, when Mayor Quincy was nominated for a second term, we went to the Democratic caucus with 220 men. I was secretary of the organization, and was appointed by the mayor custodian of the Historical Building and Old Probate Court. I received a fair compensation and from it saved all that was possible. The incoming administration being Republican, did not approve of my Democratic principles; therefore removed me in 1899 for the good of the service.

"Again I stopped, went over my accounts, and found that, including the Irving Street property, I had a balance to my credit of $11,000. I then bought my second house, and a few months later mortgaged them both and purchased the third. This one I made into flats which paid a fair percentage on the investment. I now began to realize that my capital was growing rapidly. During all this time I still continued part of my janitor work, four years later buying my fourth house. This I also converted into flats, and two years later invested in my fifth house valued at $8000. A year and a half later I made my sixth purchase, consisting of two four-story apartment houses assessed for $13,000. Very recently I made my seventh investment, valued at $8000.

"I rarely purchase property that I am not desirous of keeping, and of the property that I have purchased for investment, I have disposed of but two pieces, so that to-day when I stop and take account of stock, I find that I am paying taxes on nearly $50,000. Yes, —

"Pluck wins —
            The average is sure;
    He wins the fight who can the most endure,
    Who faces issues — who never shirks,
    Who waits and watches, and who always works.' "

in the case of some, for the purchase of other homes to be rented to their fellows not quite so far along, but on the way. The practical wisdom of putting savings into property is an ever-present theme among the Negro people. They manifest a veritable land hunger. Real-estate agents abound, and their shingles confront one at every turn — even in such unexpected places as barber shops. The Negroes are learning the lesson of property well, and are turning it to good account. As a result, the property-acquiring movement appears to be advancing at a constantly accelerating pace.

This subject leads naturally into the next one before-mentioned for consideration, — namely, that of coöperation among the Negroes for the purpose of promoting their economic welfare. For as yet such combination is confined almost wholly to the field of land investment. Allusion has already been made to the Negro's deficiency in the capacity for coöperation in general. Now coöperation in the field of industrial and business matters, to be successful, must be thoroughly definite, dependable, and permanent. As might be presumed, therefore, organization along these lines is even less developed among the Negroes than is coöperation on their part in any other respect. Nevertheless such organization is beginning to take shape. The use of funds and ownership of property by churches and societies partake of the character of business combination. All but a few of the twenty-five Negro churches hold property, though in nearly every case, as previously pointed out, this property is heavily mortgaged. The constant effort to make both ends meet, and at least to keep the interest paid, calls for the same sort of joint planning and individual yielding and helping that is necessary in collective business undertakings. That the Negroes have somehow kept their churches intact in spite of the heavy financial burden is really a substantial business achievement. In the societies, especially the more prosperous fraternal lodges, the coöperative business element enters still more largely into operation. Some years ago one lodge undertook to run a grocery store with its funds. This venture proved a failure. But most of the lodges have a surplus in the bank, the care and disbursement of which call for mutual discussion and management. As previously mentioned, two of the lodges of Odd Fellows in Boston proper own jointly a hall in the West End, part of which is rented out; while in Cambridge, several lodges of the same order own a similar hall in common.

The only examples of strictly business combination, however, consist of several small groups of persons who have formed real-estate partnerships and companies. Several concerns which solicit funds in Boston have their headquarters and their somewhat uncertain investments elsewhere, while in this city itself, the fact that self-styled companies spring up from time to time and soon pass out of existence, makes it difficult to know just how many genuine ones there really are and what they amount to. But it is safe to say that half a dozen not only make pretensions, but actually hold property which totals, as has already been estimated, to approximately $150,000 in value. Among these, the largest and most important is the organization known as the Goode Trust Company, or Jesse Goode Associates. This company, which in 1910 held about a dozen pieces of property assessed for $73,000, and which has subsequently made other acquisitions, has an interesting history. It is composed of some twenty-odd men, most of whom are waiters. Its president, Jesse Goode, who is also at the head of the large retail and wholesale grocery firm of Goode, Dunson & Henry, to which earlier reference has been made, used to be a waiter himself. He conceived the idea of taking the small weekly savings of his fellows and investing them in real estate, and on this basis the present company was gradually built up. Here, indeed, is a practical lesson by which the Negro people may greatly profit, as indicating how, by combination, individual savings petty in themselves may be massed to acquire property holdings which not only yield a good return to the individuals immediately concerned, but which also reflect credit upon, and afford substantial encouragement to, the whole Negro community. This particular organization bids fair eventually to develop into something more ambitious — perhaps a real bank or a department store — and thus to become Boston's first instance of business coöperation by Negroes on a large and successful scale.

There is promise of a further degree of economic solidarity among the Negroes in the Negro Business League. It is an interesting fact that the national organization of this body, of which Booker T. Washington is the founder and president, was launched in Boston, in the year 1900.[1] Since then it has grown to such an extent that at present it comprises more than a dozen state branches, and close to two hundred and

[1] At Parker Memorial, August 23–24.

fifty local ones.[1] Annual conventions have been held,
at which the Negro's agricultural, industrial and commercial problems are gone over and discussed, signal
instances of success described, and practical measures
of improvement recommended. The Boston branch
was the first one to be formed, and is regarded as one
of the strongest in the country.[2] There is another
branch in Cambridge. Locally, what this organization
has accomplished thus far, in the main, has been simply to bring a substantial proportion of the Negro business men together from time to time, for the consideration of their common interests; and thus to promote
some consciousness of unity among them, and some
understanding of the means by which more effective
coöperation may be worked out. This is good seed,
which must be sown; and though time will be required
for the fruition, a future crop, in the form of tangible
business progress, is certain.

The most essential features of the Negro's economic
situation are now before the reader. Looking back over
the facts, stage by stage, as they have been presented,
what is the gist of the conclusions to be drawn from
them, and what their final and net significance?

[1] For a full list of these branches, see the *Negro Year Book*, edited
by Monroe N. Work, of the Research and Record Department of
Tuskegee Institute, Tuskegee, Alabama. This publication, of about
the size of the World's Almanac and of which the price is 25 cents
(postage five cents additional) is a mine of up-to-date information regarding the Negro's conditions in the United States and elsewhere.

[2] Branch No. 1, organized August 27, 1900, at the office of Gilbert
C. Harris. Its present officers are: President, Philip J. Allston;
vice-president, J. H. Madison; treasurer, W. C. Lovell; secretary, W.
Alexander Cox.

First, the Negro is, undoubtedly, still on an industrial plane many degrees below that of the white man; the great mass of the Negro people being confined to menial or common labor. That such is the case has been shown to be due, at bottom, to the industrial unfitness of the Negro himself, arising not only from the peculiar conditions to which he is subjected, but also from certain of his own inherent shortcomings in qualities indispensable to industrial efficiency and success. A secondary factor accounting for his industrial disability consists of the pronounced discrimination against him on the part of the other race. While, on the one hand, this very prejudice is based upon the Negro's actual and amply demonstrated unfitness; on the other hand, it tends to perpetuate that unfitness by rendering all the higher avenues of industry comparatively inaccessible to the members of this race, and thereby limiting their industrial opportunities. Such is the interaction of adverse elements, which hampers and retards the Negro's economic advance.

Nevertheless, he is forging ahead. Even in connection with those kinds of labor at the foot of the industrial scale in which the bulk of his race are employed, allowance must be made for the fact that he is still relegated to such labor by tradition and the prevailing prejudice in his disfavor, without regard to any higher potentialities he may possess; and that, turning this necessity to as good account as may be, he is to a large extent deriving from these occupations very substantial earnings, with which he is becoming enabled in many cases to possess himself of a home, —or at least to provide his family with the common comforts, to educate his children, and thus altogether to rise measurably above his apparent and enforced industrial status. Better still, however, he is, in constantly increasing numbers and proportion, mounting into the ranks of those manual and clerical occupations which constitute the broad middle group of industry. Whatever of contraction has taken place in his range of employment has applied mainly to the lower forms of labor, where during recent years he has been subjected to severe competition on the part of certain nationalities of foreign immigrants; while on the higher level a steady widening of his opportunities appears to be taking place. In this intermediate field, which is of the greatest strategic importance to the rank and file of his people, the Negro is constantly becoming more strongly established. At the top also, in the sphere of the professions and business proprietorships, a substantial and continually growing number of this race are found; and here the qualities of initiative, independence, and responsibility are most fully developed, as vital assets for the further economic advance of the whole Negro community. Likewise along the more general lines of economic betterment, this race is making good strides forward. In appreciable numbers its members are taking part and benefiting in the trade-union movement. By means of practical industrial education, they are beginning to equip themselves to take a higher place in industry. As marking past achievement and definitely insuring future progress, they have contrived to acquire a rather surprising amount of property in homes. Real-estate investments are not so uncommon as would be supposed. Forms of economic combination which may introduce a new stage of collective capacity, are in a few instances beginning to take shape. The Negroes in Boston are thus not only laying an economic foundation, but are accumulating a surplus with which to rear the structure of a better family and community life.

CHAPTER X

THE FUTURE OF THE NEGRO PEOPLE

THE past and present of the Negro in Boston have now been marshaled in detailed review. But no doubt the query which is uppermost in the mind of the reader, and certainly the one which leads in interest before the public, is that having to do with the Negro's future. On the basis of the evidence contained in the foregoing account, is it possible, therefore, to forecast in some measure the destiny of the Negro people, and to predict the position which this race will probably come to occupy in the community?

This question resolves itself into two parts. First: — What is the real crux of this much discussed but seldom clearly expressed "Negro Problem"? Second: — Does this problem, thus defined, show signs of being in process either of aggravation, on the one hand, or of mitigation and solution, on the other?

In undertaking to answer these inquiries, which apply not to any one period or phase of the Negro's condition, but to his situation as a whole, the facts that have already been set forth must now be interpreted in a comprehensive way. In place of the historical and topical order, which has previously been followed, must be substituted that of synthesis and generalization. Nor will any mere restatement or summary fulfill the present purpose. It is the total and net significance of the facts at hand, in their relation to the Negro's road ahead, that is now required.

Section 1. The Problem

In all discussion regarding the Negro, two opinions, which at least on their face are widely at variance, may be distinguished. The one looks upon the colored man as inherently different *The Two Views* from and on a plane beneath the white man, and holds that its members should be kept more or less apart from the rest of the community, and definitely "in their place." The other opinion sees the Negro solely or mainly as the victim of an unreasonable and unfair race or color prejudice, and demands as a matter of justice that he be raised to a place of parity with other elements of the population, — at least in such respects as may be brought within the control of public or semi-public regulation. Many shades of opinion fall in between these points, but these are the two extremes. How far do the concrete facts which are available go to confirm either of these views as against the other, to indicate that both are in error, or to show that the truth lies in their conjunction?

It is of course undeniable that the precedent conditions from out of which the Negro popu- *Conditions of* lation of Boston is derived, have, from *Origin Inferior* the earliest period down to the present, been of a peculiarly inferior kind.

The first members of this race to appear in that city were brought, by way of the Bahamas, from their native African jungle, where from time immemorial their ancestors had lived in a state of primitive savagery. They were savages themselves, utterly ignorant of civilization, having no religion above a fear-born superstition, and lacking all conception of reasoned morality. As to the Negroes who have taken up their abode in Boston in the long period since the landing of the first shiploads of black chattels, their origin also has been of a terribly adverse character. The great mass of them have been either former slaves, or the offspring of slaves, from the South; where for two centuries and a half their race was held in a subjection even more degraded than the savage state of their ancestors, so far as concerned its prohibition of all independence and independent progress, and its disregard of any germs of personal chastity and marital loyalty. Nor in the brief span of years since slavery was abolished in law, has the Negro's lot in the Southern States, whence Boston's quota of this race is still chiefly drawn, been other than a slavish one in fact.

With regard, next, to the collective attainment of
Inferior Place in   this race in the Boston community itself;
the Community   — here likewise the Negro appears always to have occupied an inferior place.

At first he was held as a slave. Then, from the time slavery died out in the State until the national emancipation of his race, he rose only a few degrees, to the rank of a servant class, still lacking many of the manhood privileges possessed by the city's other inhabitants. Since the war, though endowed with political and civil rights equal to those of white citizens, the Negro people have nevertheless remained the most backward group in the community. In point of mere physical replacement and increase of their stock, which is surely the indispensable basis for any permanent collective progress on their part, they have not till very recently begun to hold their own; their depletion by deaths having previously exceeded their replenishment through births. Their social order and organization are still the most rudimentary. Their churches are the weakest. Their part in political affairs is the least. As concerns their industrial rank, the great majority are found at the bottom, in menial or common labor. And with reference, finally, to the inculcation among its members of any positive code of morality and any general ethical standards, this race is farthest in the rear.

This inferior attainment of the Negroes as a racial group apparently implies a corresponding and underlying inferiority on the part of the individuals comprising this group: — so far, at least, as respects their past and present abilities. Leaving out of account at this juncture the minority, made up of those who are exceptions to the general rule, and confining attention to the common mass of the Negro people, what are the facts with regard to the degree in which the average Negro measures up to the average white man?

Certain respects in which the Negro is found below par have already been specified, at appropriate points in the present account. These may now, however, be recalled and assembled together, so that their full significance may be the better understood.

Starting with the lowest plane, the physical, the Negro has been shown to evince a lesser reproductive power, and also a lesser resistance, not only to disease, but to the general wear and tear of present-day urban

conditions. The propensity of the members of this
race to rove about more or less futilely from place to
place is symptomatic of a lack of stability. In the
broadly social field, the Negro exhibits a glaring incapacity for coöperation of the underlying and permanently sustained kind, as distinguished from simple
sociability and gregariousness, which is so frequently
fickle and ephemeral. Here also, in the Negro's hesitancy to take responsible action on his own account,
and in his constant falling back upon the other race
for guidance and support, is disclosed a want of initiative and self-reliance. These same deficiencies, which
thus appear in their bearing upon social organization,
are evidenced still further in political affairs, where
they show themselves in the Negro's failure to take
fuller advantage than he now does of his potential
voting strength; and also in religious activity, where
these identical failings largely underlie the difficulties
that beset the Negro churches on the side of management and financial maintenance. In the obliquity of
many of the Negro ministers, as well as in the tolera-
tion of such culprits by their congregations, is revealed
a serious defectiveness of moral vision; while a shortage in the power of restraint and self-control are indicated by the Negro's proneness to an excess of religious emotionalism. In connection with industrial
and economic conditions, obvious shortcomings in
the basic qualities of trustworthiness, responsibility,
accuracy, and thoroughness, largely account for the
relegation of the bulk of this race to menial and other
low-grade labor; while want of persistence and of fixed
purpose, together with lack of initiative and of the

ability for combination, are further inherent obstacles in the way of the Negro's rise into higher callings and of his advance along independent and coöperative commercial lines. With reference, lastly, to the practical standards of rectitude of this race, the Negro's disproportionate commission of crime and his flagrant sexual laxity are but two of the most obvious outcroppings of a generally discernible moral and ethical undevelopment, by which he is characterized.

Thus it appears that the ordinary run of Negroes are lacking in many of the chief elements which go to make up actual competitive worth and accomplishment. The definite value of this conclusion will be enhanced, however, if the elements here involved turn out, on further scrutiny, to be not disconnected from one another, but so closely inter-related that they may perhaps be reduced to a common denominator.

To the end of determining whether such is indeed the case, the qualities in which the Negro has been shown to be deficient may now be set down more concisely, and with some approximation to their natural sequence. They are as follows: reproductive power; resistance to disease and to general wear and tear; stability; self-control; trustworthiness; responsibility; accuracy; thoroughness; persistence; constancy of purpose; initiative; self-reliance; positive morality and defined ethical standards.

When these qualities are thus lined up side by side, does it not become evident that each and all of them are characteristics the Negro's falling short in which clearly signifies an intrinsic weakness or flabbiness at the very root and core of his make-up? Let the reader go through this list of failings item by item, and he will find that every one of them bears out this interpretation. What the Negro lacks, in short, is that somewhat indefinite but nevertheless sufficiently well understood and absolutely fundamental attribute, called stamina. This is his central and underlying deficiency, in which all the others that have been enumerated have their common source, and of which they are, in truth, only the more or less differentiated manifestations. With respect to reproductive power and resistance to disease, it is more specifically with relation to physical and nervous stamina that the Negro exhibits a shortage. But even here the lack goes deeper — or higher — than the merely physical. The Negro reveals a want of that vital something which enables one to resist and overcome even physical exhaustion, with sheer force of will; and which renders one capable of standing up to his responsibilities and putting his best endeavor into the tasks before him. The element here involved is in its nature essentially moral, — not in the narrower or more conventional application of this term, but in its broadest and most basic sense. The final diagnosis of the Negro's case must be, then, that when weighed in the scale he is found wanting, in point of fundamental moral stamina.

To the previous question, therefore, as to whether any actual inferiority on the part of the individual Negro is found to underlie the backwardness of this race as a group in the community, an affirmative answer must be given. So far as pertains to the past and to the present, the *average* Negro — using this unscientific term for lack of a better — has always been, and still is, inferior to the *average* white man. Nor does this inferiority show itself in respects which are only of superficial or minor importance. It is as deep-seated as possible, and extends throughout the whole range of the Negro's character and conduct.

In the light of this conclusion, it will now be possible to take account more understandingly of the second projecting feature of the present problem, — namely, the fact that from the very beginning the Negro in Boston has been looked upon and treated as an inferior by the city's other inhabitants.

Negro Regarded and Treated as Inferior

Far back in colonial days, the plaint that he was the object of contempt and ill-usage was raised by the Negro himself, and ever since then it has kept recurring, a pathetic and monotonous refrain. "Some view our sable race with scornful eye," lamented Phillis Wheatley, her people's first poetess and prophetess. A prayer for strength to bear up under the "troubles" and "daily insults" which the members of this race had to endure, was sent up by Prince Hall, sturdy Negro leader in the years of the nation's birth. "The most degraded, wretched, and abject set of beings that ever lived since the world began," was the woe-begone characterization of this people wrung from the heart of David Walker, Negro forerunner of the Abolition struggle. On the part of the other race, during the same early period, an attempt was made to drive the Negroes out of the city, by a law which classed them in with "rogues, vagabonds, common beggars, and other idle, disorderly, and lewd persons;" while some years afterwards, this attempt having failed to accomplish its purpose, serious alarm was expressed at "the increase of a species of population which threatens to become both injurious and burdensome."

After the Negro's emancipation and his admirable record as a soldier in the Civil War, and for twenty-five to thirty years following, it is true that, speaking comparatively, with reference to the preceding period, the Negro was considerably fostered and indulged. When all is said, however, such positive favor as was extended to him was confined to a small minority of the white population; while in the case of the great mass of the other race, the aversion toward him was only somewhat softened or held in check. The particular instances of exclusion of Negroes from hotels, barber shops, and various places of entertainment, that have previously been cited, were but representative examples of much discrimination of that sort, which was in fact sufficiently pronounced to force the Negro people and their white champions into the fight for a protective statute of civil rights.

Meanwhile, moreover, an undercurrent of opinion adverse to the Negro had been setting in. It had its source partly in the disillusionment, with regard to any expectation of the Negro's immediate transcendence of his conditions, resulting from the sorry spectacle this race presented in the South during the notorious Reconstruction period of misgovernment. A second influence, working in the same direction, was the gradual inclination of the North to the Southern view of the Negro, as being a race on a lower plane of development, and therefore demanding a policy different from that followed with respect to other elements of the population. What struck closest home in Boston, however, was the cumulative influx into that city of great numbers of raw and uncouth Negro immigrants from the Southern Black Belt. Continued contact and experience with these unlovely newcomers, effectually modified the previously somewhat ideal sentiment of many white Bostonians toward the Negro in the abstract.

These several causes gradually produced a reaction of feeling, and about the signal year 1895, antipathy toward the Negro, which, as already suggested, had been more or less quiescent since the war, began to reassert itself. During recent years this antipathy has apparently been on the increase — so far as the attitude of the bulk of the white population is concerned. To show that such has been the case, not only as something rather intangibly felt or believed, but as a matter of concrete and demonstrable fact, is, however, not an entirely easy matter. Yet what would seem to be specific evidence to this effect is afforded, in the broadly social field, by the tendency to bar Negroes from semi-public institutions, especially churches; on the political side, by the decrease to zero, in recent years, of elective offices held by Negroes; and with respect to industrial conditions, by the increase of the degree of resistance which a Negro has to overcome, particularly in occupations of better grade, in obtaining employment. In general, this recent change of front toward the Negro has manifested itself in a noticeable, though as yet by no means far advanced, movement away from the Abolitionist propaganda of unrestricted inter-association between the two races, and in the direction of the Negro's segregation to some extent.

What, now, is the fundamental reason why in Bos-
Prejudice Based ton the Negro has always been looked
upon Inferiority upon and treated as an inferior ? Is it
not obviously to be found in the fact, already established, of the actual past and present inferiority of
the Negro himself?

The other possible explanations of the unfavorable
attitude in question are that it is either racial antagonism or color aversion — or a combination of the two.
As for race hostility, however, its exhibition generally
accompanies and is roughly commensurate with extreme racial differences. But it is a very interesting
fact, of which even the bare truth is seldom consciously
realized, and of which the full significance in the present connection would require extended comment,
that, except for color and certain other physical characteristics, the American Negro is very closely like the
native white American. First of all, he speaks the same
language. This means that he and his fellow-countrymen of the other race are able to talk to and understand each other; and are thus free from those barriers
of difference of speech, which so often lead to mutual
misconception and distrust. In the second place, the
Negro has the same religion as the white people round
about him. Thus is one of the most unhappily pro-
lific causes of contention among mankind absent from
the relations of the Negro with his neighbors. And
finally, most important of all, the Negro's national
traditions and allegiance are identical with those of
his white compatriots. He has been in this country
from the beginning, and is neither an adopted newcomer with a diverse past, nor an alien, intent or bound,

should need arise, to serve some other flag. Instead, therefore, of there being ground for racial antagonism between the Negro and the white members of the community, this oneness, at three of the most vital points of possible race difference, should certainly tend to reduce such antagonism to a minimum.

The one element of striking dissimilarity between the two races is, as already suggested, that of the Negro's color and certain other physical characteristics, — more particularly a strong natural odor, kinky hair, and coarseness of features. Were these characteristics accompanied, however, by intellectual and moral qualities equaling or excelling those of the white man, is it not reasonable to presume that aversion to them would either not arise at all, or would at any rate be more than offset by respect and admiration? Should a company of Martians — to employ a fanciful illustration — land upon our planet earth, and prove to be jet black, but at the same time unquestionably our superiors, in knowledge and attainment, it is hardly probable that these visitors would be ostracized on the score of their color. If in this hypothetical case any hostility should arise, it would have its origin in envy, and not in disdain. But it is not necessary to go so far afield for illustration and example. For were darkness of complexion, in and of itself, a sufficient cause of pronounced aversion toward races thus Nature-tinted, then surely such aversion should be exhibited toward the American Indians, the Chinese and Japanese, and even the swarthy-skinned southern Europeans. While it is true that more or less prejudice toward these races does exist, yet this does not appear to have arisen, except incidentally, on account of their complexion. Rather is it due to those other differences, to which attention had already been called as lacking in the Negro's case, or to the belief that these people — at least the strata of them commonly found in America — are on a lower plane of advancement, and thereby threaten our own higher standards.

That both racial antagonism and color aversion may figure as appreciable factors in the antipathy toward the Negro, the writer does not intend to gainsay. But to hold that, either singly or in combination, these are the essential elements which account for that antipathy, is a contention which, as has now been indicated, cannot be adequately substantiated. In the main and in last analysis, the aversion in question is based upon recognition of the Negro's past and present inferiority. It is not race-feeling. It is not color-feeling. It is inferiority-feeling. Differences of race and color, however, have the effect of making this as yet inferior group stand out conspicuously; whence it easily results that these features, which are in fact only incidental accompaniments of the real cause of the antipathy in question, are confused with that real cause itself.

The actual situation may be well expressed in terms of one's own everyday experience. Just as any individual, finding himself brought into association with another individual whom he perceives to be of distinctly inferior mould, naturally and almost unconsciously adapts his attitude and conduct toward that individual to conform with this fact; so, in the same way, the white race, realizing that the Negro is still at an inferior stage of development, feels and acts toward him accordingly.

But to dismiss the prevailing attitude toward the Negro, thus fundamentally explained, as something wholly in the nature of an effect, and having no separate existence in itself as *Prejudice a Second Factor* a cause, of adverse reactive influence upon the Negro's life, would be to fall far short of recognizing the full truth. For though this antipathy is ultimately and at bottom a product of real and legitimate discrimination as between different degrees of actual racial worth, yet immediately and on the surface, it is, to a large extent, patently undiscriminating and unreasonable. It manifests itself in a sweeping way toward the Negro people in the mass and as a racial group. But only in comparatively slight measure does it make distinction as between individuals of different degrees of ability, or gradations of different levels of attainment, within this group. And thus it becomes, in the strict meaning of the term, an out-and-out prejudice; — or, in other words, an adverse prepossession of mind against the Negro in general, without regard to specific evidence of exceptional merit in connection with any particular case or class.

Now at length have we reached the point where we can pass judgment with reference to the two extreme views of the Negro problem which were *The Crux of the Problem* set in antithesis at the beginning of this inquiry: — the one holding the Negro's inferiority to be the sole cause and justification of all his disabilities; the other assigning these same disabilities to an utterly unjust prejudice against the Negro, on account of his race or color. It has appeared that each of these views is partly right and partly wrong. The former is correct in so far as it makes the Negro's own inferiority the root of his difficulties; but it errs in failing to take account, as a secondary factor to the same effect, of the prejudice which this very inferiority has produced. The second of these two views is, in its turn, accurate to the extent of asserting the existence and potency of a prejudice against the Negro; but mistaken in tracing this prejudice mainly to differences of race or color, rather than to the Negro's own deficiencies; and also in advancing it as the only cause of the trials which this people is compelled to suffer. In the qualification and conjuncture of these views, therefore, is the full truth to be found.

This is,—that the two vital factors here involved are, first, the past and present inferiority of the Negro himself; and, second, the resulting prejudice against him. These two factors, moreover, constantly react upon each other. The Negro's inferiority tends, on the one hand, to perpetuate the prejudice to which he is thereby subject. This very prejudice, on the other hand, possessing a semi-independent entity and influence on its own account, has the effect of perpetuating not only the prevailing assumption of the Negro's inferiority, but also the fact itself, by grievously handicapping this race in its efforts to obtain a fair fighting chance. Such is the vicious circle which lies at the heart of the Negro problem.

Section 2. The Solution

With the nature of the problem thus clearly determined, the question relating to the future of the Negro people which still demands answer becomes, as already indicated: — Is this problem in process of aggravation, or, on the contrary, in that of measurable solution?

As there were found to be two factors in the problem itself, so now there are two corresponding lines of interrogation which need to be taken up. First, — Is there any convincing evidence that the Negro's past and present inferiority, as respects both his status and attainment as a racial group, and also his capacity as an individual, is in some degree being reduced? Or positively expressed, — Does this race appear to be progressing? If such is the case, then of course any assumption that the Negro's inferiority is irreducible, or even necessarily permanent within certain limits, is unjustified, and the whole situation pertaining to this race takes on a different aspect. Second, — Does the prevailing prejudice against the Negro, which, having already been seen to have its root in his actual inferiority, might be expected to diminish as that inferiority itself diminishes, disclose possibly, down below the surface, any hopeful tendency toward such mitigation and decrease? If so, then the barriers which this race encounters, as regards the securing of an equal opportunity to demonstrate whatever measure of capacity it may possess, are becoming less severe.

Turning now to the former of the two queries here proposed, — that, namely, which has to do with the Ne-

gro's progress, — account must be taken, at the very
outset, of an outstanding historical fact
which bears witness not merely to a
considerable but to an immense advance
on the part of this race, as respects its status in
Boston.

For whereas in the beginning the Negro was held as
a slave, to-day he is a free citizen, endowed with all
those political and civil rights and privileges which it
is within statutory power to guarantee. In this transformation of his lot, moreover, he himself has from
first to last had a vital, if not when all is said a decisive, part. Certainly this is not the record of a class
of the population without spirit or ambition, who have
been content to remain always in an inferior place.
It is that of a people who, by dint of aspiration, will,
and native capacity, have forced their way steadily
upward, from a position of nonentity, to their present
rank of full equality with their white fellow-citizens,
before the law.

This achievement constitutes the first great element
in the Negro's progress, and also the initial evidence
of his progressiveness.

Dependence solely or mainly upon the bestowment
of rights and privileges, however, could not but prove,
in the very nature of things, a far from
sufficient foundation upon which this
race, just out of slavery, and so comparatively brief a
period away from primitive savagery, might succeed
in rearing for itself any competent and independent
future. However important such legislative protection and assistance from without may be, still more

essential is it that the Negro should elicit and develop, from within, any potentialities and abilities which he himself possesses. And if there was need that he should do this before, that need has become imperative since the recent reaction and hardening of attitude toward him on the part of the other race. For the tendency now is to show the Negro no more favor than his actual merits warrant; and to subject him, besides, to an adverse prejudice which discounts even such worth as he may actually have. Under these conditions, either he must get ahead through his own exertions, or not at all.

It is significant that the Negro himself was the first to perceive this. Instinctively, the Negro people have acted upon the basic law of self-endeavor ever since their attainment of freedom. The fundamental task to which the Negro addressed himself, following his emancipation, was that of earning his daily bread, providing himself with the common decencies and comforts, obtaining an education, and, in general, gradually bettering his conditions of life. Without going through any involved course of reasoning, the great mass of this race have simply felt, intuitively, that such was the surest way by which they could improve their fortunes, and rise to a higher place in the community; and compared to which the agitation for equal rights was of secondary moment.

When, therefore, this gospel of salvation through achievement first received commanding utterance, from the lips of Booker T. Washington, its enunciation virtually amounted to raising the common sense of the Negro masses up to the plane and power of a consciously realized principle. That such was the case does not lessen, but on the contrary greatly magnifies, the mission which Washington has performed. For viewed in this light, his memorable Atlanta address appears not alone as the deliverance of a single individual, but also as that of an entire people; among whom, though till then for the most part silently and invisibly, the ideas which were by him thus definitely expressed had meanwhile been taking root and growing toward fruition. Washington's entrance into the destiny of his race, summoning it, at this time of crisis when the helping hand of the white man seemed to be failing it, to hew its own way upward with its own resources, is thus brought within the realm of those great super-events which seem to come providentially at rare intervals in the world's history, when the need is dire and the hour is ripe.

That the Negro people has evolved from within itself this deep-reaching philosophy of self-reliance, is a fact which is pregnant with promise for the future. For the Negro has shown therein that he has a fundamental grasp of his own problem. And this means that his battle is already half won.

The final and most decisive test of the Negro's ability, however, is found not merely in his recognition of the necessity for self-effort, but in the actual extent to which he is advancing by means of his own powers.

Independent Progress

That the Negro people are in truth making marked progress along all the most essential lines must surely have become manifest from the account which has here been given. The initial fact that this race has at length become physically rooted in Boston, and with an average gain, however slight as yet, of births over deaths, has begun to establish a native, self-generating Boston stock, is suggestively representative of the fundamental foothold which the Negro is obtaining at every point. His principal living districts are not only of much better quality to-day than has been the case in former years, but are in fact considerably superior to some of those at present occupied by other elements or strata of the city's population. At the same time this distribution, in respect to residence, is continually becoming wider and more scattered, tending to prevent the formation of a single segregated and congested Negro colony.

The evolution of a general social order among this people stands out clearly, while organization for broadly social ends is gradually becoming more efficient and more effective. What chiefly bears witness to the betterment which is thus being wrought, and what also affords assurance that this improvement will continue, is the evident invigoration and healthening of the Negro home and family, and of the neighborhood and community life of this portion of the population. With regard, likewise, to religious forces, this race is seen to be strengthening and raising the standards of its own independent church; and distinctly, though as yet slowly, rallying to its support, as an institution which has always held a unique place in the life of the Negro, and which may now be made one of the chief bulwarks of his racial solidarity. On the political side, the Negro has demonstrated his competency by obtaining and creditably fulfilling many positions of public trust and responsibility. Here, too, he is consciously moving, already with an appreciable degree of success, toward the effectual use of the leverage resident in numbers and cohesion, as a means of forcing due recognition of his political claims and of bringing about the adoption of measures aimed to promote his interests. With reference, lastly, to his industrial and economic conditions, upon which the whole structure of his material well-being depends, the Negro is, little by little, but in measure, withal, which neither the other race nor he himself as yet generally realizes, making his way upward into occupations of better grade, where his range of opportunity for satisfactory employment is steadily broadening. The development of initiative and of responsible management is shown by the increase of the professional element, and still more clearly by the growth of business proprietorship. The acquisition of what is, in the total, an astonishing amount of property, chiefly in the form of homes, has provided the Negro community with an economic buttress of great resisting and supporting power; while the rise of a class of Negro landlords, renting mostly to Negro tenants, together with the formation of several real-estate companies, constitutes a small but promising start in the direction of racial combination and coöperation for purposes of economic betterment.

This independent progress which the Negro is accomplishing is not ordinarily discerned in anywhere near its full proportions, for the reason that the Negro's present point of advancement is usually compared with that of the other race. But such a comparison is obviously neither fair nor intelligent. Both justice and accuracy demand that the situation of the Negro to-day be compared, not with that of the white man to-day, but with his own condition in the past. It is not necessary, however, to go back to the African jungle, nor even to the Southern slave plantation, but only to the time of emancipation and the beginning of the Negro's freedom, less than fifty years ago. Then this race was cast practically naked upon the world, without possessions, without organization of any kind, and utterly ignorant. The Negro's present plane of attainment, measured against this background, implies an advance which is, at the very least, remarkable. The assertion sometimes heard, indeed, that history affords no other example of a race which has made equal headway in its first half-century of independent existence, is probably within the truth. The fundamental task in which the Negro is now engaged — and this is the comprehensive fact which summarizes and incloses all the others — is that of laying a foundation upon which to build his future. In this undertaking, it must be acknowledged, he is notably succeeding.

Certain underlying elements of deficiency in the individual Negro, resolve themselves, in the last analysis, into a lack of moral stamina in *Negro Acquiring* the broadest and deepest sense of the *Moral Stamina* term. The progress of this racial group signifies that the Negro is to some extent reducing his individual shortcomings, and is in some measure acquiring the central and basic stamina of which he stands most vitally in need.

This quality is one of the last and most difficult products of the stern and exacting discipline of centuries of civilization. That the Negro should have become possessed of it in any high degree, as yet, would be contrary to natural law. But that he must have got a further and substantial increment of this innate ruggedness of character, is unquestionable. If such were not the case, the Negro people could not possibly have accomplished what they have. They have stood on their own feet and fought their own way forward. This they could not have done, had they not as individuals developed something of the spinal force which is essential to all achievement. Evidently the members of this race have grown tougher and stronger in the core and fiber of their make-up, and so have become better fitted to hold their own and to get ahead, on a competitive basis.

The first of the two questions at issue in the solution of the Negro problem may now, therefore, be answered. Negro's Inferiority Being Reduced This question is that which concerns the extent of the Negro's inferiority. The answer to it constitutes the most vital conclusion bearing upon the whole subject now under consideration. It is this: — that manifestly, in view of both the collective and the individual advance which this race has made, the Negro's inferiority can only be held to extend to his past and present development. Certainly it cannot be said to be an inferiority which is incapable of any diminution, — for already it has been reduced greatly. Nor can it even be presumed that, within certain limits of possible attainment, this inferiority is necessarily permanent and insurmountable. For when account is taken both of the general progress which the Negro people as a group have accomplished and are still accomplishing, and also of such high attainments by individuals of this race as some of those to which reference has been made in the preceding account, the presumption must be in favor of continued progress; to which, on the basis of any evidence now at hand, no definite bounds can at present be set. While, on the one hand, it cannot as yet be predicted with certainty that the Negro will eventually reach a state of complete inherent equality with the white man; neither can it be maintained, on the other hand, that this is outside the range of possibility. All we know is, that, though the Negro is still backward, he is steadily moving forward; and that, though he is still below the other race in point of ability, he is gradually coming up. His present incapacities, therefore, appear to be not those of the lower orders of creation as compared with man, but rather those of the growing child as compared with the mature adult.

As the Negro's inferiority was found to be at the bottom of the Negro problem, and as this inferiority is now seen to be not only reducible, but also actually being reduced, the conclusion is inevitable that the problem itself is in process of measurable solution, as regards its most fundamental element.

The other element in this problem, which still remains to be considered, is that of the prevailing prejudice against the Negro. As this also was *Prejudice Being Undermined* shown to have its root in the Negro's inferiority, it would logically be expected to show some mitigation as that inferiority is lessened. But on the surface at least, as previously stated, this prejudice appears to have increased in recent years.

In view of the sketch which has already been given of the course of development of the attitude toward the Negro, on the part of the other race, from the earliest period down to the present, it must be obvious that the antipathy which exists to-day is to some extent a survival and outgrowth of that which has existed in former years. As accounting both for the perpetuation of prejudice in this way, and also for its further increase, several sets of influences may be perceived.

The first of these consists of facts, reports, or memories, having to do with conditions of inferiority among this race in the past. The attitude of a great many people toward the Negro is without doubt determined wholly or mainly by such impressions from days gone by, with little or no regard to the present. In the case of some persons, the distant fact that this race was originally brought from a state of savagery in Africa is sufficient to stigmatize it beyond hope of redemption. Others look down upon the Negroes because they used to be slaves. With a much larger number, however, the aversion displayed is traceable to no specific source, but to a vague combination of things read, or heard, or remembered from their own experience, about the Negro at an earlier time. On the part of some of the older residents of Boston, who were living in the city in the first two or three decades following the war, when uncouth blacks were swarming in from the South, the disagreeable impressions then received stick obstinately.

A second factor working in this same direction, is that of accounts and hearsay concerning conditions among the Negroes in the Southern States. There are many white people of Boston who know practically nothing about the Negro in their own city, but who nevertheless become violently prejudiced against him, as the result of glaring newspaper reports of brutal crimes, superstitious orgies, and the like, said to have taken place somewhere in the Black Belt. Another contingent are adversely influenced by things which they hear from white Southerners, regarding the alleged ignorance, shiftlessness, and depravity of the Negroes in that part of the country. Still others, who happen for one reason or another to visit the South, return with an unfavorable verdict respecting the Negro in Boston, which is based entirely on snap-shot glimpses of the conditions of this race in, say, Alabama or Mississippi.

The third element in continuing and furthering prejudice, consists of superficial observation of the Negro in the Boston community itself. Only a slight fraction of the city's white inhabitants have even a cursory knowledge of the actual facts pertaining to its Negro population. The great majority of the former know the latter only from seeing them in the hotels, as menials, dealing with them in their homes, as servants, making an occasional curious excursion to a Negro church, or passing now and then through a Negro district; — and almost always, it must be said, with their eyes and ears open for something to make fun of, or to censure. Judgment arrived at in this haphazard fashion — and in such an attitude of mind

— can hardly be considered as either just or dependable.

These prejudicial influences, operating to exaggerate and distort the Negro's actual points of past and present inferiority, have largely produced both a survival, and to some extent an increase, of that antipathy toward the Negro which had its rise in former years, when the conditions among this race were far different from, and far below, those which at present hold true.

Leaving this side of the situation, for the moment, note may be taken of certain other influences, of a different character, which are working in exactly the opposite direction from those that have just been mentioned.

The first of these is to be found in the increase both of individual Negroes of marked ability and worth of character, and of white people who are brought into contact with such individuals. Under these circumstances, as a rule, any previously existing prejudice on the part of these particular white persons is appreciably reduced, so far as regards its exhibition with reference to these particular Negroes. Mention of many individual Negroes of this grade has been made in the foregoing account, and brief autobiographical sketches have been given of a few whose records are typical. In the case of the latter, the reader must have been struck by the fact that next to no complaint was made of any sufferings on account of prejudice; but that, on the contrary, the unanimous testimony of these individuals was to the effect that, in their own experience, they had for the most part succeeded, by dint of tact and the demonstration of capacity, in over-

coming such antipathy. White people who come to
know Negroes of this kind usually find that they do not
feel toward them as they do toward the Negro in the
mass, or in the abstract. "He is different from the rest,"
is the way they put it. But in the total, these Negroes
who are " different" constitute a very substantial and
constantly growing number; while the members of the
other race who are thrown into more or less association
with them form a total still larger and still more
rapidly increasing. Thus, it is evident, a considerable
leavening influence is at work.

And thereby arises the second factor of similar but
broader effect. Individual Negroes, of the character
which has been described, not only overcome antipathy in their own cases, but also, by their example,
blaze the way for others of the race to follow in
their steps, while at the same time they help to lessen
any prejudice which these others may encounter. For
it is improbable that white people can feel little or no
aversion toward particular Negroes, without eventually coming to feel somewhat less aversion toward
the Negroes as a race. These particular white people, moreover, can hardly fail, by force of word and
act, to influence others in the same direction. After
this manner, the number of white people whose attitude toward the Negro becomes favorably modified,
is still further increased.

The third factor in reducing prejudice grows out of
the two already remarked, but is of a more general
nature. When white people are once brought to recognize ability and accomplishment on the part of particular Negroes, they are more likely to reflect that

such individual attainment really bears witness to the latent capacity of the Negro in general; and they are also more disposed to look for and discover the progress which the Negro people as a whole are making. So marked has this progress become at many points, indeed, that it is beginning of itself to compel recognition, even on the part of an increasing number of persons whose eyes have not been opened by individual examples. In proportion as people become aware of the Negro's advance, their attitude toward him cannot fail to become more favorable.

It appears, therefore, that as regards the prejudice against the Negro, there have in recent years been two opposite tendencies. The more apparent of these has been an increase of prejudice against the mass of the Negroes, on the part of the mass of the other race. The attitude thus exhibited is based upon distant rather than close acquaintance with the facts, is impulsive or impressionistic rather than deliberately reasoned, and is undiscriminating as between individuals. It puts all Negroes in the same category. The counter-tendency consists of a decrease of prejudice, as respects both the constantly growing number of Negroes of demonstrated ability and also the Negroes as a race in proportion to their general progress, on the part of the likewise constantly growing number of white people who have an opportunity to observe such individual Negroes, and of those who are becoming aware of the collective advance the Negroes are making. The decrease of prejudice in this way is based upon close acquaintance with the facts, deliberate judgment, and intelligent discrimination as between individuals of different degrees of ability.

In view of these characteristics, the first of these two tendencies must be regarded as the more superficial; the second as the more fundamental. Inasmuch as the superficial tendency rests largely upon the assumption of the Negro's continuing inferiority, while the fundamental one grows out of recognition of the Negro's proved capacity and of his actual progress, the latter, though as yet of comparatively minor proportions, must necessarily be the one which is making the more substantial headway, and which is gradually overtaking the other. In spite, then, of the fact that prejudice against the Negro may still be somewhat on the increase so far as surface indications go, it is nevertheless evident that, at bottom, this prejudice is slowly but surely being undermined.

With regard, therefore, not only to the primary and most basic element,— the past and present inferiority of the Negro himself, — but also to that The Problem in of the resulting prejudice in the Negro's Process of Solution disfavor, which constitutes a secondary factor, the Negro problem is manifestly in process not of aggravation, but of measurable solution. This is, of course, very far from saying that as yet this problem is fully solved, or in fact anywhere near being fully solved. As to whether, even eventually, a complete and altogether satisfactory solution will be achieved, there is still, it must be acknowledged, room for question; while the period required for such a result to be worked out, granting its possibility, cannot with any definiteness whatever be predicted. But this much is

certain: — that instead of growing harder, this problem is day by day becoming somewhat less difficult.
The problem's two elements indicate the double road which the Negro will have to travel in his advance into the future. On the one hand, he must continue to make independent strides on his own account; while on the other, he must continue also to insist upon his rights and privileges as a citizen, and thus more directly to combat the prejudice against him.

The Negro's Double Road

Though not as a rule fully realized, the measure in which the possession of equal political and civil rights by the Negro in Boston conduces to his substantial progress through his own resources, is sufficiently obvious when once pointed out. Such equality not only instills this race with a degree of self-respect which it could not have as a class inferior before the law, but also results in enlarging, at practically every point, the Negro's opportunities for self-improvement.

First and foremost, the effective right to vote, without restriction either in law or in fact, is of inestimable value to the Negro. It gives him a consciousness of having some responsible part in the affairs of the community, which otherwise he would not feel, and which cannot but act upon him as a general spur and incentive. More immediately, the franchise enables him to make concrete protest against aspirants for leadership who are unfriendly to his race, and policies which are inimical to his welfare, as well as making it possible for him, from a more positive and constructive point of view, to promote measures calculated to assist him. The ballot furthermore puts him in a position to demand just political recognition, in the form of competent public offices; while the holding of such offices, and the creditable performance of the duties involved, not only give rise among the Negroes themselves to a justified confidence in their own potential abilities, but also have the effect of obtaining fuller recognition of their capacity on the part of the other race. Likewise the right to attend the same public schools and other educational institutions as those attended by the whites, renders accessible to the Negro advantages in securing an education which are undoubtedly far superior to any separate provision likely to be made for him, if a policy of segregation were followed. The freedom of this race to reside in any locality means that a considerable proportion of its members are able to live and to rear their children in much more healthful, morally salutary, and otherwise desirable surroundings, than would be the case if the Negroes were confined within such congested and evilly environed colonies as those which exist in many cities of the South. The further right to purchase real estate in any section supplies the Negroes with a stronger motive to become owners of homes, and results in their acquiring more and better property, than would be true if their holdings were restricted, as in some Southern cities, to certain inferior districts.

In addition to these rather specific considerations, there are two whose bearing is more general. The first of these is, that inasmuch as the other race is still in a much more advanced stage of development than the Negro, the present extent of the latter's contact with white people must be reckoned a factor of the utmost value in his own progress. For thus, instead of being forced back wholly upon himself and his own limitations, he is constantly enabled to derive encouragement and stimulus from the experience and example of the other race. At the same time — and this is the companion factor — such inter-racial association has the result of acquainting the other race with the Negro in a closer and more discriminating way, and of giving it a more sympathetic understanding both of the difficulties with which the Negro has to contend, and of the degree to which these difficulties are being conquered by him.

But while thus equality of public privilege greatly quickens the Negro's rate of progress, the ways in which, as already suggested, this very self-achievement qualifies him to gain and to hold such privilege, are likewise obvious. The Negro's marked advance in point of education and refinement, to begin with, secures for many members of this race an amount of helpful association with the other race which they could not possibly obtain if ignorant and uncouth. The good appearance, as regards dress and demeanor, which all but the poorest element of the Negroes in Boston usually present, obtains them admittance, and thus establishes a precedent for their admittance, in many places of semi-public character, such as theaters, churches, settlements, educational and other institutions, from which, were they a class of ragamuffins and rowdies, they would be effectually shut out.

It is the economic progress that the Negro is making, however, which is proving the surest instrument in maintaining and extending his liberties. In Boston, as is the case in most American communities, affairs regulate themselves very largely on a simple business basis of sale and purchase, with material means, rather than race or color, as the determining element. The fact that the Negro is steadily becoming better able to pay for privileges is his best guarantee of possessing these privileges. Restaurants and theaters, for instance, find that a Negro's money goes as far as a white man's toward profits. A cab driver deems it wiser to pick up a fare from a Negro than to let his vehicle stand idle. Shops of all kinds, even the most select, see no good reason for declining to sell their wares to members of this race. Banks draw no color line in accepting deposits. In the matter of residence in superior white neighborhoods, very frequently it is only by purchasing property in the locality, at a liberal figure, that the first few Negroes gain an entrance and thus make entry easier for others. Negro professional and business men could not operate among white competitors, and bid for white patronage, were they not able to pay the substantial rents which prevail in such districts. And just as white people are willing to sell to Negroes if there is profit in so doing, likewise they are willing to buy from them if they can be sure of obtaining equally good or better commodities. The underlying reason why constantly increasing numbers of Negroes are obtaining higher grade employment, among white workmen, is because in a market where the supply of satisfactory workmen is generally less than the demand, these particular Negroes are able to do this particular work satisfactorily. It is here that the immense strategic value of industrial education comes in. Such education provides the Negroes with a commodity,

industrial skill, which as a rule they can readily market at a good price. In general, moreover, the industrial advance of this race necessarily underlies its
welfare in every other respect, including that of the
safeguarding and extension of its rights and privileges. For without the material resources thus provided, the Negro would manifestly be put at a severe
disadvantage, in any efforts to protect and to assert
himself.

If independent headway through his own effort is
thus to be in the future, as it has been in the past, the
Racial Cohesion   most fundamental factor in the Negro's
and Race Pride   advance, it clearly follows that the Negro
people must obtain a position of self-reliant strength
as a racial group. As individuals, each one dependent
solely on himself and working for himself alone, they
cannot adequately cope with their peculiar problem.
More than any other people in the world to-day, the
Negroes stand in need of the mutual support and co-
operation which comes from numbers and cohesion.
They are not yet prepared to be received fully, or
even in major degree, within the general fabric and
organization of the white community. They must,
therefore, at least for the present, evolve a fabric
and an organization of their own. Instead of attempting to belittle or get away from the fact of their
race, they must, on the contrary, make as much of
this fact as possible, using it as a rallying-call for a
centripetal movement toward racial solidarity.

The individual Negro will never gain the full respect
of the other race until he first comes fully to respect
himself. This he cannot do until his own race has

reached the point where he will not be ashamed, but will be proud, to own himself a Negro. Other racial stocks —as, for example, the Slavs, Celts, or Teutons — feel no aspersion, but only the pride of historical achievement, in these corresponding designations. The Negro affords the one solitary case of which the opposite is true. And the reason for this is, that as yet the Negro has comparatively little history which warrants pride. Therefore, he must set to work to make a history for himself. He must have a creditable past upon which to build a creditable future.

That the Negro is already moving very distinctly in the direction of cohesion as a race is the most promising feature of his progress. The very reason why the gospel of self-achievement, as preached by Booker T. Washington, has taken such a deep and permanent hold upon the Negro people, is because it appeals to this call of race. The ways in which, impelled by this motive, the Negroes are beginning to draw together and to pull together, in the social, the religious, the political, and the economic fields, have already been sufficiently indicated.[1] At length, moreover, as the com-

[1] At the present time a committee, which has grown out of certain activities of the Robert Gould Shaw House, previously mentioned, and which contains representatives of both races, is considering and undertaking to promote a specific scheme of industrial betterment which calls this element of racial cohesion into play. The plan in view is to try to get a substantial number of the Negroes to withhold their patronage from such places, and especially department stores, as absolutely refuse to employ Negroes in positions above the menial grade, and particularly as salesgirls and salesmen; and at the same time to give their patronage to places which will consent to employ Negroes, if only to a very limited extent, in such positions. The expectation is that even if, at the outset, only a few members of this race are thus employed, gradually both the employers and the

bined result of the growing sense of community among themselves, the recognition of their actual past and present accomplishment as a people, and the recalling and celebration of events related to their history, the Negroes are commencing to show the germs of a genuine pride of race, and to give some evidence that they are coming to look upon the name "Negro" as not altogether a term of reproach.

The development of the Negro people as a distinct racial group, with traditions, leaders, and ideals of Articulation into their own, will run not counter, but the Community parallel to the considerably slower process of the Negro's articulation into the common life of the community. Though it may appear paradoxical to say that the surest way in which the Negro will succeed in overcoming the prevailing attitude in his disfavor will be by becoming more and not less a Negro than he is to-day, this is nevertheless the truth. For as the Negro, in proportion to his own independent progress, compels increased respect for his capacity, the other race will gradually and naturally become more willing to receive him into closer association.

This articulating process has already, indeed, reached a noticeably advanced stage. The fact that, in point of residence, the Negroes are being distributed among the city's white inhabitants to a constantly widening extent, cannot fail to promote mutual better acquaintance and to give rise to common interests. Likewise, in the ranks of industry, the interspersion

public will cease to regard their employment in such capacities as impossible, and will eventually become willing to install a larger number.

of Negro workmen among white workmen, in both
manual and clerical occupations, is steadily increasing.
The proportion of the Negro professional and business
class who are venturing to go outside those districts
colonized by their own people, and to try their fortunes among white competitors, though of course
still small, is continually growing. Cases of office-
sharing and even of partnership between persons of
the two races are less of a rarity now than in former
years, while instances of Negro proprietors or of responsible employees having white workmen in their
charge are oftener to be found. General trade contact between these two elements of the population is
gradually extending, while through the use of banks,
the ownership of property, and the paying of taxes,
the Negro is being linked, more and more substantially,
to the economic interests of the community.

Citizens of both races vote together at the same voting places and on an equal basis. Through representation on the various party committees, the Negroes
have some part in the management of party affairs,
and at all political conventions Negro delegates are to
be seen. Especially under the civil service, an increasing quota of Negroes are serving in public positions
side by side with officials of the other race. With regard
to religious activity, though on the whole the attendance of Negroes at white churches is diminishing, yet
as previously noted there are some churches which
are marked exceptions to this rule; and, on a broader
scale, cases of white churches, especially in the suburbs, which contain a few earnest and well-regarded
Negro members, are coming to constitute a significant

total. The Negro churches are admitted into the general denominational organizations, Negro delegates participate in the general meetings, and no color line is drawn on the various ministers' societies. In the public schools white and Negro children work and play together in apparent innocence of any barrier. These memories and impressions of childhood are not easily blotted out. White youth of high-school and college age find Negro youth often their equals and sometimes their superiors, both in scholarship and athletic prowess. A Negro principal, half a dozen teachers, and several school officials, represent the Negro on the side of substantial contribution to the city's educational advance.

Perhaps it may be said, however, that all such contact as this between the two races ends simply with itself, and neither signifies nor leads to social intercourse of such unconditioned character as that which takes place between the various elements of the white population. In other words, it may be held that though the Negro is in the community, and closely related to it, he is not by any means an integral part of it. This distinction is, without doubt, a real and vital one. But it is at the same time so subtle, in many respects, as to render the question raised by it extremely difficult, if not at this stage practically impossible, to answer with finality. Viewed against the background of the prevailing prejudice against the Negro people and the still outstanding fact of their separateness in the main, whatever association there is between the Negro and the white portion of the population tends easily and plausibly, of course, to appear as something of an altogether peculiar and rigidly limited nature. But, on the other hand, may it not be that these perfectly obvious elements of prejudice and separateness loom so large and so near as to bias and distort the observer's vision, and to render him incapable of perceiving, in their true light and at their full value, any facts of an opposite significance? The writer feels confident, out of years of experience, that, as regards all except possibly the most intimate personal relations, no such necessarily fixed barrier between the Negro and the white man, as that which has just been suggested, actually exists; that there is to-day a substantial measure of genuine, man-to-man association between members of these two races; and that in the future such association, based upon a fellow-feeling of human brotherhood which strikes deeper than any sense of difference, will continue to increase, tending eventually to make the Negro people an inner and component part of the general community.

As over against his present deficiencies, which, as already indicated, are gradually being reduced, the Negro will bring as his contribution to The Negro's the community and to the American Contribution complex, certain qualities of great value, of which, at least in latent form, he is either peculiarly or in superior degree endowed.

The inborn love of music, the tropically fertile imagination, and the natural eloquence of this race are gifts which are rich in promise. Already the Negro is adjudged to have given this country, in the old plantation melodies, its most distinctive folk-songs. In the future he may be expected to express himself notably in all the higher realms of musical composition and rendition. Nor is prophetic vision required to predict that some of America's poets and most powerful orators will emerge from this people. The deep religious fervor of the Negro, when raised to a plane above that of untaught emotionalism, will no doubt yield great preachers and religious leaders, and perhaps in time produce a Negro church which will set an example of heartfelt Christianity to its sister churches of pale-face hue. The Negro's capacity for taking things easily, his innate cheerfulness, and that drolly irresistible humor which is all his own, are reinforcements that will stand in good stead a nation which, from over-intensity of application and insufficiency of relaxation, is in some danger of falling victim to nerves. The spontaneous sociability and gregariousness which characterize the Negro people in such high degree are, finally, attributes which may qualify this race for an important rôle in an era of the world's progress when the individualistic and competitive motives are clearly being replaced by others of a more social and humanitarian aspect.

These suggested probabilities may, of course, strike some people as only the most distant and visionary speculations;—for the reason that, in Africa and America together, the Negro has had a long time in which to develop any inherent potentialities, and yet is still so far in the rear. It is at least within the limits of possibility, however, that — according to a well-recognized principle in biology — the eventual development and attainment of this race will be proportionate to the amplitude of its period of infancy.

There is now doubtless a final query in the reader's mind. It is this: — Are the foregoing conclusions and predictions, with regard to the Negro The Negro problem and its solution, confined strictly in the Nation to the conditions which obtain in Boston; or, if not, to what extent are they capable of general application, with reference to the country as a whole?

In reply to this query, the writer will say that, while the specific task before him has been the analysis of the Negro's situation in Boston, he has at the same time kept constantly in view the purpose of getting at the subject in a sufficiently broad and fundamental way to make the chief conclusions representative. While holding himself accountable only with respect to Boston, so far as any pretension to actual and detailed proof is concerned, he nevertheless ventures to submit, suggestively, that the problem of the Negro is essentially the same elsewhere, not only in the North but in the South as well; and that the conclusions which have here been drawn may, therefore, be extended to apply, in substance, to the position of the Negro people throughout the nation.

Certainly in all other localities it will be found that, as in Boston, the two vital elements in this problem are the Negro's backwardness or inferiority of development, and the prevailing prejudice against him. As to the problem's solution, it would appear that elsewhere also this is being worked out by the same double process: — the progress of the Negro himself, on the one hand, and the modification of the prevailing attitude toward him, on the other. In Boston, and to a lesser degree in other parts of the North, it is the Negro's advance along lines of education, refinement, and intellectual accomplishment, together with the exceptional attainment of individuals, which stands out most clearly. In the South, on the contrary, the agricultural and industrial headway of the Negro people, and their general forward movement in the mass, are most strikingly in evidence. With regard to present signs of any undermining of the prejudice in the Negro's disfavor, while, of course, such a tendency is much farther advanced in the North than it is in the South, its beginnings are nevertheless plainly discernible in the latter section. The majority of persons who are studying Southern conditions at first hand, testify to the fact that the proportion of Southern white people who are seeking to cultivate relations of mutual helpfulness and amity between the two races, though comparatively small as yet, is constantly increasing. It is true, furthermore, that while the various common interests which are operating to bind the two races together are more apparent in the North, they are in fact even more substantial in the South. For there the Negroes, by reason of their very numbers, the major share of the labor of the community which they perform, and their extensive ownership of farms, are relatively a much more essential factor in the community's life and well-being.

Because the great mass of this race have always been and still are resident in the Southern States, and because the influences drawing and forcing them together are there much more powerful, it is probable that the Negroes will develop in the South, sooner than in the North, strength of organization as a dis-

tinct and self-reliant group; while, for the same reasons, it will probably take them much longer in the
South to become satisfactorily articulated with the
other elements of the population.

But South and North the final outcome will be the
same. A people grown up, from a forlorn and helpless band of slaves brought hither from the African
jungle, into ten millions of free citizens, constituting
a tenth part of the total inhabitants of the United
States to-day; a people which has been in this country from the beginning, and has had an honorable
and, indeed, a vital part, both in its establishment
and preservation by ways of war, and in its manifold
upbuilding by ways of peace: — this people will eventually attain the position at once of self-respect and
worthy recognition. In new and fuller ways the two
contrasted races, which chiefly go to make the American nation, must and will find common cause.

"Both formed thy bulwark since thy life began,
And both together still must work thy plan."

THE END

APPENDIX

ARTICLE I

GARRISON AND THE LIBERATOR

WILLIAM LLOYD GARRISON was born in Newburyport, Massachusetts, not far from Boston, in 1805. He was of humble parentage. At the age of nine, with next to no regular schooling, he was apprenticed to a shoemaker, and later to a cabinetmaker. When he was thirteen, he obtained employment as an apprenticed printer on the Newburyport *Herald*. This marked the beginning of the remarkable self-education, especially in the mastery of language, which he eventually achieved.

In 1826, shortly after the expiration of his apprenticeship on the *Herald*, he became the editor and publisher of the Newburyport *Free Press*, exhibited marked independence in this capacity, and incidentally printed the first verses of the poet and future Abolitionist, John Greenleaf Whittier. Later in the same year, he left Newburyport and went to Boston, where, while supporting himself at his trade of printing, he displayed his fighting spirit by making a youthful but not ineffective insurgent speech, at a political convention, and by engaging later in some consequent newspaper polemics.

In 1828 he became editor of the *National Philanthropist*, of Boston, a paper devoted to the cause of temperance and other reforms. His early connection with this publication doubtless developed in Garrison the inherent impulse toward reforming which soon became the most distinguishing element of his character. His first expression of interest in slavery conditions appears to have been in the form of a comment, in the second number of the *Philanthropist* under his editorship, upon the futility of the attempts of the South to prevent teaching the slaves even simple reading and writing. The budding antipathy toward slavery, thus indicated, was greatly furthered by his meeting that same year with the Quaker, Benjamin Lundy, who was almost the only militant anti-slavery worker of that period, and who had established a paper called the *Genius of Universal Emancipation*, for the advocacy of gradual abolition. Garrison's association with and assistance of Lundy, during the latter's two visits to Boston to arouse public sentiment, resulted in his engagement, in the spring of 1829 (following a brief but highly creditable term of service as editor of the *Journal of the Times*, at Bennington, Vermont, during which his progress anti-slaveryward was evidenced by constant advocacy of gradual abolition), as associate editor of the *Genius*, then published at Baltimore.

On the way to his new post, Garrison delivered a stirring anti-slavery address, on Independence Day, at the Park Street Church in Boston. In that address, however, he still went only so far as to urge gradual abolition. But by the time he arrived at Baltimore, several weeks later, he had definitely reached the conclusion that to rest content with gradual abolition would allow slavery to drag on interminably, and that to demand immediate and total abolition was the only sure way of bringing the evil to a certain and early end. Lundy not being ready to take such an extreme stand, it was agreed that each editor should express his own views over his own signature; with the result that in the very first number Garrison declared his attitude. His uncompromisingness on this point and his radicalism on other reforms led forthwith to a steady falling-off in the *Genius'* subscription list. At the end of six months the paper was practically bankrupt, and the partnership was dissolved. Garrison had meanwhile published an article, exposing complicity in the domestic slave trade on the part of a shipowner of his native town of Newburyport, which was adjudged libelous by the court, and for the authorship of which, on his inability to pay the fine imposed, he was cast into jail. After a durance of forty-nine days, he was liberated through the payment of his fine by a wealthy philanthropist [1] of New York City, who had been moved to this action by reading an account of his trial and imprisonment.

[1] Arthur Tappan, who later became a leading Abolitionist.

Following his release, some effort was made by friends of
Lundy and himself to have the *Genius* reëstablished on the
former basis, but without result. Garrison then determined
upon the publication of an anti-slavery and general reform
paper of his own, and publicly announced that at an early
date he would begin to issue such a paper from Washington.
He left Baltimore for the North, and after delivering several
anti-slavery lectures on the way, arrived in Boston, October
1, 1830. The Boston *Transcript* of the following day had a
brief editorial referring to his coming and acknowledging his
pioneer service in a cause which, however, it went on to
predict, "he could never hope to see perfected."

In Boston, Garrison at once tried to find a hall for an anti-
slavery meeting. The fact that he was unsuccessful in his
quest till he advertised in the newspapers, and that then he
was able to secure only a hall used by a group of avowed
infidels, showed the unwillingness which at that time prevailed in Boston, as elsewhere in the North, to have the
slavery question agitated, — an unwillingness to which even
the churches, except for a scattering few, were parties. A
meeting was held on the evening of October 15. The following extracts from an account by a member of the small audience convey some impression of Garrison's personality and
convincing power of speech, and of the degree to which he
was absorbed by his cause: [1]

"Presently the young man [2] arose, modestly, but with an
air of calm determination, and delivered such a lecture as he
only, I believe, at that time, could have written; for he only
had had his eyes so anointed that he could see that outrages
perpetrated upon Africans were wrongs done to our common humanity. . . . Never before was I so affected by the
speech of man. When he had ceased speaking I said to those
around me: 'That is a providential man; he is a prophet; he
will shake our nation to its centre, but he will shake slavery
out of it.'"

The antipathy or, at the least, apathy toward the anti-
slavery propaganda, which Garrison had encountered in

[1] The Reverend Samuel J. May, who became one of Garrison's most loyal supporters.
[2] He was then only twenty-four years of age.

Boston, convinced him that the North must be aroused before there could be any hope of converting the South. The first and the several succeeding meetings held in that city gained him a few daring followers. He therefore decided to publish his paper not from Washington but from Boston. Though utterly without funds himself, he was enabled to carry out his purpose by the formation of a timely partnership with an old associate of the printing bench.[1] Dismissing counsels of moderation, he gave his paper the plain and unequivocal title of *The Liberator*.[2]

ARTICLE II

THE NEGRO'S PROGRESS IN THE ABOLITION PERIOD

GENERAL ADVANCE IN BOSTON, 1830–65 [3]

THE awakening of the Negroes in Boston, which the Abolition Movement effected, was evidenced in a number of ways and by a number of events concurrent with and related to that Movement, and yet distinct from it.

One of the earliest and most important of these developments was the demand that Negro children be admitted into the general public schools. In addition to the separate primary school opened by the city in 1820 in response to a petition from the Negroes themselves, another school, apparently of grammar grade, had been established in the North End in 1831, but had been discontinued in 1835 on account of meager attendance, owing to the facts that by that time only comparatively few Negroes were left in that quarter, and that those few were of inferior quality. In the latter year the Smith School was erected in a court off Joy Street.[4] The

---

[1] Isaac Knapp.

[2] The foregoing facts have been taken from *William Lloyd Garrison, The Story of His Life, Told by His Children*, vol. 1, chaps. I–VIII. That book, in four volumes, is not only the best biography of Garrison, but also the fullest history of the Abolition Movement.

[3] This more detailed account supplements the brief statement made at the beginning of chapter III.

[4] *Report of Primary School Committee*, June 15, 1846. The old building still stands, and is to-day used as headquarters by a Negro G.A.R. Company (Robert A. Bell Post, 134).

school took its name from a white man, Abrel Smith, who
left to the city a legacy the income from which, amounting
to $200 yearly, was to go toward the support of a school for
Negroes. The parents of the children were held to pay $1\tfrac{1}{2}$
cents a week for each child. In 1843, a primary school,
which replaced the one previously used, was started in the
North End.[1] In 1840, however, a petition signed by Garrison, Phillips, Francis Jackson, Henry W. Williams, and a
number of Negroes led by the journalist and author, William
C. Nell, son of William G. Nell, the tailor, was sent to the
School Committee, asking that the public schools be thrown
open to Negro children. In 1846, a similar petition was submitted by George Putnam, a Negro, and eighty-five others.

The Primary School Committee, in reporting adversely on
this petition, made a statement that brought out a division
of opinion, on the matter of segregation, which since that
time has assumed far larger proportions and more general
importance. "Our inquiries into the origin and history of
separate schools," they said, "have also convinced us that
the leading motive for their establishment was precisely the
opposite of a design to degrade the colored people, as has
been so frequently charged upon them. The colored children
in Boston possessed equal rights with others as every one
knows, yet very few, indeed, often not more than two or
three in all, attended the public schools. It was next to
impossible to bring them in. Benevolent individuals undertook, therefore, to sustain special separate schools for them.
And it was with great difficulty for a long time that they
could be brought even into these schools. The labor of getting them in was found to be far greater than teaching them
when once brought in. It was by the exertion of benevolent
white persons, in connection with the most intelligent of the
colored people, that this class of children were brought under
school instruction in any considerable numbers — an object
which it was found impossible to accomplish but by means of
separate schools. The question arises by what means the
views and feelings of the colored people in reference to these
special schools for their benefit have been so mysteriously
changed." [2]

[1] *Report of Primary School Committee*, June 15, 1846.
[2] *Report of Primary School Committee*, June 15, 1846.

In 1849, Jonas Clark and 227 others renewed the attack. A Negro-School-Abolition party, consisting of both Negroes and whites, was formed and set itself three tasks.[1] The first of these was to break up the existing Smith School. The agitators even went so far as to surround the school, at its opening that fall, and to make use of every means, short of actual physical violence, to prevent the children from going in. As a second expedient, they started an opposition school, open to white as well as Negro children, and taught at first by the Reverend Daniel Foster, a Negro preacher. But their principal effort was to get the Supreme Court of the State to declare separate schools unconstitutional. To this end, Benjamin F. Roberts, in behalf of his five-year-old daughter Sarah, brought suit against the city for damages on account of the refusal to receive her in the general public schools. The case was argued December 4, 1849, with Charles Sumner as first counsel for the plaintiff, and Robert Morris, the Negro lawyer, as assistant counsel.[2] Though the decision of the court was adverse, the airing which the question received was a long step toward ultimate victory. Five years later, a white lawyer, George F. Williams, made an able report to the city in favor of doing away with separate schools. This report, and a petition signed by nearly one thousand five hundred persons, Negro and white, from all parts of the State, paved the way for action by the Legislature, and a law abolishing separate schools was adopted April 28, 1855.[3] The text of the law was as follows: —

"Section 1. In determining the qualifications of scholars to be admitted into any public school or any district school in this Commonwealth, no distinction shall be made on account of the race, color, or religious opinions, of the applicant or scholar.

"Section 2. Any child who, on account of his race, color, or religious opinions, shall be excluded from any public or district school in this Commonwealth, for admission to which he may be otherwise qualified, shall recover damages therefor in an action for tort," etc., etc.

[1] *An address before the colored citizens of Boston in opposition to the abolition of colored schools,* by Thomas B. Smith, December 24, 1849.
[2] Sarah C. Roberts *vs.* City of Boston, December 4, 1849.
[3] *Laws of Massachusetts,* 1855, chap. 256.

A celebratory meeting of Negroes and whites, presided over by John T. Hilton, a leading Negro Abolitionist, was held in December, 1855, especially in honor of William C. Nell, as the Negro to whom chief credit was due for the final result of this campaign. Mr. Nell told how, as a boy, while attending the Smith School, and having been one of the Negro children to receive rewards of merit, — which were not Franklin medals, as in the case of the white children, but orders for small copies of Franklin's *Autobiography*, — he had contrived to get in as a waiter's assistant at the meeting where the prizes were being given to the white children. The principal of the schools, Samuel T. Armstrong, had whispered to him, — "You ought to be here with the other boys." "The impression made on my mind by this day's experience deepened into a solemn vow that, God helping me, I would do my best to hasten the day when the color of the skin would be no barrier to equal school rights." Besides Mr. Nell, the speakers were Garrison, Phillips, and Charles W. Slack. Mr. Slack stated that, since the new régime had gone into effect, the teachers in the schools where colored children were most numerous testified that they were as neatly dressed, and as gifted in application and understanding, as the white children.[1]

Another sign of the awakening of the Negroes was the petition sent to the Legislature in 1851, signed among others by Nell, Remond, Hayden and Joshua B. Smith, who had come to Boston as a fugitive from North Carolina in 1847, asking for the erection of a monument in memory of Crispus Attucks.[2] That request was complied with thirty-seven years later. As a further development in the direction of budding independence, the Adelphic Union Library Association was formed about 1845, and maintained for approximately ten years. The Negroes were shy about going to public institutions and meetings. As their children were excluded from the schools, so they themselves did not feel free to take advantage of such opportunities as were afforded by libraries and open lecture courses, and indeed their presence in such

---

[1] *Proceedings of meeting held in Boston, December, 1855, to celebrate Abolition of Colored Schools.*

[2] W. C. Nell, *Colored Patriots of the Revolution.*

places and on such occasions was obviously not welcome. This library association of their own served both to accustom them to make use of self-educational facilities and also to demonstrate to the whites their sincere desire for such opportunities. A number of young white men of high standing lent their assistance to the enterprise. Withal, an appreciable change of public sentiment was effected, and by the end of that decade the presence of Negroes at public lectures, theaters, and the like, excited comparatively little adverse comment.

In addition to the writings of William Wells Brown and Frederick Douglass,[1] there appeared, in 1852, William C. Nell's *Services of Colored Americans in the Wars of 1776 and 1812*, and in 1855 his larger and more complete book, *Colored Patriots of the Revolution*. The volume of *Miscellaneous Poems*, by Frances Ellen Watkins Harper, one of the most prominent Negro women Abolitionists, who was much of her time in Boston, was published in 1854.

Simultaneously with the advent of these Negro writers came the admission to the Bar and to the Medical Association of Negro lawyers and physicians. The first Negro lawyer to be admitted to the Bar in the United States appears to have been Macon B. Allen, who passed the examinations at Worcester, Massachusetts, May 3, 1845, and who had been allowed to practice in Maine two years before that. But so far as the records show, Allen did not distinguish himself. The first Negro to make an impression as a lawyer was Robert Morris, a remarkable man with a remarkable history. His grandfather, Cumono, a native African, was carried to Ipswich, not far from Boston, as a boy. There he won the esteem of the citizens, and one of the byways of the town was called, after him, Cumono Lane. Robert's father, York Morris, moved at an early age to Salem, and there Robert was born, in June, 1823. He worked as a table-boy in the home of a family named King, whom the family of Ellis Gray Loring, one of the leading lawyers in Boston at that time, were accustomed to visit. Mr. Loring was attracted by the boy, and took him into his household as a servant. Several years later, he gave him a chance to show what he

---

[1] Referred to in chapters ii and iii.

could do as office-boy, and so satisfactorily did Robert perform his new duties that his employer, seeing that the young man possessed unusual ability, helped him in the study of law. His progress accorded with his promise, and in February, 1847, he was admitted to the Bar.

He has himself described his first case in court: "There was something in the courtroom that morning that made me feel like a giant. The courtroom was filled with colored people, and I could see, expressed on the faces of every one of them, a wish that I might win the first case that had ever been tried before a jury by a colored attorney in this country. At last my case was called; I went to the work and tried it for all it was worth; and until the evidence was all in, the argument on both sides made, the judge's charge concluded, and the case given to the jury, I spared no pains to win. The jury after being out a short time returned, and when the foreman in reply to the clerk answered that the jury had found for the plaintiff, my heart bounded up and my people in the courtroom acted as if they would shout for joy."

The other Negro lawyers admitted to the Bar in Boston before 1865 were William J. Watkins, John S. Rock, and Edward Garrison Walker, David Walker's son. The first Negro physician to be taken into the Massachusetts Medical Association was J. V. De Grasse, in 1854. John S. Rock, born in New Jersey in 1825, was admitted soon afterwards. He was a man of recognized exceptional scholarship and literary ability, and on a number of occasions was invited to speak before distinguished white audiences, — twice before the State Legislature. Ill health compelled him to give up the practice of medicine, and he studied law and was admitted to practice — as above noted — in 1861. A Negro, Edward M. Bannister, had forced an entrance also into the domain of art, and had won more than local distinction as a portrait painter.[1]

The growth of the Negro population during this period,[2] coming at the same time with the general awakening which has been noted, was one of the chief causes of the increase in

---

[1] Mr. Bannister subsequently became the principal founder of the Providence Art Club, which is to-day the leading art organization in Providence, Rhode Island, and whose membership, mostly if not wholly white, includes many of the leading citizens of the city and State.

[2] See chapter III for figures.

the number of Negro churches, from two in 1830 to five by 1850. The Reverend John T. Raymond was pastor of the old Joy Street Church, succeeding the Reverend Thomas Paul about 1840 and continuing till a few years before the war. He was a man of high character, and an active worker for anti-slavery and many of the principal reforms of the day. His successor was the brilliant John Sella Martin, who came to Boston in 1859, being introduced by the pastor of Tremont Temple, whose pulpit he filled several weeks as a vacation substitute. The first pastor of the A.M.E. Zion Church, founded in 1838, was the Reverend Jehial C. Beman, born in Connecticut, and whose father is said to have taken the name "Be-Man" after escaping from slavery. The Negro minister most active in the Abolition cause was the Reverend Leonard A. Grimes, of the Twelfth Baptist Church. He was born in Leesburg, Virginia, of free parents, in 1815, worked at many occupations in various parts of the South, and as a young man became an active helper for the Underground Railway. He was concerned in nearly all the stirring events affecting the Negro from the time of his coming to Boston, in 1848, till his death.

With the founding of new churches came the formation of a number of Negro societies and organizations. Between 1844 and 1848 three additional Masonic lodges, the Union, Rising Sun, and Celestial, were established, the original African lodge having become in 1808 the Prince Hall Grand Lodge. The first lodge of Negro Odd Fellows in Boston had its beginning in 1846. The first women's beneficial society in Boston, either white or Negro, was that of the United Daughters of Zion, organized November 6, 1845, and still extant. The Female Benevolent Firm, which also has maintained itself to the present day, was formed in 1850; and the National Grand Order of Brothers and Sisters of Love and Charity, of which there are now six lodges in Greater Boston, in 1863.[1]

Though the mass of the Negroes were still employed in menial service, there had, nevertheless, been a decided economic advance. Thomas B. Dalton, who appeared in the

---

[1] *Thirty-fourth Annual Report of the Massachusetts Bureau of Statistics of Labor*, pp. 282, 283.

1829 directory as a bootblack, subsequently became the proprietor of a prosperous clothing-shop on Brattle Street, and accumulated property, as the provisions of his will later showed, to the value of nearly $50,000. With reference to the material progress made by the Negroes, William C. Nell wrote in 1855: "Boston compares favorably, in this respect, with larger cities in the United States. Several causes have combined to retard the progress of colored mechanics, but these are being removed, and, in a few years, the results will be manifest. Business and professional men are continually increasing. . . . The most popular gymnasium galleries are in the proprietorship of J. B. Bailey [1] and Peyton Stewart; the prince of caterers is J. B. Smith; a dentist highly recommended is J. S. Rock; a young artist in crayon portraits is fast winning his way to excellence and reputation; [2] and other equally meritorious aspirants — women included — are soaring to those heights that challenge the ambition of earth's gifted citizens. Real-estate to the value of, at least, $200,000 is in the hands of our colored citizens." [3] The Negroes, in fact, owned a large proportion of the property in the West End district.

ARTICLE III

NEGRO LEADERS AFTER THE WAR

When, with the war's close, the period of the Negro's freedom began, nearly all the Abolitionist leaders of that race in Boston were still alive, and the majority were in their prime. Charles Lenox Remond, born in 1810, and one of the pioneers, was the eldest of this strong group, and one of the most eloquent, having won the sobriquet of "The Colored Wendell Phillips." The leader, however, was Lewis Hayden. He had been born a slave, in 1815, and had come to Boston at the age of twenty-nine as a runaway; but his native intellectual ability and the exceptionally good education which he

---

[1] Mr. Bailey was for a time boxing-master at Harvard University.
[2] Edward M. Bannister, previously mentioned.
[3] W. C. Nell, *Colored Patriots of the Revolution.*

somehow managed to acquire are sufficiently evidenced by his writings on Negro Masonry.[1] Hayden was a man of compelling qualities and of a nature which would not brook opposition. With the Negroes he held a position almost of dictator, and with the whites he was the accepted representative of his people. His home remained a common meeting-place for councils affecting his race.[2] Joshua B. Smith, who, before he became a caterer, worked in the Shaw household, was one of the prime movers in initiating, in the autumn of 1865, the movement for the collection of private subscriptions for a monument to Robert Gould Shaw and the Fifty-fourth; — which resulted, in 1897, when $23,000 had been secured, in the erection of the present Memorial. George L. Ruffin, born in Richmond in 1838 of free parents, had come to Boston in 1853, and after earning his livelihood for some years as a barber, took a course at the Harvard Law School, and subsequently entered the law office of Harvey Jewell. Mark de Mortie, a tailor and shoe-dealer, who had come to Boston from Virginia in 1853, and George T. Downing, who, though he did not live in Boston, frequently went there,[3] were others of the "Old Guard," — the majority of whom, as well as some of those mentioned here, have already been named in other connections.

In addition to this group of men, a number of women continued to take an active part in affairs. Previous reference has been made to Eliza Gardner, who when the war ended was still a young woman of thirty-four, but in the forefront of good endeavor for her people's welfare. A co-worker was Mrs. Arianna C. Sparrow, who had come to Boston in 1852 with her mother, the latter one of the women after whom the character of Eliza, in *Uncle Tom's Cabin*, was modeled. Another zealous member of this company was Josephine St. Pierre Ruffin, wife of George L. Ruffin. Mrs. Ruffin, of mingled French, English, American, Indian, and

---

[1] *Caste among Masons; Address before Prince Hall Grand Lodge. Grand Lodge Jurisdictional Claim. Masonry among Colored Men in Massachusetts.*

[2] In the house at 66 Phillips Street, the room in which those frequent councils were held is still kept with everything as it used to be, and is proudly shown to visitors by the present tenant.

[3] Downing had a remarkable history. See the biography by his daughter, Mrs. S. I. N. Washington, printed in 1910 by the Milne Printers, Newport, Rhode Island.

African descent, was born in Boston in 1842, and was married in 1858. During the war, as a girl, she assisted in the sending of sanitary supplies to the soldiers; and immediately after the war she organized the Kansas Relief Association, which sent clothing and money to the Negro refugees who were colonizing parts of Kansas.

The ranks of the foregoing leaders, and of the others who had taken up their abode in Boston before, during, or immediately after the war, were reinforced by a number of later recruits from without. Reference will be made only to those who identified themselves closely with the propaganda for equal rights. Among such, who came in the first decade following the return of peace, were James Still, from New Jersey; W. C. Lane, from North Carolina; H. Gordon Street, from the West Indies; William H. Plummer, from Virginia; Julius B. Chappelle, from Florida; James H. Wolff and Archibald H. Grimké. Still and Lane were physicians, Street a journalist, Chappelle a barber, Plummer, Wolff, and Grimké lawyers. Wolff was born at Holderness, New Hampshire, in 1847, acquired his academic education at Kimball Union Academy and the New Hampshire State College, and studied law in the office of Hon. D. W. Gooch and at the Harvard Law School. He was admitted to the Bar in 1875. Archibald H. Grimké and his brother, Francis James Grimké, were the children, by a Negro mother, of one of the sons of Judge John F. Grimké, of the Supreme Court of South Carolina. Their father's sisters, Angelina and Sarah Grimké, were famous Abolitionists and reformers before the war, and were often heard on Boston platforms. When these sisters discovered the facts concerning the parentage of the two boys, who were then in Lincoln University, Pennsylvania, where by heroic saving their mother had contrived to send them, they forthwith acknowledged them as nephews; Angelina Grimké, who had married Theodore D. Weld, of Hyde Park, taking Archibald into her family, and Sarah assisting him in completing his education and entering the profession of law.

In the decade following, from 1875 to 1885, the principal newcomers were Edward Everett Brown, Clement G. Morgan, and Butler R. Wilson, all lawyers. Brown was a native of New Hampshire, born in 1858. He studied law in the offices of Hon. John H. White, Judge of the Probate Court in New Hampshire, and of Hon. William A. Gaston, of Boston, as well as at the Boston University Law School, and was admitted to the Bar in 1884. Morgan was born in Georgia, graduated from Atlanta University in that State and from the Harvard Law School, and was admitted to practice in Boston in 1882. Wilson, also born in Georgia, in 1860, and a fellow-student with Morgan, at Atlanta, studied law at Boston University, and began practice in 1884. Two younger men who grew up in Boston, and who entered into active service about this time, were Emery Morris, a nephew of Robert Morris, born in 1851; and William A. Hazel, born about 1850, who became a successful draftsman and architect.

In the next decade, from 1885 to 1895, the chief reinforcements were George Washington Forbes, from Mississippi, who, as noted elsewhere, has since 1895 been an assistant librarian in the West End branch of the Boston Public Library; and William H. Lewis, to whom a number of previous references have been made. Lewis was born in Virginia, in 1868, graduated from Amherst College, studied law at the Harvard Law School, and was admitted to the Bar in 1895.

STATISTICAL TABLES

TABLE I

NEGRO POPULATION AND TOTAL POPULATION OF BOSTON PROPER
1742-1865

NUMBERS AND PERCENTAGES

Year	Negro population	Increase	Per cent increase	Total population	Per cent Negroes in total
1742	1374			15,008	9.
1752	1541	167	12.	14,190	10.
1754	989 [1]	−552	−55.		
1765	848	−141	−14.	15,520	6.
1790	766	− 82	− 9.	18,320	4.
1800	1174	408	53.	24,937	4.7
1810	1468	294	25.	33,787	4.3
1820	1690	222	15.	43,298	3.9
1830	1875	185	10.9	61,392	3.
1840	2427	552	29.	93,383	2.5
1850	1999	−428	−17.	136,881	1.4
1855	2160	161	8.	158,793	1.3
1860	2284	124	5.7	177,840	1.2
1865	2348	64	2.8	192,318	1.2

In the above figures, the population as given for each year has reference to Boston as geographically constituted in that year. Additions through such annexations as were made from time to time are of practically negligible effect, so far as the comparisons from period to period are concerned.

This table shows that the percentage of Negroes in the total population was at its maximum at the time when the second count was taken, in 1752, and that from then down to the time of the war it steadily declined. It also appears that the rate of increase of the Negro population underwent a decline after 1800.

[1] The figure of 989, for the year 1754, appears to have comprised only the slaves.

TABLE II

NEGRO POPULATION AND TOTAL POPULATION
OF BOSTON PROPER AND GREATER BOSTON
1865–1910

NUMBERS AND PERCENTAGES

| | BOSTON PROPER | | | | | | GREATER BOSTON | | | | |
Year	Negro	Total	Per cent Negro	Per cent increase Negro	Per cent increase total	Negro	Total	Per cent Negro	Per cent increase Negro	Per cent increase total
1865	2,348	192,318	1.2			3,495	421,936	.8		
1870	3,496	250,526	1.3	48.8	30.2	5,648	506,999	1.1	61.6	19.8
1875	4,969	341,919	1.4	42.1	36.4	7,400	598,334	1.2	31.	17.8
1880	5,873	362,839	1.6	18.1	6.1	9,381	620,178	1.5	26.7	3.3
1885	6,058	390,393	1.5	3.1	7.5	9,481	726,832	1.3	4.8	17.3
1890	8,125	448,470	1.8	32.4	14.8	12,832	849,967	1.5	30.3	16.6
1895	9,472	496,920	1.9	16.5	10.8	16,307	1,001,474	1.6	27.	17.6
1900	11,591	560,892	2.	22.3	12.8	20,306	1,121,667	1.8	24.5	11.3
1905	11,948	595,380	2.	3.1	6.2	21,234	1,248,808	1.7	4.5	11.
1910	13,564	670,585	2.	13.5	12.6	23,115	1,373,409	1.7	8.8	12.3

The percentage of Negroes in the entire population is so small that, for purposes of this table and some others, the white population may be regarded as practically identical with the total.

These figures show that the percentage of Negroes in the total population increased from 1865 to 1900, and that it has subsequently remained stationary, at a point slightly higher in the case of Boston proper than in the case of Greater Boston.

The figures also show that, with the exception of the five-year periods 1880–85, 1900–05, and, in the case of Greater Boston, 1905–10, the rate of increase of the Negro population has been in excess of that of the white population; but that this excess has at the same time tended to diminish.

TABLE III

URBAN AND SUBURBAN DISTRIBUTION — NEGRO
POPULATION AND TOTAL POPULATION
OF GREATER BOSTON
1865–1910

PERCENTAGES

(Numbers supplied in Table II)

Year	Per cent Negro pop. in B.P.[1]	Per cent total pop. in B.P.	Per cent Negro pop. in suburbs[1]	Per cent total pop. in suburbs	Rate increase Negro pop. in suburbs	Rate increase total pop. in suburbs
1865	67.	45.	33.	55.		
1870	62.	49.	38.	51.	87.	11.
1875	67.	57.	33.	43.	12.	0.
1880	62.	58.	38.	42.	44.	.3
1885	63.	53.	37.	47.	− 5.	30.
1890	63.	52.	37.	48.	37.	19.
1895	58.	49.	42.	51.	45.	25.
1900	57.	50.	43.	50.	27.	11.
1905	56.	47.	44.	53.	6.	15.
1910	58.	48.	42.	52.	2.	8.

These figures show that, though the percentage of the
total population of Greater Boston living in the suburbs is
larger than the percentage of the Negro population living in
the suburbs, this suburban percentage has in the case of the
total population decreased, since 1865, from 55 to 52; while,
in the case of the Negroes, it has increased from 33 to 42.
Likewise, from 1865 to 1900, with the single exception of the
period 1880–85, the rate of increase of the Negro suburban
population greatly exceeded that of the suburban population
as a whole.

What this signifies is that, so far as increasing residence in
the more open and healthful outlying districts is concerned,

[1] The abbreviation "B.P." stands for "Boston proper," or the territory included
within the civic municipality of Boston. By the term "Suburbs" is meant all territory outside the limits of Boston proper, but still within the limits of Greater Boston.

the Negroes have in the main fared better than the rest of the population.

Since 1900, however, the suburban rate of increase for Negroes has markedly diminished, and has fallen considerably below that of the whites. This probably indicates a decrease — whether temporary or not remains to be seen — in the movement of Negroes from Boston proper to the suburbs. But it probably does not indicate any recent tendency toward Negro congestion in the inner sections of the city; for the reason that even within the municipality the Negroes are moving in growing, though of course still minor numbers into the more removed residential districts, which are practically the same as the suburbs in general character.

TABLE IV

NEGRO POPULATION OF GREATER BOSTON
1865-1910

IN DETAIL, BY CITIES AND TOWNS OF THE METRO-
POLITAN DISTRICT [1]

Place	1865	1875	1885	1890	1895	1900	1905	1910
Boston......	2572[2]	4969	6058	8125	9472	11591	11948	13564
Arlington....		23	28	48	61	55	62	67
Belmont.....	4	8	1		8	4	8	15
Brookline....	5	13	17	42	184	161	194	221
Cambridge...	377	1103	1689	1988	2849	3888	4290	4707
Chelsea......	150	311	513	668	693	731	566	242
Dedham.....	31	75	48		72	65	53	54
Everett......		22	24	72	455	634	801	795
Hyde Park...		78	104	98	108	116	111	87
Lexington....	10	12	17	14	17	13	22	25
Lynn [3].......	229	430	624	715	767	784	772	700
Malden......	23	30	61	107	326	446	525	486
Medford.....	8	18	21	55	169	244	248	431
Melrose......	2	11	37	48	105	130	96	110
Milton.......	5	32	36	47	53	64	67	44
Nahant......	11	1	1		2		3	4
Newton......	14	130	190	342	354	505	522	467
Quincy......	6	7	14	16	6	27	22	45
Revere......			14	24	67	43	30	33
Saugus......	1		18	14	35	27	28	55
Somerville...	16	36	87	65	72	140	229	217
Stoneham....	6	27	27	35	27	21	32	25
Swampscott..	1	1	15	16	16	44	28	14
Wakefield....		9	18	12	17	25	31	31
Waltham....	7	13	15	16	36	51	43	62
Watertown...	6	19	54	25	56	53	41	44
Winchester...	2	3	34	45	107	140	186	281
Winthrop....	3		1	28	34	43	36	47
Woburn.....	6	19	75	100	218	261	240	242

[1] The "Metropolitan District," as defined in connection with the work of certain
metropolitan bodies like the Park Commission, and as comprising the towns and
cities named above, is practically coincident with the unified and centralized social
community commonly referred to as Greater Boston.

[2] This figure is in excess of that given for Boston proper in the preceding tables,
in that here it includes the Negro population in the following outlying districts,
which were annexed to Boston during the ensuing decade: namely, Brighton,
Charlestown, Dorchester, Roxbury, and West Roxbury.

[3] In general, in this volume, Lynn is not counted a part of Greater Boston, because of its considerable population and largely independent industrial life.

TABLE V

POPULATION OF GREATER BOSTON, BY COLOR
1910

IN DETAIL, BY CITIES AND TOWNS OF THE METRO-
POLITAN DISTRICT

Place	Total population	White	Negro	All others (Chinese, Japanese and Indians)
Metropolitan District	1,373,409	1,348,424	23,115	1,870
Boston	670,585	655,736	13,564	1,285
Arlington	11,187	11,115	67	5
Belmont	5,542	5,524	15	3
Brookline	27,792	27,547	221	24
Cambridge	104,839	100,024	4,707	108
Chelsea	32,452	32,177	242	33
Dedham	9,284	9,227	54	3
Everett	33,484	32,672	795	17
Hyde Park	15,507	15,404	87	16
Lexington	4,918	4,891	25	2
Lynn	89,336	88,518	700	118
Malden	44,404	43,897	486	21
Medford	23,150	22,704	431	15
Melrose	15,715	15,592	110	13
Milton	7,924	7,873	44	7
Nahant	1,184	1,179	4	1
Newton	39,806	39,303	467	36
Quincy	32,642	32,568	45	29
Revere	18,219	18,173	33	13
Saugus	8,047	7,990	55	2
Somerville	77,236	76,956	217	63
Stoneham	7,090	7,064	25	1
Swampscott	6,204	6,183	14	7
Wakefield	11,404	11,371	31	2
Waltham	27,834	27,743	62	29
Watertown	12,875	12,826	44	5
Winchester	9,309	9,026	281	2
Winthrop	10,132	10,080	47	5
Woburn	15,308	15,061	242	5

TABLE VI

EMIGRATION OF NEGROES FROM MASSACHU-
SETTS, BOSTON PROPER, AND GREATER
BOSTON, 1890–1900

The base upon which the following table is built up consists of the figures, in the federal censuses of 1890 and 1900, showing the number of Massachusetts-born Negroes who were resident in other States in those years.

A simple comparison of the 1900 figures in this regard with those of 1890, for each State, is not, of course, sufficient to show the total accessions — if any — to that State, from the ranks of Massachusetts-born Negroes, during the decade. It is necessary also to allow for the deaths during the decade among those Massachusetts-born Negroes resident in the given State in 1890; and also for the deaths of immigrants to that State during the decade, which have occurred before the decade's close.

For this purpose, assumption has been made of a death rate of 2.5 per cent (25 deaths per 1000 persons), this being a point between the prevailing Negro death rates North and South. As there are no figures which indicate the number of Massachusetts-born immigrants entering a given State each year, the deaths among such immigrants are calculated roughly by taking one half the increase in the number of immigrants during the decade (this being a mean between the number arriving in the year 1891 and the larger number arrived by 1900) as a numerator; to which the death rate of 2.5 per cent is applied. In many cases the numbers involved are so small that the deaths are practically negligible in quantity, and are therefore not taken account of.

Further emigration of Massachusetts-born Negroes, out of any given State into others, is another factor involved; but as the interstate total of such migration remains the same, this element need not be included in the calculation.

A. Negroes of Massachusetts Birth Emigrating from Massachusetts as a Whole

State or Territory	Mass.-born Negroes 1890	Mass.-born Negroes 1900	Excess 1900	Probable deaths 1890 pop.	Minimum immigration Mass.-born Negroes 1890–1900	Deaths among immigrants of the decade	Total immigration Mass.-born Negroes 1890–1900
Ala.	20	19	− 1	4	3	–	3
Alas.	0	8	+ 8	0	8	–	8
Ark.	33	14	−19	7	−12	–	–
Ariz	3	31	+28	0	28	3	31
Cal.	94	68	−26	21	− 5	–	–
Col.	43	41	− 2	10	8	–	–
Conn.	395	454	+59	88	147	16	163
Del.	6	12	+ 6	1	7	–	7
D.C.	99	132	+33	22	55	6	61
Fla.	32	39	+ 7	7	14	1	15
Ga.	42	65	+23	9	32	3	35
Ha.	0	1	+ 1	0	1	–	1
Id.	1	1	0	0	1	–	1
Ill.	76	117	+41	17	58	6	64
Ind.	18	30	+12	4	16	2	18
I.T.	0	3	+ 3	0	3	–	3
Iowa	9	10	+ 1	2	3	–	3
Kas.	13	10	− 3	3	0	–	–
Ky.	11	17	+ 6	2	8	–	8
La.	55	38	−17	12	− 5	–	–
Me.	24	56	+32	5	37	4	41
Md.	69	85	+16	15	31	3	34
Mich.	33	32	− 1	7	6	–	6
Minn.	19	16	− 3	4	1	–	1
Miss.	19	17	− 2	4	2	–	2
Mo.	34	37	+ 3	7	10	1	11
Mont.	5	5	0	1	1	–	1
Neb.	15	14	− 1	3	2	–	2
Nev.	1	1	0	0	1	–	1
N.H.	46	44	− 2	10	8	–	8
N.J.	101	156	+55	22	77	8	85
N.M.	3	3	0	0	0	–	–
N.Y.	462	606	+144	104	248	27	275
N.C.	21	24	+ 3	5	8	–	11
N. & S. Dak.	7	2	− 5	1	− 4	–	–
Ohio	143	64	−79	32	−47	–	–
Ok.	1	3	2	0	2	–	2
Or.	11	12	1	2	3	–	3
Pa.	197	294	+97	44	141	15	156
R.I.	320	406	+86	71	157	17	174
S.C.	19	16	− 3	4	1	–	1
Tenn.	24	22	− 2	5	3	–	3
Tex.	38	51	+13	8	21	2	23
Utah	1	1	0	0	0	–	–
Vt.	65	67	+ 2	14	16	2	18
Va.	58	114	+56	13	69	7	76
Wash.	16	12	− 4	3	− 1	–	–
W.Va.	6	10	+ 4	1	5	–	5
Wis.	5	12	+ 7	1	8	1	9
Wy.	1	0	− 1	0	− 1	–	–
						Total	1369

Total emigration of Massachusetts-born Negroes from
Massachusetts, 1890–1900........................... 1369
Average yearly emigration, 1890–1900................... 136.9

B. ENTIRE EMIGRATION OF NEGROES; BOTH MASSACHU-SETTS-BORN AND OTHERS

1. EMIGRATION FROM MASSACHUSETTS AS A WHOLE

The emigration from Massachusetts of Negroes of Massachusetts birth having been ascertained, it is now possible to estimate the entire Negro emigration from the State, on the basis of the ratio between that part of the State's Negro population which is native, and the total.

The mean native-born Negro population of the State for the decade 1890–1900 may be reckoned roughly as one half the sum of that of 1890 and that of 1900: — i.e., $\frac{9455+11,747}{2}$, or 10,601.

In the same way, the mean total Negro population of the State, for the decade, may be reckoned as $\frac{22,144+31,974}{2}$, or 27,064.

The native Negro population of Massachusetts, therefore, stands in relation to the entire Negro population of the State as 10,601 to 27,064; forming a proportion of 39 per cent.

Assuming now that the emigration from Massachusetts of the Negroes who are native to the State corresponds roughly in rate with that of the non-native element; the former, 1369 for the decade 1890–1900, may be reckoned as 39 per cent of the total for that decade, — which would thus amount to $\frac{1369}{39} \times 100$, or 3510.

Total emigration of Negroes from Massachusetts, 1890–1900 **3510**
Average yearly emigration, 1890–1900................... **351**

2. EMIGRATION FROM BOSTON PROPER

The entire Negro emigration from Boston proper may now be calculated in the same way, on the basis of the ratio between the Negro population of Boston and that of the State as a whole.

The mean Negro population of Boston for the decade 1890–1900, was $\dfrac{8,125+11,591}{2}$, or 9858; which stood in relation to the mean Negro population of the State as 9858 to 27,064; forming a proportion of 36 per cent.

The total emigration of Negroes from Massachusetts for the decade being 3510, the emigration from Boston proper would then be reckoned, on a strict percentage basis, as 36 per cent of 3510; — $\dfrac{3510}{36} \times 100$, or 1263. As a matter of fact, however, Boston, on account of its more intensive city conditions and its position as a metropolis, is undoubtedly subject to a shifting or emigration of its Negro population which is considerably larger in extent than its proportion of the Negro population of the State; and which must amount, at a reasonable estimate, to 50 per cent of the State's entire emigration, — or, for the decade concerned, to 1755.

Summary

Total Negro emigration from Boston proper, 1890–1900... 1755
Average yearly emigration, 1890–1900.................. 175.5

3. Emigration from Greater Boston

The mean Negro population of the Greater Boston district, for the decade 1890–1900, was $\dfrac{12,832+20,306}{2}$, or 16,569. This stood in relation to the mean Negro population of the State as 16,569 to 27,064; forming a proportion of 61 per cent. The emigration from Greater Boston for the decade would, therefore, on a strict reckoning, be 61 per cent of 3510, or 2141. But, for the same reasons that hold true in the case of Boston proper, the emigration from the urban district of Greater Boston is relatively larger than for the rest of the State; amounting, doubtless, to not less than 75 per cent of the whole, — or 2632.

Summary

Total emigration of Negroes from Greater Boston, 1890–1900 2632
Average yearly emigration, 1890–1900................... 263

SUMMARY

TABLE VII

IMMIGRATION OF NEGROES TO BOSTON PROPER AND GREATER BOSTON

To calculate the extent of Negro immigration, it is necessary to add to the net increase of the local Negro population, during the given period, the estimated local emigration of Negroes during the same period; inasmuch as immigration, besides yielding a net increase, has also filled the space left by emigration. Strictness of procedure would require furthermore that any excess of deaths over births, for the period, should be taken into account; since depletion from this cause also has to be made up for by accessions from without, before any net gain is shown. But as the births nearly, if not entirely, offset the deaths, for the two decades in question, this factor may for practical purposes be omitted from the present calculation.

A. Boston Proper, 1890–1900

Increase of Negro population of Boston, 1890–1900........ **3466**
Estimated Negro emigration from Boston, 1890–1900 (Table
VI, B, 2)... **1755**
    Total Negro immigration to Boston, 1890–1900......... **5221**
    Average per year, Boston, 1890–1900................. **522**

B. Boston Proper, 1900–10

Increase in Negro population of Boston, 1900–10........... **1973**
Estimated Negro emigration from Boston, 1900–10......... **1317** [1]
    Total Negro immigration to Boston, 1900–10.......... **3290**
    Average per year, Boston, 1900–10.................... **329**

C. Greater Boston, 1890–1900

Increase in Negro population of Greater Boston, 1890–1900 **7474**
Estimated Negro emigration from Greater Boston, 1890–
1900 (Table VI, B, 3)............................... **2632**
    Total Negro immigration, Greater Boston, 1890–1900... **10,106**
    Average per year.................................. **1010**

---

[1] This figure is estimated, rather than calculated, on the assumption, borne out by observation and report, that the emigration of Negroes from Boston, in the decade 1900–10, was probably at least 25 per cent less than that (as above given) of the decade preceding.

D. Greater Boston, 1900–10

Increase in Negro population of Greater Boston, 1900–10... 2809
Estimated Negro emigration from Greater Boston, 1900–
1910... 1974

Total Negro immigration, Greater Boston, 1900–10........ 4783
Average per year.................................... 478

[1] This figure is estimated on the same assumption as in the case of section **B**, above; — i.e., that the Negro emigration from Greater Boston, in the decade 1900–10, was at least 25 per cent less than in the decade preceding.

Table VIII

STATE NATIVITY OF NEGROES IN BOSTON PROPER AND MASSACHUSETTS

In Percentages, from 1900 back to 1860

The numbers put before the percentages show the numerical rank of each State, for each year given, as respects the quantitative contribution of that State to the nativity of the local Negro population.

For States contributing less than 100 individuals, no percentages are indicated.

The figures for Massachusetts as a whole are given for 1880, as no figures for Boston alone are obtainable in the case of that particular census year.

	Boston 1900	Boston 1890	Mass. 1880	Boston 1870	Boston 1860
Massachusetts........	[1] 28.2	[1] 32.9	[1] 54.9	[1] 41.1	[1] 46.6
Virginia.............	[2] 27.6	[2] 29.9	[2] 19.1	[2] 24.8	[2] 15.3
North Carolina.......	[3] 11.5	[3] 7.4	[4] 3.4	[6] 3.4	
Maryland............	[4] 4.7	[4] 4.5	[3] 4.1	[3] 7.7	[3] 8.4
Georgia.............	[5] 3.8	[8] 2.5			
District of Columbia..	[6] 2.9	[6] 2.7	[9] 1.4		
New York............	[7] 2.9	[5] 2.8	[5] 3.4	[4] 4.5	[4] 6.4
South Carolina.......	[8] 2.8	[7] 2.6	[8] 1.7		
Pennsylvania........	[9] 2.5	[9] 2.5	[7] 1.9	[5] 3.9	[5] 5.4
Connecticut.........	[10] 1.1		[6] 2.2		
New Jersey..........	[11] .9				
Maine..............	[12] .9	[10] 1.5			
Rhode Island........			[10] 1.2		

TABLE IX

NATIVITY BY SECTIONS OF THE COUNTRY
NEGROES OF BOSTON PROPER
AND MASSACHUSETTS

IN PERCENTAGES, FROM 1900 BACK TO 1860

This table, of course, applies only to Negroes of American birth.

	Boston 1900	Mass. 1900	Boston 1890	Mass. 1890	Mass. 1880[1]	Boston 1870	Mass. 1870	Boston 1860
North.........	39	50.3	44.	59.5	67.8	55.6	66.3	69.8
South.........	59	45.2	54.	38.4	31.4	43.2	33.7	29.1
Central and Western States	2	4.5	2.	2.1	.8	1.2	0	1.1

[1] No figures for Boston alone are obtainable for the year 1880.

TABLE X

NEGROES OF FOREIGN BIRTH AND FOREIGN
PARENTAGE — BOSTON PROPER
AND MASSACHUSETTS

IN PERCENTAGES, FROM 1900 BACK TO 1860

For years in which no figures are given for Boston, such figures are not available. Figures of foreign birth are lacking prior to 1890.

	Boston 1900	Boston 1890	Mass. 1880	Boston 1870	Boston 1860	Mass. 1860
Foreign born........	10.2	14.2	6.4 [1]	10.8	14.9	6.3
Foreign parentage...	16.8	18.8				

[1] The percentage for Boston in 1880 was probably (estimated) about 13.6.

TABLE XI

MARRIAGE RATE — NEGRO AND WHITE POPULATION

BOSTON PROPER, 1900–06

The following figures apply to the number of marriages per one thousand of population.

Year	Negro Rate	White Rate
1900	18.3	18.7
1901	17.8	18.1
1902	16.6	17.7
1903	19.5	18.2
1904	18.1	18.2
1905	17.7	18.5
1906	21.5	24.3
Average, 1900–06	18.5	19.1

The proportion of Negroes in the total being practically negligible, the figures quoted for the white population in the above table are those reported for the total population by the Municipal Registry Department, for each year; on the basis, for non-census years, of the estimated population.

In the case of the Negro population, however, where such yearly estimates are less dependable, the population for each non-census year has been calculated, for the table above, by adding to the population of the last census year, preceding, one, two, three or four fifths, respectively, of the increase recorded by the following census, taken at the close of the given five-year period.

TABLE XII

BIRTH AND DEATH RATES — NEGRO AND WHITE POPULATION

BOSTON PROPER 1900–10

The figures below apply to number of births and deaths per one thousand of population.

	Negro birth rate	Negro death rate	White birth rate	White death rate
1900....	27.7	28.4	29.1	20.8
1901....	24.4	27.4	27.1	19.6
1902....	26.6	28.3	26.3	18.6
1903....	25.1	25.4	26.	17.6
1904....	23.4	23.2	25.	17.4
1905....	23.	23.	26.	18.4
1906....	26.9	27.6	28.2	18.8
1907....	26.9	25.5		
1908....	27.5	26.9		
1909....	25.8	20.		
1910....	22.8	23.7		
Average	25.4+	25.4+	26.9+	18.7+

The Negro birth and death rates are calculated on the same basis as that followed in the case of the Negro marriage rate (Table XI). The rates given for the white population are those reported for the total population by the Municipal Registry Department. Though the latter figures, as here cited, come down only through the year 1906, it may safely be assumed that the average would remain substantially the same if the figures were brought down to 1900.

Table XIII

NEGRO BIRTH AND DEATH RATES
BOSTON PROPER 1865–1910

Averages for Five-Year Periods

The purpose of the following table is to afford a more stable basis for the study of the trend of the local Negro birth and death rates, than is possible when recourse is had only to rates for single years. Owing either to inaccuracies in the estimates of the size of the Negro population for non-census years, or possible under- or over-counts in the yearly recording of births and deaths, rate figures for single years are almost sure to be somewhat uncertain, and therefore more or less unreliable. When the average rates for five-year periods are taken, however, a more substantial set of figures is provided, making possible more reliable conclusions as to tendencies extending over a term of years.

In order to eliminate from the figures given below the element of doubt arising from estimates of population for non-census years, one half the sum of the Negro population at the beginning of the five-year period and of that at its close, is regarded as the mean population for the period. The sum of the Negro births and deaths for the period are divided by the number of years (six, including both beginning and ending year), in order to get the yearly average. On the basis of this mean population, and this yearly average, the average rates for the period are reckoned.

Five-year period	Birth rate	Death rate
1865–70	26.	35.2
1870–75	30.9	41.3
1875–80	29.5	30.4
1880–85	34.9	39.
1885–90	29.	36.2
1890–95	26.4	32.1
1895–00	22.	27.9
1900–05	25.4	26.5
1905–10	25.8	24.3

These figures show a decline, in the Negro death rate, which has been uninterrupted since 1880, and also a small increase in the birth rate since 1895; as the joint result of which factors — though chiefly of the former — the death rate has finally, in the decade 1905–10, declined to a point which leaves an excess of births.

Table XIV

A COMPARISON OF THE WHITE AND NEGRO POPULATION OF BOSTON PROPER

As respects Sex, Marital Condition, Proportion of Children, and Age Groups — In Percentages, for the Year 1895

The year 1895 is selected for this comparison because the Massachusetts census for that year supplies the requisite information in fullest detail. It may safely be assumed that a similar comparison for any subsequent year would show substantially the same results.

As the Negroes form such a small fraction of the whole population, the latter is considered, for comparative purposes, as virtually identical with the white population.

A. Sex

Negro population; — men exceed women by about 1 per cent of the whole.

White population; — women exceed men by about 4 per cent of the whole.

B. Marital Condition

1. Women

Single	Per cent
Native-born Negroes	49
Native-born Whites	67
Foreign-born Negroes	36
Foreign-born Whites	36
Combined native- and foreign-born Negroes	47+
Combined native- and foreign-born Whites	55

Married

Negroes	38+
Whites	34

Widowed

Negroes	13.6
Whites	9.9

Divorced

Negroes	.29
Whites	.19

2. Men

Single   Per cent
  Negroes.................................... 56
  Whites 56
Married
  Negroes.................................... 38
  Whites 36
Widowed
  Negroes.................................... 3.8
  Whites 3.4
Divorced
  Negroes.................................... .14
  Whites .... .07

C. PROPORTION OF CHILDREN

Children, age 1–14   Per cent
  Negroes.................................... 18
    Average number children per married woman... .72
  Whites 25
    Average number children per married woman... 1.12
Infants under one year
  Negroes.................................... 1.7
  Whites 1.9

D. OLDER AGE GROUPS

Persons 15–49   Per cent
  Negroes.................................... 71
  Whites 60
Persons 50 and above
  Negroes.................................... 9.7
  Whites 13.6
Persons 60 and above
  Negroes.................................... 3.8
  Whites .... 6.

TABLE XV

CAUSES OF POVERTY AMONG DIFFERENT RACES

BASED UPON A TABULATION OF 7,225 SPECIFIC CASES REPORTED TO THE ASSOCIATED CHARITIES OF BOSTON AND CERTAIN OTHER CITIES [1]

CLASSIFICATION	PERCENTAGES						
	American	Negro	German	Irish	English	All Other	Totals
1. Indicating misconduct . . .	**27.35**	**13.76**	**16.67**	**30.43**	**28.01**	**18.64**	**25.11**
Drink	15.16	6.24	7.75	23.62	16.98	8.27	15.28
Immorality	0.63	0.92	0.12	0.27	0.32	0.30	0.44
Shiftlessness and inefficiency	9.19	5.69	7.39	5.78	7.12	7.52	7.52
Crime and dishonesty . .	0.74	0.73	0.47	0.38	1.11	1.05	0.68
Roving disposition	1.63	0.18	0.94	0.38	2.53	1.50	1.19
2. Indicating misfortune . .	**69.58**	**83.31**	**78.64**	**67.55**	**69.46**	**79.11**	**72.03**
A. Lack of normal support	*6.04*	*4.96*	*5.17*	*7.04*	*6.33*	*8.12*	*6.32*
Imprisonment of breadwinner	0.67	0.37	0.12	1.20	1.27	0.60	0.76
Orphans and abandoned children	0.37	0.37	–	0.38	0.63	0.30	0.35
Neglected by relatives .	0.89	1.28	0.82	0.38	1.27	1.96	0.91
No male support . . .	4.11	2.94	4.23	5.08	3.16	5.26	4.30
B. Matters of employment .	*33.40*	*27.15*	*38.73*	*26.14*	*30.85*	*34.59*	*31.60*
Lack of employment .	24.57	17.43	28.40	18.88	24.68	25.87	23.17
Insufficient employment	6.64	8.62	7.51	6.38	4.75	5.11	6.52
Poorly paid employment	2.08	0.92	2.58	0.82	1.42	3.61	1.81
Unhealthy and dangerous employment . .	0.11	0.18	0.24	0.06	–	–	0.10
C. Matters of personal incapacity	*30.14*	*51.20*	*34.74*	*34.37*	*32.28*	*36.40*	*34.11*
Ignorance of English . .	–	–	0.47	0.06	–	3.76	0.42
Accident	2.67	1.47	3.52	3.11	2.69	3.46	2.86
Sickness or death in family	20.31	39.63	22.65	19.80	22.94	21.66	22.27
Physical defects . . .	3.41	5.51	4.70	3.49	1.74	4.51	3.70
Insanity	0.93	–	0.70	0.93	1.27	0.90	0.86
Old age.	2.82	4.59	2.70	6.98	3.64	2.11	4.00
3. Miscellaneous	**3.07**	**2.93**	**4.69**	**2.02**	**2.53**	**2.25**	**2.86**
Large family	0.52	0.55	1.17	0.87	0.79	0.75	0.73
Nature of abode	0.07	0.18	0.12	0.06	0.47	0.15	0.12
Other, or unknown	2.48	2.20	3.40	1.09	1.27	1.35	2.01

The above classification is arranged in three main divisions, sections 1, 2, and 3 totaling to one hundred, and the subdivisions thereunder adding to the percentage line of each section. The first section indicates poverty caused by misconduct, and has details of five causes which resulted in the poverty of the persons considered; the second indicates mis-

[1] Warner's *American Charities*, 1894 ed., Table VIII.
The date of these cases is not stated, but it was presumably about the time of the date of publication of Mr. Warner's book, — i.e., not long prior to 1894.

fortune, with three main causes, each being subdivided into direct causes which could be classified under each head; and third, miscellaneous, or causes which were of a nature not readily classifiable under either misconduct or misfortune.

Examination of the foregoing figures shows that in the case of the Negroes the percentage of poverty due to misconduct was lower than in the case of any other race; while, on the other hand, the percentage of poverty due to misfortune in some form or other was highest among the Negroes.

Analyzing these statistics still further, it appears that the Negroes exhibit the lowest extent of poverty due to drink. "This low percentage has been corroborated by the investigation of John Koren,[1] whose conclusions are: that comparatively few Negroes are habitual drunkards; that intemperance is only accountable for a small part of the Negro's poverty; and that only in exceptional cases are drinking habits a barrier to steady employment." [2]

"Those who know the colored people only casually or by hearsay may be surprised to find the misconduct causes running so low among them, while sickness as a cause is of greater relative importance than in any other nationality. But to one who has worked in Baltimore or Washington it seems a natural result, and indeed a confirmation of the reliability of the statistics. The colored people are weak physically, become sick easily, and often are without visible resistance to disease. At the same time, they have a dread of being assisted, especially when they think an institution will be recommended; and this, together with a certain apathy, will often induce them to endure great privation rather than ask for help. Besides this, there are many associations among them for mutual help, and the criminal and semi-criminal have a brutal way of making their women support them. That the percentage for 'lack of work,' 17.43, is the lowest, and that for 'insufficient employment,' 8.62, is the highest, under these two heads, perhaps reflects their hand-to-mouth way of working at odd jobs rather than taking steady work." [3]

[1] Koren (Committee of Fifty), *Economic Aspects*, etc., p. 176.
[2] Warner's *American Charities*, 1908 ed., p. 59.
[3] Warner's *American Charities*, 1908 ed., pp. 59–60.

TABLE XVI

OWNERSHIP OF PROPERTY BY NEGROES OF BOSTON PROPER, THE SUBURBS, AND GREATER BOSTON, FOR THE YEAR 1910

(The following figures are supplementary to those given in chapter IX, pp. 384–5.)

A. PROPERTY ACTUALLY REPORTED.

Area	Owners	Pieces	Value
Boston..................	183	241	$1,143,500
Cambridge..............	175	275	869,000
Other suburbs (15).......	283	310	693,000
Total..............	641	826	$2,705,585

B. ALL PROPERTY — ADDITIONS ESTIMATED.

Area	Owners	Pieces	Value
Boston..................	215	265	$1,250,000
Cambridge..............	200	300	950,000
Other suburbs (15).......	365	407	900,000
Total..............	780	972	$3,100,000

Total private ownership, Greater Boston....... $3,100,000
Total corporate ownership, " " 400,000
Grand total, individual and corporate ownership,
   Greater Boston............................ $3,500,000

C. ACTUALLY REPORTED — FIFTEEN SUBURBS

Area	Owners	Pieces	Value
Winchester.............	21	24	$48,400
Chelsea................	28	39	82,950
Woburn................	30	30	45,285
Everett................	71	76	191,100
Dedham...............	6	7	11,350
Melrose................	3	3	6,000
Malden................	25	25	59,800
Somerville.............	13	14	51,800
Medford...............	37	37	68,000
Hyde Park.............	11	12	34,150
Milton................	3	3	4,500
Stoneham..............	3	3	6,850
Wakefield..............	1	1	4,500
Newton................	30	35	74,400
Waltham...............	1	1	4,000
Total..............	283	310	$693,085

INDEX [1]

Abolition Movement, the Boston Negroes' specific share in, 30; as forerunners of, 36–38; as participating in formation of New England Anti-Slavery Society, 42–43; in response to Garrison's appeal, and use of the "Liberator" as a medium of expression, 46; in distinct organization at first, 46; as regards Boston committee appointed by free Negroes, 46; in formation of separate societies, 46; as received into white societies, 47–48; as elected to board of New England Anti-Slavery Society, 47; Charles Lenox Remond, first Negro Abolitionist platform speaker, 47; increasing participation of Negroes in Movement, 48; Remond in British Isles, and his return with Address from Irish People, 53–54; entrance of Frederick Douglass into Movement, 54–56; activity of William Wells Brown, 56; assistance given runaway slaves, 57–64; council meetings, 57–58; prayers for slavery's destruction, 69; Negroes' part in celebration of the Proclamation, 70–71; as forerunners, further reference, 405; women, 450; ministers, 452.

Abolition Movement, Boston source and center of, 30–71; enthusiasm of Abolitionists for Negro, following the war, 81; effect of Movement in arousing the Negro, 82–84, 446; results in broadening Negro's rights, 94; passing away of Abolitionists, 112–13; effect on Negro's sense of citizenship, 267–68; propaganda of racial inter-association, 407.

Acting, 202, 359.

Adams, Mrs. Agnes, leader in organization of Negro women, 212 *f.*

Adams, John, w., 8, 11.

Adams, Samuel, w., 11.

Addams, Jane, w., 126.

Advocate, the, Negro newspaper, 103 *f.*, 216.

Africa, 1, 1 *f.*, 45, 160, 172, 173, 198, 238, 257, 317, 422, 438.

African, 1, 164 *f.*, 172, 173 *f.*, 252, 399, 450, 455.

[1] To avoid frequent use of racial designations, the abbreviation "w." is put after all names of white persons. Names not so marked may be assumed to be those of Negroes.

African Abolition Free-Hold Society, 46 *f.*

African Female Anti-Slavery Society, 46 *f.*

African Meeting House, the, establishment of, 21–22; Negro private school located in, 23; organization of New England Anti-Slavery Society in, 43; Negro "Cradle of Liberty," 43; Rev. Thomas Paul, pastor in early Abolition period, 46 *f.*; become known as old Joy Street Church, 61; meeting to recruit Negro volunteers for war, 73; evolution of name, 241; in Abolition period, 452.

African Society, 21.

"Afro-American," the term, 164.

Agitation. (*See* Discrimination and Rights.)

Alabama, 108 *f.*, 423.

Aldermen, Negro, 274, 275, 282, 283.

Allen, Isaac B., on Governor's Council, 283.

Allen, Macon B., earliest lawyer, 450.

Allston, J. Henderson, on Common Council, 102 *f.*, 271 *f.*; address as presiding officer, 272–73; last Negro member of, 273.

Allston, Philip J., autobiographical sketch, 352 *f.*; officer Negro Business League, 394 *f.*

Amendments to Constitution, proposal of, following the war, 86; passage of Thirteenth, 87; of Fourteenth, 91; of Fifteenth, 93; Negro's disaffection with Republican party on account of non-enforcement of, 120.

American Anti-Slavery Society, 48, 88.

American House, 324.

American Journal of Religious Psychology and Education, 173 *f.*

Amherst College, 456.

Andrew, John A., w., "War Governor" of Massachusetts, 72–74.

Anglo-Saxon, 287, 388.

Anti-Negro riots, during Civil War, 74.

Anti-Slavery, early movement, 36 *f.* (*See* Abolition, and Slavery.)

Anti-Slavery Harp, The, 56.

Anti-Washington agitation, by Negroes, 122–25.

Antipathy. (*See* Discrimination.)

Aristocracy, the Negro, 179, 181–183.

Arkansas, 33 *f.*, 34 *f.*, 51, 108 *f.*

Arming of Negroes, decided upon by Federal Government, 72.

𝕮𝖍𝖊 𝕽𝖎𝖛𝖊𝖗𝖘𝖎𝖉𝖊 𝕻𝖗𝖊𝖘𝖘

CAMBRIDGE . MASSACHUSETTS

U . S . A